HINDU PASTS

the fox knows many things,
but the hedgehog knows one big thing

HINDU PASTS

Women, Religion, Histories

VASUDHA DALMIA

"Hindu Pasts: Women, Religion, Histories" by Vasudha Dalmia was first published by Permanent Black D-28 Oxford Apts, 11 IP Extension, Delhi 11092 INDIA, for the territory of SOUTH ASIA.

Not for Sale in South Asia

Cover design by Anuradha Roy
Images: Kupuldhara Tulao, Benares, 1834 (front); Thurtheree Bazar,1831 (back); both by James Prinsep

Published by State University of New York Press, Albany

© 2017 Vasudha Dalmia

All rights reserved

No part of this book may be used or reproduced in any manner whatsoever without written permission. No part of this book may be stored in a retrieval systemor transmitted in any form or by any means including electronic, electrostatic,magnetic tape, mechanical, photocopying, recording, or otherwise without the prior permission in writing of the publisher.

For information, contact State University of New York Press, Albany, NY
www.sunypress.edu

Library of Congress Cataloging-in-Publication Data

Names: Dalmia, Vasudha, 1947- author.
Title: Hindu pasts : women, religion, histories / by Vasudha Dalmia.
Description: Albany, NY : State University of New York, 2018. | Originally published: Ranikhet : Permanent Black in association with Ashoka University, 2015. | Includes bibliographical references and index.
Identifiers: LCCN 2017007771 (print) | LCCN 2017041461 (ebook) | ISBN 9781438468075 (e-book) | ISBN 9781438468051 (hardcover   ) | 9781438468068 (paperback   )
Subjects: LCSH: Hinduism--India--History--19th century. | Vaishnavism--India--History. | Hindu women--Religious life--India. | Hindi fiction--19th century--History and criticism.
Classification: LCC BL1153.5 (ebook) | LCC BL1153.5 .D35 2018 (print) | DDC 294.50954--dc23
LC record available at https://lccn.loc.gov/2017007771

10 9 8 7 6 5 4 3 2 1

Contents

Acknowledgements　　　vii

Introduction: Where these Essays are Coming From　　　1

I: Colonial Knowledge-Formation

1. Friedrich Max Müller: Appropriations of the Vedic Past　　　21
2. Sanskrit Scholars and Pandits of the Old School: The Benares Sanskrit College and the Constitution of Authority in the Late Nineteenth Century　　　45
3. Sati as a Religious Rite: Parliamentary Papers on Widow Immolation　　　66
4. Mosques, Temples, and Fields of Disputation in a Late-Eighteenth-Century Chronicle　　　91
5. Vernacular Histories in Late-Nineteenth-Century Banaras: Folklore, Puranas, and the New Antiquarianism　　　110

II: Vaishnava Renewals c. 1600–1900

6. Forging Community: The Guru in a Seventeenth-Century Vaishnava Hagiography　　　141
7. Women, Duty, and Sanctified Space in a Vaishnava Hagiography of the Seventeenth Century　　　173

8	The Sixth *Gaddi* of the Vallabha *Sampraday*: Narrative Structure and Authority in a *Varta* of the Nineteenth Century	189
9	The Modernity of Tradition: Harishchandra of Banaras and the Defence of Hindu Dharma	210

III: THE HINDI NOVEL: NINETEENTH-CENTURY BEGINNINGS

10	A Novel Moment in Hindi: *Pariksha Guru*	231
11	Generic Questions: Bharatendu Harishchandra and Women's Issues	251
12	Pilgrimage, Fairs, and the Secularization of Space in Modern Hindi Narrative Discourses	286
13	The Locations of Hindi	309
14	Hindi, Nation, and Community	335

Acknowledgements

An earlier version of 'Where I am Coming From', in French translation as 'Franchir barrières et frontièrs' (Crossing Borders and Boundaries) in Jackie Assayag & Veronique Benei, eds, *L'Est dans l'Ouest. Intellectuels en diaspora et théories nomades à l'âge de la globalisation*. Special Issue of *L'Homme*, 15/6, October–December 2000, pp. 47–56. English version: 'Crossing Borders and Boundaries", in *At Home in Diaspora: South Asian Scholars and the West*, Delhi: Permanent Black, 2003, pp. 66–76.

'Friedrich Max Mueller: Appropriation of the Vedic Past', in *Representations in History*, Special Issue of the *Journal of Arts and Ideas*, ed. Kumkum Sangari, 17/18, June 1989, pp. 43–58.

'Sanskrit Scholars and Pandits of the Old School: The Benares Sanskrit College and the Constitution of Authority in the Late Nineteenth Century', in *Journal of Indian Philosophy*, 24, 1996, pp. 321–37.

'"Sati" as a Religious Rite. Parliamentary Papers on Widow Immolation, 1821–30', in *Economic and Political Weekly*, January 1992, pp. 58–64.

'Mosques, Temples and Fields of Disputation in a Late Eighteenth Century Chronicle', in *Studies in History*, 20/1, 2004.

'Vernacular Histories in Late Nineteenth Century Banaras: Folklore, Puranas and the New Antiquarianism', in Nita Kumar, ed., *The Dilemma of the Indian Intellectual*, Special Issue of the *Indian Economic and Social History Review*, 38/1, March 2001.

'Forging Community: The Guru in a Seventeenth Century Vaishnava Hagiography', in *Charisma and Canon: Essays on the Religious*

History of the Indian Subcontinent, ed. Vasudha Dalmia, Angelika Malinar, and Martin Christof, Delhi: Oxford University Press, 2001.

'Women, Duty and Sanctified Space in a Vaisnava Hagiography of the Seventeenth Century', in *Constructions hagiographiques en Inde: entre mythe et histoire,* ed. Françoise Mallison, Paris: École Pratique des Hautes Études, IVè Section—Sciences historiques et philologiques, Serie II: Hautes Études Orientales, 2001.

'The Establishment of the Sixth *Gaddi* of the Vallabha *Sampraday*: Narrative Structure and the Use of Authority in a *Varta* of the Nineteenth Century', in *Studies in South Asian Devotional Literature, Research Papers, Proceedings of the Fifth International Conference on Devotional Literature in New Indo-Aryan Languages, Paris, 1991,* ed. Alan Entwhistle and Fransoise Mallison, Delhi: Manohar, in Association with École Française d'Extrême-Orient, 1994, pp. 94–117.

'The Modernity of Tradition: Harischandra of Banaras and the Defence of Hindu Dharma', in *Vivekananda and the Modernisation of Hinduism,* ed. William Radice, Delhi: Oxford University Press, 1997.

'A Novel Moment in Hindi: *Pariksa Guru* or the Tutelage of Trial', in *Narrative Strategies: Essays on South Asian Literature and Film,* eds. Vasudha Dalmia and Theo Damsteegt, Leiden: CNWS, 1998; Delhi: Oxford University Press, 1999, pp. 169–84.

'Generic Questions: Bharatendu Harischandra and Women's Issues (1850–1884)', in Stuart Blackburn and Vasudha Dalmia, ed., *India's Literary History: Essays on the Nineteenth Century,* Delhi: Permanent Black, 2003.

'Pilgrimage, Fairs and Secularisation of Space in Modern Hindi Narrative Discourse', in *Patronage and Popularisation, Pilgrimage and Procession: Channels of Transcultural Translation and Transmission in Early Modern South Asia,* Wiesbaden: Harrassowitz, pp. 117–33.

'The Locations of Hindi', in *Economic and Political Weekly,* April 2003.

'Hindi, Nation, and Community', Introduction in Shobna Nijhawan, ed., *Nationalism in the Vernacular: Hindi, Urdu, and the Literature of Indian Freedom,* Ranikhet: Permanent Black, 2010.

Introduction

Where these Essays are Coming From

I CAME TO GERMANY AS A 22-YEAR-OLD. LITTLE IN MY upbringing and education had prepared me for life in Europe. On the face of it, I was a typical example of Indian upper-class upbringing. I had, like so many others, been schooled in a convent, studied English in Miranda House (a well-known girls' college in Delhi) and been brought up to believe in the infallibility of English literature. My favourite teacher in school had been an English nun of upright gait, forthright in her opinions, sweeping in her judgements. She had taught us to read the newspapers, discuss politics, become familiar with Jane Austen. Living in a middle-sized German city made me realize that my English education was skin deep. My way of life had been coined much more by the orthodox Marwari household, modified and softened in its ways by my educated Kayastha mother from Lucknow—ways to which I lived in deep resistance even as they remained my point of reference.

I spent the first ten years of my life at home. My younger brother and I had not been sent to primary school because my father felt it was a waste of time. He was a leading industrialist who rose to the top between the two wars; he was closely connected to the cultural politics of Hanuman Prasad Poddar, the founder of the Gita Press in Gorakhpur, a formidable bastion of Hinduism from the 1930s on.

Tauji (Uncle)—as he was called by our generation—preached in fact a modernized version of traditional Hinduism, published Sanskrit and Bhasha texts in the original and with translations in easily accessible editions, and brought out a monthly journal in Hindi, *Kalyan*, which was widely disseminated. We were surrounded with this literature. We read our way through a number of the beautifully printed volumes, but most of all we avidly awaited the annual number of the journal, a thick volume densely printed and packed with stories, articles, and some illustrations. Here the two ways of life, the Indian and the Western, were presented as opposed to each other in every essential dimension. In the issue devoted to women (*nari amka*) I remember well the black-and-white illustrations; they looked like photographs. On one side of the page were pictures of the Hindu woman, modest in dress and demeanour, counselling and serving her husband in graceful submission. Lined up on the other side of the page were pictures of the club-frequenting westernized woman in sleeveless dress, smoking, dancing with her husband and, we somehow recognized, being self-serving, faithless. The West corrupted.

Besides, as my father often asked, of what use was a school and college education which turned out essentially similar products? He was referring to the scores of jobless MAs and BAs. He wanted us to develop our own individuality. He told us countless stories, one tale melting into the other, of transgressive gods who populated Indra's heavens, and of *rakshasas* banished to the worlds below who fought for justice and their own space. We were to be educated at home, mainly in Sanskrit grammar and religious texts; that would be best. We were put in the hands of a young Sanskrit tutor and memorized Panini with him. Soon we could begin taking the Sanskrit exams administered by the Sanskrit University in Banaras. I had worked out in my mind that, by the time I was 12, I could attain their highest degree, become a 'shastri'. An 'acharya' might follow. I remember the lonely triumph of composing my first shloka.

We were to demonstrate our learning at a huge gathering of pandits in Calcutta. I have a mercifully dim memory of stuttering into the microphone and sharp recollections of the arguments between my parents which followed fast upon it. My mother managed to extract us from our somewhat haphazard education. We were thrust into school, a newly opened convent in the heart of 1950s Delhi, and with that into a colonial educational environment which barely took note of the newly won political independence of the country.

I had learnt a little English and had some knowledge of arithmetic. But the other children regarded my brother and me with suspicion and were quick to point out that we were not allowed to speak Hindi on the school grounds, not even during the recess. In a thousand barely tangible ways we learnt to despise Indianness. Hindu gods and the ritual life at home receded, to be entirely rejected later. We had moved from one kind of hostility to another. We worked with colonial texts and memorized poems about the English countryside, which was happily dotted with daffodils and fairies. Our history books, printed in England, taught us about the vital onrush of Aryans into the subcontinent, and of Dravidians who gave way. We became acquainted with vaguely sketched portraits of Mughal emperors and then, larger than life almost, with Clive, Dupleix, Hastings, Bentinck, Dalhousie. The roads in Delhi, at this time still named after them, were a reminder that these European generals, adventurers, and administrators still peopled the imagination of bureaucrats and diplomats. And then there was the Independence movement, which apparently just happened.

The way had been evened for a BA in English Literature: Chaucer, Spenser, Bacon ('"What is truth", said jesting Pilate and would not wait for an answer'); Shakespeare, more Shakespeare; the Enlightenment: man as the measure of all things; Wordsworth (*The Prelude*, the French revolution: 'Bliss was it in that dawn to be alive'), Keats, Browning, Tennyson, T.S. Eliot. Entering this world was heady, an entirely legitimate and blissful way of becoming the individuals we had been told to become.

But I was thrown off course in Germany. Once I had learnt the language and been granted admission to the university, I began to delve into German literature. I read the works of the Romantics, accosted Novalis and his strange tale *Heinrich von Ofterdingen*, the mysterious blue flower which he sought. I read Goethe's *Wilhelm Meister, Elective Affinities*; I discovered Thomas Mann's *Magic Mountain*, Kafka's *Metamorphosis*. German literature relativized English and its lone dominance of world culture, at least as we had been taught to believe. It opened up new worlds, of melancholy, of yearning, of different layers of being. But it was vast and I was just beginning to dip into it. I turned to Indology, as yet in an unreflective way.

My Sanskrit was rusty and the German Professor of Indology in Cologne was forthright in his rejection. Did I have Latin? No, but as an eager student of 23 I was willing to learn. It would not be possible even then, he said firmly. It would take years for me to understand the approach. Besides, as he told my partner at a later meeting, I was a lady. I should stay with English. The professor for English played tennis, he said. East in the West was an entirely Western concern. I continued then with my study of English, William Blake, more Shakespeare, and for the subsidiary subjects turned to German literature and Ethnology instead of Indology; no one objected to that.

Soon I moved to Tuebingen, a university town in South Germany. Indology could mean different things in different settings. Here, as a young adult, I again encountered Panini and discovered the German reverence for the Veda. The Professor of Indology here was an internationally recognized authority in these fields. His immense enthusiasm spilled over to his students. He was generous with his time, barely noting the Indianness of my existence. Panini had known about the zero suffix in the fifth century before Christ. This discovery had revolutionized, if not founded, the discipline of linguistics in the West. And the Vedic gods represented moral values which the world had not known in quite this way until then. Here was unexpected revalidation of my early education. I would devote my life to the study of these texts.

I re-learnt Sanskrit the Western way and cautiously ventured into deeper waters, into what they called philology—once again, a heady experience, for this science of philology prised open words so that they revealed their innermost kernel. The accretions of centuries fell off as so much dirt. Armed with a good grammar and a dictionary I could pore over texts, over one line of verse, over a single Vedic hymn, for weeks on end, till the inner self of words was laid bare. If I could then connect these selves with each other, a world of unalloyed feeling and perception, when gods and men inhabited the same universe of meaning, could become accessible. And so I went on, with great zeal, semester after semester. The wonderful tales enlivened dry grammatical reflections. It took me five years to realize that this was knowledge rooted in itself. It had little connection to anything else, it barely needed India. The raw material had been supplied in the nineteenth century. And, I was to realize slowly, it revolved upon itself, leading nowhere.

Somewhere in between I had acquired an MA from my former German university and begun to teach Hindi, mainly as an intensive language course considered an appendage to the main course of study. Painfully, I learnt to teach Hindi the way I myself had been taught German and Sanskrit. Perhaps I could write a dissertation on the compound verb in Hindi, prising open the secret of its combinations?

A linguistics degree in Delhi University was a technical impossibility. But, for various reasons, after seven years in Germany, I did return to Delhi. As I ran from pillar to post, seeking employment, I was told that with my knowledge of languages I belonged in the university. However, all I was equipped to do there was teach German. So now the boot was on the other leg: I was appointed to teach German certificate classes in the evening in New Delhi's Jawaharlal Nehru University. If I wanted to stay on in the university, I needed a PhD. Yes, but researching what?

The 1960s and 1970s had seen a great flowering of urban theatre. Folk forms had begun to be used, sometimes with reckless abandon, to create new theatrical modes and address new issues. Brecht's epic theatre offered many possibilities for absorbing these forms creatively. Here was German presence on Indian soil. I read his plays, his theoretical essays and reflections, I read Walter Benjamin. It was from Brecht that I learnt what historicization meant. I learnt about the importance of Chinese theatre aesthetics, of the epic form, of oral traditions, of Brecht's use of Russian formalism for his own theoretical edifice. He was 'A child of all nations', to quote the translated title of the second volume of Pramoedya Ananta Toer's great Buru Quartet.

Brecht's theatre was political theatre. I talked to theatre people, I met Habib Tanvir, pioneer in the use of folk theatre in North India. I met Ebrahim Alkazi, who brought modernity and modernism to the capital of the new nation in the 1960s. My friends in my new field of interest taught me to understand something about post-Emergency politics in India. There was still buoyancy in the air, hope of change. I researched laboriously, analysed the translations of Brecht's plays into Hindi, what the directors of Brecht's plays in India thought and said. Together with my partner I puzzled out the creative misunderstandings of theatre traditions which made possible new combinations, which changed the very premises of the encounter. But in the meantime new questions also began to be thrown up. When did modern Hindi drama begin? What was the function of this drama? When did the proscenium arch come to frame Indian drama, creating new illusions of reality, of psychological verisimilitude of character and new visions of the historical past? When did East meet West? It was in Banaras, in the nineteenth century, within the plays of Bharatendu Harischandra, that Western drama and Shakespeare came to coalesce with the newly created plays in modern Hindi. I wrote my dissertation on Brecht in the Hindi-speaking theatre. I acquired a PhD.

Personal circumstances took me back to teach Hindi in Tuebingen, at my old department, newly validated with the presence of a new Professor of Indology, and thus to re-learn Hindi literature. I had trudged through the length and breadth of all this over my childhood and youth. For, though my mother had sent me to a convent school, she herself had gone to college and university in the high noon of nationalism and had ever reminded us children of the importance of Hindi literature. She had pushed me, while still in school, to sit through all the Hindi exams administered by the Panjab University in Patiala and the Hindi Sahitya Sammelan in Allahabad. I had come into the reluctant possession, which I now discovered to be a treasure, of their highest degree. For the next fourteen years I taught Hindi language and literature, but with a new consciousness of its historicity, of its embeddedness in the politics of colonialism and nationalism. It was a different kind of teaching now. It was connected to Sanskrit, and it was connected to contemporary scholarship in India. Friends made in my Brecht days were situated in/at the heart of a new kind of scholarship and of historiography in India.

It was then that I embarked upon my second dissertation, aiming this time to obtain my Habilitation in the German academic system. For the next many years I was to stay in the nineteenth century, trying to understand how tradition had reasserted itself in colonial North India. I focused on the figure of Bharatendu Harishchandra in order to work out what it meant to be a Hindu in colonial India. The many modes of interaction, the multiplicity of bylanes and alleyways, were dense and intricate. There were many wishes and agendas that I carried into this research, but my friends and foes knocked my thoughts around till I learnt to acknowledge that India and the East had used Western notions of nation and the state, of post-Enlightenment notions of history, to reinforce and reassert themselves, to build new edifices of power. And thus it was also that Hindi literature had been born as the autobiography of the nation, as the new story of an old people. I came to the firm realization, over this time, that if there was one world to which I could belong, intellectually and emotionally, it was the universe of Hindi literature, and that its urban heartland lay in Banaras.

Of my first visit to Kashi as four-year-old, I have dim memories. Of a house perched high on one of the many ghats lining the river, of white marble interiors, of my parents talking to a very ancient grandmother with a deeply lined face, and of my baby sister awaiting her first ritual tonsure on the banks of the Ganga. A city of death and of new life. A classic image, one could almost say, of a classic city.

Later that decade, it must have been in 1957, my grandmother died in that marble interior. It had been built to house her in her last years. Two paternal aunts would follow the same route to the other world. When my sister and I, accompanied by my partner and little daughter, visited the house almost two decades later, the younger of the two aunts still lived in that house. We had only known her in her joyless widow's white. Despite apparent disapproval, she kept back from scolding us, as the other elderly women in the family did, for wearing our hair short, for the way we dressed, the way we talked. She busied herself with *satsang* with the many other women in white who came to sing joyless bhajans in the evenings.

The city fascinated us, even as its dirt repelled us. The wide riverside terraces of the house were haunted by monkeys; boat people lived in its low-roofed terrace, we could hear them sing in the evenings. The marble courtyard of the house was filled with miniature Shiva temples, with lingams in their inner sanctums and Nandis posted outside. And there was that view of the ghat, with a lone sadhu or two and the silent river, the sandy and unpeopled banks on the other side underlining the timelessness I associated with the Ganga. The spectacular evening arati in the Vishwanath Temple performed by shaven priests only reinforced the image—of death, solemnity, filth, and holy grandeur. Half a decade later my sister and I would carry the urn which contained my father's ashes to the city and immerse it in the river. The city remained distant, ensconced in a distant past.

What took me to Banaras again to look for completely different things—things that I could never have associated with that city of temples and *panda*s? By this time, in the late 1980s, I had lived in Germany for many years and had written that doctoral dissertation on Bertolt Brecht and the impact of his theatre in North India, particularly the Hindi-speaking belt, with Delhi at its centre. It was then, as part of the quest to understand the beginning of modern Hindi theatre, that I first lit upon Bharatendu Harishchandra, the young merchant prince of late-nineteenth-century Banaras, who had 'fathered' modern Hindi. Of the three thick volumes of his *Granthavali* (Collected Works), one was entirely devoted to drama of many kinds: farces, comedies, history plays, translations from Sanskrit and English. Bharatendu had wished to see his plays performed. He had acted in one or two of them on an amateur stage of his own creation, but the Hindi belt, which was just coming into its own, entirely lacked the kinds of audience that theatres in the Presidency port cities of Calcutta and Bombay could entice. Performance culture in North India existed at this time in the salons of courtesans, and in the streets. So Bharatendu's plays lived on in print, since the theatre he envisioned never really got going.

But Bharatendu's works had then formed one short chapter in a thesis focused on contemporary drama which had taken me to theatres in Germany, to the Brecht Archives in East Berlin in order to better understand Brecht, and to many different kinds of performances in Delhi and North India. Bharatendu's Banaras, encountered primarily in print, had remained hazy, of little further interest.

But now that I was working in Tuebingen, at the Institute for Indology and the Comparative Study of Religions (we are speaking of the mid-1980s), and had turned to teaching Hindi and modern Hinduism, while looking for the modern turn in traditionalist, rather than reformist, religious discourse of the nineteenth century, my interest in Bharatendu revived. This merchant prince, known as much for his extravagant lifestyle as his generosity, was not only writing sharp-tongued satirical plays, not only reading and translating Shakespeare and experimenting with a variety of genres—all things I could relate to, given my undergraduate training in English literature—but also arguing out an overarching scheme for a national religion rooted in Vaishnava bhakti. During my exam-filled childhood I had also taken a series of exams on the works of Tulsidas. This was part of my Marwari legacy, of belonging to a family closely related to Hanuman Prasad Poddar and the Gita Press. These were resources to which I could now revert; there were ways, it seemed, to relate to this modernizing bhakti culture, regardless of the varieties of alienation I had gone through over the many years of my Western education.

A first reading of Bharatendu's texts on religion—poems, essays, and tracts—yielded a puzzle, for they seemed to be going both ways, in the direction of openness as well as closure. Was there some hope of finding a generous vision of Hinduism at this early stage of nationalist thought? Or were these the first traces of the Hindu communalism that seemed all set to tear the country apart in the late 1980s and early 1990s? I went first to what was then the India Office Library in London, to catalogues, librarians, and archivists. The material I found opened up a whole new world. James Prinsep's *Benares Illustrated* (1831–2) gave me glimpses of fine architecture, of the roof terrace of Kashmiri Mal's grand merchant house, of portraits of courtesans and courtiers, of Burhwa Mangal, the river festival with its procession of decorated barges, of narrow city lanes lined with shops. Prinsep also offered an illustration of the British presence in Banaras and of their perspective. I had visited those crowded lanes with no inkling of the layers of modern history embedded in them. Bharatendu was born a few decades after the world displayed in Prinsep's book, but he emerged in this world all the same: from a devout Vaishnava merchant household in close interaction with the anglicized education which overtook the Benares Sanskrit College in the 1830s, from the lectures and discussions held in the Benares Institute, and from the conversations between the city literati, British officers, and missionaries. Stray issues of Bharatendu's pioneering Hindi journals of the 1870s and early 1880s provided some sense of the wider network of his addressees, of Hindi enthusiasts scattered across the North West Provinces. What, precisely, had come together in Banaras in the decades following the uprising of 1857, making it the cultural capital of the new Hindi–Hindu world of North India— a position it was to retain till well into the 1930s when the scene shifted to Allahabad? It was becoming increasingly clear that I would have to go to Banaras, to work out the links between literature, performance, religion, politics, and modernity. For this was connected to me, to all of us late-twentieth-century moderns looking for the roots of our modernity and all that lay beyond, in both directions, past and present. Yet, I must confess that I somewhat dreaded this looming encounter with the city. Would I once again encounter traditional Hindus who would scold, as my aunts had scolded once, and be confronted with temples and *pandas*?

My sister Ila, who was intimately connected to the Hindi cultural world (her partner being the Hindi poet Agyeya), got me access to Rai Anand Krishna, Professor Emeritus of Art History, who invited me to stay with him and his family. It took me only a few days in Sita Niwas, their tree-shaded residence on the Banaras Hindu University campus, to realize that I had found the kind of resource I was looking for, a compound of knowledge, warmth, and hospitality. From Raja Bhaiya (as Anand Krishnaji was called by family and friends) and his family I learnt most of what I know about Banaras. He was not only an art historian, at home in the world of Maurya sculpture as much as in Mughal and Rajput miniature painting, but also his deep love and knowledge of music, literature, and culture at large, and his family history, connected him to the city's many networks. Rai Krishnadas, Raja Bhaiya's father, one of Bharatendu's grand-nephews, had given his rich collection of art works to Bharat Kala Bhavan, the university art museum of which he was both founder and first director. He had been at the heart of a vibrant circle of writers, artists, intellectuals, and the stray visitor from Europe who could not tear herself away from the holy city—such as Alice Boner and Alain Danielou.

As I began to view it through Bharatendu's eyes, the city grew on me. He had loved this city, he had known it inside out; he had eulogized its learning, ancient and modern; he had shown the attractions of the gleaming towers and palaces that adorned the ghats in his play *Satya Harischandra* (1875), even as he had had no illusions about his city's darker underbelly, its rogues and thieves, Brahmin and non-Brahmin, who pervaded the temples, the ghats, and the newly built railway station at Mughal Sarai. The city was holy, the city was unholy. In the brief span of his life he had literally called Hindi literature into being. He had created lilting prose in a language just beginning to find its feet and given it body with his writings. This was work which would help provide legitimacy for Hindi in the family of modern Indian languages, clearing the path for it to later stake a claim to being the country's national language.

What did I find in this vast corpus of work that Bharatendu managed to conjure up in the thirty-five years of his life? What was the Hinduism that had emerged from this brave new world, launching itself, as much as being launched, by the force of colonial circumstance into the modern? The answer had begun to stare me in the face, there was no ignoring it. The Hindu–Muslim polarization had unmistakably set in at this time. Not only had Hindi and Urdu forked sharply, all but denying their linguistic origins in the same fount, but Hinduism was increasingly consolidating into a whole that seemed to need the 'other' in order to project its own identity more clearly. Bharatendu's vision of bhakti-rooted Hinduism, though expansive and seeking to integrate the diverse streams that the forces of modernity were also pushing into some kind of unity, was also exclusive. It differentiated itself sharply on many sides: from folk belief, from pirs, from village and tribal deities, as much as from Islam at large. The story of the divisive colonial politics that exacerbated and cemented this division is too well known to be rehearsed here again—the 1905 partition of Bengal, the Morley–Minto reforms, electorates for Muslims, all climaxing in the communalism of the 1920s. But it was also clear that this communal Hinduism could not be read back wholesale into the late nineteenth century, at which time it still carried traces of the old porous borders of the Mughal-era bhakti traditions of the North.

Once I had written my book on Bharatendu, I thought my work in Varanasi was over. In the meantime, this being the late 1990s, I found myself in the University of California, Berkeley, as a Professor of Hindi, looking now to focus on the very Hindi literature of which Bharatendu had laid the foundation. The study of Hindi literature had flourished in Berkeley since the early 1960s. Agyeya had helped to found the fledgling Hindi programme then, which flowered all the way to the mid-1980s, when, for a variety of reasons, it trailed away. At the time I came to Berkeley there were only faint traces of a once-vital area of study. The resolve I formed then was to contextualize the canonical authors of the twentieth century, in the way I had learnt to do for the late nineteenth, and in order to do this my students, three successive generations of them, and I turned to the literary journals of the first half of the twentieth century, to Premchand and to Hindi's first romantic poet, Jaishankar Prasad, both based in Banaras.

For all his vivacity and irreverence, Bharatendu had circumvented 'tradition' even while questioning it. Premchand, by contrast, occupied another social and political location, he lived in a different time. *Sevasadan* (1918) and *Karmabhumi* (1932), his two Banaras novels, had taken venerable institutions head on, storming the citadel that was the holy city of Kashi. *Sevasadan* had questioned the very foundations of modern upper-caste marriage. By the turn of the century, the choice of a bridegroom for a high-caste Hindu girl, depended entirely on the right caste status and dowry. More than ever, women were on sale. The narrative skilfully counterposed to this world the relative freedom enjoyed by a successful *tawaif* (courtesan): she had money, social power, and some control over her life. As Suman, the young girl at the centre of the novel, bitterly observes, the only difference in her situation from that of a *tawaif* consists in being confined to a single client, her husband, who has bought her by virtue of the power given him by his caste and gender. I looked for Benia Bagh, the colonial park which then had its zoo and aviary, its stone benches and shaded avenues, which had shooed away Suman, the wife of a poor man, but welcomed Suman the famed courtesan. I wandered down Dalmandi, a narrow street located in the heart of the city, to get some sense of what had once been courtesan quarters. I went in the early morning, before the shops opened and the place filled with clamour, to look for other sights and sounds, to echoes from another past: graceful *jharoka*s set in slim buildings from which music poured, the sound of dancers' anklets in the evening, the areas where dandies on horseback paraded on stone-paved streets. Premchand's vivid descriptions recorded that past, more with fascination than disapproval. Perhaps he had embarked on *Sevasadan* with an indictment of 'marriage as market transaction' in mind but ended up by portraying with great empathy the world of the courtesan. The book shows many talented, beautiful, and sometimes strong women embedded in this world. It shows also the wretched universe of latter-day marital unions where neither man nor woman finds mental stability or satisfaction; the narrative has not one couple in it who might serve as the possible model of a happy union. At the centre of it are scenes in the increasingly communalized municipality of the city, the 'Hindu' side portraying courtesans as examples of a larger Muslim depravity. They look to remove them from the heart of 'their' town and are backed by pig-headead social reformers, as they strain to realize their fantasy. To rescue the 'Hindu' woman from the life of the bazaar, Premchand showed, could only lead to her confinement in puritanical reform institutions. This could neither erase the stigma of her former life nor end her social isolation, her only fault having been to seek a meagre, ephemeral measure of power and happiness for herself. This was a radical feminist stance far ahead of its time.

When I visited Banaras now, in the first decade of the twenty-first century, I stayed in Ganges View, a riverside hotel on Assi Ghat run with great aesthetic sense and personal warmth by its proprietor-director Shashank Singh. Scholars and artists met here, in search of one kind of Banaras or another. I was, at this time, writing about *Karmabhumi*, Premchand's second-last novel, set in the early 1930s. And once again I was in luck. Shashankji's scholar-father had grown up in those very decades, and his old books on the city and its culture were strewn in the hotel.

Karmabhumi is worlds removed from *Sevasadan*. An educated middle class has come into being, providing a counter-force, however subdued, to colonial rule. Professors, lawyers, judges, even the Indian members of the civil service and the police force, are succumbing to the strong nationalist wave and the modernization that is part of it. It is a world full of protest, almost entirely coloured by Gandhi. His famous salt satyagraha has just taken place, and he has concluded his epic fast against the move to establish a separate electorate for Dalits. Yet, though his presence is all-pervasive—whether in non-violent peasant protest and village uplift work or in the cause of Dalit temple entry—there is only one reference to the Mahatma in the course of a public speech and he is not directly mentioned even once in the novel. This seems paradoxical, but it is appropriate in a way, for the novel's whole tone, its support to the working poor of the city, its projection of women as leaders of political protest and beyond—to their public role for the rights Premchand thinks they should have in the private sphere—goes much further than Gandhi. The utopian cast of the novel allows for the storming of many citadels. Under Gandhian leadership, and with the support of youthful activists, Dalits manage to enter a key temple in the city; civil servants are moved enough to concede that some negotiation be possible with starving peasants over unfair revenue demands; the municipality gives in on a major land scam so that the poor get housing within the city. These are fictional moves, in no way reflecting the reality of city politics, but they do take place in a puritanical urban environment, marking the long way the city has travelled since the first stirrings of social reform in the first two decades of the twentieth century.

When looking back on my work in Banaras, it seems clear to me how far I too have travelled—from my childhood impressions of the holy city to a fuller picture of its history, its centrality within a dominant variety of Hindi–Hindu life and culture. In my early almost entirely secular Banaras-based work I recognize the seeds of my own rebellion against the tradition I had grown up in. The only temple I visited was Vaishnava rather than Shaiva, in this Shiva-centred city, and that was because it was connected to the Bharatendu family. With time, I think I have better understood what went into the making of my world. The image of the 'classic' holy city has never quite gone away, but the accretions of the many layers which went into the construction of that image have become clearer. For all that, I have remained an outsider, eager to understand but not always able to do so. This combination of being an insider as well as an outsider, of understanding and not understanding, has taken me back to the city again and again.

Over the years my students and I have faced and tried to answer innumerable questions about the whys and hows of Indological knowledge, of East as taught in the West. Nineteenth-century Indology was a strong presence in Tuebingen, exerting great authority, enjoying great prestige. We needed to investigate what it was that had moved the great scholars of the last century. We needed to understand that the questions posed in Germany, then and now, were different from those posed in India while being of concern to each other.

Together, we learnt to understand in greater historical depth the relationship between religion and society, the ever-changing role of religious and social institutions, understanding for the first time that traditions I had been taught to regard as monolithic consisted in fact of a multiplicity of autonomous and semi-autonomous strands. What was old clearly reached into the present and what was new stretched into the past. There was no real cut-off point between classical and modern, between East and West. On the other hand, there were no utopias and no encounters innocent of power. Then as now, there have always been keepers of knowledge, sometimes self-appointed, from whom it has had to be wrested, and this is a never-ending exercise.

Working within the frame provided by the Western academy, the questions I have needed to ask again and again are: On what basis do I collect the data for teaching and research? What is the validity of the conclusions drawn from what I collect? Can the knowledge produced here be extracted from this context and continue to be regarded as knowledge in completely different social and political contexts? I have come to believe that resolving these issues is in fact also a never-ending process. The knowledge produced in the Western academy, as elsewhere, can only be tested out in various contexts, to see how it measures up to lived reality.

Clearly, there are many Indias now, and we can only understand them together. They even look different from the vantage of the two coasts of North America, West and East.

The essays collected here offer a glimpse of the various stages of my journey, of the passionate intellectual quest to understand and come to terms with the contradictions of my existence, as one representative of that generation of 'Midnight's Children' who grew up with one foot still rooted in older tradition, the other pulling West. That the concerns which drove my research were connected to my personal and cultural history, I often understood only retrospectively. The Panini I grew up with and the Vedas—why were they so revered in Germany? What authority did the pandits I had been taught to respect retain after Indology emerged as almost the sole authoritative voice on the Indian past in India and the West? What meaning did now-discarded customs carry in the past? A visit to Shekavati in my early Tuebingen years had disclosed that a sati, the sati, who had survived a bloody Rajput–Vaishya dispute in our ancestral village two centuries ago, was the first known member of our clan. Soon thereafter I came across the *Parliamentary Papers on Widow Immolation* recording the discussions around sati in the list of new acquisitions by the Tuebingen library. How could I not engage with them? What did it mean to be Hindu in the poisoned communal environment of the early 1990s? Being Vaishnava, being Hindu, I had taken these facts for granted. So also the locations of the Hindi we had been discouraged to speak in the school playgrounds—all these became questions that have followed me for over three decades. I offer here the answers I found, in the form I found then, when there was still an element of surprise in the things we, who were born around Indian Independence, seemed to see clearly for the first time. Much water has flown under the bridge since then—there is so much literature on sati for instance, almost every aspect has been considered—but to change and add now would be to distort that excitement of discovery. Perhaps the essays collected here still have a story to tell, as part of the trajectory of one Indian scholar wrestling with her past? Within that larger frame, perhaps they still carry meaning?

PART I

Colonial
Knowledge-Formation

1

Friedrich Max Müller

Appropriations of the Vedic Past

THE GERMAN ROMANTIC ATTACHMENT TO INDIA'S ancient past, being unconnected with colonialism in any direct way, has been widely accepted as disinterested. Here I try to show that it was not: that in fact as an 'interest' it was part of a cultural politics seeking to establish a new basis for the German national tradition—a complex and often contradictory process, coherent primarily in the framework of an internal European dialogue. Three figures stand out as significant in the unfolding scholarly activity of the nineteenth century: Johann Gottfried Herder (1744–1803), Friedrich Schlegel (1772–1829), and finally Friedrich Max Müller (1823–1900), who occupies a remarkable position between scholar and poet and whose works provide a climax to the concern with India's ancient heritage.[1] These three also demonstrate a shift in perspective during the course of the century.

I shall confine myself to an analysis of one early influential work each by these authors, the three works under discussion having been conditioned by the quality and quantity of the source material available. The author's personal relationship to India, which

---

[1] All translations from the German in this essay are mine. Cf. Rocher 1978: 224.

in Schlegel's work shows many stages, is an area too large for the discussion here.

J.G. Herder

In the 1780s a variety of travel literature on the Orient had become available in Europe, the kind written in English by missionaries, tradesmen, and civil servants of the East India Company. There was evidently an eager readership for these works; the moment they appeared they were translated into other European languages. Primary textual material was at this time scarce and consisted of preliminary translations of maxims, Puranic legends, and moral-philosophical dialogues of dubious origin.[2] In spite of this paucity of first-hand knowledge, Voltaire had not hesitated to locate the place of origin of the human race—expressly against the biblical tradition—on the banks of the Ganges. His readiness to use any supportive evidence for this thesis had been enabled by the Jesuits, whose labours provided access to a manuscript of the *Ezourvedam: A French Veda of the Eighteenth Century* (1760). A mixture of Puranic and Christian teaching, this work was a forgery but was only discovered to have been so several decades later.[3] Herder's *Auch eine Philosophie der Geschichte zur Bildung der Menschheit* (Yet Another Philosophy of the History of the Formation of Humanity) was published in 1774. Expressive, dynamic, and provocative, this work has been widely regarded as the manifesto of historicism. Though rooted

---

[2] Bhartrihari's maxims were available in a Dutch translation by Abraham Rogerius, *De Open-Deure tot het Verbogen Heydendom*, Leyden, 1651, with the German translation appearing in Nuremberg, 1663; there were fragments of Bramah's 'Chatah Bhades' (possibly 'Satapathagrahmana') in John Z. Holwell, *Interesting Historical Events Relative to the Provinces of Bengal and the Empire of Indostan*, London, 1776, a German translation by J.F. Kleuker appearing in Leipzig, 1778; passages from a 'Sastra of the Vedanga', the original of which it is not possible to identify, appeared in Alexander Dow, *The History of Hindustan*, 1768.

[3] For a contemporary interpretation and speculations regarding possible authorship, see Rocher 1984.

in the eighteenth century, it is at the same time a critique of the progressionist historical view of the Enlightenment whereby contemporary technical and civilizational achievements were regarded as unquestionably superior to any in the past—making these, in fact, a yardstick for measuring the past, which by comparison appeared as steeped in superstition and prey to cynical priestly betrayal. But, as has been pointed out,[4] Herder did not totally reject the ideas of the Enlightenment; rather, he qualified them: each age was to be regarded in light of what it was capable of accomplishing. Herder was as yet far removed from an uncritical, romantic glorification of the past.

Though he polemicized against Voltaire's scepticism of all human endeavour and refusal to see any hope for the future of mankind, Herder followed him in identifying the Orient as the cradle of the human race. But there was yet another difference, for, unlike Voltaire, Herder left the Christian claim to infallibility untouched. Since the Jewish people had no place in his historical universe, he had qualms about the locations of the origin of the Christian faith 'amongst the naked hills of Judea! Shortly before the overthrow of the whole of this ignominious people, even in the last miserable epoch of these very same people, in a manner which will always remain miraculous...'[5] This, then, made a case for the Orient being the childhood of man. Herder's use of the metaphor of the ages of man for both universal history as well as for individual peoples and states was an effort to organize historically, but without any claim to absolute consistency. For in his scheme successive ages did not transcend those preceding, and nor were later ages seen as inevitably inferior.[6]

The significance of the Orient in Herder's thought is part of his debate with the classicism of J.J. Winckelmann (1717–68), the well-known scholar of Greek art. Herder had accused Winckelmann of paying too little attention to the Asiatic and the Egyptian in his *Gedanken über die Nachahmung der Griechischen Werche*

---

[4] Gadamer 1972: 103.
[5] Herder 1982: 75–6.
[6] Meyer 1981.

(Reflections on the Imitation of Greek Works, 1755). Winckelmann had attempted to delineate the significance of Greek works of art, particularly sculpture, for contemporary artistic production. 'If the artist allows his sense and hands to be led by the Greek regulations of beauty, then he is on the way which will lead him most securely to the imitation of nature. The concept of the Whole, of the Perfect in the nature of the Ancients will purify and make more sensuous the concepts of the Divided in our nature . . .'[7]

Herder's attempt to relocate the place of the Greeks in the historical sequence of the cultural history of mankind was an attempt to free himself from the classicism of Winckelmann and the claim that the imitation of nature was possible only by imitating Greek art. Even though Herder's eloquent rhetoric would tempt one to think so, it would be an error to regard his evaluation of the Orient in isolation.[8] It is not as if Greek culture and its achievements are being questioned: they are—following the metaphor of the ages of man, of which Herder makes consistent use in the first part of his book—the blossoming youth of mankind.[9] But Greek culture is now

---

[7] Szondi 1974: 34.

[8] This has been the traditional practice since the beginning of the twentieth century, as for instance in Hoffmann (1915: 6), who seeks a psychological interpretation for Herder's enthusiasms, rather than one within the totality of his concept of cultural history: 'It is with apparent pleasure that the soft-hearted Herder depicts the tender dreamy docility of the Hindus. And when he hears of the hard Muhammedan yoke, under which India lies heavily oppressed, then he sees the cause of it not in the political incapability and indolence, in the spirit which has been confined by caste; instead, he assumes there to be a friendly, yielding patience which is his own characteristic.' Similarly Willson (1964: 48): 'The lines above, in which Johann Gottfried Herder refers to the chief figures in the Sanskrit play *Sakuntala,* identify India as a holy land for which he yearns. These lines might serve as a motto to characterize his attitude towards India, an attitude of extreme reverence and adulation, which resulted finally in the formulation of a mythical image, whose development can be traced in the fancy of Herder.' Gerard (1963) seeks a more political explanation.

[9] 'Greece! Primeval image and proto-image of all Beauty, Grace and Simplicity! Blossom of the youth of the human race—oh if only it could have lasted an eternity.' Herder 1982: 59.

conceived of as part of a historical development rather than as some aesthetic absolute; it appears as a form in its turn affected and formed by the Orient and Egypt. Greek mediation is now no longer the sole way to nature; undivided nature is present most prominently in the childhood of mankind, the description of which bears close resemblance to the biblical world of pastoral patriarchs.

The supreme height of manhood is seen as having been achieved in the Roman imperial age, but it is significant that, despite an ample critique, Herder nowhere explicitly dwells over his own epoch as deteriorating. For, just as he resolves the absolute hegemony of Greek culture, he questions the contemporary European political claim to direct the affairs of the world, to reign supreme over it:

> we have only allowed ourselves this one thing, to use three parts of the world as slaves, to dispose of them in silver mines and sugar mills, but they are not Europeans, not Christians . . . The savages everywhere, in the same measure as they grow to love our brandy and opulence, become ripe for our proselytism! When, all over the world, they approach the proximity of our culture, through brandy and opulence . . . God help us—all men will be the same as we . . .![10]

Herder's historicism also explicitly questions the achievements of the European Enlightenment: 'this luminous century . . .' (41), 'our gigantic progress in religion' (107). He sees the political order, the absolute monarchies of the age, as 'impoverished, impoliced Europe, which eats up all its children, or relegates them . . .' (82), a social order mechanized, inhuman, which increasingly pushes back family ties (94). The hope then lies in regeneration by way of the Orient: 'the childhood of the race will work upon the childhood of each individual . . .' (115). In that patriarchal world of 'mild fatherly reign'—the original form of all social order—there is no despotism of the kind denounced by the uninitiated (44), much more an authority radiating with 'godliness and fatherly love'. It is posited as an age lacking in the subsequent division between philosophy and religion, and in which there is no difference between state polity and theology (48). 'With the simplest, most necessary, pleasantest

---

[10] 'Trade and Popery', in Herder 1982: 101.

inclinations! Human being, man, wife, father, mother, son, heir, God's priest, regent, father of the house, for all centuries shall he be formed there . . .' (44). 'The life of the herdsman in the most beautiful climate of the world thus anticipates and helps to meet the simplest needs' (43). This image of an 'Urzeit', with its many biblical associations, therefore merely awaited discovery, in a way which seems almost pre-programmed, within the ancient scriptures of the Hindus.

In sum:

1. The childhood of mankind is not restricted to the search for European ancestry; the human race is universally traced back to the Orient, locally and temporally.
2. The Greek ideal remains intact, but without the power to rejuvenate.[11]
3. Politically, especially with regard to the politics of religion, Herder is critical of the mainstream thought of his time. He sees his own social order as repressive, and as hiding behind the façade of a 'general love of people, full of tolerant subjugation, exploitation and enlightenment' (48). He considers colonial politics ruthlessly exploitative, under cover of the claim to civilize and proselytize.

Friedrich Schlegel

Till the end of the eighteenth century Friedrich Schlegel, one of the most influential thinkers of the early Romantics in Germany, had like Winckelmann before him attempted to demonstrate that 'a generally valid science of the Beautiful and of Representation, as well as the proper imitation of the Greek originals . . . [are] the necessary conditions for the recreation of the truly fine arts.'[12] This was the thrust of Schlegel's 1795 essay *Über das Studium der Griechischen*

---

[11] One of the reasons being that when Greece had a second opportunity to influence Europe, 'it could not work without mediation. Arabia was the muddy channel, Arabia was the "underplot" to the history of the formation of Europe.' Herder 1982: 116.

[12] Szondi 1974: 119.

Poesie (On the Study of Greek Poetry). But if Schlegel's beginnings were classicist, shaped and influenced by the Weimar School, he had moved away from this position by the turn of the century. In 1805 he left for Paris in order to pursue Persian studies. Here he made the acquaintance of Alexander Hamilton, professor of Sanskrit at the East India Company's Haileybury College in England, and from him learnt, in a remarkably short period, what he knew of Sanskrit.[13] In the meantime, much more source material had become available than Herder could ever have known: the *Law Books of Manu*, the *Bhagvadgita*, and Kalidasa's *Sakuntala* had since been translated into English. Learned articles and treatises published by the Royal Asiatic Society of Bengal, many translated into German, were also now available.

In 1808 Schlegel published *Über die Spracheund Weisheit der Inder* (On the Language and Wisdom of the Indians). The title of the book alone is sufficient indication of the significance for him of the science of language. William Jones (1746–94) had already proclaimed that the classical European languages, Greek and Latin, were closely related to Sanskrit and Persian, and speculated about their common historical past.[14] Schlegel went further. He raised language itself to the status of a historical document. 'The old languages, whose family tree we seek to follow . . . from their roots to the main branches, are the original document of the history of mankind, more instructive and more reliable than all monuments in stone.'[15] As Schlegel saw it, each work constituted in itself the history of the people who spoke the language, the root of the word being at the same time the root of a concept. And further, just as in Comparative Anatomy, whole family trees of genetically related languages could now be constructed. The botanical metaphors that he used and which prevail throughout the book are an extension of this analogy. It was the grammatical rather

---

[13] On Hamilton and Schlegel's scholarly pursuits in Paris, see Rocher 1968 and Struc-Oppenberg 1969.

[14] For a vivid, if disturbingly partisan, account of the early British Orientalists, see Kopf 1969; for excerpts, Marshall 1970; for the translation into German, Willson 1964.

[15] Schlegel 1976: 257.

than the lexical similarity, an organic rather than surface similarity, which bound languages decisively into a family bond, a similarity which reached into their innermost structure: 'The affinity then is not casual, which it were possible to explain as stemming from intermixture; on the contrary, it is elemental and points to a common origin' (115). The organic languages, the Indic—and the Greek, Latin, and Persian which stem from it—are counterposed to the inorganic languages. The organic possess inflection, each root being truly that which the word denotes: 'a living germ' (157). As against this, the inorganic languages possess roots which bear 'no fertile seed, on the contrary, they are like a heap of atoms, which each casual wind can drive asunder or together' (159). Similarly, Schlegel maintained on the origin of languages that the inorganic were largely onomatopoeic, 'merely an emotional cry' (171), and unlike the organic in no way constituted of meaningful syllables and fertile seeds. Later research was to demonstrate the arbitrariness of this division.[16]

The dichotomy organic/inorganic was related to the divergent characters of the respective families of peoples. Schlegel maintained: 'it is true, that practically all of the Indian language consists of philosophical or much rather religious terminology' (173). Sanskrit, then, was not the language of the universal childhood of mankind, it was the proto-language of one branch of mankind which had its origin somewhere in Asia; from here its speakers had spread over parts of Asia and all of Europe.[17] Schlegel went on to speculate: 'not only the external pressure of necessity but some other miraculous concept of the high dignity and splendour of the North, such as

---

[16] Timpanaro (1977: xxxv) situates Schlegel's linguistic-ethnographic ideology within the general context of the historiography of comparative linguistics in eighteenth- and nineteenth-century Europe. Whereas he views Herder as a corrective to the Enlightenment's 'intellectualizing narrowmindedness', he points out that Schlegel's is 'a kind of Manichaean, potentially racist, mysticism which splits the human species in two.'

[17] Schlegel converted to Catholicism in 1808, the year in which his Indian study was published. In spite of the change in faith, and the awareness that this kind of glorification of Sanskrit as the most ancient language should actually have been reserved for Hebrew, all his life he held fast to the belief in Sanskrit as the most ancient language of his family of peoples: Nusse 1962: 67.

we find spread all over the Indian legends, led them northwards' (293). This then was an important consideration 'for the history of our fatherland' (ibid.).

It was amongst the Indians, the 'most cultivated and wisest people of Antiquity', that 'traces of divine truth' (209) were still to be found. While on the one hand it was true that Indian sources no longer contained the original revelation, 'an upsurge of innermost feeling, the feeling for the true' (207), at all events there still existed the first system that had come to replace the original, authentic system. It was the same with poetry. Schlegel believed that it was the Indians who were the nearest to the original source:

> From a worship of nature and superstition still fructified by the thoughts of the eternal and the divine, there first sprang the abundance of originally wild and gigantic compositions; as the beautiful light of a gentle and noble enthusiasm was added to it, through just this moderation, the raw fable became poetry ... If it were not too bold to dare to speculate after such few fragments, then I would plead that Indian poetry is not so different from older Greek poetry in its essence, only that it offers the same in a still greater measure, partly in that the original fable is stranger and wilder, but partly also in that the later moderation is spiritually more tender and more lovely, more sensuous and more moral, more beautiful than the charm even of Pindar and Sophocles.[18]

As regards nature worship, Schlegel assured his readers that Indian religion did not revere 'the wild and destructive, lasciviousness and death, but only the pure and benevolent, fire and light, in fact, free life and the inner spirit' (231). He described Vishnu as the most benevolent of deities, as a king and sage whose repeated incarnations occurred in order to destroy the evil and protect the good. The notion of God becoming man was proof of the Indian depth of thought and

---

[18] Schlegel 1976: 261 and 263. The Oriental poetry that Schlegel spoke of was not to be considered the same as the extravagant variety generally known as 'Asiatic'. This latter was to be confined to some Asian peoples, foremost to the Arabs and Persians—'Raw and uncultivated as the exuberance of the arrogance in the teachings of Mahomed'—as well as those portions of the *Old Testament* which were generally regarded as merely poetic rather than religious in character.

of the level of their knowledge (233). The history of their philosophy and of the oriental way of thinking was the most beautiful and most instructive commentary on the Christian Holy Script (297).

Herder is mentioned once, though only in a note: 'Glorious indications are to be found about this (traces of divine light in Indian religion) in Herder's *Älteste Urkinde des Menschengeschlechts* (Oldest Document of the Human Race). Except that I would not wish to derive each murky stream of degenerate mysticism from the pure fountainhead of divine revelation. Otherwise the abundant Oriental spirit flows through this work, as also several other early theological works of Herder' (297). Parallels of Herder's thoughts are present most of all in the suggestion of that age which preceded the one preserved in the Indian works. In the first epoch of the Vedas, Philosophy, Religion, and Poetry were still one with each other, suggestive of a yet nobler age, not divided as they almost were in the Greek and the European (265, 307–9). Priests and Warriors must have also been united in one stand, suggestions of this being preserved in the Roman patriarchal system. It was the severe constitution of Manu, the rigidification into a caste system, which drove the Kshatriyas away from the priestly stand, fostering feuds amongst them, such as the battles in the *Mahabharata*, and forcing them to flee as well as later to found new colonies (281–3).

The Vedas were still largely unknown to the Western world;[19] but to Schlegel it seemed that in times to follow these 'most antiquated and most mysterious works would attract the most desire for knowledge' (251). His expectations regarding the fruits of Indian studies are summarized thus at the conclusion of his book:

> And if a too one-sided and merely playful preoccupation with the Greeks has estranged the spirit of the last century far too much from former earnestness or even from the source of all higher truth, then the deeper

---

[19] The travel literature had reported the sacred character of the Vedas—for instance Dow, and excerpts in Marshall (1970: 109–13). H.T. Colebrooke had written his essay 'On the Vedas, or Sacred Writings of the Hindus' in 1805 in the *Asiatick Researches*, but it has not been possible to determine whether Schlegel knew this work.

we delve into this completely new knowledge and contemplation of Oriental antiquity, the more so might it guide us back to the recognition of the divine and to that rigour of conviction, which first bestowed light and life on all art and all knowledge.[20]

The following may then be concluded:

1. For Schlegel, the study of language is of primary importance; a scientific method, comparative philology has been evolved in order to accomplish this backward thrust into the history of mankind.
2. For Schlegel in 1808 the Orient, India, is not the cradle of all mankind, as it was for Herder, but it is the original home of his own family of languages and peoples. He draws a sharp boundary between his own and the Semitic languages, which form a loosely assorted group along with the languages of the savages existing in need and penury on the African continent and the Americas.
3. Herder had denounced colonial politics on humanitarian grounds; his philosophy of history had universal aspirations. Schlegel on the other hand regarded it as a task for his own family of peoples to see to it that 'some of the supply and seed of higher intellectual activity, learning, and flexibility' become available to other countries (273).
4. For Herder all of the Indian tradition was a potential source of regeneration for European society. For Schlegel there were only traces of the original revelation in the religion and poetry of the Indians, to be found primarily in their earliest works, which were still largely unknown.

Friedrich Max Müller

The Veda remained unexplored territory for scholars. Max Müller, son of the romantic poet and scholar of Greek Wilhelm Müller (1794–1827), took upon himself the task of compiling and editing the Veda for the first time from manuscripts and making it known

---

[20] Schlegel 1976: 317.

to the Western world, and he invested energy in this venture as no other Indologist of his generation had done before him. More than anything else it was Schlegel's work which inspired Max Müller, as so many others at the time, to turn his attention towards Indian studies, for as he noted in 1860: 'This work was like the wand of a magician. It pointed out the place where a mind should be opened; and it was not long before some of the most distinguished scholars of the day began to sink their shafts and raise the ore.'[21]

His pioneering and painstaking edition of the *Rgveda* (1849–73), along with the medieval commentary by Shayana, gained him an immense reputation in India as well as Europe. In 1859 his *A History of Ancient Indian Literature* was published.[22] In it he offered the fruits of his own philological research and summarized—within the bounds of his conceptual framework—all the available information on the literature and religion of the Vedic period. The book was an instant success. The first edition was sold out within five months of publication; in the following year a second edition appeared.

Max Müller stated the aims of his work in no uncertain terms: 'to discover the first germs of the language, religion and mythology of our forefathers, the wisdom of Him who is not the God of the Jews alone.'[23] Right at the beginning, then, he draws a clear distinction between his own branch of language, religion, and mythology, and that of the Semites. To the ancestors of his own race, Max Müller

---

[21] Müller 1965: 176. Schlegel's work proved to be an inexhaustible source of inspiration for the pioneering generation of German Indologists: Franz Bopp, A.W. von Schlegel, Christian Lassen, to name a few.

[22] Reprinted in India (Delhi, 1965) with the following justification: 'It is however true that some of his conclusions have, now, become back-dated, some of his cautious conjectures have proved futile, in a number of cases he might have been mistaken, due to insufficient data then at his disposal, to determine the true spirit and value of ancient Indian culture, but the method he followed to reconstruct the cultural history of India's past, the scholarly sincerity he displayed at every step of the work and, over and above the love he cherished for India can never be devalued; so the intrinsic merit of the work is still held in high esteem.'

[23] Müller 1968: 3.

assigned the designation 'Aryans', a term with a remarkable historical reception.[24]

> They have been the prominent actors in the great drama of history and have carried to their fullest growth all the elements of active life with which our nature is endowed. They have perfected society and morals, and we learn from their literature and works of art, the elements of science, the laws of art and the principles of philosophy ... these Aryan nations have become the rulers of history, and it seems to be their mission to link all parts of the world together by the chains of civilization, commerce and religion. In a word, they represent the Aryan man in the historical character.[25]

This active side of the Northern European Aryans was still extant in the poetic compositions of the Vedic *rishis*. Later, in the rich, fertile plains of Central India, this energy was turned inwards; it was to become abstract and passive with time. This was the explanation for the absence of history and the failure to establish political dominance over wide tracts of the earth's surface. It was this notion again which prompted Max Müller to maintain that there was in fact no heroic poetry after the Vedic age. The germinal sections of the two epics, the *Ramayana* and the *Mahabharata*, belonged to the Vedic period, since identical genealogies could be traced in the Veda. In character and behaviour the figures of the later epics differed from the heroic typology of the shorter hymns of the Veda, these latter being then much more amenable to comparison with Homeric hymns.

The criteria for the division of Vedic literature into successive epochs were not only thematic, they were also formal: metrical

---

[24] The term 'Aryan' was not originally coined by Max Müller. It was introduced into German by J.F. Kleuker in his translation of Anquetil Deuteron's *Zend Avesta* (Riga, 1776–81). Friedrich Schlegel used the term for the Indo-Persian languages and peoples. A.W. von Schlegel's pupil C. Lassen used it first as a designation for the so-called Indo-Germanic peoples. For further details, see Roemer 1985: 65–6. Max Müller, however, bears full responsibility for the popularization of the term, a responsibility he willingly acknowledges in the *History* as well as in a later essay, 'Aryan as a Technical Term', German version in Müller 1879, 333–45.

[25] Müller 1968: 13.

innovation signalled a new epoch. Since the *anushtubh shloka* was not familiar in the Vedic age, the epics, Manu's Law books, the Puranas as well as the Shastras and Darshanas were excluded from this period. The rest of the works were then classified chronologically into four periods: Chandas, Mantra, Brahmana, and Sutra.

Max Müller constructs his edifice with care, with a certain amount of suspense inbuilt. He begins his descriptive analysis backwards, starting from the Sutra period, i.e. the six Vedangas, or the six disciplines necessary for the right understanding of the Veda: phonetics, ritual, grammar, etymology, metrics, and astronomy. The Sutra period was apparently an age when a spontaneous understanding of Vedic hymns was no longer possible. Max Müller describes the style of the Sutras thus: 'It is impossible to give anything like a translation of these works, written as they are in the most artificial, elaborate and enigmatical form. Sutra means a string . . .' (64). 'There is no life and no spirit in these Sutras' (65). The various Sutras had been composed for practical purposes: to disentangle the theological and mystical meandering of the Brahmanas, to teach and make them widely comprehensible. Max Müller recounts attempts to date the Sutras, and compares these with the chronology of the Buddhists. Half of the *History* consists of this documentation. Only towards the end does he allow himself to remark that, with the passing of time, the Sutra style degenerated further. Of Panini he says: 'He is no longer writing and composing, but he squeezes and distils his thoughts and puts them before us in a form which hardly deserves the name of style . . .' (260). Katyayana is 'algebraic', Pingala possesses the greatest possible measure of 'enigmatic obscurity' (280).

It is in the third Vedic period, that of the Brahmanas, that Max Müller apprehends most clearly the fall from original clarity. In this, as in the section on the Sutra period, he likes to speak of the ancient Hindus, not of the Aryans.

He treats the Aranyakas and the Upanishads briefly, conceding that they have a virtually unlimited range of ideas and speculations. According to his conceptions of the natural and the originally authentic, he judges them to be 'a most extraordinary medley of oracular sayings . . . all tending to elucidate the darkest points of philosophy and religion, the creation of the world, the nature of God and similar subjects. That one statement should be contradicted by another seems never to have been felt as a serious difficulty' (288). The reason for contradictions and half truths being that the authors were poets who composed according to fantasy, seeking to follow their own subjective visions of reality. In a degenerate social order there could be no question of knowledge, leave alone any kind of spiritual enlightenment. Degenerate, since this philosophizing was meant for forest ascetics who had retired from active participation in social life. 'In a healthy state of society these questions were discussed in courts and camps: priests were contradicted by kings, sages confounded by children, women were listened to when they were moved by an unknown spirit' (304).[26]

The Brahmanas, theological tracts, were related only distantly to the original faith and rituals of the Aryans. After a conscientious recounting of all the schools and teaching traditions, Max Müller comes to the following conclusions: 'No one could have supposed that at so early a period, and in so primitive a state of society, there could have risen a literature which for pedantry and downright

[26] Later, Max Müller's attitude to the Upanishads and Vedanta philosophy changed considerably; the latter was in any case not discussed in the *History*, since it was allotted to a period later than the one his book dealt with. He was to translate the Upanishads for the 'Sacred Books of the East' series, which he edited, but most of all, in *Three Lectures on the Vedanta Philosophy* (1894) he was to speak of his admiration for the teachings of Badarayana and Sankara. He was also ready to settle his previous differences with the Upanishads: 'To us the Upanishads have, of course, a totally different interest. We watch in them the historical growth of philosophical thought, and are not offended therefore by the variety of their opinions. On the contrary, we expect to find a variety, and are even pleased when we find independent thought and apparent contradictions between individual teachers although the general tendency of all is the same' (33–4). However, when concluding he qualified this verdict: 'Remember that all this Vedanta Philosophy was never esoteric, but it was open to all, and was elaborated by men who, in culture and general knowledge, stood far below any one of us here present . . . should the wisdom reached by the dark skinned inhabitants of India two or three thousand years ago be too high or too deep for us?' (171).

absurdity can hardly be matched anywhere' (352). Moreover, 'These works deserve to be studied as the physician studies the twaddle of idiots and the ravings of mad men' (353). Or, he says, as an example of how 'the fresh and healthy growth of a nation is blighted by priestcraft and superstition' (353). He cites extensively from passages on the initiatory ritual *diksaniya* in the *Aitareya Brahmana*, a ritual once simple and spontaneous but now distorted beyond all recognition. In the beginning, all ritual was spontaneous and intrinsically significant. Apparently, the composers of the Brahmanas harboured the belief that all the Vedic hymns had been composed exclusively for the purpose of ritual sacrifice. Hence the development of Vedic exegesis in India, and the creation of new deities out of words which had never been conceived of as names for divine beings: mythology as the sickness of language, originating in the second Vedic period, and enthusiastically elaborated upon in the third.[27]

Small wonder then that for Max Müller the Brahmanas presuppose 'a complete break in the primitive tradition of the Aryan settlers of India' (417). These tendencies did not exist in this age alone; they went back to the second Vedic period, in which the later hymns of the *Rgveda*—according to Max Müller the greater mass of them— had been composed. 'A spirit was at work in the literature of India, no longer creative, free and original, but living on the heritage of a former age, collecting, classifying and imitating' (ibid.). No longer the age of 'poets, but no priests, prayers but no dogmas; worship but no ceremonies' (ibid.). The vast number of priests needed for rituals was alone sufficient indication that the later hymns were composed in a period when there was no memory of the time when the patriarch, the father of the family, was priest, poet, and king all in one person. In order to distinguish between the first and second periods of Vedic literature, language alone did not suffice as criterion. Oral tradition

---

[27] Schlegel had called this 'worship of the wild forces of Nature', and this 'sinking from the Creator to his works': 'Oriental Materialism', in Schlegel 1976: 219. The Christian Occident could only distance itself from it, 'for it is always the highest and the noblest, which becomes hideously malformed, once it runs wild and degenerates' (ibid.: 221).

had levelled out all difference and created uniformity to an extent 'which baffles the most careful analysis' (454). The only criterion which could then be available was a kind of unerring intuition: 'We feel that we move in a different atmosphere . . . listening to priests rather than poets' (450).

Finally it was important to register that this period was innocent of any knowledge of script. As evidence Max Müller noted that in the Vedic pantheon no place was reserved for a deity responsible for the signs of a script. This corresponded well with all the other authentic mythologies of the Aryan world. Once again, distinct polarities were established. It was the Semites, Moses in the Old Testament, who had known of the script. Clearly, it was being implied that the written was a less spontaneous and less natural means of transmission than the oral.

The last section of the *History*, relatively short, based on little that admits of direct evidence, is devoted to the period towards which the reader's suspense has been directed all along: 'The three periods all point to some earlier age which gave birth to the poetry of the early Rishis' (481). We have now reached the depiction of the golden age of Aryan history. Max Müller speaks exclusively of the Aryans, no more of the ancient Hindus. The songs of the *rishis* lived and were understood, he says, by a simple, pious race. The rites of Vedic sacrifice, later spun out so monstrously, 'were dictated by the free impulse of the human heart, a yearning to render thanks to some Unknown Being, and to repay, in words or deeds, a debt of gratitude, accumulated from the first breath of life' (481). Here there was no trace of elaborate ritual—not as the later superstitious age knew it. As an example he cites a hymn to Ushas, the glow of dawn (*Rgveda* VII, 77). Here, no technical expressions for ritual operations were used, it was a 'natural vision of a visible deity' (505). Moral order reigned supreme here, not priestly craft. He quotes a hymn to Varuna, who watches over this order (489). In short, the kernel of all religion, whether natural or revealed, was preserved in these hymns. 'There is belief in God, the perception of the difference between good and evil, the conviction that God hates sin and loves the righteous' (492). These realizations almost deserved to be recognized as revelation: God is gracious, He is judge, but also Father (495). Later this first, flexible, organic state of affairs became rigid, ossified into Mythology; the power of nature, behind which the Aryans had first discerned God, assumed the shape of independent deities. 'Dyaus' the luminous sky, was now worshipped as a divine being.

Finally, in the well-known hymn, *Rgveda* X, 121, which Max Müller accepts as late, the kernel of which he however dates back to the first period, he discerns the idea of one God—monotheism proper—clearly stated: 'it will make us hesitate before we deny to the Aryan nation an instinctive monotheism' (521). Max Müller has already taken the precaution of drawing a clear distinction between the primitive Aryans and the really barbaric tribes, such as the African negroes and the American Indians, to whom this instinctive monotheism was denied (511).

In conclusion, then:

1. Max Müller discovered the ancient age of the Aryans in the earliest Vedic period. Schlegel had supposed this to have preceded the tradition that the Indians preserved. The image of the prehistoric past, first envisaged by Herder, was thus confirmed by the findings of Vedic philology.
2. The difference was that Herder had been concerned with the universal history of the human race; Max Müller, however, just as Schlegel before him, was concerned primarily with the past of his own branch of the family of mankind. With philological evidence to support him, he sought to demonstrate that the ancient Aryans were in fact most akin to the ancient Germans as described by Tacitus, 'agricultural nomads . . . they had recognized the bonds of blood and the bonds of marriage; they followed their leaders and kings, and the distinction between right and wrong was fixed by laws and customs. They were impressed by the idea of a Divine Being, and they invoked it by different names.'[28]

---

[28] Müller 1965: 245. For the Germanic ideology of the nineteenth century and the Tacitus-enthusiasm in the twenties of the twentieth century, see Roemer 1985: 85–102.

3. Herder had been a vehement critic of European politics. Schlegel's critique of Western society was restricted by 1808 to the poetical-religious sphere. Max Müller, convinced of the unmatched progress achieved by Europe, refrained from all criticism. The Aryans of north-western Europe dominated the rest of the world as a natural privilege: 'the Teutonic race, the most vigorous and enterprising of all members of the Aryan family . . . planted new states in the West and regenerated the effete kingdoms of the East . . . they preached among the slaves of West Indian landholders and the slaves of Brahmanical soulholders, until they greeted at last the very homes from which the Aryan family had started . . .'[29]

4. The gains of Indian studies were for Max Müller no longer the regeneration of European society. What had been gained was knowledge of the European Aryans' past. Nearly half a century later, he could still maintain (and here the choice of imagery is noteworthy) 'Many of Bopp's, Grimm's and Pott's etymologies have had to be *surrendered* and yet *our suzerainty* over that distant country which they *conquered*, over the Aryan home, remains.'[30] The images are of war, booty and territory seized. In his veneration of the achievements of Vedic philology, in his estimation of the Vedic Aryans as the ancestors of the Indo-Germanic family of peoples, in his denigration of the later Brahmanic tradition, and finally in his attempt to draw a clear line of demarcation between the Aryans and the Semites, Max Müller is no lone specimen of early German Indology. He belongs in fact to the mainstream of Veda research in the nineteenth century.[31] Similar attitudes are for instance also typical of even so sober a scholar as Rudolph von Roth, coeditor of the Petersburg-Sanskrit dictionary. For

---

[29] Müller 1965: 236.

[30] Müller 1974: 148, emphasis added.

[31] Academic German Indology has tended to view what it regarded as Max Müller's popular and non-scholarly activities with disfavour. For a recent example, see Hermann Berger: 'Max Müller: What Can He Teach Us?', in Rau 1974.

him, too, race, language, and religion form a single unit. For him, too, the literature of the ancient Indians and Persians offers the only access to the ancient history of that family of peoples 'who are now the bearers of Christianity, as in the pre-Christian era, they were the bearers of universal history.'[32] Light was characteristic of the Indo-Germanic type of religion, just as the love of night was typical of the Semitic religions.

It would not be difficult to locate and cite any number of similar examples from nineteenth-century German Indology.

In the foregoing no attempt has been made to treat the manifold aspects of Max Müller's relationship to India and Indians. The central focus has been rather to scrutinize the functions of the Veda research which was centrally situated in his own works. Later, as in many other aspects of his scholarly activities, he modified his position. The kernel of his original thesis, however, remained intact.

Towards the end of his long career, Max Müller was overtaken by the laws of phonetic change—with which many of his carefully constructed etymologies inevitably collapsed—as well as by an anthropology which had gained increasingly in confidence.[33] He distanced himself from the gross misuse of racial theories in his often publicized speech at the University of Strassbourg in 1872.[34] Most of all, however, in his book *Biographies of Words* (1888) he took care to draw a clear line of distinction between himself and the most fervent propagators of racial theories, whom he then also expressly named: Theodor Poesche, Wilhelm Tomaschek, Karl Penka.[35] In his later

---

[32] Roth 1857: 171. For a descriptive analysis of Roth's theories of language and religion, see Nanko 1980.

[33] Andrew Lang was one of Max Müller's most vehement and sharp-tongued opponents. For a specimen of his critique, see 'Fetishism and the Infinite', in Lang 1970: 212–42.

[34] Though even here there are passages which are strongly reminiscent of his earlier writings: for instance Müller 1876: 113.

[35] For details on Penka, see Roemer 1985: 23ff., 64ff.

works he was on the defensive; he was more cautious when matters of race could be detected in his works. He did not speak of 'race' or 'folk'; he replaced these with terms like 'the Aryan family', 'the Aryan man, whom we know in his various characters as Greek, Roman, German, Celt and Slav', 'Northern Aryans', 'Aryan humanity'.[36]

In response to and in an effort to integrate Darwinian evolutionary theories and Tylor's views on primitive religion, Max Müller modified and altered his perspective by many minor adjustments of terminology. But here again 'most of these modifications are designed to reconcile his original position with those of his critics, while at the same time preserving the most fundamental principles of his original view . . . Issues to the fore in the initial encounters still remain at the end, though displaced from bold and prominent to hidden and esoteric areas of rhetoric and theory.'[37]

In his estimation of the Vedic period, Max Müller remained unshaken. Even in his later oft-cited book, *India—What Can it Teach Us?*, which is frequently held up as an example of his admiration for the country, he maintained expressly that his India was ancient India, 'such as it was a thousand, two thousand, it may be three thousand years ago . . .'[38] He would also include as his India the unchanging Indian countryside, which had remained untouched by Muslim and British influence, an idealization of the eternal countryside and the unchanging peasant best represented by Sir Henry Maine's well-known apotheosis of the Aryan village in *Village Communities in the East and West* (1871), itself much influenced by the German historical school and the findings of comparative philology. As such, only the history of Hindu India, up to the year 1000, was of real interest to Max Müller.[39] This, with the reservation that only Vedic

---

[36] Müller 1883: 23, 95, 102, 112. Here, once again, there is the North–South division of the Aryan linguistic family with the by-now-familiar typology, North: active, South: passive, meditative. Here and there, also, instances of the use of 'race': 'the civilization of the Aryan race, that race to which we and all the greatest nations of the world . . . belong . . .' Ibid.: 116.
[37] Schrempp 1983: 102.
[38] Müller 1883: 7.
[39] Ibid.: 54.

literature was to be considered true to nature and thus authentic, the later literature being modern and artificial: 'The modern Sanskrit literature never was a living or national literature. It here and there contains remnants of earlier times, adapted to the literary, religious and moral tastes of a later period . . . But the great mass of that later literature is artificial and scholastic, full of interesting compositions, and by no means devoid of originality, and occasional beauty, yet with all that, curious only . . .'[40] If on the one hand the glorification of the Aryan-Vedic past and the theories of subsequent decadence were to have considerable bearing on the Indian self-image and assessment of the national past, they were conversely also to justify and support the policy-making of the colonial government.[41] The general consensus in Europe regarding the national character, racial typology, and cultural history of the Indian peoples was to find reification in the anthropocentric and the classificatory categories of the Indian Census Survey of 1901: 'the record of physical characters bears out the conclusion suggested by philology.'[42]

References

Gadamer, Hans Georg, 1927. 'Herder und die geschichtliche Welt', in *Kleine Shriften III. Idee und Sprache.* Tuebingen.
Gerard, Rene, 1963. *L'Orient et la pensee romantique allemande.* Paris.
Herder, Johann Gottfried, 1982. *Herders Werke* (Selected Works), vol. 3, selected and introduced by Regine Otto. Berlin/Weimar.
Hoffmann, Paul Th., 1915. 'Der Indische und der Deutsche Geist von Herder bis zur Romantik, Eine literar-historische Darstellung', Diss. Tuebingen.
Kopf, David, 1969. *British Orientalism and the Bengal Renaissance.* Calcutta.

[40] Ibid.
[41] Leopold 1974: 593.
[42] Risley 1969: 35. Here it seems only fair to put on record Max Müller's protest regarding the 'unholy alliance' of ethnology and philology in a letter to Risley, who was then conducting an ethnographic survey of Bengal (Risley 1969: 7). However, by registering the protest Max Müller seemed only to be denying the possibilities of interpretation inherent in his own work.

Lang, Andrew, 1970. *Custom and Myth*. London, 1885. Repr. Oosterhout, Netherlands.
Leopold, Joan, 1974. 'British Application of the Aryan Theory of Race to Indian, 1850–1870', in *English Historical Review* 89.
Marshall, Peter James, ed., 1970. *The British Discovery of Hinduism in the Eighteenth Century*. Cambridge.
Meyer, Heinz, 1981. 'Ueberlegungen zu Herders Metaphern fuer die Geschichte', in *Archiv fuer Begriffsgeschichte*, vol. XXV, Bonn.
Max Müller, Friedrich, 1879. *Essays*, vol. 1, 2nd edition. Leipzig.
———, 1883. *India—What Can it Teach Us?* London.
———, 1888. *Biographies of Words and the Home of the Aryas*. London.
———, 1894. *Three Lectures on the Vedanta Philosophy*. London.
———, 1965. *The Science of Language*, 1860. Repr. Delhi.
———, 1968. *A History of Ancient Indian Literature*, 1859. Repr. Delhi.
———, 1979. *My Autobiography. A Fragment*, 1901. Repr. Varanasi.
Nanko, Ulrich, 1980. 'Die Geschichte des Lehrstuhls fuer Vergleichende Religionswissenschaften an der Universitaet Tuebingen'. Unpublished Master's thesis, Tuebingen.
Nuesse, Heinrich, 1962. *Die Sprachtheorie Friedrich Schlegels*. Heidelberg.
Rau, Heimo, ed., 1974. *Max Müller. What He Can Teach Us*. Bombay.
Risley, Herbert, 1969. *The People of India*, 1908. Repr. Delhi.
Rocher, Ludo, 1978. 'Max Müller and the Veda', in Melanges Armand Abel, ed. A. Destree, vol. 3, Leiden, 1984.
———, ed., with an Introduction. 1984. *Ezourvedam. A French Veda of the Eighteenth Century*. Amsterdam/Philadelphia, Pa.
Rocher, Rosanne, 1968. *Alexander Hamilton. 1762–1824: A Chapter in the Early History of Sanskrit Philology*. New Haven.
Roemer, Ruth, 1985. *Sprachwissenschaft und Rassenidelogie in Deutschland*. Muenchen.
Schlegel, Friedrich, 1976. *Kritische Ausgabe* (Critical Edition), vol. VIII, ed. Ernst Behler and Ursula Struc-Oppenberg. Paderborn.
Schrempp, Gregory, 1983. 'The Re-education of Friedrich Max Müller', in *Man*, 18/1, March.
Struc-Oppenberg, Ursula, 1969. 'Zu Friedrich Schlegels orientalischen Studien', in *Zeitschrift fuer deutsche Philologie*, 88.
Szondi, Peter, 1974. 'Poetik und Geschichtsphilosophie I', *Antike and Moderne in der Aesthetik der Goethezeit*, ed. Santa Metz and Hans-Hagen Hildebrandt. Frankfurt am Main.

Timpanaro, Sebastian, 1977. Introductory article transl. from the Italian by J. Peter Maher, New Edition of 'Ueber die Sprache and Weisheit der Indier', Amsterdam Classics in Linguistics 1800–1925, vol. I. Amsterdam.

von Roth, Rudolph, 1857. *Die Heiligen Schriften der Arier: Jahrbucher fuer die deutsche Theologie*, vol. 2. Stuttgart.

Willson, A. Leslie, 1964. *A Mythical Image. The Ideal of India in German Romanticism*. Durham.

2

Sanskrit Scholars and Pandits of the Old School

The Benares Sanskrit College and the Constitution of Authority in the Late Nineteenth Century

THE HISTORY OF THE BENARES SANSKRIT COLLEGE, founded in 1791, provides an opportunity to follow the stages of one variety of East–West encounter in which knowledge-formation and pedagogy themselves formed the core of the debates. The encounter could be said to climax in the debate between an Orientalist and an 'Oriental' at the end of the nineteenth century. After thorough mutual exposure to the method of each other, it was the learned 'Oriental' who, far from being silenced, showed a breadth of vision and generosity that remains rare in the academic world.

Kashi's reputation as a learned and religious centre was registered at the very onset of colonial rule;[1] and it soon acquired multi-dimensional authority with British administrators, travellers, and

---

[1] There is an instance in 1778 of the British requiring a *vyavastha* from Banaras pandits, over the question whether an adopted son could inherit the full share of his father's estates. Governor General Hastings questioned the Banaras pandits via Raja Chait Singh. The *vyavastha* which followed was signed

historians, who initiated the development of a parallel Western tradition regarding the significance of Kashi as an eminently Hindu city.[2] The information they received from the Brahmans, who remained their main informants on this point, confirmed the reputation of the city as the ancient centre of a Hinduism conceived as a unitary—however unwieldy—religious tradition. And they understood the Brahmans of the city, again viewed as a single body, as a centralizing force, regulating, ordering, and administering the religious and learned tradition of Hindus from the earliest historical period. The first generation of British administrators, following the policy laid down by Warren Hastings of ruling the subject population by their own laws and customs, and inspired by the work of William Jones and the Asiatic Society in Calcutta, attempted to draw benefit from the authority of the learned traditions of the city. They developed a concern for rescuing and preserving for posterity the knowledge preserved both in the minds of such men and in manuscripts. This salvaging motif, an anxiety peculiar to the Western discovery of other cultures, was to remain a constant preoccupation.[3]

William Robertson, in his *An Historical Disquisition concerning the Knowledge which the Ancients had of India* (1791–1804), put it

---

by 31 pandits. There was, then, a group of pandits in the city whose knowledge of law was supra-regionally recognized. Cf. Gabriel 1979: 83–4.

[2] The Muslim presence there was minimal by comparison, as James Prinsep was to point out when compiling the results of the 1823 census of the city, which he had conducted: 'The *Muselmans* apparently form but one-fifth of the population, and are not more numerous than the *Brahmans* alone; very few of them reside within the City, properly so called, which is almost exclusively *Hindu*'. Prinsep 1932: 477. Of these Muslims, the larger number were involved in the weaving trade.

[3] Cf. Marcus and Fischer 1986: 24; Clifford and Marcus 1986: 1139; as also Williams 1973/1985: 9–12, who, in initiating his own investigation into the relationship of vanishing cultures and landscapes in English literature, offers the critical framework for placing the sense of loss relating to them. This framework, according to Williams, is determined by the respective historical perspective and 'the criticism which the retrospect supports: religious, humanist, political, cultural.'

thus: 'Benares has been from time immemorial the Athens of India, the residence of the most learned Brahmins, and the seat both of science and literature', adding: 'There, it is highly probable, whatever remains of the ancient astronomical knowledge and discoveries of the Brahmins is still preserved.' But all this knowledge, or what remained of it, seemed doomed to perish. It was the task of the ruling power to rescue it from oblivion.

> In an enlightened age and nation, and during a reign distinguished by a succession of the most splendid and successful undertakings to extend the knowledge of nature, it is an object worthy of public attention, to take measures for obtaining possession of all that time has spared of the philosophy and inventions of the most early and most highly civilized people of the east. It is with peculiar advantages Great Britain may engage in this laudable undertaking. Benares is subject to its dominion; the confidence of the Brahmins has been so far gained as to render them communicative; some of our countrymen are acquainted with that sacred language in which the mysteries both of religion and of science are recorded; movement and activity has been given to a spirit of inquiry throughout all the British establishments in India; persons who visited that country with other views, though engaged in occupations of a very different kind, are now carrying on scientific and literary researches with ardour and success . . . Thus Great Britain may have the glory of exploring fully that extensive field of unknown science, which the Academicians of France had the merit of first opening to the people of Europe. (257–8)

Apart from the laurels that Great Britain would acquire in mediating this knowledge to the rest of the civilized world, more pragmatic concerns motivated the interest in the city at this early stage of colonization. The knowledge not only of the science, but also of the religion of the Hindus, was needed in order to govern the country effectively.

What were the learned traditions which existed in the city before the arrival of the British, and by what means were they further transmitted? Travellers' reports from the mid-seventeenth century testify that there were *pathshalas* or institutions of learning attached to some of the larger temples. These *pathshalas* as well as the tuitions in the houses of learned pandits were financed and supported by wealthy merchants, as also by Rajput and Maratha chiefs.[4] This was presumably the situation as the British encountered it in the early nineteenth century. In 1818 the British missionary William Ward published a major work on the history, literature, and mythology of the Hindus. He recorded the names of the famous teachers of Kashi and the disciplines they taught, their place of residence, and the number of students. According to his information, small groups of teachers were scattered throughout the city. The subjects taught were the Vedas, Shastra, Panini's grammar, Kavya, Vedanta, Mimamsa, Nyaya, Dharmashastra, and astronomy. Teachers of a particular discipline tended to live in one area; the number of pupils varied from ten to twenty-five. They spent up to twelve years with their teachers. The majority of the names were Maharashtrian, and, not surprisingly, they were clustered around the ghats built by the Marathas.[5] These schools were to continue to operate till well into the British period. A report of 1850 records 193 Sanskrit schools with a total of 1939 scholars in the city, in addition to 318 Hindi and Sanskrit mixed schools with 1949 scholars.[6]

British patronage began to play a prominent part from 1791 onwards, when the Benares Sanskrit College was founded. The British Resident, Jonathan Duncan, specified the main objectives, in his letter to the Earl of Cornwallis, Governor-General-in-Council, on 1 January 1791:

> Having in view to the surplus Revenue expected to be derived from the permanent settlement, it appeared to me that a part of those funds could not be applied to more general advantage or with more local propriety than by the Institution of a Hindoo College or Academy for the preservation and cultivation of the Laws, literature and Religion of that nation, at this centre of their faith, and the common resort of all their tribes.

[4] Cf. Moticandra 1962/1985: 217ff.
[5] Cf. Gabriel 1979: 34ff.
[6] As against this, there were only six of the type of school listed as 'Sanskrit-Nagari-Mahajani'. Henry Stewart Reid, *Report on Indigenous Education and Vernacular Schools* (Agra: Secundra Orphan Press, 1852), cited in Kumar 1998.

Two advantages seemed derivable from such an establishment, the first to the British name and nation in its tendency towards endearing our Government to the Native Hindoos; by our exceeding in our attention towards them and their systems, the care shown by their own native princes; for although learning has ever been cultivated at Benares, in numerous private seminaries, yet no public Institution of the kind here proposed ever appears to have existed; . . . to accumulate at only a small and comparative expense to Government, a precious library of the most ancient and valuable general learning and tradition now perhaps existing on any part of the globe.

The 2nd principal advantage that may be derived from this Institution will be felt in its effects more immediately by the natives, though not without being participated in by the British subjects, who are to rule over them, by preserving and disseminating a knowledge of the Hindoo Law and proving a nursery of future doctors and expounders thereof, to assist the European judges in the due, regular and uniform administration of its genuine letter and spirit to the body of the people.[7]

Duncan, then, recognizing the claims of the city's learned traditions to encompass the knowledge of the laws, literature, and religion of the nation, proposed that the British salvage, institutionalize, and administer this knowledge. A public institute was to replace or supersede the existing private seminaries. Radical structural changes, as we shall see, would be gradually introduced.

The college began to function from the end of 1791. Enough 'custom' had to be preserved if the institution was to gain native recognition. 'Hindu literature' was understood as the study of the Vedas and Vedangas. With the exception of medicine and grammar, which could be taught by a scholar of the *vaidya* caste, all other teachers were to be Brahmans. They were to receive comparatively high salaries as part of the plan to enhance the prestige of the college. The curriculum was left entirely to the teachers. However, there were obvious structural departures from the traditional system. For one thing, not only were the students to receive education free of charge, they were in fact to receive stipends from government. This was to lead to the first misunderstanding, since the first rector of

---

[7] Nicholls 1907: 1. Further citations from this work will appear as page references within the main text.

the college, Pandit Kashinath, who was also Duncan's pandit, simply retained the stipends of the students, which he considered a part of his own fee.

There were several other occurrences, a result of cross-cultural misunderstanding, which were viewed as 'abuses' by the English. A committee was appointed in 1799 to review the organization of the college. The conclusion was almost foregone: 'The President, Mr. John Neave, declared the Rector Kashinath Pandit to be the greatest villain he ever saw' (6). The pandit was subsequently dismissed. But the incompatibility of the two systems of learning was not to be easily resolved. The pandits were not familiar with the practice of public teaching, and there was consequent malfunctioning at this most fundamental level of pedagogical communication. The Minute of F. Brooke, Second Judge of Banares and Acting President of the Committee, was to affirm on 2 January 1801: 'The college instead of being looked up to by the natives with respect and veneration is an object of ridicule; instead of an assemblage of learned Hindus, it resembles a band of pensioners supported by Government' (9). Amongst other recommendations to streamline and structure the chaos in the college, the committee recommended that the pandits revert to the personal methods of teaching. This formed the backbone of the traditional pedagogical relationship between teacher and pupil, i.e. the *guru–shishya parampara*, and would make the college functional rather than an anomaly. A recommendation was made 'that the Professors be selected from amongst Pandits who may have a reputation for learning, and that they be required to teach their pupils, and to read their lectures at their own houses, and not in a public college' (13).

The college continued to languish in the confusion created by cross-cultural systems of patronage and pedagogy. A radical overhauling of the system occurred in 1820, when annual examinations were introduced for the first time, as also public displays of the skills of debate acquired in the college. From this time on an effort seems to have been made to create a new public image of the college and to co-opt the traditional patrons of learning into countenancing and financing the institution under the headship of the British. The prize-giving ceremony held on 1 January 1821 was organized for the first time as a public occasion. British civil and military officers were invited, as were 'a numerous party of the most distinguished residents residing at and near Benares' (47). In his address to students and pandits during a public distribution of prizes to students for proficiency, Captain Fell, secretary of the committee appointed for the occasion, proclaimed:

> The attention shown by the Pandits to their respective classes has not escaped the serious consideration of the committee, and it affords them the greatest pleasure in thinking that the name of the Benares institution must with the same care on the part of the Pandits and perseverance on the part of the pupils, be most fully established as the seminary of the first order, and further that the proud consolation of being a material cause in the revival of Sanskrit Literature will be applicable to this institution. Indeed it becomes you all most seriously to reflect that the restoration of fading Hindu lore as well as the fame of the college rests entirely on the exertions and talents displayed by you as the members of this Government establishment.[8]

Hindu lore, fast fading, required the pandits to perform the proud task of reviving Sanskrit literature under British patronage. At the public disputation in January 1821 the Raja of Banaras presented Rs 1000 to the institution, and 'the higher class of natives' presented it Rs 4387. The college authorities feared that the motives of the presentees were suspect: they merely wanted to be in the good graces of the government without being interested in the college. However, the patronage remained steady, even if the amounts donated varied considerably. The report of 1832 recorded that the rajas of Banaras and Vizianagaram, as well as the rajas Kalisankar Ghosh and Putnimul, attended the annual prize-giving function. From this time on the college maintained a high public profile.

In addition to refurbishing the image of the college, there was a steady anglicization of the structure, this being seen as a necessary measure of reform. Age limitations were introduced as well as entrance examinations. At the termination of their studies, students were awarded certificates of proficiency, which were to serve as a qualification for employment in any line of service in the Company.

[8] *Calcutta Gazette*, 22 March 1821, in Das Gupta 1959: 749.

One of the recommendations made in 1820 by a committee—which consisted amongst others of the Sanskritist H.H. Wilson—was that a European rector be appointed: 'We are indeed of opinion that the appointment of a native to that station will always prove useless, and perhaps worse; and cannot expect that the duties of the college will be systematically and sedulously attended to under any other than a European Superintendent' (31).

By the end of the second decade of the nineteenth century the changes in the intellectual climate in Calcutta made themselves felt in Banaras as well. Once the effects of the Anglicist–Orientalist controversy on the merits of the two systems of learning began to filter through to Upper India, Sanskrit learning could only be considered to be of limited practical use. Thus Captain Thoresby, in March 1829 to the General Committee of Public Instruction, Fort William, on the necessity of establishing classes for imparting knowledge of English language and literature, argued: 'for the object is to stock the mind of a certain portion of the rising generations with a true and useful knowledge and to communicate instruction in that kind of literature, an acquaintance with which will tend to assimilate tastes and feelings and models of thinking, reasoning etc. between those so educated and their foreign Governors; if successful in the execution, the scheme may incalculably be beneficial in its result *both morally and politically*' (68, emphasis added). In March 1829 funds were released for the establishment of an English College at Banaras, and in June 1830 the Benares Anglo-Indian Seminary, after November 1836 called Benares English Seminary or Benares Government School, was inaugurated.

In 1839 the college authorities registered a gradual falling off of pupils. This was mainly caused by the drastic reduction of stipends which followed the change of government policy regarding Sanskrit education. The traditional learning which had first been brought under British patronage and recast in structure was now being reduced in size. The law pandits had not been in demand for some time. In 1843 Mr Thomason, lieutenant governor of the province and devout Evangelical, proposed that the English and Sanskrit Colleges come together under the same roof. The 1843 report by

John Muir (1810–82),[9] on the progress of the Sanskrit College, recommended the study of useful works rather than the study of 'the abstruse systems of Hindu philosophy'. In 1844 Muir was appointed to supervise the reorganization of this Sanskrit College, the very institution created to uphold the religious tradition he had only recently tried to uproot in a well-known Sanskrit tract.

Muir's appointment can be regarded as evidence of pressure of the circle around Thomason to bring Christian influence to bear upon the college.[10] In a memorandum submitted to the education department, Muir took a clear stand on the religious and philosophic contents of the *darshanas* as taught in the college: 'The metaphysical systems are notoriously characterised by grave errors, the Vedanta being decidedly pantheistic, the Nyaya maintaining the eternity of matter, and the Sankhya in one of its branches being of an atheistic tendency: and even the astronomy which the scientific books of the Hindus teach is the exploded ptolemaic.'[11] Muir attempted to so manipulate the curriculum that the *darshanas* were deprived of all pretence to being revelations. Astrology, which provided the Brahmans with a livelihood, was for reasons of its inaccuracy in the light of modern research removed from the curriculum. The English and Sanskrit seminaries were henceforth to be united. Apart from one learned language, the study of one of the vernaculars was now a requirement.

In May 1845 J.R. Ballantyne was appointed principal of the college. He was much more fiercely committed to the cause of Christianity. It was his intention to make 'every educated Hindu a Christian'.[12] At the close of 1846 a report by him urged the study of Hindi. Further:

> The object of such an institution, I conceive (and I understand Mr. Muir to have considered) ought to be this, to produce Pandits, not merely

---

[9] Muir was a fierce Evangelical but also a Sanskritist of note who was later to edit the five volumes of the *Original Sanskrit Texts* (London, 1868–73).
[10] Cf. Young 1981: 53.
[11] Ibid.
[12] Ibid.: 55.

with Sanskrit learning equal to that which can be acquired in the native schools, but with minds so far tinctured with European habits of thought as shall render each of them in some degree a moral light amongst his country men.

The great influence which the Europeanized ideas of the learned Brahman, Ram Mohun Roy, exerted upon the native mind of Bengal, when contrasted with the comparatively slender influence exerted by well-educated and intelligent men of a different class, has always struck me as pointing to the combination of conditions which we must strive to bring about if we would aim successfully at raising the native character.[13]

Though the primary object of the college was still the study of the most valuable branches of Sanskrit learning, a secondary 'though not subordinate object' was the study of 'those works which constitute the glory of the nation which founded this college.'[14]

From the time of Muir and Ballantyne, then, traditional Sanskrit learning began to be evaluated critically and its importance reduced in comparison with Western philosophy and science. Ballantyne, in spite of his own considerable learning in the language and literature, had little use for traditional methods in learning: he questioned the whole pedagogical approach of the pandits. In a series of articles written in 1849 and published later in the college journal *The Pandit*, he demonstrated at length the tediousness of the traditional system of grammar; the entire irrelevance of the vast commentarial literature—which explained the most obvious of points at length; the obscure scholastic quibbling of the classical schools of philosophy which nurtured the equally obscure mental gymnastics needed to practise the art of debate or *shastrartha*, cultivated so assiduously by the pandits; and finally the intricate and ornamental art of Rhetoric, which revolved so ponderously upon itself.[15]

---

[13] Nicholls 1907: 102.

[14] Ibid.: 103.

[15] *The Pandit* began to be issued from 1866. It was to continue till 1917. The main objective was 'to publish rare Sanskrit works which appear worthy of careful editing hereafter; to offer a field of discussion of controverted points in old Indian Philosophy, Philology, History and Literature, to communicate ideas between the Aryans of the East and of the West—between the Pandits of Benares and Calcutta—and the Sanskritists of the Universities of Europe.'

The authority of the pandits in matters concerning literature and religion was considerably diminished by the seventies and eighties of the century, as evinced in the debate in 1884 between George Thibaut, then principal of the college, and Babu Pramadadas Mitra, formerly assistant professor in the Sanskrit department. The debate can be seen as the formal expression of the clash between the two systems, for here the two met head on. Dr Thibaut's memorandum, which set off the controversy, was occasioned by the proposal to revive the Anglo-Sanskrit department, which had been temporarily abolished in spite of public protest, in 1877, in the wake of an economy drive. The task of the old Anglo-Sanskrit department had been to impart as much English or European education as the young Brahmans were able to assimilate. 'But the leading idea remained at all times the same, viz., to superimpose on a liberal Sanskrit education a liberal European education' (109). Thibaut saw the revival as a necessary step, since it would fulfil

> the task, I mean, of gradually improving the methods on which the study of Sanskrit is at present carried on in the Benares Sanskrit College and of converting Pandits of the old school into accomplished Sanskrit scholars, in the European sense of the word. I do not by any means wish to under-rate the Sanskrit learning possessed by the Professors and many of the students of our Sanskrit College. Their deep and extensive reading, their most accurate knowledge of the technicalities of the Sanskrit Shastras, and their command of the Sanskrit language may well raise the envy of European scholars.
>
> On the other hand, not even the best of our Pandits can be said to possess a critical knowledge of the Sanskrit literature and language. They know nothing of the history of their language and the place it occupies

---

Ballantyne's article, 'The Pandits and their Manner of Teaching', was serialized in the journal from 1867 to 1868 and is available in the selections from the journal edited by Mishra (1991: 44–82). The condescending and heavily jocular tone of the article itself speaks volumes: 'It would not be easy to imagine a prospect more probably pregnant with plague, perplexity and disappointment—*in a small way*—than that of a person of mature years, who, having some leisure at his disposal, and being commendably inclined to employ it not unworthily, shall resolve to commence studying Sanskrit with a Pandit' (44, emphasis added).

among cognate languages. They have no idea of the gradual growth of their literature and the fact that it mirrors different phases of national and religious life. They are quite unable to discuss intelligently historical and chronological questions. They proceed most uncritically in editing texts etc. etc. It would of course be a hopeless undertaking to attempt all at once a radical reform of the entire Sanskrit College . . . And yet it appears only natural that in institutions maintained by a European Government some efforts should be made to render the study of Sanskrit more critical and—viewing the matter from a European point of view—more fertile than hitherto. (110)

Thibaut allowed that the pandits possessed a sound and even vast technical knowledge of their subject even as he undermined the very grounds and fundamentals of their learning—in that he applied solely European criteria, the historical-critical scholarship developed in the wake of Bible criticism, to evaluate the knowledge and methodology of the pandits. The course of studies recommended, once the students had acquired a sound knowledge of the English language, was to consist of

such English books as would have a direct bearing on their Sanskrit studies and enable them to form wider and more enlightened views of Indian literature, history and antiquities. Books, for instance, like Muir's Sanskrit Texts, Max Müller's and Weber's Histories of Indian literature, the Essays of Colebrook and Wilson, &c (to mention only a few of the many suitable works). The student might finally be made acquainted with the elements of comparative grammar and the researches of European scholars in the history of Indian languages. Last of all—and this is a point to which I would attach great importance—the ablest and most advanced students of the Department would under the guidance of their Professor attempt to turn their acquired scholarship to use by attempting independent research in the wide and unexplored field of Sanskrit literature. (111)

The students were to be offered professional prospects, which deflected them from the traditional course, that is: 'The hope of obtaining a degree of recognised value would determine many a student resolutely to turn his back on the old ways and lines of study to which custom, the influence of his surroundings and, in many cases, the anxiety for his future tie him at present and to turn to the new course opened for him' (ILL). In order to revamp the system it would be necessary to appoint a European professor who would guide and direct the course of studies and acquaint the students with the results of European research in the field of Indian languages, literature, and history. The European professor would add immensely to the prestige of the department. This would add to the financial burden of the college, but pecuniary assistance could be expected from rich natives, since 'Benares is still the foremost seat of Sanskrit learning and the Government College by far the most eminent among the different Sanskrit schools in Benares' (113). The kind of patronage traditionally offered to Sanskrit learning was now to be re-routed through a European principal.

Babu Pramadadas belonged to the Mitra clan, one of the prestigious Bengali merchant families in the Chaukhambha area. With all the rootedness and tradition as well as the self-confidence of one well versed in the new knowledge, he took a spirited stand on the issues raised by Thibaut. In his letter of 2 April 1884 he questioned the absolute validity claimed for historical knowledge. He took up Thibaut's terminology, he spoke in his terms, but he turned the phrases around, as befitted his perspective. The object of the proposed Anglo-Sanskrit department, as he understood it, was 'to convert a genuine Indian Pandit into a Sanskrit scholar of the European type.' His own opinion was unequivocal: 'The attempt at such a conversion, I am clearly of opinion, would be a sad mistake and a positive failure' (114). He brought forward three arguments to support his view. First, there was no doubt, even in European quarters—he invoked the names of Jones, Colebrook, Wilson, and Max Müller—regarding the intrinsic value of Sanskrit literature. But this Sanskrit literature was the outcome of a system of culture which neither knew the modern principles of historical criticism nor had brought forth a single work on history proper (that is, history as understood in the modern sense). Historicity made neither for creativity nor necessarily for depth in the given field of study. Historicizing a particular piece of work could tear it out of the contextual field in which it was embedded.

If the poetry and ethics, philosophy and theology, of ancient India have any value of their own; if the works of Valmiki and Vyasa, Sankara and Vacaspati, Sri Harsa and Madhava, Udayana and Abhinava Gupta, may be studied for intellectual delight and moral elevation, the culture and wisdom that they afford, then it is desirable that [the] class of men who study them deeply should be encouraged to study them still more deeply, and to flourish and grow in numbers as well as in intellectual vigour. (114)

Second, it was this kind of knowledge, possessed by 'Pandits of the true Indian type', which could provide the necessary cross-references from which European scholars, who had yet to learn a good deal about the numerous philosophical systems of India, drew nurture. The multi-referential works of the authors referred to above had come into existence in spite of 'history' and required more than history to explicate them: 'Indeed, if the great authors of India have not laboured only to furnish materials for a conjectured history of the rise and growth of a national and religious life, there are higher objects to be aimed for by a Sanskrit scholar' (114). It was not that history was not important: it provided, however, but one perspective.

Third, as regards the course of studies, the works recommended by Thibaut could be referred to two heads: (1) historical theories and conclusions, and (2) expositions of religious and philosophical systems. Historical knowledge could not, in spite of its claim, be free of error, prejudice, or partisanship of judgement, or claim universal validity so long as the criteria applied remained bound to the cultural, religious, and racial prejudices of the historian. Mitra was most explicit in his rejection of the universalist claims made by Western historical-critical scholarship:

> With regard to the first topic, historical theories, etc. it must be remarked that in the absence of any history in Sanskrit literature, they must necessarily be based in the main upon mere conjectures naturally influenced by the author's own social and religious sentiments. Again, without detracting from the great values of those works, I may venture to assert, and I think I shall not be guilty of presumption in so doing, that they are not altogether free from errors, errors sometimes serious and radical. So long as criticism, as employed in ascertaining dates and framing

historical theories, is not reduced to a system of universally recognised scientific rules, so long as there is an ample range for the imagination, and consequently a facility for religious prejudice or race feeling being unconsciously led into misrepresentations, the result of such a criticism, however elaborate and learned, cannot be properly laid into the hands of a student as possessing any historical authority. (115)

The periodization of literary and religious history as, for instance, Max Müller undertook in his *A History of Sanskrit Literature* (1859), was loaded with value judgements. The criteria applied here, both for dividing into periods and then evaluating their creativity, were based on Müller's concept of Aryan history. The Vedic age was glorified, and all that came after was seen as progressive decay, linguistic and religious, caused in part by India's luxuriant tropical climate and foliage.[16] Mitra referred to such scholarship obliquely when he spoke of racial and cultural prejudice. However, graver still were the consequences of placing works so squarely in past ages since their present validity was then relativized, for the diachronic sequencing tore knowledge out of its synchronic embedding in contemporary systems of thought and experience. The expositions of religious and philosophical systems could be safely left in the hands of the pandits of the old school, for 'learning in Sanskrit has not so completely died out of its native land as to require the Pandits themselves to resort to the works of European scholars (however valuable they may be for their own countrymen or persons unacquainted with the Sanskrit language) for the purpose of gleaning the most correct notions about their own religious and philosophical systems. Let not our paternal Government hasten that day of universal lamentation for India when her glorious past shall be divorced, irrevocably torn off from the present' (115).

Mitra did not ask for the mere conservation of traditional knowledge and pedagogy, as proposed by Duncan at the end of the eighteenth century. He had himself benefited from Western knowledge. But, as against Thibaut, he asked not only that the methodology developed in the West be extracted from their sciences and imparted

---

[16] Cf. Dalmia-Luderitz 1987.

to Oriental students only so far as it could be considered applicable to Sanskrit texts, but that the knowledge of these sciences itself be transmitted to them, to 'train up a class of men combining Eastern wisdom with Western enlightenment' (116). And it was in this sense that he asked that the course of studies for the proposed Anglo-Sanskrit department comprise 'standard English works on constitutional history and political economy, the principles of jurisprudence, science, and philosophy: in short, such subjects as address themselves much more specially to the reasoning powers than to memory' (116).

Mitra was asking for the enrichment of Sanskrit learning, for the cultivation of fresh fields of knowledge as well as of fresh criteria which would make possible the composition of works of a standard comparable with those of the past, works which in fact had been created without the aid of historical knowledge. It was imperative that Sanskrit works, both past and contemporary, remain in their own context, but that the horizons be widened. Complementarity, then, not superimposition.

Thibaut's response was energetic. He admitted that though 'the Hindus have a right to expect that their national learning should be maintained and fostered to a certain extent', the Babu and he did not 'think exactly alike with regard to the value and importance of Sanskrit scholarship of the old type.' However, for the time being he concurred with the Babu, since 'even from the European point of view, the maintenance of the old learning appears highly desirable as it will be a long time before European scholars have learned from the Pandits *everything* that the latter can teach them about Sanskrit literature and philosophy' (121, emphasis added). He envisaged a period, once the treasures of Oriental knowledge had become accessible in their entirety to Western scholars, when learning of the old type would become entirely obsolete.

Thibaut, however, also brought forward questions which remain pertinent even today. Mitra wanted Eastern wisdom combined with Western enlightenment. 'But how can things be combined which, in very many points are of an essentially conflicting nature?' How was astronomical information, as in modern English books, to be reconciled with that in the *Vishnu Purana*, which maintained that the sun revolved around Mount Meru in twenty-four hours? 'If they accept the European teaching, as it is to be hoped, after a special department is established for their enlightenment, their views regarding the "intrinsic value" of the Vishnu Purana will certainly undergo some modification.' Thibaut genuinely believed that the European system annulled the Eastern, not only that of the natural sciences but in every department of knowledge. 'Everywhere the Hindu will have in the end to confess to himself that the absolute value of his country's literature is smaller than he used to think before he had begun to study English books' (122).

Thibaut brushed aside jurisprudence, political economy, and constitutional history (nationalist concerns), all as unworthy of the prospective pandit's attention. These were matters one could occupy oneself with only if there were students who progressed beyond an elementary knowledge of English. All in all, he considered it advisable that no student be overly attracted—'too much at least for the wishes of patriotic Hindus'—to the culture and sciences of the West. Which is the reason for his proposal that only the historical-critical method developed in the West be taught, so that, the methodology acquired, the attention of Indian minds could be redirected to India and Indian things (123).

As regards the advantages of the historical method, he believed Mitra was not really competent to speak about its validity. 'A controversy on this point would recommend itself only if Babu Pramadadas Mitra were *fully* acquainted with all that has been accomplished during the last 30 or 40 years by the scholars of England, France, Germany and America, and that he really is so I do not feel convinced, in spite of the very decided tone of his judgements' (emphasis added). The Indian indifference to history was responsible for the fact that so many important Sanskrit works had been lost to posterity, not having been considered worthy of preservation. The salvaging motif surfaced once more: if the pandits possessed more historical spirit 'we—including the Pandits—would not have to regret at the present time the irretrievable loss of so many of the most important works of Sanskrit literature, and the endeavours made by Government to rescue from final loss as much as can yet be rescued would be rewarded by considerably greater success' (123).

Though not all of Thibaut's suggestions regarding change of curriculum and organization were adopted, his view echoed opinions widely held in official circles. In the wake of the educational decision in favour of Anglicist as against Orientalist study, British scholarship in Oriental studies had declined, and its former place of eminence increasingly occupied by German Indology. The Asiatic Society of Bengal had difficulty in finding qualified Englishmen to edit texts; to carry out this task the aid of pandits was increasingly being sought. By the seventies the society had succeeded in attracting the most able Sanskrit scholars of the day, but the quality of their work came in for criticism. Thus, for instance, Max Müller in the *Contemporary Review* in 1871: 'Some of the Calcutta texts are not edited as they ought to be . . .' The pandits were not used to the methods of higher criticism, they relied on traditional authorities, they did not use a sufficient number of manuscripts in preparing their editions, they failed to give all variant readings, and they did not rely sufficiently on internal evidence in resolving apparent inconsistencies.[17]

The prestige of being attached to the Benares Sanskrit College remained immense, for it continued to offer attractive conditions of employment. The pandits continued to receive patronage from the maharaja—they were the learned pillars supporting the dharma sabha of the Maharaja of Banaras—as well as from the merchants of Kashi. But the final burden of supporting them financially could not but shift to the British, who had taken this task upon themselves and had at their disposal the salaried posts at the College.[18] After an initial shying away, at the beginning of the nineteenth century, from so blatant a selling of their knowledge, the pandits had sought salaried posts which ensured a regular livelihood. The most

---

[17] As cited in Gunderson 1970: 174.

[18] Cf. Upadhyaya 1985: 158–66, 169–80, 181–91, where also a mass of information on the prominent learned Brahmans and ascetics of the period is available.

renowned of them were engaged in the college, and in their turn benefited from its authority. They took Western-style examinations, so that they could be employed in one institution or another. When they became redundant in the law courts, they sought teaching employment in schools and colleges.

But there could be no doubt that in the course of the nineteenth century the pandits had suffered a general loss of authority. With the historicization of knowledge, the final source of authority could, in the eyes of the educated, only be Western Orientalists who had the resources of the historical-critical method at their disposal. Thus it came to pass that, though indigenous scholarship was also mobilized for support, it was the Orientalists who were most often cited as the final authority by nationalists in support of one argument or another proffered in the cause of Hindu religion and culture. And thus within Western 'Orientalism' there was a radical shift from awe and a certain mystification of the wisdom of the East at the end of the eighteenth century to a marginalization of this knowledge, and the degradation of the bearers of it to the position of native informants. The pandits had to deliver the raw material, so to speak; the end-products were to be finally manufactured by the superior techniques developed in Europe. In other words, their knowledge became valuable only once it had gone through the filter of European knowledge.

The pandits, however, were not silenced, nor did the traditional sources of patronage completely die out. The loss of authority, I would submit, was not due to the intrinsic worth of either system, it was occasioned by the weightage awarded to Western scholarship by the political power it commanded. Today, historical knowledge itself has been questioned and its absolute authority has been relativized in the West. Structuralist and poststructuralist thought is by and large much more open to non-European belief systems and their embeddedness in tradition, though the newer trends can be as uncritical and as self-convinced as nineteenth-century historicism. Yet the process cannot be reversed. The rehabilitation of traditional systems, whether in structuralist or poststructuralist reinterpretations, comes, once more politically reinforced, from the West.

References

Ahmad, Aijaz, 1992. 'Orientalism and After: Ambivalence and Metropolitan Location in the Work of Edward Said', in *In Theory: Classes, Nations, Literatures*. Bombay: Oxford University Press.

Clifford, James, and George E. Marcus, eds. 1986. *Writing Culture. The Poetics and Politics of Ethnography.* Berkeley: University of California Press.

Dalmia-Luderitz, Vasudha, 1987. 'Die Aneignung der vedischen Vergangenheit: Aspekte der fruhen deutschen Indien-Forschung', in *Zeitschrift fur Kulturaustausch* 3/37.

———, 1993. 'Reconsidering the Orientalist View', in *Perceiving India: Insight and Inquiry*, ed. Geeti Sen. Delhi: Sage Publications and India International Centre.

Das Gupta, Anil Chandra, 1959. *The Days of John Company. Selections from Calcutta Gazette, 1824–1832.* Calcutta: The Superintendent, Government Printing.

Gabriel, Ruth, 1979. 'Learned Communities and British Educational Experiments in North India: 1780–1830'. PhD dissertation, University of Virginia.

Gunderson, Warren, 1970. 'The World of the Babu. Rajendralal Mitra and Cultural Change in Modern India'. PhD dissertation, University of Chicago.

Kumar, Nita, 1998. 'Sanskrit Pandits and the Modernization of Sanskrit Education in the Nineteenth to Twentieth Centuries', in *Swami Vivekananda and the Modernization of Hinduism*, ed. William Radice. Delhi: Oxford University Press.

Marcus, George E., and Michael M. Fischer, 1986. *Anthropology as Cultural Critique. An Experimental Moment in the Human Sciences.* Chicago & London: The University of Chicago Press.

Mishra, B.N., ed. 1991. *Pandit Revisited*, part I, Varanasi: Sampurnanand Sanskrit University.

Moticandra, 1962/1985. *Kashi ka itihas.* 2nd ed. Benares: Vishvavidyalaya Prakashan.

Nicholls, George, 1907. *Sketch of the Rise and Progress of the Benares Patshalla or Sanskrit College, Now Forming the Sanskrit Department of the Sanskrit College* (written 1848). Allahabad: Government Press, United Provinces.

Prinsep, James, 1832. 'Census of the Population of the City of Benares', in *Asiatic Researches* 17.

Robertson, William, 1791/1804. *An Historical Disquisition concerning the Knowledge which the Ancients had of India; and the Progress of Trade with that Country prior to the Discovery of the Passage to it by the Cape of Good Hope. With an Appendix containing Observations on the Civil Policy—the Laws and Judicial Proceedings—the Arts—the Sciences—and the Religious Institutions, of the Indians.* 4th edn. London: T. Cadell and W. Davies, and Edinburgh: E. Balfour.

Upadhyaya, Baldev, 1985. *Kashi ki panditya parampara.* Banaras: Vishvavidyalaya Prakashan.

Williams, Raymond, 1973/1985. *The Country and the City.* London: The Hogarth Press.

Young, Richard Fox, 1981. *Resistant Hinduism: Sanskrit Sources on Anti-Christian Apologetics in Early Nineteenth Century India.* Vienna: Publications of the De Nobili Research Library.

3

Sati as a Religious Rite
Parliamentary Papers on Widow Immolation

WHILE 'HINDU FUNDAMENTALISM' IS A HANDY EXplanation for the recent resurfacing of the practice of 'sati', it blurs the vision and pre-empts the need for analysis of the nature of the contradictions inherent in policies inherited from the British. There is also need to look more closely at the constitutive elements of the legal discourse around it, which suffered no rupture after Independence but became in fact yet more opaque than before. In this context, the *Parliamentary Papers on Widow Immolation, 1821–30* (henceforth PP),[1] are of immense historical value not only for the evidence of the colonial denigration of Hindu women and religion, but for the tensions and contradictions which they reveal, the unravelling of which has significance for understanding contemporary attitudes .

'Sati', as the practice of widow immolation came to be generally known under British rule, is still prevalent as isolated incident in India.[2] The case of an 18-year-old widow being burnt alive with

---

[1] The official title of these is *Papers Relating to East India Affairs, viz Hindoo Widows and Voluntary Immolations*, by order of the House of Commons from 1821 to 1830, cited hereafter with year of publication and page.

[2] As a Sanskrit term, sati, meaning a 'good or a virtuous woman', is exemplified most of all in the devotion to the husband. Since the qualities were

the body of her husband in Rajasthan in September 1987 provoked a nationwide discussion, as well as some ripples of excitement in the international press. The key terms of the discussion, however, 'superstition', 'pagan practice', 'coercion', and 'free decision',[3] have a history which reaches far back into the debates enshrined in the *Parliamentary Papers*. If recent controversies are to be understood rather than taken for granted, then these papers can yield information beyond statistics and place names; they can help disclose the interpretive framework, the contradictions inherent in the colonial situation, and the situation bequeathed to us, clarifying thereby some of the preconditions of the present response.

There had been queries from district magistrates in Bengal regarding the official attitude towards sati since the 1790s.[4] Since 1812 the government of Bengal had sought to regulate the practice in accordance with the Shastras, the legal treatises of the Hindus. The practice, it was ascertained, was authorized though not enjoined

---

held to climax in the supreme act of self-immolation after his death, women who underwent this sacrifice retained the appellation as long as they were remembered. The British usage restricted the term to the sacrifice alone, the act as well as the agent.

[3] Used variously, for instance in the report published in *India Today* (15 October 1987); as also the controversy around these very issues in the *Illustrated Weekly of India* (4 February 1988, 28 February 1988, 1 March 1988); the Hindi *Hans* (October 1987) castigates the reporting style of the Hindi *Jansatta* (18 September 1987). For a sample from the German press, see the *Frankfurter Allgemeine Zeitung* (23 December 1987), as well as the Berlin daily *taz* (23 November 1987).

[4] The legal and political history of sati has been dealt with extensively by the following: *Calcutta Review* 1868, Thompson 1928, and Seed 1955; all three representing the British stand with varying degrees of identification. For a study of Western reactions, see Sharma 1979; for excellent analysis of the official discourse and debate, Mani 1985 and Mani 1987. For a historical survey of the rite from ancient times up to the present, with reformist, apologetic tendencies, see Datta 1988, useful also for data on Rajasthan not easily accessible elsewhere. For the pre-British legal history of the rite, the only sources at present are Kane 1941 and Alickar 1956. There is obvious need to re-evaluate the material they collected.

by the later lawgivers of the Hindus. A number of restrictions were more or less clearly defined: coercion was discouraged, as was the carrying out of the ritual in cases of extreme youth, pregnancy, states of impurity ensuing from the period after pregnancy, menstruation, and the existence of infant children. Women of the Brahman caste were only allowed to burn with the remains of the husband rather than with articles belonging to the deceased. Otherwise, women of all the four 'clean' castes were allowed to burn.

After 1815 detailed statistics specifying name, age, caste of husband, and date of immolation were maintained, and at the end of the year duly scrutinized and evaluated. Strict vigilance as to the enforcement of the Hindu regulations was periodically emphasized, but there was little change of policy till the rite was banned in 1829 by the governor general, William Bentinck.

Since 1815, however, the statistics had exhibited a tendency to increase. The figures for the six divisions of Bengal for 1815 are 378 satis as against 442 for 1816. The year 1817 recorded a total of 707, in 1818 it rose to 839. The years 1817 and 1818 had been cholera years, which could be a possible explanation for the rise, as also the increased vigilance of the law officers in ascertaining and reporting cases of sati. But even though the figures decreased subsequently, they never went back to the original figures of 1815, whatever the justification for the increase.

The fact that under British administration the practice became more widely prevalent than previously was noted and discussed at length by British legislators and officials. It is not surprising, therefore, that sati became the occasion for the most extensive documentation centring around women in the nineteenth century. In the first three decades the sati issue became, in fact, the battleground for conflicting ideologies, for violent missionary attacks on the nature and basis of Hindu civilization, for agitated proclamations of faith, and for legal wrangling as well as bureaucratic insistence on detail. Thus, though women are centrally located in the debate, they become so enmeshed in a network of structures and issues, political and social, not to say religious, that they often seem peripheral to the issue at hand. In reconstructing the debate a century and a half later it becomes imperative, then, to consider the conceptions and preconceptions which colour the documentation and its evaluation.

The first part of this essay will be concerned with the categories within which the woman as a legal subject deserving scrutiny becomes an object of documentation. The *Parliamentary Papers* seem to call specially for this treatment, since it was the express aim of the legal discourse which constitutes them to encompass and control social reality through a set of concepts linked in a manner deliberately schematic.

By a regulation of 1772 Hindus and Muslims were allowed to carry on their religious and social practices and were administered according to their own legal codes, for, as Nathaniel Halhed, the first translator of the *Code of Gentoo Laws*, clearly saw, 'Nothing can so favourably conduce to these two points [i.e. the affections of the natives and the stability of the territorial acquisition] as a well-timed toleration in matters of religion, and an adoption of such original institutes of the country, as do not immediately clash with the laws and interests of the conquerors.'[5] In keeping with this policy, pandits and maulvis as legal exegetes and advisers had been attached to the Supreme Court since 1777, and to the rest of the courts, following the Cornwallis Code, in 1793.

The clash between religious institutes and post-Enlightenment principles of rationality, which were held to be universally valid— though they were based on principles which served 'the laws and interests of the conquerors'—was to occasion much debate. But the imperial Romans whom Halhed held up as the model for such governance had apparently managed to negotiate such difficulties.[6] It was imperative therefore that stable criteria be established, for 'prescribed rules' were necessary in order to pronounce judgment, as William Jones specified in his address to the Grand Jury in Calcutta in 1783. 'Law' was to stand above individual sense of justice.[7] But Halhed's compilation came to be considered inadequate for

---

[5] Halhed 1776/1781: ix.
[6] Ibid.
[7] Jones 1799: 4–5.

these purposes by the generation that followed his. Manu was the legendary legislator of the Hindus and Jones set about translating his 'Institutes' for the benefit of his fellow judges in Calcutta. He was moved, while underlining its importance, by 'its austere majesty that sounds like the language of legislation and extorts a respectful awe', and added: 'It is system of despotism and priestcraft both indeed limited by law, but artfully conspiring to give mutual support, though with mutual checks: it is filled . . . with *idle superstitions*, and with a scheme of theology most obscurely figurative and consequently liable to dangerous misconception.'[8] Jones juxtaposed this to the humanitarian practice of European society: 'Whatever opinion in short may be formed of Manu and his law, in a country happily enlightened by sound philosophy and the only true revelation, it must be remembered, that these laws are actually revered, as the word of the Most High, by nations of great importance to *the political and commercial* interests of Europe.'[9]

In addition to Manu, there was a vast corpus of legal literature which had been compiled through the ages and which seemed to defy all attempts to derive a uniform code applicable in all parts of the subcontinent. Besides the tension between local usage and the code as the British attempted to standardize it,[10] there was the dual nature of the authority—it existed in British law as well—that the state 'uphold the church's decrees, by secular penalties.'[11] Since in the Indian case the religion in question was alien, there was bound to be further tension between the two legislating instances.

The derivation of a uniform code regulating the practice of sati proved to be an awkward task. The attempts to establish consonance between 'Shaster' (the legal treatises) and 'humanity', the two authorities which were invariably juxtaposed in this discourse, led to an uneasy balance. 'Regard for the religious opinions of the natives' (PP 1821: 64), 'erroneously derived from the superstition

---

[8] Ibid.: 89, emphasis added.
[9] Ibid.: emphasis added.
[10] Cohn 1965.
[11] Derrett 1961: 81.

they possess' (PP 1821: 136), inevitably clashed with 'feelings of humanity' (PP 1821: 64). But since judges had no feelings, the sole resort was to find within the Shaster scope for the principles of humanity; and thus, practically through the back door, the means 'to confine those sacrifices within as narrow bounds as the rules permit' (PP 1821: 64). So, if on the one hand 'the strict adherence to the ordinances of the Shaster' (PP 1821: 101) was advocated, the actual practice in the case of sati was never described as other than 'this perversion of humanity' (PP 1821: 65), 'this inhuman custom', 'present bigotry . . . uncivilised and ignorant' (PP 1821: 176).

Superintendent Ewer of the Lower Provinces could stretch this so far as to claim that the rite was not religious at all, since it was not prescribed by Manu. It was merely local practice, and 'sacred authority is subsequently produced to enforce the merit of an act originating in the mortal feelings of affection, grief, despair, or some other passion of the mind, equally incapable of affording a hope that it could be acceptable in the eyes of the deity. Such can never become religious . . .' (PP 1821: 231). The dichotomy between bigotry and enlightened religion could only be resolved, as Lord Amherst (governor general from 1823 to 1828) observed, by plans for encouraging native education, for '[t]he well-meant and zealous attempts of Europeans to dissuade from and to discourage the performance of the rite, would appear to have been almost uniformly unsuccessful; and prove but too strongly, that even the best informed classes of the Hindoo population are not yet sufficiently enlightened to recognise the propriety of abolishing the rite' (PP 1825: 7).

British as Vindicators and Expounders of Hindu Law

The British had to cope with a predicament which, though obviously caused by their own policy of conciliating Hindu orthodoxy, had consequences which they could not have foreseen and which led to repeated protests by members from their own ranks. In order to effectively execute Hindu law regarding sati, they had necessarily to become exponents of it where it was not yet sufficiently known;

seek and provide amplification where there were gaps or where clarification was called for; and, finally, supervise that it was legally enforced by actual presence during the course of the rite, and by active interference if any violation were detected.

Lord Moira (governor general, 1813–23) most clearly realized the impotence of alien rulers as propounders of indigenous law, and their powerlessness to introduce effective change: 'We directed our opinion to be stated that the greatest caution was requisite on the officers of our government, in dissuading widows from the performance of this ceremony, in order to avoid the imputation of interfering with the religious opinion of the inhabitants, to which the government of a *brahmin prince* could not be liable' (PP 1821: 243, emphasis added). Yet, in effect this was the position that British policy-makers seemed to arrogate—to govern the country as enlightened Brahman princes.

The Board of Directors in London, writing to Lord Amherst in 1823, declared itself unwilling to participate in this rite: 'It is, moreover, with much reluctance that we can consent to make the British government, by a specific permission of the suttee, an ostensible party to the sacrifice; we are averse to the practice of making British courts expounders and vindicators of the Hindoo religion, when it leads to acts which, not less as legislators than as Christians, we abominate' (PP 1824: 45). This was obviously an echo of the missionary discourse in India as well as the parent organizations in Britain, who were at the forefront of mobilizing public opinion against the rite. The language in which they did so was vehemently critical and tended towards a wholesale dismissal of the Hindu religion.[12] It was obvious that missionaries recommended drastic action.

---

[12] On the efforts of missionaries to mobilize public opinion against sati, see Ingham 1956: 44–54. On the petitions sent to the House of Commons by citizens holding meetings for the specific purpose in several towns, see Peggs 1830. Here is a sample of Peggs' style, as one in the forefront of the campaign, citing a sympathetic review of his pamphlet on the subject: 'There is a voice that must be heard, that will require it—the voice of *an enlightened and Christian people*—that voice (Oh, let it be loud and solemn!) must, we are confident, awaken a power and move an arm that, sooner or later, will extinguish the

A Calcutta Baptist paper, the *Quarterly Friend of India*, advocated that if the British 'possess discretionary power over the Hindoo laws', then 'the helpless widow has a strong claim on our compassion' (PP 1823: 22).[13]

Though the *Parliamentary Papers* were ordered to be printed from 1821 onwards, the extensive documentation had begun in 1813. As we saw, the returns for the years 1817 and 1818 had shown a dramatic increase in the number of satis. Though officials tended to view this as a consequence of cholera epidemics, and the numbers did decline thereafter, it was obvious that they had increased substantially under British jurisdiction. The zealous watchmanship seemed to encourage rather than inhibit the practice, and it was seldom that a case declared illegal was actually prevented, since this often happened in retrospect and the punishment meted out tended to be cautious rather than cautioning.[14]

Suttee fires of India.' For one of the earliest and most detailed reports from the missionary perspective, see Ward 1811: 544–66.

[13] The report cited here is part of the documentation included in the PP. From the missionary perspective also there is complete identification with the ruling race, as the report testifies: 'Are the sacred principles of justice to be abrogated because private individuals are mistaken in their notion of the worship which is acceptable to the Deity? The admission of this principle would rend asunder the bonds of society; for if the highest crime, that of murder, may go unpunished when committed under a religious pretext, what crime can we consistently punish in India? There is no species of abomination which the Hindoo code does not sanction under some shape or other. But the whole course of our judicial proceedings demonstrates that we have never acted on these principles' (PP 1823: 21). This is supported by the quotation of a long passage from Locke.

[14] Exemplified in the reply to the magistrate, Southern Concan, 14 March 1822, by J. Farish, secretary to government: 'The honourable the governor general in council instructs me to inform you, that under the orders given to him, the sirkurnaviesdar of Rutnagerry did his duty in prohibiting the suttee on this occasion, and the disregard of his prohibition was illegal, and might without injustice be punished; such a step however in this instance would be highly impolitic and you have shown great prudence and judgment in forbearing to adopt it' (PP 1824: 49).

The term 'sanskritization' to describe a process whereby lower castes effect upward mobility by emulating the customs of the higher castes, and sati would seem to be a case in point.[15] Yet it could also be seen as a case of inverse sanskritization—norms imposed from above on castes and groups originally outside the scope of jurisdiction of high-caste Hindu law. The British tended to a uniform, undifferentiated application of the legal code they had been at such pains to devise, a code which cast all manners of Hindus on the subcontinent, regardless of actual caste customs and regional practice, into the social mould prescribed by the Brahmanic tradition as they understood it.[16]

The *Parliamentary Papers* offer ample evidence of this inadvertent sanskritization. As an indignant magistrate reported (PP 1821: 243), from Chandernagore, a French possession, those wishing to perform sati simply moved to British territory, giving credence to the argument that the British seemed actually to be offering protection, if not encouragement, to the practice. In Farrukhabad, in the Upper Provinces, a sati took place where the bewildered family had never before witnessed the rite. It was the insistence of the newly bereaved widow which apparently obliged them to carry out her wishes, though there was some perplexity as to the appropriate ritual procedure. After submitting a lengthy report, the magistrate was moved to register protest: 'But I beg to observe, with all deference, that it might be attended with good effects, if some punishment were awarded, and operate as a check to the growth of this barbarous custom, which though it was at one time wholly unknown in these provinces, appears under the British government, to be gaining ground once more' (PP 1821: 212). A 'chandala' woman, though belonging to an 'unclean' caste, was permitted to ascend the social scale since the local pandit allowed that she belonged to the fourth, or 'Shudra', caste. So she was given permission to burn (PP 1825: 42). But a woman

---

[15] Srinivas 1962 for the term 'sanskiritization'. See also Ahmad 1965; for a more provocative formulation, see Nandy 1980. For an attempt at social analysis by breakdown of caste and occupation figures, see Roy 1987.

[16] Cohn 1968: 7.

who had lived in adultery was not to be allowed to burn, since the couple could not be considered legally married. Though the sacrifice was suspended, the woman managed to burn: thus the unfortunate consequences of the British attempt to function as a moral instance authorizing correct ritual conduct (PP 1823: 44). Similarly, women in the Bombay Presidency were to be prevented from burning with the bones of the husband, since Brahman women, according to the shastras as interpreted in Bengal, were not to be burnt if much time had elapsed after the death of the husband (PP 1824: 46).

The 'jogis', a weaver community, observed the practice of burying widows alive with the bodies of their dead husbands, instead of immolating them. As a low-caste social community, their resistance to change had little political weight. They were brought under the jurisdiction of Hindu law; the rite was summarily terminated. In its proceedings of 4 June 1818 the Nizamat Adalat tersely recorded:

> as the Hindoo law does not sanction the practice which prevails amongst the jogee tribe of burying the widow alive with the body of her deceased husband, the Vice-President in Council entirely concurs with the nizamut adawlut in thinking that the practice in question should be positively and entirely interdicted . . . It appears, however, to be highly objectionable that so inhuman a practice, without legal sanction, should be continued. (PP 1821: 179)

It is not on record whether it was forthwith considered permissible for the jogis to burn their widows instead. All in all, it was a question of policy: 'politic' and 'impolitic' are frequently used terms, the British colonial attempt to absorb the authority of former Indian ruling classes to assimilate, and if convenient temper and thus render unobjectionable to themselves.

A Legal Subject for Sati

In this section I will consider the conceptualization of Hindu women as legal subjects, as the subject emerges from this documentation. It is important to emphasize that the account which follows is in no way in defence of an act which belongs to a world to which there is no direct access for urban Indians today, except as part of history. It is difficult, if not impossible, for us to read between the lines in order to provide even a speculative account of the social experiential reality of the cases recorded. It is possible, however, to see *how* the women were seen, without necessarily seeing *what* there was to determine the verifiability of the criteria applied to the women concerned, for them to qualify as 'a legal subject for a suttee' (PP 1821: 38).

The police officers present on the scene of the rite were required to be notified in advance. They were to determine and record the age of the woman—whether below the age of puberty—finally fixed at 16, whether pregnant or not, the age of her children, caste and name of the husband; but the most important task was to ascertain whether the act was voluntary or not. There were a number of eyewitness reports of force having been applied to prevent the woman from escaping the burning pile, for it was often a question of fiercely upheld family honour. The point was stated repeatedly and with great emphasis, as in the *General Rules and Circular Instructions to the Magistrates and Police Officers Regarding Suttees*, promulgated by the Nizamat Adalat, the chief criminal court in the Presidency of Bengal, in 1817: 'These ordinances require that the sacrifice be in all instances, perfectly voluntary; that the widow be of a competent age to judge and choose in a matter of so much consequence to herself and her children . . .' (PP 1821: 137). The premise was clear enough. Theoretically, at least, the woman was considered to be an agent capable of free choice. The very concept occasioned protest. While submitting the report and statement of satis for the year 1815 to the Nizamat Adalat, E. Watson, fourth judge, Calcutta Court of Circuit, stated categorically: 'It appears to us, that the assent of the woman should be utterly void, and that the persons killing her at her desire or command should, in the eyes of the law, be murderers' (PP 1821: 99). The question, then, was whether the power of legitimate volition could be ascribed to Hindu women. Magistrate Bird of the city of Banaras suggested the promulgation of an additional rule to safeguard against the *whims* of women, for there had been three cases of illegal sati. He proposed that they burn immediately upon receiving the news of the husband's death and not later; this in order 'to put an end to a practice, not at all unusual, of becoming a suttee many years subsequent to the husband's death, in a fit of caprice or of worldly disappointment, after having in the first instance neglected to become a suttee; a practice which I understand, is neither recognised nor encouraged by the doctrines of the Hindoo religion' (PP 1821: 134).

The most detailed paraphrase of this view was once again supplied by Superintendent Ewer of the Lower Provinces. He maintained that there could in fact be no such thing as a 'voluntary suttee' because 'few widows would ever think of sacrificing themselves, unless overpowered by force or persuasion; very little of either is sufficient to overcome the physical or mental powers of the majority of Hindoo females.' Therefore, Ewer reasoned, 'her opinion on the subject can be of no weight, and whether she appear glad or sorry, stupid, composed or distracted, is no manner or proof of her real feelings' (PP 1821: 227). It was evident that once it was possible to abstract the woman's real feelings from her environment and upbringing, there could be no motivating ground for the sacrifice. Women were at all times victims of persuasion, since in any case they had no direct access to the shastras and could form no independent opinion. 'Now it is well known that the education of Hindoo females, of all ranks, precludes the possibility of their having, of themselves, any acquaintance whatever with the contents of the shastras' (PP 1821: 228).

Ewer had sent a questionnaire regarding the sati regulations to several magistrates of the Lower Provinces, and while analysing their response he proposed the following thesis regarding the evolution of the practice. He was voicing a general opinion, when, within this theory, he located the woman as a creature who could not be actuated by reason but was moved by feeling alone, with the feeling ever amenable to manipulation. Ewer posited an *ur*-sati whereby one woman, from overpowering devotion and grief, voluntarily committed the heroic act, 'not with any idea that such an act could be acceptable to the gods, or of any benefit to herself in a future existence, but solely because her affection for the deceased made her regard life as a burden no longer to be borne' (PP 1821: 231). This was an acceptable stand; the act of the woman was at the time not rooted in superstition but, motivated by an excess of emotion, was part of a world comprehensible to enlightened thought. Essentially the same tendency was to be observed in Europe *vis-à-vis* the mythological, miraculous aspects of religious life—an effort to reduce these 'to events which could be narrated in the common sense language of the cafe. To popularise, to render plausible, to make credible the incredible persisted as the great heroic act of the age.'[17] Now this original heroic sati, according to Ewer, excited admiration and possible emulation as a novelty, but it would never have been installed as a rite if the interested relatives and the Brahmans had not stepped in at this stage. This was also the opinion of E. Molony, acting magistrate of Burdwan district, where the practice was frequent:

> It is needless here to remark, the influence which education has upon the reasoning powers of the human mind; the total want of anything like a system of education among the natives is also well known . . . We have known, that whatever little education is given to the males is never extended to the female sex; I have never met an instance of a Hindoo woman, of whatever rank, who could write even her name. If, therefore, we find that the greater proportion of the men are unable to give a reason for the performance of the sacrifice, it is surely fair to infer that the women are not better informed on the subject; and therefore it is fair to suppose that the resolution to become suttees *cannot proceed so much from their having reasoned themselves* into a conviction of the purity of the act itself, as from a kind of infatuation produced by the absurdities poured into their ears by ignorant Brahmins, most of whom, if asked, would be found unable to give a reason for the doctrines which they inculcate. (PP 1821: 235, emphasis added)

The woman was therefore uniformly referred to as 'the victim', 'the poor creature', 'the infatuated victim'. The possibility of ever forming 'free, voluntary, unbiased, and uninfluenced' (PP 1823: 63) judgement was forever precluded in the case of Hindu women; for as the Governor-General-in-Council, Lord Amherst, himself concluded after studying the report and statement for the year 1821: 'the women are taught from infancy to believe that by consenting to the

---

[17] Manuel 1959: 124–5.

immolation, they perform an act, if not of imperative duty, at least one that will rebound to their own credit and raise the reputation of their families. On the other hand, that a refusal involves the reproach of cowardice, or of the want of true devotion to their husbands (PP 1824: 43).

Such then was the predicament of 'law' and the legislators. Women in order to be legal subjects were to function autonomously, but they could not in effect be free agents because they had early internalized the virtues of custom. It is not remarkable, then, that no judgement is passed upon women, since in a way they could not be held responsible for their actions. They existed, not unlike savages, in a kind of pre-moral state, neither good nor evil, moved by social instinct and feelings, defenceless, since reason could not be a regulating principle in their lives, making them all the more exposed to corrupting influence. They could, ultimately, only be protected.

Intimately connected with this vision of the woman is the stereotype of the crafty priest. If religion as practised on the subcontinent was viewed largely as a corpus of superstitious beliefs—or 'prejudices' in the language of the day—then the Brahmans were the fostering agents, both as 'priests and legislators',[18] this being a view common since its popularization by the Deists in the seventeenth and eighteenth centuries; and as 'sacerdotal plotters . . . themselves enveloped by the vapors of darkness which they had originally generated.'[19]

In the *Parliamentary Papers* they are constantly referred to as 'hungry brahmins', 'necessitous brahmins' (PP 1821: 227, 270). It is once again Superintendent Ewer who explicitly thematizes the link between law-making and the execution of it, both of which functions are seen as being opportunistically used by the Brahmans. Contemporary Brahmans, he allows, were an ignorant breed, unable to provide grounds for their dogma, but originally they had known better. After the first sati took place, 'in a short time the Brahmins began to perceive, that if properly managed, suttee might be made a very productive source of emolument; and the most esteemed authors

---

[18] Halhed 1781: liv.
[19] Manuel 1959: 69.

of the age were induced to recommend it as a most meritorious act, productive of good effects to the souls of the widow and her husband, and to those of the surviving members of their families; they also prescribed forms and ceremonies in which the attendance of brahmins was of course indispensable' (PP 1821: 231). William Jones had remarked that in the *Institutes of Manu* despotism and priestcraft, though operating as systems of mutual check and balance, ultimately reinforced each other. Half a century later, matters had practically come full circle: the new legislators, while ostensibly supporting the old laws, were to protect the woman from the old law-makers: they sought to check and overrule what they themselves set up as the absolute authority of the priests. Thus the Nizamat Adalat was urged by Judge C. Smith to 'interfere with a vigorous hand for the protection of the weak against the strong, of the simple against the artful classes of its subjects' (PP 1823: 63).

As the final document for the year 1825, an extract from the *Bombay Courier* is included in the *Parliamentary Papers*. It is the report of an exceptionally articulate encounter between on the one hand an Englishman, who inquires and describes his experience in unbureaucratic language, free from legal encumbrance, and on the other a young Indian woman about to perform sati, whose answers are clearly recorded. In the encounter, two worlds, apparently mutually exclusive, accost each other with near-total incomprehension. It is worth quoting at length:

> *The poor wretched woman* I found seated on a mat, and surrounded by about forty or fifty females who all seemed to be in a state of perfect indifference, and were frequently laughing to each other, she seemed to be in the possession of all her faculties and gave distinct answers to all my questions . . . she obeyed the commandment of God, and was certain of everlasting happiness. I endeavoured to set before her the absurdity of such conduct, and how much it was in variance with the character of the Divine Being . . . and assured her, that if poverty had driven her to her present resolution, if she would only abandon it I would find her adequate support. After *reasoning* with her for a long time, I took higher ground, and plainly told her she was a self-murderer; and that, instead of finding happiness after death as the reward of her conduct, she must be visited with the punishment, which a murderer deserves. She told me

that she was not poor; that she had never committed any sin; that her heart was holy, that she had gone to God, and that He had ordered her to do what she was about to do. This last expression she explained by saying, that she had gone to the idol, and that it had told her to burn. It immediately struck me, that perhaps some interested individual had induced her to go to the temple, and had employed means to give her such an answer; but on this subject I could obtain no information, as her answers were vague and unsatisfactory.

After bathing and praying, the widow distributed some betel-nut and spice to those around, who fell at her feet and did her reverence, as a being of superior nature. She ascended and calmly laid herself down on the pile, without the smallest assistance; and nothing I have ever witnessed surprised me more than the indifference with which she went through the whole. She was a young woman of perhaps about twenty-two, in the full vigour of health and strength. There appeared no symptom of grief for her departed husband, and I should certainly have thought her in a state of stupor, but for the answers she gave to our questions and the composure with which she performed all the ceremonies . . . When I saw the *poor deluded creature* actually mounted the pile I really felt so agitated as not to be able minutely to observe if she took a light along with her. (PP 1825: 212–14, emphasis added)

The beliefs of the two could obviously not be subsumed under a single global category, religion, though each was convinced and rested in her or his position. The inquirer could not believe that there was no manipulation and that the woman seemed to perform the act voluntarily. The woman seems not to have grasped the implication of the question. Here it needs to be emphasized once again that, in providing the viewpoint of the woman, there is no attempt to vindicate the practice. But it is important to take note of the nature of the mutual incomprehension, of the one perspective remaining incomprehensible in terms of the other. Whose was the true god, whose belief in the nature of life after death the more legitimate? What is the distinction between 'superstition' and 'religion'? On what premises does 'reason' rest and when does 'voluntary decision' become plausibly applicable to women? How adequate are these categories and how do they correlate to the social and religious phenomena under review? Analysis of the *Parliamentary Papers* would suggest that the terms of their discussion cannot, without further reflection and modification, be applied in the construction of an alternative view of sati. Perhaps it is worth the effort for us, as modern Indians who have inherited the humanistic concern of the Englishman, to make an attempt to redefine our stand before we disqualify and condemn the women performing sati in terms too sweeping and too uncritical of their historical legacy and basis.

As is well known, in the year 1829 Lord William Bentinck, newly appointed Governor General of India, passed a regulation making sati an offence punishable by law. His justly famous Minute of 8 November 1829 tackles issues which had long been skirted and remains noteworthy in its attempt to resolve the contradictions of the colonial situation. He insists emphatically that 'nothing has been yielded to feeling, but that reason, and reason alone, has governed this decision' of abolishing 'this inhuman and impious act'.[20] He feels impelled to quote the testimony of a contemporary Indian in support of his claim that the rite was not part of the original religion of the Hindus: 'that enlightened native Rammohun Roy, a warm advocate of the abolition of suttee and all other superstitions and corruptions engrafted on the Hindoo religion, which he considers originally to have been a pure deism.'[21]

With the help of reason, then, these later engraftings are to be removed, and religion cleansed of immorality: 'I know nothing so important to the improvement of their future conditions, as the establishment of a proper morality, whatever their belief, and a more just conception of the will of god. The first step to this better understanding will be dissociation of religious belief and practice from blood and murder. They will then, when no longer under this brutalising excitement, view with more calmness acknowledged truths.'[22] Thus could 'a foul stain upon British rule' be washed, and

---

[20] Datta 1988: 237. Bentinck's *Minute* and the regulation are on pp. 237–50, 251–3.

[21] Ibid.: 241. Rammohun Roy's role in the abolition of the rite has always excited a great deal of comment. He was against the practice, but also initially against legislation as being inappropriate, and accepted this at a very late stage. Besides his own writings, the most pertinent contemporary compilation on Roy is Joshi 1975.

[22] Datta 1988: 249.

religion and humanity become once more reconciled. Bentinck claimed: 'I write and feel as a legislator for the Hindoos.'[23] The British government seemed to have—at least for the time being—come to terms with the position it had long eyed with unease, that of a Brahman prince, albeit enlightened, who could confidently propose and carry out reform. A network of power relationships had emerged, alliances established in the last century seemed to have matured—the rich landed proprietors were beholden to the British for their position and the native army had no present cause for discontent. Bentinck could confidently maintain: 'We are supreme.'

With this self-appointed task of protecting the 'innocent victim', the British took over the function not only of potent legislation, but also of *manly* protection: 'Were the scene of this sad destruction of human life laid in the Upper instead of the Lower Provinces, in the midst of a bold and manly people, I might speak with less confidence upon the question of safety.'[24] In Bengal, where the practice was most rampant, the people were not bold and manly enough to offer any violent resistance to the measure. Henceforth, the regulation proclaimed, 'all persons convicted of aiding and abetting in the sacrifice of a Hindoo widow, by burning or burying her alive, *whether the sacrifice be voluntary on her part or not*, shall be deemed guilty of culpable homicide.'[25] It was final acknowledgement of that which had vexed legislators for at least two decades—it really was of no consequence whether the sacrifice was voluntary or involuntary, the woman could be no other than an innocent victim.

At least on the surface of it, Bentinck seemed to face up to the responsibility of legislating for the Hindus as one actually involved and implicated in the system; it did not seem that he was merely administering and supervising the proper observation of the Hindu legal code from the outside and above, while at the same time barely countenancing it. A consideration of his motives, political, evangelical, utilitarian, and otherwise, is not feasible here. The solution he found, however—of purging the religion of aspects he believed to be 'immoral'—could also be viewed as high-handed and

[23] Ibid.
[24] Ibid.: 240.
[25] Ibid.: 253, emphasis added.

peremptory, as something to be expected of an alien ruler attempting to determine the nature of religious beliefs held by a subject people. It is possible that though the regulation terminated the wide spread of the practice, the symbolic value of sati was intensified on a scale much determined by the policy of what I have for convenience labelled inverse sanskritization. There is ample literary evidence of the glorification of sati through the nineteenth century to support this; however, it needs to be sifted dispassionately. For mere suppression does not terminate 'superstition'; it finds other modes of expression, and the contradictions, far from being resolved, continue to coexist.

The *Parliamentary Papers* are of immense historical value, not so much for the evidence they contain of the colonial denigration of Hindu women and religion, nor for all that they do not disclose about women, as for the tensions and contradictions which they reveal, the unravelling of which has vital significance for the awareness of attitudes today. I have tried to demonstrate that the categories discussed here are far from self-explanatory or self-justificatory. Their application to the Indian situation, even superimposition, at a particular historical period was part of an attempt by a European colonial power to come to grips with an awkward task—that of ruling an alien people in interests which, in their turn, could only be alien to the people concerned. Enlightened mistrust of ritual, of superstitious belief, of credulous women and crafty priests, was offset by pragmatic concerns regarding alliances, which often meant support for the very forces which reactivated certain strands of tradition. It can hardly be regarded as a coincidence that the collusion of these forces with the political structures of authority meant counter-reformatory authorization and reinforcement of the practice of sati. This led to an apparent ideological contradiction, which condemned and vilified even as it supported and codified Brahmanic tradition, which supervised the practice of sati while attempting ostensibly to weed it out in the interests of humanity, and which, finally, highlighted the importance of voluntary immolation while maintaining that, in effect, Hindu women could have no free will.

In order to avoid being caught up in these contradictions, we need today to emancipate ourselves from the categories of post-Enlightenment thought, to effect a conceptual shift such as, partially at least, has taken place in anthropology.[26] This critical perspective is most urgently required in the matter of establishing a distinction between 'superstition' and 'religion', without trying to find global definitions: for a discourse cast in universal terms would necessarily be a denial of the historically specific functions of these terms.[27] What the British felt compelled to elevate to 'religion' and what was discarded as 'superstition' needs at least to be evaluated once again, and the beliefs of the participants need to be taken into account. Only then could there be a dialogue with those actually involved in the rite today, or with those in the past, whose testimonies are recorded in the *Parliamentary Papers*, however inadequately.

Both Bentinck and the officials involved in the correspondence recorded in the *Parliamentary Papers* denied women the capacity of free volition. If we are to treat women as not alone in being victims of their respective belief systems, but restore at least a measure of agency and autonomy to them, then we would be compelled to consider seriously the amount of legitimate authority and formal recognition we accord to them, to review the spheres of power reserved in 'traditional' and neo-traditional societies for women as well as for men. Anthropological literature bears testimony to the complex set of attitudes and social constellations whereby a special status was reserved for widows, for the power of women, when not contained in the benign aspects of 'wife' or 'mother', has often been regarded

---

[26] An awareness indicated for instance in the critical reflection, from a feminist point of view in Strathern 1987; on a general anthropological level in Marcus and Fischer 1986 and Clifford and Marcus 1986; a feminist critique of the latter two titles is in Gordon 1988.

[27] See Kippenberg 1983 for a suggestive summary of the stand regarding definitions of religion.

as 'uncontained', as threatening and signalling danger.[28] These are questions which need detailed study, in specific historic detail. Then it could become possible to explore the putative differences between the social status of the widow in India and, official claims notwithstanding, the condition and social insecurity of unattached women—spinsters and widows—in nineteenth-century England.[29] And this, not in order to establish distance from a practice to be viewed as a malformation of some norm, which remains to be established, but in its specific social configuration, which needs to be investigated rather than castigated—in spite of the awesome spectre of human sacrifice.

'Religion' and 'superstition', as also the 'reason' and 'feeling' polarities—equating respectively with 'culture' as part of a higher or later stage of evolution and 'nature' as continuing to remain mired in unreasoning superstition, as applied to gender considerations in Europe and Asia respectively—were the product of eighteenth-century Enlightenment thought.[30] These were by no means simple categories, because though they defined each other negatively as well as complementarily, each contained, through this very process of definition, also a critique of the other. 'Feeling' was a complex conceptualization of the feminine developed both by the French philosophers of the period,[31] as well as by a physiology which purported equally to consider biological, psychological, and social phenomena.[32] By the turn of the nineteenth century the broad consensus was that women were the products of 'feeling'—both biologically as being, in their reproductive function, identical with 'nature', as well as socially, by virtue of the functions they were called upon to fulfil. Thus, on the one hand, they were dependent on

---

[28] See Rosaldo 1974 for some discussion of the issue, as also Rosaldo 1980 for later qualifications of the results of her survey.

[29] An approach initiated by Stein 1978, which needs to be concretized with regard to the attitudes of important figures in the sati debate, such as Superintendent Ewer.

[30] Bloch and Bloch 1980; Jordanova 1980.

[31] Steinbrugge 1987.

[32] Jordanova 1980.

manly judgement and enterprise, since they lacked 'reason', on the other they were credulous, 'the negative aspects of female naturalness', which made them prone to superstition. 'The classic example of the problem was the uneducated woman under the thumb of her priest, who fed her a diet of religious dogma, urging her to believe things which served his interests alone.'[33]

In England, this restrictive definition and corresponding socialization was particularly linked to Evangelical Christianity, and church and chapel remained central to the articulation and diffusion of beliefs and practices relating to femininity and manliness.[34] This was a mode of thinking mainly current among the educated middle class, though popularized and readily accessible to all those who would be literate in the lexica of the first half of the nineteenth century.[35] It was an ideology obviously closely linked to the modes of production, as also professional life in industrialized society, and the spheres—public and domestic—henceforth to be regarded as proper for each sex, with the occupations correspondingly reserved for men and women. That these characteristics and criteria were applied indiscriminately by British officials to the Indian situation from the turn of the nineteenth century—in an age confident of the right to evaluate by its own standards—should offer little cause for surprise. But there is an obvious need to clarify the relationship of these concepts to the social reality of different sections of Indian society, to the past as far as there is available data, and certainly anew to the present. Perhaps some degree of correspondence can be established as regards the restrictive function of gender conceptualization, but this would also need to be identified rather than taken for granted.

Further, the political implications of the resurfacing of the rite amidst popular acclaim need to be probed. 'Hindu fundamentalism' is a handy caption, but it blurs the vision, for it relegates phenomena which fill us with unease to a convenient category. This pre-empts

---

[33] Ibid.: 51.
[34] Davidoff and Hall 1987.
[35] See Hausen 1976 for the descriptions of 'female' and 'feminine' in the popular German lexica of the period, as well as for the economic aspects of the polarization of gender roles in middle-class family and professional life.

the need for analysis of the nature of the contradictions inherent in policies inherited from the British, and of the constitutive elements of a legal discourse almost unchanged till the present.

References

Ahmad, A.F. Salahuddin, 1965. *Social Ideas and Social Change in Bengal 1818–1835.* Leiden: E.J. Brill.

Altekar, A.S., 1956. *The Position of Women in Hindu Civilisation.* Delhi: Motilal Banarsidass.

Bloch, Maurice, and Jean H. Bloch, 1980. 'Women and the Dialects of Nature in Eighteenth Century French Thought', in Carol MacCormack and Marilyn Strathern, ed., *Nature, Culture and Gender.* Cambridge: Cambridge University Press.

Calcutta Review, 1868. 'Suttee', XLVI, 92.

Clifford, James, and George E. Marcus, 1986. *Writing Culture: The Poetics and Politics of Ethnography.* Berkeley: University of California Press.

Cohn, Bernard S., 1965. 'Anthropological Notes on Disputes and Law in India', in *American Anthropologist*, vol. 69, no. 6, pt 2 (Special Issue: The Ethnography of Law, ed. L. Nader).

———, 1968. 'Notes on the History of the Study of Indian Society and Culture', in *Structure and Change in Indian Society*, ed., Milton Singer and Bernard S. Cohn. New York: Wenner Gren Foundation for Anthropological Research.

Datta, V.N., 1988. *Sati: A Historical, Social and Philosophical Enquiry into the Hindu Rite of Widow Burning.* Delhi: Manohar.

Davidoff, Leonore, and Catherine Hall, 1987. *Family Fortunes: Men and Women of the English Middle Class 1780–1830.* London: Hutchinson.

Derrett, J. Duncan M., 1961. 'Sanskrit Legal Treatises Compiled at the Instance of the British', in *Zeitschrift fur vergleichende Rechtswissenschaft*, vol. 63.

Gordon, Deborah, ed., 1988. *Inscriptions* (Special Issue: 'Feminism and the Critique of Colonial Discourse'), nos 3 and 4.

Halhed, Nathaniel Brassey, 1776/1781. *A Code of Gentoo Laws, Or Ordinations of the Pundits, From a Persian Translation. Made from the Original, Written in the Shanscrit Language.* (London, 1st edn, 1776.)

Hausen, Karin, 1976. 'Die Polarisierung der "Geschlechischaraktere"— Eine Spiegelung der Dissoziation von Erwerbs—und Familienleben', in *Sozialgeschichte der Familie in der Neuzeit Europas*, ed. Werner Conze. Stuttgart: Klett.

Ingham, Kenneth, 1956. *Reformers in India 1793–1833: An Account of the Work of Christian Missionaries on Behalf of Social Reform*. Cambridge: Cambridge University Press.

Jones, William, 1799. *The Works of William Jones*, vol. VII (*Containing: Institutes of Hindu Law; Or, The Ordinances of Manu, According to the Gloss of Calcutta*) *Indian Report*. Delhi: Agam Prakashan, 1979.

Jordanova, L.J., 1980. 'Natural Facts: A Historical Perspective on Science and Sexuality', in Carol MacCormack and Marilyn Strathern, eds, *Nature, Culture and Gender*. Cambridge: Cambridge University Press.

Joshi, V.C., ed., 1975. *Rammohun Roy and the Process of Modernisation in India*. Delhi: Vikas.

Kane, P.V., 1941. *History of Dharmasastra*, vol. 11, pt 1. Poona: Bhandarkar Oriental Research Institute. (Article on Sati, pp. 624–35, 2nd edn, 1974.)

Kippenberg, Hans G., 1983. 'Diskursive Religionswisenschaft—Gedanken zu einer Religionswissenschaft, die weder auf einer allgemein gultigen Definition von Religion noch auf einer Uberlegenheit von Wissenschaft basiert', in *Neue Ansatze in der Religionswissenschaft*, ed. B. Gladigow and H.G. Kippenberg. Munich: Kosel.

MacCormack, Carol, and Marilyn Strathern, ed., 1980. *Nature, Culture and Gender*. Cambridge: Cambridge University Press.

Mani, Lata, 1985. 'The Production of an Official Discourse on "Sati" in Early Nineteenth Century Bengal', in *Europe and Its Others*, vol. 1: Proceedings of the Essex Conference on Sociology of Literature, July 1984, ed. Francis Barker, *et al.*, University of Essex.

———, 1987. 'Contentious Traditions: The Debate on "Sati" in Colonial India', in *Cultural Critique*.

Manuel, Frank E., 1959. *The Eighteenth Century Confronts the Gods*. Cambridge, Massachusetts: Harvard University Press.

Marcus, George F., and Michael M. Fischer, 1984. *Anthropology as Cultural Critique*. Chicago and London: University of Chicago Press.

Nandy, Ashis, 1980. 'Sati: A Nineteenth Century Tale of Women, Violence and Protest', in *At the Edge of Psychology: Essays in Politics and Culture*. Delhi: Oxford University Press.

Papers Relating to East India Affairs: viz Hindoo Widows and Voluntary Immolations, Printed by Order of the House of Commons, 1821–30.

Peggs, James, 1830. *India's Cries to British Humanity*. London: Seely. (2nd edn, Indian Report: *Cries of Agony*. Delhi: Discovery Publishing House, 1984.)

Ray, Benoy Bhusan, 1987. *Socio-economic Impact of 'Sati' in Bengal and the Role of Raja Rammohun Roy.* Calcutta: Naya Prokash.

Rosaldo, Michelle Zimbalist, 1974. 'Woman, Culture, and Society: A Theoretical Overview', in *Woman, Culture and Society*, ed. M.Z. Rosaldo and L. Lamphere. Stanford: Stanford University Press.

———, 1980. 'The Use and Abuse of Anthropology: Reflections on Feminism and Cross Cultural Understanding', in *Signs*, vol. 5, no. 3.

Roy, Rammohun, 1982. *The English Works of Raja Rammohun Roy*, ed. J.C. Ghose, 2 vols. New Delhi: Cosmo.

Seed, Geoffrey, 1955. 'The Abolition of "Sati" in Bengal', *History*, October.

Sharma, Arvind, 1979. 'Suttee: A Study in Western Reactions', in *Thresholds in Hindu Buddhist Studies.* Calcutta: Minerva Associates.

Srinivas, M.N., 1962. *Caste in Modern India and Other Essays.* Bombay: Asia Publishing House.

Sitin, Dorothy K., 1978. 'Women to Burn: Suttee as a Normative Institution', *Signs*, vol. 4, no. 2.

Stembrugge, Liselotte, 1987. *Das moralisehe Geschlecht: Theorten und literarische Entwurfe ueber die Natur der Frau in der franzoesischen Aujklaerung.* Weinhein and Basel: Beltz.

Strathern, Marilyn, 1987. 'An Awkward Relationship: The Case of Feminism and Anthropology', *Signs*, vol. 12, no. 2.

Thompson, Edward, 1928. *Suttee: A Historical and Philosophical Enquiry into the Hindu Rite of Widow Burning.* London: George Allen.

Ward, William, 1811. *Account of the Writings, Religion and Manners of the Hindoos. Including Translations from their Principal Works*, 4 vols. Serampore: Mission Press.

4

Mosques, Temples, and Fields of Disputation in a Late-Eighteenth-Century Chronicle

*B*ULWUNTNAMAH, A LATE-EIGHTEENTH-CENTURY CHRO- nicle written by Fakir Khair-ud-din Khan, covers the times of the first three heads of the Banaras royal house. It tells of the deeds of Mansa Ram, the founder; his son Raja Balwant Singh, the first officially recognized chief of the house, in whose last years the British enter the scene; to then recount and wind up the tale with the rise and fall of Raja Chait Singh. Written at the behest of the British, and of particular interest for the politicization of religion, the *Bulwuntnamah* is the record of a period of transition and in its hybrid orientation is a cross between a court chronicle and colonial archive.[1]

This text is valuable testimony precisely because it is a relatively dispassionate account of a time when the religion-based frontiers that were to harden in the colonial period had not yet formed. It is an account by a participant-observer who belonged distinctly to a pre-colonial world, though he would later become a part of the colonial

[1] For a survey of the historiography of the Banaras royal house, see Dalmia 1996.

order. The latter half of the eighteenth century was a turbulent period for the Awadh region, as power passed from the nawab of Awadh, who was still operating under the aegis of the Mughal emperor, into the hands of the East India Company, still ill equipped to undertake the tasks, civil and juridical, which this power would bring with it. In what follows I focus not on the political battles and intrigues that the chronicle chiefly records, but on the disputes—territorial, theological, and juridical—which involve 'Hindu', 'Muslim', and 'native', identities variously acquired by the populace under the classificatory system of the colonial state. In 1875, almost a century after its composition, the Persian original was considered to be of enough moment to be found worthy of translation via Urdu into English. Since it is the English text that we consider,[2] its character as colonial archive comes yet more sharply into focus.

Though the *Bulwuntnamah* is an officially commissioned history, it is in many ways a very personal document.[3] The Fakir has intimate knowledge of power struggles in the countryside: in fact, we discover in the course of the chronicle that he is himself implicated in them. His family has claims that date back to the pre-*nawabi* era in Awadh, to certain *madad-i-ma'ash* (revenue-free) villages in the Banaras region.[4] He is a man of learning, though impoverished,

---

[2] See Khan 1875.

[3] The Fakir seems to have become a professional chronicler for the British, for, according to his own testimony, he wrote two further chronicles, *Karnama Gwalior* and *Ibratnamah*.

[4] Muzaffar Alam has described the four categories of persons deemed eligible by the Mughal government for the grant of *madad-i-ma'ash*: 'i) scholars, who were "seekers after truth and renounced the world", ii) persons who "eschewed the urge for greater gain and chose a life of seclusion and self-abnegation", iii) the destitute and the poor "who were incapacitated to earn their livelihood", and iv) "persons of noble lineage who ignorantly deemed it below their dignity to take to any employment".' The grantees increased their power and wealth by purchasing zamindaris and accumulating enough wealth for moneylending, while managing to retain their earlier facilities and revenue-free possessions. This led to increased conflict between them, but also with the zamindars. However, as Alam also points out: 'Their divergent interests notwithstanding, the zamindars and the *madad-i-ma'ash* holders formed two sections of the same class that thrived and flourished on the expropriation of agrarian surplus. There

and, despite his youth, inspires respect because his family has a reputation for religious learning. It is likely that he also has explicit Sufi affiliations; at a later stage in the chronicle he refers to Dara Shikoh in the course of a theological debate. In his dealings with the various political figures he encounters, it is the pride he takes in his 'fakir' lineage that determines for him his own position in relation to them. He states this clearly while recounting an episode that he sees as sharply offensive to his dignity as a *'fakirzadah'* (descendant of a fakir). When there is jealous intrigue against the Fakir and he seems to fall into disfavour with the British agent, he is taken aside by the intriguing deputy who is causing the discord. This deputy tries to make him believe that:

> It was the usual custom in Lucknow for the Government mookhtar to stand in his presence, and that in future, when transacting any business before him, I was to stand. I replied that the dignity of my position was from him, while no act of mine could increase his dignity; that although I was a fakirzadah, yet my father and my grandfather had appeared before kings and princes, and had been treated with utmost respect; that I was a man of some learning, and respect was everywhere paid to that; that since I had had any connection with the English such a request had never been made; that he himself had seen [in] what manner the Governor-General had received me; that in the previous year I had sat on equal terms in the presence of Sir Eyre Coote and the other English gentlemen; that when in attendance at the court of the Nawab Wazeer, where it was not permitted to anyone, either of his own subjects or of the English, to sit in his presence, I had usually sat on the ground; that I would not now consent to any other agreement in Lucknow; and that as I perceived it was displeasing to Mr Johnson my remaining in his service, I begged to retire from it.[5]

The Fakir's father had obviously been attached in some capacity to the retinue of Fazl Ali, who had been awarded the government of

---

appears to be little difference in the character of the property of a *jagirdar* and a *madad-i-ma'ash* holder.' See Alam 1986: 110, 120–1. For the troubled relationship of the landlords with the nawab of Awadh, see Fisher 1987: 42–9.

[5] Khan 1875: 157.

Ghazipur by the nawab of Awadh. Fazl Ali was later to be ruthlessly ousted by Balwant Singh. As chronicler of the dynastic lineage set up by this very man, the Fakir is not altogether neutral, though he maintains a certain distance from the events narrated. He betrays his own opinions only in asides and epithets, or in that he ends an account of a particularly disreputable encounter between Balwant Singh and some hapless Rajput or Muslim landowner with events that followed much later, often in the Company period, when the aggrieved person was finally able to pay back Balwant Singh and his descendants in their own coin.

The chronicle is divided into three chapters of varying length. The first is the shortest (sections 1–20). It deals with the family and kinship net of Mansa Ram, who began to manage the revenue of the province from around 1717, though he held officially recognized power only from 1734 until his death in 1740. The second is longer (sections 21–63), consisting of a year by year—one could almost say blow by blow—account of the reign of Raja Balwant Singh (1740–70). The third (sections 64–178), which makes for two-thirds of the book, has to do with the troubled reign of Raja Chait Singh (1770–81). The Fakir is a subterranean presence in the first two chapters; he is acquainted with the descendants of most of the participants in the events, and though he nowhere explicitly acknowledges it, his data is often based on personal information. During the course of the third chapter he enters the narrative abruptly, appearing suddenly in the streets of Banaras. He has, he tells us, completed his years of study, *Lehrjahre*; he is in his early twenties and has now set out to see the world, the *Wanderjahre*. The world seems to receive him almost as eagerly as he enters it, and he is promptly embroiled in the thick of political events.

The narrative perspective of the third chapter is varied and tends to shift with the physical location of the Fakir himself. We often find him in the fort of Ramnagar, at the side of Raja Chait Singh. From incidental information in stray passages we discover that his family has also settled in Ramnagar. There is thus some reason to suspect that he has been for a while in the employ of the raja, but he never confirms this. The recurrent theme of the third chapter is the fate of his *mafi* villages, as the English translation designates them, and the hope that they be restored to him, and for this, necessarily, his constant reference point is the raja.[6] But he clearly finds favour with various English officials, accompanying and advising them, and, at least periodically, working for them. Astute, possessed of a dry wit, the Fakir carefully picks his way through the jungle of intrigue and corruption surrounding the various seats of power. What position does he take with regard to the chief actors? Conforming to the chronicle as a genre, the account focusses on the density of the Banaras lineage, but the Fakir neither eulogizes the rajas nor, for all his implicit critique, ever entirely rejects them. There seems even to exist some bond of loyalty to Raja Chait Singh: the Fakir sees him for the faint-hearted, shuffling, and luxury-loving ruler that he is, but time and again he tries to steer him past the worst disasters.

As for the British, the Fakir is cautious in his estimate of them. He is no flatterer, he pays them no more than their due when in their presence or when narrating of them. They are dependable to a degree, and they inspire awe, for they control the *subas* of Bengal, Bihar, and Orissa. He quotes Sheikh Ali Hazin, 'one of the holiest men of his times', who from his seat of authority in Banaras has prophesied in the presence of the nawab of Awadh and the Mughal emperor that the English armies will rule over Hindustan.[7] In his personal dealings with the English the Fakir treads softly, choosing as patrons only those whom he can trust and whose character he can morally condone. The chronicle then reflects a world of variegated hue. The Fakir has claims to religious authority, at the very least he has knowledge of his own faith, but also of the religion of the Hindus. It is as a man of learning that he works for Muslim, Hindu, and Christian masters. He is a fine and discriminating observer of the changing times. Are the religious communities, so self-evidently present on the political landscape today, represented in any

---

[6] The Fakir's villages were confiscated by Raja Chait Singh, who later promised to return them to him. He failed to keep this promise. Eventually he was pressed into doing so, when it was conveyed to him that the British held the Fakir in great respect. Ibid.: 69, 148, 156.

[7] Sheikh Hazin (1697–1766), a Persian poet of distinction, left his native land to live in India. He settled in Banaras where he received much respect from Raja Balwant Singh. For details of his life, see Khatak 1944.

self-contained sense in his narrative? What impression does he have of the ruling culture of the English?

Once the British enter the scene, political and cultural conflict increases as people of every religious hue scramble for power. But in this early period there also continues to be some theological dialogue between 'Hindu' and 'Muslim'. The three episodes that I briefly depict and analyse here are spread over the three districts of Jaunpur, Banaras, and Chunar, which the nawab of Awadh had first put under the charge of Mir Rustam Ali, and which were thus administratively linked with one another over a period of time. All three districts had come under the control of the rajas of Banaras. This transition from 'Muslim' to 'Hindu' rule, from the nawab of Awadh to the Banaras lineage, led to a reshuffle of power in the countryside. It also meant some readjustment of city space. What was the ideological frame, if any, under which these changes occurred?

The first of the three episodes concerns the battles surrounding a temple and a mosque in Jaunpur, the second treats the theological debate with which the Fakir establishes his reputation within the new power constellation in Banaras, and the third, which may seem initially unconnected with our theme, has to do with small, even trifling, incidents in Chunar. These incidents relate to early measures taken by the newly installed British to dispense justice, accompanied by the Fakir's attempts to correct the misapprehensions and prevent the violence provoked by the imposition of a new order upon the old. It seems clear from these incidents that the British would not long remain silent on the matter of religion. Here, too, they would seek to dispense justice from an ostensibly neutral standpoint, with misapprehensions and violence ensuing.

The Mosque–Temple Dispute in Jaunpur

Even after the nawab of Awadh ceded the province of Banaras to the British, Raja Chait Singh was allowed to retain the administration and revenue collection of the province. For this he had to pay the Company an annuity of Rs 2.5 million. A British agent, Fowke, was posted in Banaras and enjoyed considerable political power. Thus, over 1775–87 the English ruled the province of Banaras indirectly. It was in this period of layered authority that the mosque incident took place.

The *Bulwuntnamah* records there being in the reign of Chait Singh, in the year 1190 Hijra, a disturbance in Jaunpur:

> In this year Sewan Mahajun, a resident of Muhulla Humman Durwaza in Jounpoor, began the erection of a heathen temple between the musjid of 'Asar qudam Sharif' and 'Punjah Moobarak', on land in Mouzah Kunhyapoor, planting a grove of mango trees about it, and celebrating idolatrous worship with conch blowing and other ceremonies. The attendants at both the musjids forbade these proceedings from the commencement, but Sewan heeded not their remonstrances, and finished the building with profuse expenditure, placing a gilt trishool at the top of the dome.[8]

Jaunpur, a city first founded by the Tughlaks, was densely strewn with mosques and madrasas, many dating from a period as early as the fourteenth century.[9] In this landscape, dominated by Muslim learning and patronage, building a temple between two mosques could not, given the clear opposition to it, have been an entirely innocent enterprise. As C.A. Bayly has pointed out in his much discussed essay on the prehistory of 'communalism', in the late Mughal period and in the early years of Company rule Jain and Vaishnavite merchants from Rajasthan began to build up their power throughout the Ganges valley. Sewan Mahajun presumably belonged to this category of people. He was clearly the catalyst in the round of hostilities that was to follow the building of the temple. According to Bayly, who follows Muzaffar Alam's lead in this matter, the records of the period show clearly that the *qazis* (chief registrars)

---

[8] Khan 1875: 77–8.

[9] Ahmed 1968, a history of the city and the district, offers a detailed account of the political rise and fall of this region. The city of Jaunpur was founded in 1361 by Feroz Shah Tughlak. It saw the peak of its power in the reign of Ibrahim Shah (1402–42) of the local Sharqi dynasty. The city's stately mosques and madrasas later enjoyed the patronage of the Mughals. Dara Shikoh also built his own mosque to rival those of the Tughlaks and the Sharqis on the banks of the river Gomati.

and the *kotwals* (chief executive officers) often took a leading role in religiously inspired violence. They appear, on several occasions, to have incited and led anti-Hindu activity.[10] There are thus at least two sets of people who claim religious affiliation as some kind of driving force when reacting to the changed power situation.

The narrator could hardly be expected to sympathize with Sewan Mahajun's endeavour. However, his report here, as elsewhere, strives for neutrality. Two students, he tells us, fell into a 'pious rage' at these doings and the temple was pulled down. Next day, the Hindus of the city closed their shops and 'Sewan, the builder of the temple, Bhowani Dustooria, Shewpershad and others, the leaders of the assembly, determined in revenge for the destruction of their temple, to pull down the "Punjah Moobarak" Musjid and with this intent, some 2,000 men assembled at the tank "Tikka Sahoo".'[11] Meanwhile, the Muslims who had collected in the Jama Masjid of the town also went out in procession. There was an encounter with the Hindus. In the ensuing skirmish, two Hindus were killed.[12]

The Hindus refused an offer of peace from the Muslims, who sent envoys urging the 'Hindoos to settle the quarrel and return to their former friendly footing with the Musulmans, and most of them seemed disposed to do so.'[13] But one of their crowd managed to agitate them once again and, determined to go to Banaras, they presented themselves to the British agent, Fowke, who, not ready or willing to intervene in the affair, referred them to Raja Chait Singh.[14]

---

[10] Bayly 1985: 196, 198.

[11] Khan 1875: 78.

[12] Ahmed lists 'Hammam Darwaza' as a *mohalla* (residential neighbourhood) of Jaunpur. He says the 'Panjah Sharif' mosque was built in 1766, not long before our episode; it was situated two miles east of the city, in Mohalla Babupur. Presumably, this was in the *mauza* (village) of Kanhaiyapur, mentioned in our text. The Qadam Rasul mosque had been in existence from an earlier period. Ahmed gives a terse and heavily edited account of the above episode, which took place in 1776. He seems intent on glossing over the religious nature of the tensions and the violence, ascribing the whole to miscreants of one kind or another. See Ahmed 1968: 285, 479, 835, 842.

[13] Khan 1875: 79.

[14] Fowke's residency lasted till 1777.

The raja, 'on learning of the wrongs suffered by the Hindoos, was much perplexed and annoyed.'[15] He seemed to be somewhat affected in his 'Hindu' sensibilities by the skirmish, but within bounds, for he did not exhibit particular religious zeal. He sent one Jaykaran Chaudhari to investigate the matter. The ring leaders, the qazi and the mufti, as well as the principal weavers of the city, were sent to the raja.[16] The weavers absconded. The qazi and the mufti remained under surveillance for three months, after which they were fined and let off.

However, events in Jaunpur did not stand still and the Muslim party, not content with destroying the temple, were determined to erect a mosque at the site. The raja sent 'Jutimul, a Vakeel', to pacify the ring leader, who was duly bribed, but he could not convince his excited brethren to withdraw, and the new mosque was completed in the amazing period of eight days. The raja gave orders to the neighbouring zamindars to destroy the mosque. Did he want to prevent the Muslim participants in the skirmish from triumphing over the Hindus? We do not know. It does seem clear that he wanted the balance of power not to tilt overmuch. However, in the skirmish that followed it was the Hindu party that was defeated. The zamindar of Machalishahar, himself a Muslim,[17] persuaded his fellow men to retreat, whereupon the Hindu party stormed the place and finally pulled down the mosque. The conflict was clearly not on 'religious'

---

[15] Khan 1865: 79.

[16] Gyanendra Pandey has written at length of the Muslim weavers who were concentrated in towns, where the possibilities of serious and violent conflict were greater than in the countryside. In the nineteenth century, they would become increasingly vulnerable to the play of market forces: 'It is hardly surprising to find that as part of the weaver's fight to preserve (and improve) their economic status, a vigil was maintained by prominent groups of weavers in what they considered to be *their* towns, *their* mohallas, *their* mosques, to guard against any innovations that might go to reduce the importance of their religious festivals and places of worship.' Pandey 1990: 102.

[17] According to Ahmed, the zamindars of Machalishahar had adopted a Bhumihar Brahman boy (of the same caste as the rajas of Banaras) to set forth their lineage. Thus, Raja Chait Singh may have had some connection to this particular zamindar.

grounds alone, but was already beginning to assume the character of a political power conflict, though there were surely many amongst the contestants whose religious sensibility was truly provoked.

Further trouble was brewing in town, a reprisal seemed inevitable. The raja, propelled increasingly into the position of protector of the Hindus, apparently more irked than honoured and 'in great vexation', sent his troops to put an end to these disturbances. The leaders of the skirmish, which had originated in the Muslim quarters, were expelled from the city, 'and they not being able to resist, and being deserted by their party, quitted the place and went with their families into the territories of the nawab.'[18] When it came to seeking protection, the religious affiliation of the rulers did therefore count. The afflicted parties had now to send delegations to Fowke in Banaras, who in such matters obviously preferred to defer to the authority of the raja.

Before relating this episode the Fakir nowhere designates the people who play a role in his narrative as Hindu or Muslim, though obviously it has constantly to do with men who belong to one or the other religious group, whether in Banaras, Awadh, or the countryside. The various landholders are referred to as Rajputs, Goutam Brahmans—as the Bhumihars are designated in the chronicle. The Muslims are mentioned merely by their names, without further specification. There is plenty of conflict among the various Muslim groups, as also among the different Hindu *jati* groups. The Fakir is keenly conscious of group differences and affiliations. Later we see what trouble brews between Raja Chait Singh, of mixed Bhumihar–Rajput descent, and Ausan Singh, his chief minister of pure Bhumihar blood. Ausan Singh chooses to flee from the service of the raja rather than dine with him in public. In all these altercations, no homogeneous group of Hindus or Muslims emerges. Why then does Sewan Mahajun figure primarily as Hindu, and the students and weavers primarily as Muslims, in this particular episode? The answer seems to be that they assume these primary identities only in specific situations.

Jaunpur was a city of mosques. The Hindu merchant makes a bid to carve out a religiously symbolic space in what could possibly be an

[18] Khan 1875: 84.

opening created by the new power constellation and, willy-nilly, the raja finds himself being thrust into the role of defender of the Hindus: when called upon, he cannot escape this role. But some at least of the ring leaders seem aware that beyond him there are also the English, whose leanings cannot yet be ascertained. However, Fowke refers the matter to the raja, preferring to stay aloof. The interventionist state is not yet in place. But in the final run the culprits prefer to play safe and shift to the territory of the nawab.

The temple–mosque affair follows a well-known pattern of disturbance and is apparently only one of many such incidents.[19] Can we regard it as a transitional period also in the matter of communalism, perhaps literally pre-communal and not connected or leading up to it? After the episode, the Fakir goes back to his dealings with the various groups, whom he continues to designate Rajput, Afghan, and the like, apparently untouched further by this violent scuffle for local redistribution of religiously symbolic ground. As a group, the Hindus and Muslims, then, appear suddenly in the *mandir–masjid* episode, to disappear as suddenly thereafter. But religious spaces were beginning to be redefined, a process which would be further accelerated once the British assumed absolute power.[20] The religious difference that came into play in such situations, however, seemed to function without reference to theologically, philosophically, or even

[19] For further examples of 'religious' strife, see Bayly 1985: 186–91, 194–201. Bayly's points are well taken; the examples he cites show clearly enough that there was little homogenization of categories in this period. Pandey's refutation of his thesis (Pandey 1990: 15–22) may be slightly overdrawn. However, Bayly's conclusion regarding the kind of religious strife prevalent in the late Mughal and early years of British rule providing 'pre-existing lines of social fracture' in the twentieth century remains problematic. See Bayly 1985: 203. If there was no homogenization in the earlier period, how can we maintain that the lines of social fracture were given? We would need, in fact, to investigate and determine the kinds of continuities that exist between the older and the newer lines of social fracture.

[20] See Asad 1993, particularly the introductory essay, 'The Construction of Religion as an Anthropological Category' (27–54), for an extensive discussion of the importance of the authorizing discourses that systematically redefined religious spaces in the history of Western/Christian society.

socially grounded theories of difference. In fact, the Fakir himself would take some pains to lay out his thoughts in this regard: as far as he was concerned, there was more similarity than difference in the religious systems of his countrymen.

Religious Disputation in Banaras

Soon after the mosque–temple episode, the Fakir enters the scene in his own person. He is drawn into religious debate with Brahmans. It is in this context that he is led once again to speak of Hindus and Muslims. He is new in Banaras. He notices a crowd of travellers at a gateway, attendants of the rich Bengali Durgacharan, former diwan to a Mr Marmot. Durgacharan, he is told, 'held no communication with Mussulmans and avoided even the shadow of a Mahomedan.' The Fakir's curiosity is aroused, 'I thought to myself, I am travelling to see strange things, and the religion of the Bengalee is certainly among them.'[21] Note, he does not say 'religion of the Hindus'.

He enters the building to see a hundred Hindus sitting around Durgacharan. Contrary to expectation, Durgacharan turns out to be friendly, welcoming, and, in his turn, curious. When he tries to take his hands, the Fakir recoils instinctively: 'As by your religion Mussulmans are unclean, and you avoid their shadows even, and bathe after the least touch, so according to my religion you are utterly unclean.'[22] Durgacharan laughs heartily, and seizing the Fakir's hands draws him towards himself. When the Fakir tells him of his years of intensive study and the thirst for knowledge that now drives him into the world, Durgacharan, sceptical of the claims to knowledge made by this tender youth, provokes him into speaking to the Brahmans by mocking the cosmogony of the Muslim. Unafraid, the Fakir launches into his own account of creation. There were many men who lived before Adam, but he was the ancestor of the Muslims, and therefore it is from his time that they reckon the creation of the world. The

---

[21] Khan 1875: 87.
[22] Ibid.

Fakir then proceeds to recount the years of Adam, Noah, Abraham, Moses, Jesus, and the Holy Prophet. He then recapitulates the belief of, as he calls them, 'your sages': the creation by the almighty Brahma of the five elements and the theories concerning these. He explains the yuga cycle, a thousand of which make a day of Brahma, and so on. In each of the Dvapara yugas, Brahma creates a male personage called Dulja and endows him with beauty and strength.[23] This Dulja, the Fakir proclaims, is identical with Adam and is thus 'our common ancestor'. After this statement, it can come as no surprise that he quotes Dara Shikoh who, he says, 'knew all your books'. It is to his authority that the religio-mythological narrative that now follows is attributed. It consists of a rich mixture of godly beings, demons, epic heroes, and yuga cycles, and culminates in an account of the origin of idol worship in Hind. The 2000 years between Noah and Soorajrai, that is, just before the coming of Muslim conquerors, were chaotic:

> As in this time there was no guidance or authority, Iblis, taking the form of a Brahmon, appeared to man, and falsifying the descent of man from Ham, the son of Noah, gave out his ancestors to be Mahadeo, Ram and Luchmaun, and making images of them in wood and stone caused them to be worshipped as deities; but as the history of the time of Ham could not be shaken, he upheld and taught it. So, according to your own sages, all the men now existing are the descendants of Adam, and not of any race of Jins of the Kuljoog period. Our Prophet in his day declared the truth, and your own sages pronounce such stories to be fables and unfounded, and your learned men consider such idolatry as abominable; yet for the instruction of children and the ignorant, they allow them to place before them the images of their guides and teachers, to excite them to devotion and worshipping God.[24]

The reaction of the Brahmans to these startling revelations could not but be mixed. Some denied the truth of these statements, while

---

[23] I have not been able to identify 'Dulja' with any known mythological figure in the Hindu systems. It could be a reading of '*dwija*', the Sanskrit term for the 'twice born'. Adam was also 'twice born'. I am indebted to Catherine Clementin-Ojha for this thought.

[24] Khan 1875: 91–2.

others, as the Fakir tells us, 'older and better acquainted with their sacred writings . . . corroborated my statements, and said that, with slight verbal discrepancies, all that I had uttered was in their books.' Durgacharan went so far as to proclaim: 'You are a Pundit of my religion.'[25]

The Fakir was able to establish not only that he had knowledge of the system of the Hindus, but that there were clear points of agreement between Hindu and Muslim sacred lore. And apparently he won recognition for this knowledge from Durgacharan—whose views may or may not have been representative of those of his fellows. In either case, he was of the breed of men from which would later issue such free spirits as Raja Ram Mohan Roy. The Fakir's views cannot be regarded as indubitably representative of the times either, though it is possible he was far from singular in holding them. The ideal of religious intermingling, which the ill-fated Mughal prince Dara Shikoh personified, had been influential enough to generate others of his kind.

Even in the Fakir's generous eclecticism, the religions of the Hindus and Muslims do not entirely meld. There is a clear consciousness of 'you' and 'we', of difference—if not in matters of cosmogony then surely in practices such as idol worship—and at least some apprehension of the treatment to be expected from the other. Yet he is looking for equivalence, and there is no trace of the hostility that could be expected if he were to see himself as a partisan in the mosque–temple affair. The levels of dispute in Banaras are entirely separate from the skirmish in Jaunpur. The Hindus who raze the mosque to the ground are not brought into connection with Durgacharan. He draws no line of connection between them. The enlightened view of religion that he presents at once enables friendship with the Fakir. Durgacharan carries the news of his exposition to the chief British officer in Chunar, who is none other than Colonel Alexander Dow.

The year is 1192 Hijri and the British have established themselves in Chunar. Colonel Dow has cultural as well as political presence.

---

[25] Ibid.: 92.

MOSQUES, TEMPLES, AND FIELDS OF DISPUTATION 105

He has already written extensively on the history of the subcontinent and on the Hindus.[26] Besides translations from Persian, he has published two volumes of the *History of Hindostan* in 1768, adding a third in 1772. The first volume of the *Dissertation on the Hindus* has appeared in the first volume of the *History*, and it is from this that the following citation on Dow's views on Hindu cosmogony is drawn:

> These repeated dissolutions and renovations [of the world] have furnished an ample field for the inventions of the Brahmins. Many allegorical systems of creation are upon that account contained in the Shasters. It was for this reason, that so many different accounts of the cosmogony of the Hindoos have been promulgated in Europe; some travellers adopting one system, and some another. Without deviating from the good manners due to these writers, we may venture to affirm, that their tales, upon this subject, are extremely puerile, if not absurd. They took their accounts from any common Brahmin, with whom they chanced to meet, and never had the curiosity or industry to go to the fountainhead.
>
> In some of the renovations of the world, Brihma, or the wisdom of God, is represented in the form of an infant with his toe in his mouth, floating on a comala or watery flower, sometimes upon a leaf of that plant, upon the watery abyss . . . Brihma, in one of the renovations, is represented in the form of a snake, one end of which is upon a tortoise which floats upon the vast abyss, and upon the other, he supports the world. The snake is an emblem of wisdom, the tortoise is a symbol of security, which figuratively signifies providence, and the vast abyss is the eternity and infinitude of God. What has already been said has, it is hoped, thrown a new light on the opinions of the Hindoos, upon the subject of religion and philosophical inquiry. We find that the Brahmins, contrary to the ideas formed of them in the west, invariably believe in the unity, eternity, omniscience and omnipotence of God: that the polytheism of which they have been accused, is no more than a symbolical worship of divine attributes, which they divide into

---

[26] Alexander Dow, probably born in Scotland in 1735 or 1736, began as an ensign in the Company's Bengal army to rise to the rank of colonel by the time he died in India in 1779. Extracts from Dow's works are conveniently available in Marshall 1970.

three principal classes. Under the name of Brihma, they worship the wisdom and creative power of God; under the appellation of Bishen, his providential and preserving quality; and under that of Shibah, the attributes which tend to destroy.[27]

Colonel Dow's views on moral, religious, and political questions were enlightened and it was clearly his intention to credit the religion of the Hindus with all the features that would make for its validity as a theological and philosophical system that commanded respect. He was at pains, therefore, to discredit the accounts of those travellers who would make it appear merely fantastic. The Brahmans believed in the 'unity, eternity, omniscience' of God. However, though he spoke of going to the fountainhead for his knowledge of Hinduism, he admitted elsewhere that he was unable to learn Sanskrit, and that he relied on translations of the sacred texts of the Hindus into Persian and into the 'vulgar tongue of the Hindoos'.[28] A person such as the Fakir, who claimed to have knowledge of both Hindu and Islamic thought, would have been of special interest and value to him. Small wonder that Dow wishes to hear the discussion that the Fakir had with the Brahmans. For Dow as much as for the Fakir, it seemed viable and legitimate to establish equivalences between religious systems, to look for their underlying truth, to see allegory in myth. A certain fluidity in the boundaries that marked off religious systems from one another seemed entirely possible at this stage of the encounter.

Dow is an admirer of Persian poetry and he seeks the Fakir's help in translation. The Fakir stays with the colonel for a month. It is here that two small incidents take place which show that British notions of justice had little universal validity, that they were frequently misplaced, and, more often than not, made for serious harm to the populace. The Fakir records them in dry detail.

The British Settle Disputes in Chunar

Dow's diwan is a Bengali. One day he brings into the colonel's presence a Muslim in irons. The colonel orders that he receive 150 stripes and then be released. The Fakir learns that the prisoner's of-

[27] Ibid.: 138.

fence was that he had lost an important decree which established his rights over certain possessions. The prisoner had offered the diwan Rs 250 to affix the signature anew on a similar document; in short, he had asked that the document be forged. 'The dewan told him [the colonel] of the affair, which is a grave offence in his country, where the signature is relied upon, and not the seal on a document.'[29] It does not take the Fakir long to realize what has actually happened. The diwan had probably first agreed to the forgery, the prisoner had then possibly questioned the reliability of the diwan: if he could forge the signature once, he could forge it twice. How was he to know that the diwan would not similarly help possible opponents? At which the diwan had taken alarm and thrown the consequences onto the prisoner. The Fakir communicates his reading to the colonel, to then remonstrate with him: 'The prisoner is an ignorant man, quite unacquainted with the rules and customs of the English, while the Dewan is an intelligent man, who has been for a length of time in association with Englishmen, and knows their laws and habits; why then did he consent to the prisoner's proposals?'[30] We have the satisfaction of seeing the Bengali diwan grow yellow with fear. The prisoner is released and the diwan issued a stern warning. But the regulations continue to be issued. They attempt to establish order; instead they cause further malfunctioning and corruption. Chaos ensues when all the inhabitants of the town are asked to produce the title deeds of their houses or lands in court. Dow asks for the Fakir's opinion. The Fakir comments:

> It was a strange circumstance that, while he [the colonel] was only anxious to do justice and relieve the poor from oppression, they suffered injustice and oppression without bounds, that the officials had fixed such a rate of fees that rich men only were able to pay them, and by this means had obtained the title-deeds of poor men, who could not afford them, and that they considered it hopeless to attempt to establish their rights.[31]

[28] Ibid.: 7.
[29] Khan 1875: 94.
[30] Ibid.
[31] Ibid.: 95.

It is no wonder that the qazi of the town is soon so infuriated with the Fakir that he himself considers it wise to take leave of the colonel, and we soon find him back in Banaras.

In the Fakir's dealings with the British we find little trace of servility or of any notion of being in the presence of a superior culture. The British are misinformed, if often well disposed, towards those they attempt to rule. In introducing their sweeping notions of justice for all, in trying to deal globally with local problems, they fail to realize the misuse to which their barely comprehensible notions of government can be put.

The disturbances and debates discussed lend themselves to at least two radically different interpretations. One could see in these episodes the seeds of all later violence: in short, see them as pointers to all later developments that evolved naturally from these preconditions and were consolidated into full-fledged 'communalism' a century and a half later. The other interpretation, the one that I have sought to follow, would see these events as indications of how much state intervention determines the direction strife can take. Raja Chait Singh's initial ire, but lack of subsequent religious zeal in the matter, allows for a certain rude equilibrium to be established. The temple is pulled down, so is the mosque, the miscreants are allowed to abscond, and peace is restored. In this state of affairs, which we can only describe as fluid, if notions of difference are beginning to take the form of definite cultural and religious identities, they can be viewed as transitory, as yet unfixed. They appear on certain occasions, when the question of rights—ritual, theological, legal—has to be negotiated anew under a novel political authority. They subside once a resolution to the immediate questions at hand has been found. In the debate at Banaras, the Fakir is at pains to establish that there is little difference between the religion of the Hindu and that of his forebears. A tolerant, even syncretic, view of religion seems at least within the realm of the possible for men like Durgacharan, Fakir Khair-ud-din Khan, and Colonel Dow.

But once the colonial state, which only partially comprehends the social and religious issues at stake, begins to intervene and regulate, the directions it gives make for large-scale homogenization and violence. A linear, official narrative begins to evolve. As the Fakir points out: 'It was a strange circumstance that, while he [the colonel] was only anxious to do justice and relieve the poor from oppression, they suffered injustice and oppression without bounds.'

However, I should not like to conclude this brief essay by laying the blame for the present communalization of religion once again at the door of the colonial state. As the mosque–temple episode in Jaunpur demonstrates, it is the role that the given state plays in resolving the conflict that finally determines the direction of events. There can be disturbances, but they can be allowed to subside if the state does not choose to make capital out of them or support others in doing so.

References

Ahmed, Syed Iqbal, 1968. *Sharqi Rajya Jaunpur ka Itihas*. Jaunpur.
Alam, Muzaffar, 1986. *The Crisis of Empire in Mughal North India*. Delhi.
Asad, Talal, 1993. *Genealogies of Religion. Discipline and Reasons of Power in Christianity and Islam*. Baltimore and London.
Bayly, C.A., 1985. 'The Prehistory of "Communalism"? Religious Conflict in India, 1700–1860'. *Modern Asian Studies*, vol. 19, no. 2.
Dalmia, Vasudha, 1996. *The Nationalization of Hindu Traditions: Bharatendu Harischandra and Nineteenth-Century Banaras*. Delhi.
Fisher, Michael H. 1987. *A Clash of Cultures: Awadh, the British and the Mughals*. Delhi.
Khan, Khair-ud-din, 1875. *The Bulwuntnamah*. Trans. from *Tuhfa-i-Taza* of Fakir Khair-ud-din Khan by Fredrick Curwen. Allahabad.
Khatak, Sarfaraz Khan, 1944. *Sheikh Muhammad Ali Hazin: His Life, Times and Works*. Lahore.
Marshall, P.J., 1970. *The British Discovery of Hinduism in the Eighteenth Century*. Cambridge.
Pandey, Gyanendra, 1990. *The Construction of Communalism in Colonial North India*. Delhi.

5

Vernacular Histories in Late-Nineteenth-Century Banaras

Folklore, Puranas, and the New Antiquarianism

Even a cursory glance at the vast amount of periodical and pamphlet literature produced in the second half of the nineteenth century would confirm that all new literary endeavours in modern Hindi were shot through with an urgent sense of history. Not only were the claims to antiquity and nationhood stated historically, all spheres of social activity, including literature, were fast acquiring 'history'. The authors of each literary genre, newly created or assimilated, sought to prove their linear descent and legitimacy by establishing links with ancient texts. The most obvious example of this antiquarian enterprise was the attempt to link the novel, a manifestly new literary genre, with *Kadambari*, the ornate seventh-century Sanskrit courtly romance in prose.[1] The

---

[1] *Acknowledgements*: I should like to record my gratitude to Nita Kumar for her participation in the writing of this article. She has invested more than editorial labour in shaping the argument and in tying up the many loose ends.

On the beginnings of the novel in Hindi, see Dalmia 1999: 169–84. For a broad perspective on the development of the novel in India, see Mukherjee

historical essay, which came into being at this time, had no obvious predecessors in the immediate past. It could, however, cite and relate to various works in Sanskrit and the vernacular which helped reconstruct the past.

Several knotty problems were linked with this endeavour, most centrally the question of dating the works thus used in order to bring them within the chronological scheme acknowledged by Western historians. Only then could the data contained therein be validated. The Puranas, once considered works of history, had been widely discredited even as a historical source. This could obviously and radically change the very nature of historiography, as has been shown for Bengal. If, in the early nineteenth century, it had seemed entirely plausible to think in terms of the cosmic time-cycle of the yugas, to locate Bharatavarsha in a topography equally cosmic, and to accept the genealogies of the Puranas as given, the latter half of the century had seen a complete reversal of this scheme of things. Not only were the Purana genealogies of royal houses considered entirely suspect, the very idea of thus chronicling history was radically modified.[2]

If the transition from the old to the new was made abruptly in Bengal, the response in Banaras was both less precipitate and more complex. For one thing, historiography in late-nineteenth-century Britain and Europe had itself undergone change. Anthropology and folklore were widening the bounds of old-style history, and this made itself felt in the colonies almost immediately. Further, Banaras faced

---

1985. On the introduction of various new literary genres into modern Hindi, see Dalmia 1997: 222–337.

[2] 'We have passed from the "history of kings" to the "history of this country" . . . This history now is periodized according to the distinctive character of rule, and this character, in turn, is determined by the religion of the rulers. The identification here of country (*des*) and realm (*rajatva*) is permanent and indivisible. This means that although there may be at times several kingdom and kings, there is in truth only one realm which is coextensive with the country and which is symbolized by the capital or the throne. The *rajatva*, in other words, constitutes the generic sovereignty of the country, whereas the throne represents the centre of sovereign statehood.' Chatterjee 1995: 115.

changes introduced by the colonial state much later than in Bengal, retaining tenacious links with both Sanskrit tradition and local history. Thus, while the representatives of the modernizing elite in the North West Provinces and particularly Banaras sought to adopt the new and the newest, they also found other ways to authenticate the traditional. They continued to value the Puranic and the local-oral, and to remain bound to it, even as they bowed to the authority of the Orientalist which both Sanskritized and homogenized.

In the first part of this essay I will look at notions of history as they reconstituted themselves in both Britain and its colonies in the last quarter of the nineteenth century. In the second part I will retrace the path trod by Harishchandra of Banaras (1850–85) who, as litterateur and amateur historian, tried his hand at writing manifold histories in Hindi. Situated at the heart of Banaras society, this merchant prince of immense cultural influence became heir to a dual historiographical heritage—the local-customary and the pan-Indian Orientalist. His explicitly historical writings, published in pamphlet form or in his periodicals, are worth analysing for the uses to which he put his sources and the ways in which he sought to resolve a major dilemma of the intellectual of his time in South Asia. In this regard it is instructive to follow the delicate manoeuvres he made to resolve the tensions between the newly minted caste, regional, Hindu, and pan-Indian identities. In doing so he seemed to be following the nationalist models forged first in Bengal, but he also differed from these in his approach, for he both touched and parted ways with Puranic history and the European historiography of India.

Centrifugal and Centripetal Forces

Viewed within a larger time frame, the Orientalist as well as the nationalist historiographical agendas can be seen as a culmination of an old struggle, that of negotiation between centrifugal and centripetal forces, pulls operative for many centuries in the subcontinent.[3] Put somewhat differently, it was a struggle between Sanskritic and

---

[3] Cf. Hardy 1995: 35–50.

non-Sanskritic forces, to be regarded not so much as two monoliths but as individual entities partaking in multiple, overlapping traditions which encountered each other regionally and locally. 'Sanskritic' is used here both in the sense of the term coined by M.N. Srinivas—that is, as signifying upward caste mobility by adopting Brahmanic customs—and also as the move by these Sanskritic forces themselves to appropriate popular, folk, or simply other traditions through the centuries.

The situation in the nineteenth century was somewhat more complex, since the negotiations involved a third force, the colonial presence in the subcontinent, which followed its own agenda. This presence was obviously linked with the desire to control the subject population most effectively. Sanskritization as effected in this context was an administrative, centralizing move, concerned less with creative evolution or adaptation than with codification. What it elected to view as normative, it endowed with an inflexibility and universality unparalleled in the history of the subcontinent, and also sought to freeze this in time. The British understanding of Indian culture thus took place largely through selective and sometimes even fresh interpretations of the Sanskritic traditions, as mediated by Western Orientalists, who came to exercise an authority which superseded that of the Brahmins, especially when it came to historiography. Their eagerness to gain access to the stores of traditional knowledge and wisdom and learn from Sanskrit pandits in the late eighteenth century had, by the end of the nineteenth, given way to an attitude bordering on contempt for the pandits. The Sanskrit College in Banaras, founded in 1791, was now run with the conviction that, without sound training in modern historical-critical methods, native teachers and students of the college would gain little of whatever remained of the old. They needed to study Western histories of Sanskrit literature and Western editions of Sanskrit texts before they could 'form wider and more enlightened views of Indian literature.'[4]

---

[4] The latter half of the century saw a rich crop of work emerging from such civil servants turned anthropologists and philologists. C.A. Bayly seems, rightly, to be somewhat sceptical of Shahid Amin's proposition that the ethnographic

The late-nineteenth-century nationalist endeavour, though closely allied with the Brahmanic-Sanskritic and the Western Orientalist moves to codify tradition, was possibly even more concerned with being comprehensive in its efforts to enfold what it came to view as 'tradition'. However, it differed from the Western Orientalist in that it sought also to modernize under the protective umbrella of the old. The desire to merge in the great national stream and direct it could take very different forms. Once again, however, it is important to look closely at the respective social groups and religious communities involved in this process. Some groups ended up insisting on greater specificity, even to the point of polarity, if merging did not suit their interests. This polarization could be expressed through 'naming' and new 'identities', such as 'Muslims', 'Aryans', and 'Dravidians'.

In the process of merging or assimilating with the great nationalistic-Sanskritic stream, the nationalizing forces often cited the early- and mid-century European Orientalists either to confirm the positions they adopted or to question those which they rejected. In late-nineteenth-century Banaras, when following their own special agenda, they found that they could absorb newer tendencies within British officialdom and other intellectual currents flowing in

---

work of civil servants such as William Crook 'was, in effect, a discursive strategy to bury change within tradition.' See Bayly 1996: 354. Crook and others were much more 'conservationists as well as Orientalists, and their perceptions owed much to the turn in contemporary European sensibilities towards popular culture represented in the British case by the legal thought of Sir Henry Maine. This new thinking about race, popular culture and authenticity was consciously radical and modern' (ibid.: 355). Their representation of Indian life was indeed, as Bayly observes, informed by powerful undercurrents in Indian life itself (ibid.: 357). However, I would see these undercurrents as the ever-present centripetal forces that were genuinely difficult to reconcile with visions of a monolithic Aryan, Brahmanic, or Sanskritic culture. Both British and Indian amateur ethnologists and antiquarians (in the terminology of the day) had, in fact, to undertake a series of manoeuvres in order to reconcile the contradictions which surfaced whenever they attempted to fit their findings within the frames of the newly constructed monolithic Aryan-Sanskritic culture.

from the West—in so far as they were felt to confirm, support, or extend their own approach. These currents included concern with folklore, with peasant cultures, and with tribes and castes, most of which were non-Sanskritic in their style and content. The interest of British civil servants turned anthropologists in these matters could serve to revalidate whole literary genres, such as caste histories and genealogies, set within one later Purana or the other, which in the past had also been concerned with Sanskritizing a variety of social groupings.

Folklore, Local History, and Nationhood

In reviewing these processes today, journals such as *Indian Antiquary*, founded in 1872 by James Burgess and published in Bombay, acquire great interest and value. Not only was every civil servant a potential antiquary and scholar, but every native with access to English education could also aspire to this position, though in the first decades of the journal's existence there were obviously few native contributors.

> We invite all our readers to aid us with their pens; there is no country where fresh information of the most varied sort lies so near to everyone's hand as in India; and whoever tries to write, we feel sure, will find his field widen and deepen in interest, the oftener he makes the attempt to put it into form for the interest and instruction of others.[5]

In the pages of this one journal alone both centrifugal and centripetal forces can be observed in operation. There is a strong Sanskritizing, appropriating current which attempts to fit all data into a larger scheme of things, but there is also the dispassionately documentary, detailing the manners, customs, and languages of tribes and castes which had remained firmly outside the pale of varna society. It was quite clear that not everything could be neatly packaged. Social and cultural tensions, caste based and otherwise, continued to prevail. The data pulled in various directions, spilling over the boundaries provided by the Dharmashastras.

[5] Burgess 1872: 2.

It is worth noting, however, though it was nowhere expressly stated, that the data thus collected, or rather its summation, transformed the very concept of what constituted the history of the country, poised as it was on the threshold of nationhood:

> The scope of this [journal] will be as wide as possible—addressing the general reader with information on Manners and Customs, Arts, Mythology, Feasts, Festivals and Rites, Antiquities and History—in which every one, in any way connected with the country, ought to feel an intelligent interest—and at the same time it is intended as a *medium of communication* between Archaeologists in the East and West. Its Correspondence columns will afford ample opportunity for the amicable discussion of many questions, on which more information is yet required before any fixed opinion can be formed, and for propounding *Queries* on all matters fairly within the domain of Oriental Research. By presenting its readers with abstracts of the most recent researches of *savants* in India, Europe and America, and by its translations from German, French and other European languages—it will make fully accessible to the many Native Scholars, unacquainted with these languages, the latest results arrived at by the greatest continental scholars.[6]

The common ground created by the journal was expressly for East and West to meet, and pool and exchange information. However, since cultural and social rather than political history was being solicited, it was going to be found embedded in myth and legend, in oral narratives, and in the manners and customs which had survived the ravages of time.[7] If these were modern, progressive notions,

---

[6] Ibid.: 1.

[7] See Dorson 1968 on the anthropologist Edward Burnet Tyler and his notions of cultural history as accessible in myth and folklore. In his *Researches into the Early History of Mankind and the Development of Civilization* (London, 1865), 'Tyler considered with obvious relish two vexing problems posed by myths: What degree of historical truth, if any, do they contain? Were similar myths the result of diffusion or independent invention?' (Dorson 1968: 188). Tyler placed mythical narratives on a broad spectrum running from the historically valid to the purely inventive. In *Primitive Culture: Researches into the Development of Mythology, Philosophy, Religion, Art and Culture* (London, 1871), Tyler codified his observations on the behaviour of folklore within a

they could and did, for all their modernity, merge and meet with older notions of history. Myth and legend had not only figured as history but had also carried various other forms of historical narrative within themselves. As Romila Thapar has demonstrated so lucidly, generational history existed within mythic time, just as linear notions of time, astronomic and mathematical, could be contained within the ritual and the circular. Cyclic time had a genesis and predicted termination; it did not preclude other categories of time. The listing of generations in the *Vishnu Purana*, for instance, begins with a description of the progeny of Manu, the mythical father of mankind, to then go on with a sequential reckoning of generations which, as Thapar has pointed out, is for all practical purposes an exercise in linear time.[8] Other kinds of generational histories, such as bardic chronicles and caste histories, drew on the Puranas for legitimating purposes, though they were not identical with them. For instance, they relate the succession of later rulers and then go on to emphasize the major concerns 'perceived as important to historical change'. These included primarily 'the recognition of the importance of acquiring caste status, the emergence of institutions linked to state formation and the establishing of new religious sects supportive of caste hierarchy.'[9] Ethnologists and antiquarians now turned to

---

new concept—'Survival in Culture'—which made it possible to view practices once labelled 'superstition' as fragments of an earlier culture. His study of myths and folklore from all over the world demonstrated the similarities and interrelationships in the traditions of primitive and civilized peoples. 'Folklore could now take its place with the new empirical sciences': (Dorson 1968: 193, 195). Collecting local data and comparing it with textual source material, Sanskrit, and the vernacular were trends that motivated much of the fieldwork by imperial ethnographers (ibid.: 333). See also Burke 1990: 6–11, for the shifts in mainstream European historiography towards the end of the nineteenth century.

[8] 'The term used for a succession list of any kind of a genealogy is *vamsa*, derived from the name for bamboo. This is an appropriate image where each node marks a new generation of growth. This itself would suggest linear time.' Thapar 1996: 37.

[9] Ibid.: 37.

these genealogies and chronicles with a new curiosity, as also to oral narratives and tales current in the social world of various groups.

Journals such as *Indian Antiquary* were only one medium for these documentations and reflections. What was not articulated in English found space in the vernacular press in the guise of the historical essay, termed variously *itihasa* and *puratattva*, which emerged as an independent literary genre.[10] Sanskrit terms were taken over, but new meanings were attached to them; thus *puratattva* stood for antiquities and *itihasa* for a new historiography influenced by Europe. Though the colonial periodization of subcontinental history into Hindu, Muslim, and British was thereby unquestioningly accepted, what occurred with varying degrees of emphasis—and this was where nationalistic history parted ways with the imperial—was a reinterpretation of the whole stretch of history in terms of the Hindu period, understood not only as constituting past history but as determining the contemporary political and cultural identity of the Hindus. If local and national history were thus to be reconstituted in terms of the Hindu, there was indeed much territory to be traversed.

Such antiquarian and historical essays, then, need to be considered part of a larger enterprise—compiling a comprehensive national history. Their perspective differed from the older Brahmanic-Sanskritic. They comprised both the constitution of the political, social, and cultural history of an increasingly Hindu India as well as the attempt to popularize it and link it to the local. They also drew on manifold sources. Though early British chronicles such as James Tod's *Annals and Antiquities of Rajasthan* and Grant Duff's *History of the Mahrattas* had set the tone, it was from the first a question of wresting this power from civil servants and Orientalists; the reappropriation of this knowledge meant converting it into a category of Indian nationalist thought.[11] Caste histories, newly validated,

---

[10] Morrison 1984. Morrison has coined the term 'miscellany' for this genre of writing.

[11] As Ranajit Guha has pointed out: 'the production of colonial historiography was from the very outset an exercise in dominance and not an act of charity.' See Guha 1988: 3.

could be referred to, as also current traditions and field observations. The Puranas remained a vital source, but though history was to be deduced from them they did not present it pure, so to speak; it was inherent, embedded in them.[12]

In the mid-nineteenth century there existed only two general surveys in modern Hindi which tried to encompass the history of the subcontinent: Bansidhar's *Bharat ka Vrittant* (1845),[13] and the better known text by Raja Sivaprasadsingh, *Itihasa Timirnashak* (1864). Both relied on the models created by British historians and the textbooks written by them. Their main source of information were the Orientalists. Yet even Sivaprasadsingh did not endorse or absorb uncritically all that the British historians had seen fit to report. In his Preface to *Itihasa Timirnashak* he says:

> I was not fully aware of the difficulty of my task when I promised to prepare a little work on the History of India in Hindi and Urdu, for the use of our Village Schools. I knew how imperfect and full of errors the so-called histories are, which have hitherto been written in the Vernacular, but I had not imagined for a moment that even so cautious a writer as Elphinstone was liable to commit such mistakes . . . Or that a talented author like Mr. Marshman would forget the topography of the country.[14]

The need to constitute the information anew in the new narrative framework of vernacular historiography is clear.

However, historiography in Hindi did not consist only of these larger works, though it is often maintained that apart from Sivaprasadsingh's oeuvre there was no historical writing worth the mention.[15] Many of the historiographical essays scattered in Hindi

---

[12] See Thapar 1986: 27, for the notion of the Puranas as containing 'embedded history'.

[13] Cf. McGregor 1974: 89; and idem1966: 118.

[14] Sivaprasadsingh 1864.

[15] Thus: 'In the later period Bharatendu Harishchandra and his associates made a great contribution to the growth of a prose literature, but historical writing did not catch up with the progress. Writers were largely concerned with the production of school text-books, many of which are translations, and of small biographies which, as a rule, are of very poor quality.' Singh 1961: 461.

literary journals of the period, some of which I shall examine in the next section, have been disregarded merely because they neither appeared as comprehensive accounts nor as monographs, but were, rather, even as essays, fragmentary and with abrupt endings. Piecing together these fragments affords new insights into the intellectual dilemmas of the day and the creative solutions being sought. By looking closely at them it becomes possible to discuss the complex historiographical response to the Orientalist and nationalist challenge that they embodied.

Regional and Caste History as National History

Hindi journalism, particularly in the format of the literary journal, reached maturity only in the 1870s.[16] It was pioneered and dominated by magazines published in Banaras under the editorship of Harishchandra, the leading literary figure of his day. Though he belonged to one of the most influential and wealthy families in the city, it was as a poet and as the son of one that Harishchandra legitimized the publication of the *Kavivacansudha*, a journal (as it described itself) of literature, news, and politics which acquired a legendary reputation even in its own day. In the years that Harishchandra was its editor and proprietor (1868–77), this journal examined contemporary issues with a confidence that belied the years and experience of its editor. *Harishchandra's Magazine*, later renamed *Harishchandrachandrika*, followed fast upon it.[17] It was in these two journals that most of Harishchandra's literary works were published.

In addition to being a *kavi* (poet) himself, the editor was connected to the most varied associations and institutions and had as such a uniquely mediating function. The very names of these associations point to the diversity of their fields of operation. There was the Kashi Dharma Sabha, most centrally representing the sacral authority that the city possessed for the subcontinent. Here disputed

---

[16] For details on the beginnings of modern Hindi journalism, see Dalmia 1997: 227–32.

[17] For details on these two journals, see Dalmia 1997: 232–45.

matters from all over—Punjab to Nepal to Calcutta—were sent for clarification and final judgement. The maharaja of Banaras was an authority, but it was a medley of Kashi pandits, who met at various places to discuss, dispute, and adjudge, who finally ruled. Socially binding as well were the festive and ritual activities of a group of merchants belonging to the Vallabha Sampradaya who lived in and around Gopal Mandir. In addition to these citadels of tradition as it was newly defining itself, there was the Benares Institute, founded by men of new learning, or *nai shiksha* as Western education was called, but later largely taken over and managed by British civilians, missionaries, and non-officials. The institute had of late become the playground of Sivaprasadsingh and Syed Ahmad Khan and was treated with much sarcasm by *Kavivacansudha*. The editor himelf had, however, early become an honoured member of the institute and was implicated in its activities.

In fact the titular 'Bharatendu' (Moon of India) prefixed to Harishchandra's name was endowed by his countrymen through the medium of the press. It was the work, if we are to believe later reports, of the Hindi journal *Sarsudhanidhi*, which began coming out in Calcutta in 1879 and proposed that the poet be honoured thus. Public consensus was sought by the journal in lieu of the recognition not forthcoming from the British. The British had seen fit to bestow the Sitar-e-Hind (Star of India) on Sivaprasadsingh, who, for all his efforts to further the education of his countrymen, was regarded by the British as their lackey. These matters were discussed freely in the journals of the day. The press was fast becoming a counter public instance of authority; it could award titles which came to be widely used; the British were not the sole title-awarding instance.

Harishchandra of Banaras, as one of the leading cultural voices in the city, also wrote a series of shorter histories. He used the information provided by the British, but, as against Sivaprasadsingh,[18]

---

[18] In the Preface to Part III of his *History*, Sivaprasadsingh had stated clearly: 'No sober man is expected to go through these pages and again believe in the mythology of the Puranas or long for some of the old regimes.' Sivaprasadsingh 1864.

he continued to regard Puranic sources as valid. I understand this attitude not as naive traditionalism but as one that regarded myth, epic, and genealogy as embedded in historical consciousness.[19] These had served various functions in the past and continued to do so in the nineteenth century. They legitimized changed social and political conditions and provided social sanction. Besides Puranic material, Harishchandra presented, in the tradition of the best of the new ethnological documentation, local legends and explications in support of his theses. Local history was not discarded as mere fabulation but considered worthy of antiquarian interest. He was familiar with the *Indian Antiquary*, which he repeatedly refers to, as well as with works such as Sherring's *Hindu Castes and Tribes*. His historical essays, then, are an intricate though not always satisfactorily resolved amalgam of ethnography, so-called hard historical facts gleaned from newer histories, and the more complex information from the Puranas. A critical vocabulary for distinguishing between the different kinds of source material in any consistent fashion had not yet evolved. But two factors do remain consistent: the vital importance of establishing links with the Sanskrit tradition alongside a new process of fanning out to include contemporary fare. Muslim chronicles are thereby firmly discounted as biased. Western antiquarians form clear points of reference, but Harishchandra is as acutely aware of the fact that their beliefs can at all times degenerate into dogma and serve only their own imperialist ends. As he was to point out in the opening paragraph of his antiquarian essay *Ramayan ka samay* (The Age of the Ramayana [1885]):

> Once you set about thinking and reflecting upon matters connected with the ancient age [you will find that] there is no way to form an immediate estimate of things. The number of new works you consult will determine the range of ideas revealed about them. Present-day intellectuals (*budhiman*) have two views about this branch of knowledge (*vidya*). The one follow, without due reflection, the path laid down by the older European scholars (*vidvan*) while the other insist on nothing and accepts new facts as they emerge. The latter view is the more proper and correct but the former makes it more convenient to lay claim to

---

[19] Cf. Thapar 1986: 354.

being 'antiquarian'. One need only proclaim some cliches in order to become 'antiquarian'. A man can become an antiquarian merely by making pronouncements such as these: all newly discovered statuary stems from the Jains, the Hindus are sure to have come from Tartar or from somewhere in the west, there was no image worship in former times etc. Be that as it may, we shall not insist on this line of thinking. Here we shall select only such few matters from the Valmiki *Ramayana* that have to date received no attention from scholars.[20]

By relativizing the absolute authority of the Orientalists, Harishchandra was validating other sources as equally authoritative if not more. Hereupon follow a series of facts, social and technological, gleaned from Valmiki's text.

Armed with this approach to source material, Harishchandra tried his hand at three kinds of historical writing: (1) on *desha* (territory), that is, regional histories such as *Maharashtra desh ka itihas* and *Udayapurodaya*; (2) on various caste groups, such as Khatris, Agravals, and the like; and (3) a whole series of smaller pieces documenting texts of inscriptions and copper plates, sometimes translated and commented upon, which are scattered through the pages of his journals. I shall consider the first two.

Desha

An exclusively Hindu history is presented here. Since 'Hinduness' was increasingly coeval with the territory inhabited by Hindus, the history of respective regions was seen in terms of when Hindu kings reigned and when they had to retreat. In keeping with the trend discussed earlier, nationalist history from the mid-nineteenth century turned away from older forms of historiography which had worked with Puranic notions of time and space and were more chronicles of kings than histories of territory, or *desha*. It would not have occurred to older chroniclers that, for instance, the history of the kings of Delhi could be the history of a nation.[21] But in late-nineteenth-

---

[20] Harishchandra 1954: vol. III, 377–8. Hereafter *Granthavali*. This and all ensuing translations from the Hindi are mine.

[21] Cf. Chatterjee 1995: 115.

century Banaras it was possible for Harishchandra, more traditionally rooted than his Bengali counterparts, to reincorporate the Puranic or mythic sense of time and space, newly revalidated as it was by anthropologists and folklorists. It was within this contextual frame as a context that he sifted and reorganized his material.

Maharashtra desh ka itihas begins,[22] ironically with the coming of the Muslims, since, as Harishchandra has to confess, there is no consistent information available for the period before that: 'A chronological history of Maharashtra country is not available. Raja Shalivahan is counted amongst the ancient kings there. He started the Shaka era and it is also well known that he killed a certain Vikrama. Prasthan, which is called Paithan now, was his capital. The kingdom of Devagiri was independent till the coming of the Muslims and Ramdev was the last independent king there.'[23] Harishchandra does not disclose his sources or mention the vastly influential *History of the Mahrattas* by Grant Duff in three volumes published in 1818, which was the obvious source of even this information and which glorified, even if reluctantly, the exploits of Shivaji.[24] This reticence is unusual because it is unlikely that Harishchandra did not know of this work,

---

[22] Published first in the journal *Harishchandrachandrika*, vol. 3 (8–12), May–September 1875, the full text has been included in *Granthavali*, vol. III, 167–79, from which I have the quotations that follow.

[23] *Granthavali*, vol. III, 171.

[24] The short character sketch that Grant Duff provides makes this abundantly clear: 'Sivajee was patient and deliberate in his plans, ardent, resolute, and persevering in their execution; but even in viewing the favourable side, duplicity and meanness are so intermixed with his schemes, and so conspicuous in his actions, that the offensive parts of a worse character might be passed over with less disgust. Superstition, cruelty, and treachery are not only justly alleged against him, but he always preferred deceit to open force when both were in his power. But to sum up all, let us contrast his craft, pliancy, and humility with his boldness, firmness, and ambition; his power of inspiring enthusiasm while he showed the coolest attention to his own interests; the dash of a partisan adventurer, with the order and economy of a statesman; and lastly, the wisdom of his plans which raised the despised Hindoos to sovereignty, and brought about this own accomplishment, when the hand that has framed them was low in the dust.' Grant Duff 1826: 297.

and he does not shrink otherwise from mentioning his sources. His own attitudes are, however, very clear. The Muslims are regarded as an interruption in Hindu history. Their period is discounted, blocked out; it is the time before their coming that must provide the base for restoring the country to its original glory.[25] The first part of Harishchandra's history deals with the exploits of Shivaji and his efforts to keep the country free of Mughal and Muslim influence. Not even the most determined efforts of Aurangzeb could really win control over the country during Shivaji's time.

At no stage is their varna affiliation discussed, though Grant Duff had been somewhat sceptical of their claims to Kshatriya or Rajput status.[26] Harishchandra ends with an account of the dissolute heirs to

---

[25] Grant Duff, in the Preface to his *A History of the Mahrattas*, makes it clear that his interest is to record the exploits of the immediate predecessors in power: 'The want of a complete history of the rise, progress, and decline of our immediate predecessors in conquest, the Mahrattas, has long been felt by all persons conversant with the affairs of India; in so much that we cannot fully understand the means by which our own vast empire in that quarter was acquired, until this desideratum be supplied.' Grant Duff 1826: vii. He took a very dim view indeed of the ultimate source of their success: 'The rise of the Mahrattas was chiefly attributable to the confusion of other states, and it was generally an object of their policy to render everything as intricate as possible, and to destroy records of rightful possession. As their armies overran the country, their history became blended with that of every other state in India, and may seem to partake of the disorder which they spread.' Ibid.: xiv. Though, as Stewart Gordon has pointed out: 'It should he noted however, that it was Mountstuart Elphinstone, the well-known Bombay administrator of the early nineteenth century who, in his *History of India*, first referred to the Marathas as a "nation" and to Shivaji's activities as a "war of independence".' Gordon 1993: 3.

[26] As Grant Duff stated: 'The reader will now understand, from what has been said of the most conspicuous classes of the inhabitants in Maharashtra, that the name of Mahratta is applicable in some degree to all of them, when spoken of in contradistinction to men of other countries; but amongst themselves a Mahratta Brahmin will carefully distinguish himself from a Mahratta. That term, though extended to the Koonbees, or cultivators, is in strictness, confined to the military families of the country, many of whom claim a doubtful but not improbable descent from the Rajpoots.' Grant Duff 1826: 18.

this country, which finally fell into the hands of the British in 1818. The second part then goes back in time to begin with an account of Balaji Vishvanath, and deals with the reign of the Peshwas: 'Sadasiv Rav Bhau with the aid of Ramchandra Baba Senabi established new and firm order within the territory of the Maharashtras [Harishchandra seems to be avoiding the term "Marathas"]. The Maharashtrian power was fully entrenched at the time and they roamed and freely attacked all over Hindustan. The emperor of Delhi was their puppet.'[27] However, as matters stood, the short account of the Marathas had to end with the victory of the British forces, which are not explicitly vilified. Though the British had originally come to settle the infighting and squabbling in the subcontinent and carried out this task with some fairness, they claimed payment for this. The reader is prepared for the final catastrophe through information such as the wealth and power of the Maharashtra kingdom went with Nana Phadnavis when he died in 1800. The triumph of the British is noted with due reserve: '[The British] government took control of Maharashtra and entrusted the arrangements of it to Elphinstone. The aforesaid official respected the dignity and customs of the Maharashtrians and satisfied the people there to such an extent, by making over the estates of some to be the responsibility of some others, that the people of the place remember him to this day.'[28] In that they are made out to have willingly acquiesced, the Marathas' valour and dignity are preserved.

Udayapurodaya, an account of the rise of the dynasty of Udaypur, published two years later in the journal *Kavivachansudha* (hereafter *KVS*), is Harishchandra's better-known historical essay.[29] It has three long chapters and is more ambitious in its scope, the author's aim being to review the history of a dynasty which claimed ancient roots and which preserved its independence through most of Muslim

---

[27] *Granthavali*, vol. III, 175.
[28] Ibid.: 179.
[29] It was published in 1877 in the *KVS*. The issues for these years have been scantily preserved. There is at all events an instalment in vol. 8, no. 29, 8 December 1877. The booklet as a whole was published independently in 1878 and is available in *Granthavali*, vol. III, 211–43.

and Mughal rule. After citing a popular legend to indicate how this dynasty came to be called Sisaumdhiya, its most ancient roots are invoked in solemn and ringing tones:

> This is the lineage which is the most ancient and the most respected in all of Bharat. It is in this lineage that there have been such gigantic kings as Mandhata, Sagar, Dilip, Bhagirath, Harishchandra, Raghu and others and it is in this lineage that Bhagvan Ramchandra took incarnation. It is of this lineage that Kalidasa, Bhavabhuti, as also Vyasa and Valmiki have written charitras, or biographies, which still bejewel Indian literature. This is the only lineage remaining in Bharatvarsa which has remained on the throne in eternal sovereignty since the satyayuga.[30]

Since Bharatkhand and Hindustan are repeatedly mentioned in this account, the premise appears to be that Hindus once reigned over this whole territory, that it was their natural right to do so, and that they had done so since the beginning of time, i.e. *satyayug*. Much has been lost since, but this one dynasty, which can boast of the most illustrious names in Indian/Hindu history, and which has been celebrated in the most famous literary works, has preserved itself intact through time and never given way to alien power. Even if, on the whole, the territorial importance of the Hindus has shrunk, this one lineage has remained in power continuously, however shrunk it may now appear. Like a kernel which can again branch out and bear fruit, this dynasty has ever preserved its life energy, its hauteur, and its dynamism.

The sources for this history could not be of alien origin alone, however sympathetic their tenor. The information collected had to be incorporated into a new narrative of Hindu valour which validated Hindu sources while utilizing them:

> I have sat down today to write a history of this gigantic, valorous and ancient lineage. My main sources are Tod's *Rajasthan*, vernacular works on the lineage of Udaypur and ancient copper plates. Just as the beginnings of the chronicles of most kings of the world are filled with many miraculous tales, so there are many wondrous tales set at the beginning of this one. No one need harbour suspicion on the historicity (of

---

[30] *Granthavali*, vol. III, 213.

this lineage) on this account, since ancient chronicles are often filled with miraculous episodes and historians apply their intelligence to deduce from them the essentials of their history.[31]

Harishchandra then proceeds to relate these tales. But before doing so he cites Orientalist sources and juxtaposes the dates proposed by William Jones and H.H. Wilson to refute them with information published in more recent articles in the *Bombay Journal* and *Indian Antiquary*. The main figure, whose exploits have been related at such length by Tod, is the legendary founder of the present dynasty, Bapa Raval. The account proceeds at a leisurely pace; Tod is cited but also refuted. At all times Harishchandra displays an independence of judgement surprising in one so young and so amateur. The third chapter deals rather summarily with the history of Bapa's successors, shrouded as it is in the mists of time. With that the narrative comes to rather an abrupt end.

Apart from several other shorter articles, Harishchandra wrote the *Kashmirkusum*, a history of the kings of Kashmir, depending this time on the *Rajatarangini*. He also wrote the *Badshadarpan*, on the Mughal kings of Delhi, though none of these were published in the journals.[32] He cannot thus be accused of confining his attention to Hindu dynasties and territories. But his intention is clear. As he stated expressly in *Kashmirkusum*:

> The moon of history cannot be sighted in the clear sky of Bharatvarsa, since along with other ancient branches of knowledge, history has also disappeared. Partly there was no tradition of writing chronological history in older times, and what was left has disappeared in the jaws of grim time. The Jains destroyed the works of the Vaidics, and the Vaidics those of the Jains . . . As if this was not enough, the Muslims came and burnt whatever was left. Thus were we relieved of our burden. Such black clouds gathered that the valiant glow of the moon of Bharatvarsa was cast over.[33]

---

[31] Ibid.: 214.

[32] Both these articles were published as independent booklets by the Medical Hall Press in 1884. They are available in *Granthavali*, vol. III, 271–312, 313–45.

[33] Ibid.: 275.

The purpose behind writing a history of the Muslim kings is equally clearly stated. There was no dearth of chronicles pertaining to this period, yet these were often distorted; they failed to present the Hindu side of the history, let alone chronicle any tales of Hindu valour. They virtually made the Hindus disappear from the pages of history. It was necessary to redress this imbalance:

> The very Bharatvarsa which was once the crown of this earth, whose glory was recognized the world over, which was the mainstay of knowledge, valour and wealth—it is also one aspect of time that this very Bharatvarsa stands lean and inferior today.
>
> There is no chronological history of the period before the sun of independence set here. The histories that Muslim writers have written have caused the glory of the Aryas to disappear. It is to be hoped that there will be some mother's son who will undertake the labour of writing the history of his ancestors to make everlasting their glory.
>
> In this work there are only the biographies of those people who first made slaves of us. There are small character sketches of those lusty elephants who uprooted and then trampled upon the lush lotus groves of Bharatvarsa and tore these apart. Chief amongst these are Muhammad, Mahmud, Alaudin, Akbar, Aurangzeb and so on.[34]

The yoke which bore down so heavily upon the country was depicted, all said and done, as a burden to be borne by the Hindus alone, and blame placed squarely on the shoulders of the Muslims who had initiated the process. The humiliation and misery were projected backward and hostility for the alien projected on them as well. The significance of these short accounts cannot be emphasized enough, for it was thus in small steps that the grand narrative of Hindu India was being constructed, the vocabulary coined, the perspective clarified. The nationalist historians who followed had mainly to put the pieces together. Each part of the subcontinent had been territorially reclaimed by the Hindus in the name of Hindu dynasties which traced their roots back to Vedic times.

Harishchandra could not have been entirely unaware of the fact that he was cutting and pruning in order to fit his information into

---

[34] Ibid.: 315.

the national frame. Since he obviously also resorted to Grant Duff's *A History of the Mahrattas* for information on the Marathas, he could not have failed to observe that Shivaji fought with his own kind as well, that he was a marauder of no mean stature. But for Harishchandra's purposes it suffices that the Marathas were the last Hindu rulers, and that they had a misty past which linked them to illustrious and legendary names such as Salivahana and Vikrama. He does not touch upon the vexed issue of their varna affiliation. However, he has a much freer hand when it comes to the history of the Rajput kings of Udaypur, and draws generously on the Puranas and Sanskrit court poetry, such as that of Kalidasa himself, to endow them with epic dimensions.

The history of these regions and royal houses is interpreted from a perspective entirely different from that of the Orientalists. Not only are they not always acknowledged as sources, their authority is recognized only tangentially. They stand in need of correction, supplementing, expansion.

Jati

Harishchandra had very early in his career written a history of his own jati, the Agravals.[35] Their varna status as Vaishyas was not disputed. Apart from describing manners and customs, he had here considered in detail the Puranic sources regarding their origin and spread. However, in the nineteenth century there were several other jatis with uncertain claims. These could not be located specifically in any one of the varnas, though they had clearly belonged to privileged groups in the past. One such group was the Kayasths. There was heated discussion regarding their claims to kshatriyahood. Though they were repeatedly classed as Sudra, they repeatedly pressed their claims to higher status. Questions of ritual status had become intimately linked to employment in the colonial army, police force, and

---

[35] Entitled *Agravalom ki utpatti*, the tract was first published by the Medical Hall Press, 1871. It is available in *Granthavali*, vol. III, 3–12. For a short discussion of this tract, see Dalmia 1997: 118–19.

bureaucracy.[36] Thus, judicial note was taken of ethnological speculations and such information was also collected directly by local colonial administrators. The colonial government was the largest single employer in the country, and it was now officially possible to be excluded from employment on the basis of caste.[37] Numerous caste sabhas (associations) had begun to spring up from the late nineteenth century. All historical and ethnological writing on caste issues had assumed a new significance.

Another group of uncertain varna status was the Khatris, merchant and trader castes with their home in the Punjab and the North West Provinces. Harishchandra chose to unequivocally support their Kshatriya ambitions. In *Khatriyom ki utpatti*, an account of the origin of the Khatris, he brought forward a number of arguments to support these claims.[38] He had long wanted to collect *jati ka puravrtta*, the antiquities connected with this jati, but had been unable to do so for lack of material. His sources in the present study were his friend Sri Radhakrishnaji from Lahore, the book *Mihirprakas* by Munsi Budhsingh and finally Sherring's *Hindu Tribes and Castes*.

The situation was such that all kinds of jatis were busy laying claims to higher status. Hence there were the Dhusars, who were barely recognized as Vaishyas, since their women could remarry, claiming Kshatriya status; similarly there were the Kayasths, who

---

[36] '(F)or the award and denial of favours (e.g. public employment, political representation) the colonial forced a predictable Indian response: those seeking patronage or protesting proscription had to speak in the name of the bureaucratically recognized category . . .' Carroll 1978: 249. There was a clear 'distribution of patronage through caste categories.' Ibid.: 250.

[37] The Kayasths were not recognized as Kshatriyas, but had been classed as Sudras instead, with the result that 'Official circulars declared Kayasths ineligible for the police service (1860) and the army (1883).' Carroll 1978: 244.

[38] The first and longer part of the article was published in *Harishchandra's Magazine*, vol. 1, no. 1, 15 October 1873; vol. 1, no. 3, 15 December 1873; the final instalment, more in the nature of a supplement, appeared in *Harishchandrachandrika*, vol. 6, no. 5, November 1878. The full text is also available in *Granthavali*, vol. III, 245–60, whence the following citations.

had been classed as Sudras, to say nothing of the Jats. The writer's illustrious Jat friend Raja Thakur Giriprasadsingh was among those who pressed this claim. What then of the Khatris, *Jo mukhya arya jati ke nivassthal panjab aur pascimottar des meim phaili hui hai aur jis meim sarvada acche log hote aye haim* (who were spread over the Panjab, the chief place of habitation of the Arya jati, and the North West Provinces and who have always consisted of good folk.) This, in fact turns out to be one of the chief arguments of the essay, that the Punjab was the main area of Aryan settlements. This was asserted by all the English histories of Hindustan and here it is their authority that is invoked: 'Let no one harbour any suspicion, since I have used the word 'Arya' twice in the foregoing, that I have insisted on this out of any partiality for the country. This is indeed the prime abode of the Arya people and it is from here that they have spread to all of Bharatvarsha; this will become clear from the study of English histories of Bharatvarsha.'[39] John Muir himself had written to Pandit Radhakrishnaji, Chief Pandit of Lahore, that in his study of Vedic literature he had found corroboration for the fact that the Aryans inhabited the territory which stretched from the Punjab to Prayag. Citing a number of Vedic hymns which testified to this, he concluded that the Khatris were the *param aryas*, the highest kind of Aryas.

Once their Aryahood has been accepted, and this does form the premise of his argument, there arose the vexed question of the varna status of this jati. Oral history provides the main corpus of evidence:

> Now there is the dispute regarding the varna to which they belong. So we maintain that in general they are kshatri (that is, Kshatriyas). There is great controversy about how they became Khatri from kshatri. It is the belief of many people that the people of Punjab cannot pronounce ksha, that is the reason why they came to be called Khatri rather than kshatri. Some say that when Parashuram destroyed the Kshatriyas, some children were called khatris and thus saved. They were raised in the houses of Brahmans, Vaishyas, and Sudras. Thence it was that many subcastes came into being, such as Khatri, Arora, Bhatiya, and their cus-

[39] *Granthavali*, vol. III, 248.

toms also became like those of their guardians. A third lot maintain that this difference between Kshatri and Khatri has come into being since the times of Emperor Chandragupta since Chandragupta had been born from the womb of a Sudra woman and when he killed Raja Nanda through the strategems of Chanakya Brahman, all the Kshatriyas sought marriage alliances with them. But many Kshatris separated from them and hid in the foothills of the Himalayas, and when he began to annihilate the Kshatris, many saved themselves by becoming tradesmen and calling themselves Khatris.[40]

Tale piles upon tale. There is one version which maintains that those Kshatriyas who first became Jains only to reconvert to being Hindu were received back into the fold not as *kshatris* but as *khatris*. Guru Govindsingh and Guru Nanak had spoken of the *kshatris* as *khatris*. The evidence thus provided by linguistics, local lore, and Sikh literature is incorporated.

Conclusive evidence is also provided by the Puranas, where the story of the annihilation of Kshatriyas by Parashurama is related: 'We have proved conclusively in the above thus the conclusiveness of oral evidence! That Khatris are Kshatriyas and we have also documented the many options of opinion that people have offered. But we retain no uncertainties, it is clear that they are Kshatriyas from the pronouncements we bring below on Parashuramji's conquest of the world within the section on the ten avataras, or incarnations of Vishnu.'[41] He then cites as evidence slokas 24–43 from the *Sarasangraha* of the Puranas and Upapuranas which in its *Dashavataraprakarana* relates the story of Parasurama's conquest of the world. It was important for Harishchandra to cite the text in Sanskrit on account of the authority that the language and the author's access to it generated, even if it was unlikely that the majority of his readers understood it readily. Instead of going into a lengthy translation, which would have testified to the importance of the text quoted as a whole, Harishchandra translates or rather summarizes excerpts from these, thus:

[40] Ibid.: 249–50.
[41] Ibid.: 251.

When Parasuramji set out to conquer the world, the earth was filled with gladness since he destroyed the wicked whose weight had caused her distress. Wandering the breadth of the earth and winning by his arm's strength, he went to the land of the five rivers and fought a great battle with the king. Though the godly one was alone, he killed the entire army of the king etc.

A Vaishya by the name of Laksmivilas took the wives and children of the brave thus killed and righteously protected them. And nurtured the sons and carried out the *yajnopavita* and other *samskaras* for them. In this way the wives and children of the brave men thus killed acquired the customs of the varnas of the men to whose houses they went and the cluster of Kshatriyas belonging to the vamsas of Agni, Surya, Chandrama and the Nagas, that went to the house of Laksmivilas, acquired the characteristics of the Vaishyas even though it had originally received Kshatriya samskaras.[42]

Two long passages from the *Purvardha* of the *Bhavishya Purana* are then cited. The language of this text fragment is so simple, says Harishchandra, that it is unnecessary to translate. All that is important to know is that here it is once more clearly stated that after Parasurama's act of destruction, the Kshatriyas of the Punjab laid down their warriorhood. Though their present habits and customs, in that they so nearly resemble those of the Vaishyas, belie their kshatriyahood, it is quite obvious that their origin was Kshatriya.

It is characteristic of Harishchandra's approach in this period, contextualized as it was in the kind of ethnological information granted pride of place in journals such as the *Indian Antiquary*, that he presents dispassionately the evidence of the many stories, which he expressly designates as *kahani*. They are neither presented as fictive accounts, nor discounted. As cumulative evidence they serve to prove that there has always been the need to account for the status of the Khatris, and that there was some kind of radical change from one status to another which has been preserved in folk memory—and not only in the Puranas.

To sum up the evidence presented in the body of his essay, Harishchandra cites a genealogical poem, a *nrpavamsavali* consisting

---

[42] Ibid.: 252–3.

of twelve couplets, by Sivaramsingh, a local, presumably Khatri, bard, which once more puts forward the Khatri claims to kshatriyahood:

> The earth once took the shape of Kamadhenu, the wish fulfilling cow
> Thrilling with ecstasy, its body hair standing on end, it shed its body well
> From the root of those hairs emanated the Khatri clans
> I shall recite now the names of each [clan] according to its rank.[43]

Harishchandra is acutely aware that all kinds of jatis were pressing their claims to higher varna status, or even to acquiring varna status. He was equally aware that Khatri claims to kshatriyahood were based on thin evidence and ran counter to their actual professional profile. Yet he declared his unqualified support for these claims largely on the basis of oral tradition, putting to use thereby the new ethnologizing trend in British India. Though his arguments are based on the Orientalist claim that Punjab is the prime country of the Aryans, it is liberally and generously expanded by citing both vast quantities of oral tradition and long passages from the Puranas. It is more expansive than the older forms of Sanskritization, since it is not only the Brahmanic varna scheme which is being revalidated but also the newly forming nation itself which is laying claim to these dynamic clans.

Conclusion

The centripetal forces at work, straining to pull all regions into the nationalist frame and all Hindu groups into the fourfold varna scheme, seem all-powerful in such historiography. Yet, Harishchandra's approach has a freshness and newness since it is made so early. There is a self-aware, self-confident use of sources other than the Orientalist, a new revalidation of oral tradition as ethnology, and of the Puranas as history. It is Hindu history but it comes from a modernizer who has a more open relation to tradition than would be possible for a rationalist like Bankimchandra, at least as interpreted by contemporary scholarship. In Sudipta Kaviraj's reading of his works, for instance, Bankim wrote and spoke as a Hindu:

---

[43] Ibid.: 259.

It is significant that Bankim was not among those of his generation who stayed within the received Hindu tradition, and attempted to fashion intellectual defence in its favour. He was a person who returned to a position that was of a reconstructed Hinduism very different from its traditional form, and from that point of view, rightly regarded with suspicion by those more devoutly inclined. On at least two points, this reconstructed philosophy diverged sharply from its conventional form. The apparatus of argument it used was almost wholly rationalistic, and it was prepared a little too easily, to surrender as nonsensical a great deal of the deeply held certainties of traditional religion. A traditionalist could therefore ask what was historically Hindu in his construction of philosophic and ethical doctrine. A vaisnava could object on similar lines to a vaisnavism which so casually dismissed Caitanya. Bankim's answer, stated explicitly, was that this was the only way Hinduism could survive in history.[44]

But I would argue that in fact Hinduism has many local and regional forms and many levels of discourse and that possibly even Bankim's notions of Hinduism may need to be evaluated in a more nuanced manner to determine whether modernity could have had the unilinear impact it seems to have had if we judge from interpretations such as those cited above. Harishchandra, as a man of the late nineteenth century and more specifically of the self-consciously holy city of Banaras, could not but span many time schemes. And if he was looking back, by making deliberate use of sources formerly declared ahistoric, he was in many ways also looking forward. As literary historians of the period and place, we could also do worse than recognize with Bharatendu, that there are more cultures and ways of worship within Hinduism than one.

As we take leave of the nineteenth century, we see the new intellectuals in colonial India using both older and newer forms of historiography to press nationalist claims which ran both diachronically and synchronically. But mainstream nationalist historiography would choose to follow the newer alone, cutting off the many untidy local odds and ends. Harishchandra's anthropologizing, which in setting forth an older Puranic tradition found corroboration in the

---

[44] Kaviraj 1993: 141.

newer one of folklorists, did not find any sustained perpetuation. It would take many more decades for folklore and anthropology to establish themselves institutionally and stake their claims to historicity.

References

Bayly, Christopher A. 1996. *Empire and Information. Intelligence Gathering and Social Communication in India, 1780–1879.* Cambridge: Cambridge University Press.

Brajratnadas, ed., n.d. *Kavivachansudha 1.1.* Banaras.

Burgess, James, 1872. 'Prefatory' to *Indian Antiquary*.

Burke, Peter, 1990. *The French Historical Revolution: The Annales School 1929–89.* Stanford: Stanford University Press.

Carroll, Lucy, 1978. 'Colonial Perceptions of Indian Society and the Emergence of Caste Associations'. *Journal of Asian Studies*, vol. 37, no. 2. February.

Chatterjee, Partha, 1995. 'History and the Nationalization of Hinduism', in Vasudha Dalmia and Heinrich von Stietencron, eds, *Representing Hinduism: The Construction of Religious Traditions and National Identity.* Delhi: Sage.

Dalmia, Vasudha, 1997. *The Nationalization of Hindu Traditions: Bharatendu Harishchandra and Nineteenth Century Banaras.* New Delhi: Oxford University Press.

———, 1999. 'A Novel Moment in Hindi: Pariksa Guru or the Tutelage of Trial', in Vasudha Dalmia and Theo Damsteegt, eds, *Narrative Strategies: Essays on South Asian Literature and Film.* Delhi: Oxford University Press.

Dorson, Richard M., 1968. *The British Folklorists: A History.* London: Routledge.

Gordon, Stewart, 1993. *The Marathas: 1660–1818. New Cambridge History of India*, vol. II, no. 4. Cambridge: Cambridge University Press.

Grant Duff, James, 1826. *A History of the Mahrattas*, 3 vols. London: Longmans.

Guha, Ranajit, 1988. *An Indian Historiography of India: A Nineteenth-Century Agenda and its Implications.* Calcutta: K.P. Bagchi.

Hardy, Friedhelm, 1995. 'A Radical Reassessment of the Vedic Heritage—The Acharyahridayam and its Wider Implications', in Vasudha Dalmia and Heinrich von Stietencron, eds, *Representing Hinduism: The Construction of Religious Traditions and National Identity.* Delhi: Sage.

Harishchandra, Bharatendu, 1954. *Bharatendu Granthavali: Teesra bhag.* Banaras.

Kaviraj, Sudipta, 1993. *The Unhappy Consciousness: Bankimchandra Chattopadhyay and the Formation of Nationalist Discourse in India.* Delhi: Oxford University Press.

McGregor, Ronald S., 1966. 'Krishnacharya', *Hindi ke adimudrit granth.* Banaras.

———, 1974. *Hindi Literature of the Nineteenth and Early Twentieth Centuries,* vol. 8, fasc. 2, in Jan Gonda, ed., *A History of Indian Literature.* Wiesbaden: Harrassowitz.

Morrison, Charles, 1984. 'Three Styles of Imperial Ethnography: British Officials as Anthropologists in India', in Henrika Kuklick and Elizabeth Long, eds, *Knowledge and Society: Studies in the Sociology of Culture Past and Present,* vol. 5.

Mukherjee, Meenakshi, 1985. *Realism and Reality: The Novel and Society in India.* Delhi: Oxford University Press.

Singh, H.L., 1961. 'Modern Historical Writing in Hindi', in C.H. Philips, ed., *Historians of India, Pakistan and Ceylon.* London: Oxford University Press.

Sivaprasadsingh, Raja, 1864. 'Preface' to *Itihasa Timirnashak: Teen Khandom Meim.* Banaras.

Thapar, Romila, 1986. 'Society and Historical Consciousness in the Itihasa and Purana Tradition', in Sabyasachi Bhattacharya and Romila Thapar, eds, *Situating Indian History: For Sarvepalli Gopal.* Delhi: Oxford University Press.

———, 1996. *Time as a Metaphor of History: Early India.* Delhi: Oxford University Press.

PART II

Vaishnava Renewals c. 1600–1900

6

Forging Community

The Guru in a Seventeenth-Century Vaishnava Hagiography

MODERN HINDUISM IS BASED TO A LARGE EXTENT on the great monotheistic devotional movements, many of which, emerging from the South, swept through and occupied North India from the fifteenth century. The transformations in these great movements, which set in during the eighteenth century with colonialism, and the subsequent reconfigurations within them, have never really been subjected to close scrutiny. Nor has there been a systematic study of the theological and sociological relationship of the devotional communities to each other and to the Brahmanical orthodoxy of the day.

The movements themselves fall into two somewhat heterogeneous clusters. The first cluster consists of those communities of believers that practised *nirguna* or aniconic devotion, the second comprises communities which believed in *saguna* or iconic worship. There were antagonisms within these clusters as well as between them. What were the bonds which forged the respective devotional communities, what made for the similarities, and what distinguished them from each other? What, if any, were the features shared by the two clusters? *Saguna* and *nirguna* are valid theological classifications, but should they also be extended to the social dimension?

Scholars today often suggest that belief in a personal god, in reincarnation, and in *varnashramadharma* are to be regarded as some of the main features of the vastly influential *saguna bhakti* (iconic devotional traditions).¹ With the exception of the belief in *varnashramadharma*, as I hope to show below, it would be possible to accept these features as characteristic of the *saguna* traditions. However, the question is whether these features alone justify the contemporary view, which is to see these *saguna* movements as Brahmanical, catering only to the elites, and ultimately fathering what is today known as Hindutva.²

An approach which confounds Hindutva with the loose coalition which is modern Hinduism can, I would suggest, at best be described as reductive. A perspective so coloured by contemporary prejudices can only serve to distort rather than clear any view of the past. In

---

¹ Thus for instance Lorenzen in the introduction ('The Historical Vicissitudes of the Bhakti Religion') to his edited volume on the bhakti religions of North India: 'The second pillar of saguni ethics is, of course, the doctrine of varnashramadharma (the law of social classes and stages of life). According to this doctrine, one obtains a better rebirth precisely by following the rules of conduct appropriate to the varna (roughly "class") and *jati* (caste) in which one was born. The rules of behaviour for *varnas* are set out in elaborate detail in the legal texts of Hindu tradition: the dharmasutras, dharmashastras and legal digests.' Lorenzen 1995: 16. The Vaishnavas, as I hope to show in the course of this essay, in fact developed their own ritual and social codes in express opposition to the *Dharmashastras*.

² To quote Lorenzen once again: 'Kings are more often portrayed as the allies of *saguni* saints, while their opponents may either be fellow Brahmin philosophers (with whom they have mostly polite intellectual debates) or low "heretics" who are generally dispatched by force (either by the saint's magical power or by the physical power of his royal ally) . . . Is it too far fetched to see these alliances as early precursors of the curiously similar political alliances of present-day India between the social base of the Congress and Janata Dal Parties (richer peasants, Untouchables, poor labourers, and Muslims), on the one side, and the social base of the Bharatiya Janata Party (merchants and traders, lesser peasants, and my white-collar professionals), on the other?' Lorenzen 1995: 189. Have the same groups retained elite positions across the centuries? In which category would we, by this definition, include the Sikhs, surely a *nirguna* formation?

fact, much spadework remains to be done before we can even begin to formulate satisfactory questions, leave alone provide answers, regarding religious constellations in post-medieval India and their relationship to Hindu formations today. How elitist were these *saguna bhakti* formations and in what relationship did they stand to the orthodoxy of the day? The information we have at this stage is tentative; it has to be drawn from texts which speak, in however convention-ridden a manner, about actual people and the social groups initiating and participating in the fledgling movements. In reviewing the representation of community formation in a central text from the Vallabha *sampradaya*—one of the Vaishnava *saguna bhakti* traditions which emerged at the end of the fifteenth century—what I shall be putting forward, then, are explorations rather than final results. My focus will be on the guru as the charismatic figure in the process of winning over disciples and welding them into fellowship.

The four great Vaishnava communities, or *chatuhsampradaya* as they were collectively known, existed in some kind of a loose coalition from the seventeenth century on.[3] The lifespans of the founders of two of the most prominent movements, Chaitanya (1476–1533) and Vallabha (1478–1530), were almost coterminous. The remarkable coincidence of the rise and spread of their *sampradayas*, as also their relationship to each other, await detailed study.[4] The founders'

[3] Burghart's pioneering essay (1978) on the meeting of the four *sampradayas* in Galta which brought about the coalition still remains the only sustained treatment of the theme.

[4] As Satish Chandra has pointed out, '[w]e have yet to assess the social and economic background and the historical significance of this second phase of the bhakti movement as it was, or popular (saguna) bhakti as distinguished from the earlier movement which has been called popular monotheism. Was the "success" of saguna bhakti in large parts due to its being more traditional, and hence arousing less hostility from the orthodox Brahmans? Was its appeal specifically more rural, as compared to the earlier movement which drew support from city based artisans and traders?' (Chandra 1996: 130). Chandra then does go on to postulate that 'the triumph of saguna bhakti over the more radical school of popular monotheism in the Gangetic valley may, to some extent, be considered as the triumph of the conservatism of the countryside over the latent radicalism of the towns' (ibid.: 131). As my investigation to date

decisive role in the actual formation of community has also tended to be overlooked by scholars. This is because more attention has been devoted to the *nirguna* or aniconic devotional traditions—which were more obviously centred around the figure of the guru.[5] It is certainly true that in the *saguna bhakti* traditions there were a number of other authoritative instances which bound the devotional community and embedded it in a tradition which claimed immemorial existence. Apart from the central image or icon of the deity worshipped, there were the older scriptures—the *Bhagavatapurana* for the Krishnaite and the *Ramayana* for the Ramaite traditions—which could be viewed as fountainheads of the newly forming canons. Yet, though linking up with the older canonic texts, the founders of the new *sampradayas* were opening up radically new paths which were also to find expression in popular literary genres. Two other categories of religious literature proliferated under the patronage of the *sampradaya*, that of the *pada* or verse composed for singing; and the hagiography, termed *varta* by the Vallabhites.[6] Both addressed a completely different audience than did the Sanskrit works. This audience was often a non-literate one, and the transmission of these literatures required congregational activity, since they were primarily oral in character. The *varta* literature is particularly valuable for the investigation undertaken in this essay. It contains a mass of information about the social and political formations of the day, but most of all it offers

---

shows, it is not really possible to stipulate any kind of rural–urban divide. The followers of the *sampradaya* in fact come much more from lower to middling castes, and from small town and city rather than village, though later the *sampradaya* does seem to profit from Rajput patronage. There is, then, even in this second *saguna* phase of the bhakti movement, a decided radicalism which has been largely overshadowed by later developments.

[5] Here there seems to have been some inadvertent glorification of the *nirguna* tradition (in such accounts necessarily viewed as homogeneous), which is celebrated somewhat uncritically as radical and resistant from often rather hazy beginnings in time through the Mughal period (Akbar's role remains fuzzy in such narratives) into the present. See Gold 1987: 210, 211.

[6] For a comprehensive account of the hagiographic literature of the periods, see Dube 1968.

insights into the nature of the popular appeal of the founding figures and the ideologies they embodied.

The first two preceptors of the *sampradaya*, Vallabha as a migrant from the South and his son Vitthala (1515–85), had written learned treatises in Sanskrit, the pan-Indian elite mode of communication amongst various 'Hindu' formations. From the third generation onwards, Brajbhasha, which was understood and spoken by a majority of the *sampradaya*'s following, took over as the literary and liturgical language. The *padas*, devotional verse, of poets who later came to be known collectively as the *ashtachhap*, eight seals, vividly expressed an emotional relationship to the lord. This relationship was newly vested with a literary-religious aesthetics of its own. These *padas* became part of the official canon, endowing both the language and the *sampradaya* with new prestige. The earliest extended narrative prose in Brajbhasha, relating the lives of devotees, was also a major literary contribution. This popular narrative genre, *bat* or *varta*—loosely translatable as tale—which was taken over and transformed for this purpose, had originally consisted of incidents strung together, chiefly with the aim of sustaining suspense as to the outcome of the story. These were now endowed with a new didactic goal. Tales which related the lives of devotees who had had the fortune to be initiated by the first two preceptors were collected, and then ordered and enriched with a commentary in the century and a half following Vallabha.[7]

The *Pushtimarg*, or 'way of fulfilment', as the *sampradaya* came to be known, boasts of two major hagiographic compilations. The first relates *prasangas* or episodes in the lives of 84 followers of Acharyaji, or preceptor (as Vallabha was called in the narrative). The second is a collection of the lives of the 252, i.e. three times 84, followers of his son Vitthala. Here I concentrate upon the first collection,

[7] The central motifs in the individual tales, as Lorenzen (1995: 181–211) has shown, often repeat themselves in the hagiographies of the various *sampradayas* crossing, as I have found, the boundaries of *nirguna* and *saguna*. However, since the frame of reference does not stay the same, it is entirely legitimate to treat each episode, even if it has already occurred in another compendium, as unique in its own context.

the *Chaurasi vaishnavan ki varta*, or Tales of the 84 Vaishnavas, of which a good edition based on the manuscripts of 1695 and 1721 is fortunately available.[8] The lives of the *bhaktas* as related in these compendia came to form an explicit part of the official canon. They were *daivi jivas*, godly beings, whose specific destiny it was to serve according to the will of the lord and the guru. Their peculiar form of bondage to this will, and to each other, served to distinguish them from all the other communities surrounding them.

Hagiography as Canon

According to the tradition current in the *sampradaya* and recorded in the second compilation, the *vartas* came into being as part of the pious ritual of telling and hearing of the lives of the men and women who had first formed the core of the community. Acharyaji himself had been known to indulge in this virtuous pastime, but it became the particular addiction of Gokulnathji (1557–1640) who, in the third generation, came luckily to possess a version written by an ardent devotee. This written version was reduplicated and continuously added to, till his nephew and pupil Harirayji (1590–1721!), in the fourth generation, placed the episodes within the framework of a *Bhav prakash* or commentary. This commentary related details of the previous lives of the devotees, thus providing motivation for the course of events related in the main *vartas*.[9] It added incidents from

---

[8] The citations in this essay are from this text as edited by Dvarikadas Parikh (1971).

[9] The commentary began always by providing information about the devotees' favoured initial position in Krishna's heaven, from which they fell temporarily only to be gathered up and taken into the fold again by the deity, after their lives on earth were spent. As Caroline Bynum, in her study of women's religiosity in the Christian middle ages, has noted: 'Indeed medieval hagiographers pointed out repeatedly that saints are not even primarily "models" for ordinary mortals; the saints are far too dangerous for that. Like Christ himself, they could not and should not be imitated in their full extravagance and power. Rather (so their admirers say), they should be loved, venerated, and meditated upon as moments in which the other that is God breaks through into the mundane worlds, saturating it with meaning.' Bynum 1987: 7.

the lives of those connected with the devotees, and interpreted the whole in the light of theological developments in the late seventeenth century.[10]

In his commentary Harirayji drew an explicit axiom—he called it *siddhanta*—from each life, and it was with this that he rounded up each *varta*. It was the *siddhanta* that endowed the compendium with lasting value and raised it to canonical status, for it was here that the teachings of Acharyaji, his charisma and authority, were explicitly articulated in the life of the devotee. This is how the compendium introduces itself in the *Bhav prakash* of Harirayji: as *bhagavadvarta*, or godly discourse, in stature and splendour higher than the *Bhagavatapurana* itself, or Acharyaji commentary thereof, the *Subodhini*. It called forth ecstatic listening:

> So one day while discoursing on the eighty-four Vaishnavas, Sri Gokulnath was so immersed in *rasa*, pleasure, that he heeded not to the daily ritual of the telling of the *katha*, the tales of the *Subodhini* and midnight approached. Then one Vaishnava asked Sri Gokulnath, Maharajadhiraj, when will you relate the tales today? Midnight is past. Then with his illustrious mouth Sri Gokulnath said, you must take all fruits [of the *katha*] to be in the discourse on the Vaishnavas. There is no other *padartha*, principle, besides the Vaishnavas. This is the path of *pushti*, fulfilment, which gains fruition through the Vaishnavas. Acharyaji himself used to say, Damla [the name of his first disciple], this path has been manifested for you. Hence the discourse on the Vaishnavas is to be understood as supreme. The eighty-four Vaishnavas are to be considered foremost in the *nirguna* or qualityless aspect of Acharyaji. (2)[11]

Thus the central importance of the tale of the devotees, for whom the path was created and who, by moving on it, kept it intact. However,

---

[10] The *vartas* are available in three kinds of compilations: the first seem to be random collections of tales, without any discernible organizational pattern; the second, possibly later, compilations, have been arranged in the sequence of 84 and 252 lives as we know them today; and the third go further still and arrange the tales within a commentarial frame. For details, see Tandan 1960: 44ff.

[11] All translations are by the author. The *saguna* aspect was ordered and subsumed under Gosaimji.

the listeners and readers of the compendium were ever reminded that the life of the devotee, as centrally constituent of the canon, was not related for any intrinsic value but selected and steered by the guru for his specific ends. It was the charisma that he radiated which formed the central focus of the compendium.

Since the individual *vartas* can stem from different stages in the evolution of the community, they are not always theologically consistent or homogeneous in style and perspective. Inevitably, there are certain contradictions and tensions, as also an occasional need to interpret and temper the original radical message. Vallabha's teachings are sometimes overlaid with the workings of the much more sensuous Gosaimji, as Vitthala was called; he was said to incorporate *parakiya bhava*—the extramarital erotic relationship to the Lord as beloved and as one path of access to the Lord. Later redactions also tended to place Gosaimji at par with his father, or even at times to supersede him. Right at the beginning of the compendium, for instance, the first disciple, Damodardas Harsani, is made to recognize the primacy of Gosaimji after Vallabha. However, obviously in some faithfulness to the historic situation, Damodardas cannot be kept from chiding the new incumbent for, upon occasion, simply whiling away time in laughter. It is, as he points out, a serious and painful task that Gosaimji has taken upon himself; it demands study, self-control, and concentration.

Acharyaji as Mediator of Direct Access to the Lord and as Identical with the Lord

The main *varta* text begins by proclaiming that the way of bhakti was created for Damodardas Harsani. However, it is at pains to emphasize the prime role of the guru as mediator. Before initiating Damla, Acharyaji is seen to be steeped in anxiety:

> There this anxiety grew in Acharyaji. Why? Thakurji, the lord, has ordered that *jivas*, human souls, be bound to him (*brahmasambandha*), but as Acharyaji reflected, if human souls are full of *dosha*, impurities, and Sripurushottama is the treasure of good qualities, how can this binding take place? As this anxiety grew, he became exceedingly restless.

At this moment, and at once Thakurji manifested himself and asked Acharyaji, why are you so restless and anxious? Then Acharyaji himself said, you know the *svarupa*, self-form or image, of human souls, it is full of impurities. So how can this binding/bonding with you take place? Then Thakurji said, if you impart the name to human souls, then all their impurities will be checked, therefore accept them as your own [the term used is *angikar kar*]. (4)

It thus becomes clear that only when Acharyaji mediates and hands over a devotee to Thakurji does he become the eternal concern of the Lord. It is Acharyaji who decides what form of initiation is best suited to a particular devotee, and what kind of *seva* or service to the Lord he or she is best capable of fulfilling thereafter.

Initiation consisted of (1) *nam nivedan* or *nam sunana*, that is, communicating the name of the Lord to the devotee; (2) *brahma-sambandha*, imparting the *mantra*; and, finally (3) *lalji padhrana*, presenting a *svarupa* or self-image of the Lord. Not all three were followed with each devotee, and the kind of initiation determined the kind of *seva* to be undertaken by the devotee.

The *seva* at home, as described in the *varta*, was a private, even secret, ritual, intensely intimate and tender. No priestly mediation was necessary. *Karmakanda*, and Brahmans who specialized in it—as the tales are at pains to emphasize—were absolute anathema to Acharyaji. The *seva* could even be idiosyncratic, provided it was performed with intense devotion. Once a *sevak* had proved his or her mettle, then it was in this private sphere that Thakurji himself began to hold communion with the devotee and communicate his wishes. *Sanubhavata janana*, or causing experience of the Lord, is the term that the *varta* uses for this communion. This intimate experience of the Lord was the prime fruit of the path. However, even here Acharyaji remained mediatory, he was present even in his absence. If a devotee disregarded some intimate need of Thakurji, he complained immediately to Acharyaji or Gosaimji, who then reprimanded and corrected him.[12] This form of domestic devotion,

---

[12] When Thakurji was served a *khir* dish too carelessly prepared and it scalded his mouth, he complained at once to Acharyaji (173).

this intense immediacy of experience—at once intimate and transcendent, unmediated by Brahmanical ritual, not requiring years of withdrawal, asceticism, and self-discipline—seems commonplace to us today. It needs to be stressed that it was obviously the radical innovation of its time.

The stories relate what befell devotees from the time that they had been initiated and received instructions on *seva* till such time as they attained the state of grace. The devotees were by no means perfect models of virtue. If there were some amongst them who followed a relatively straight path, there were those who faltered, fell, and had to be picked up. It was left to Acharyaji to intervene and correct them. Often, their failings were then highlighted, for these served to substantiate a *siddhanta* more effectively than virtues.

Acharyaji's following was numerous and heterogeneous in its composition. His followers came from all walks of life and from a variety of castes—mostly lower to middling.[13] In principle, the

---

[13] Thus the Bhatiya and Lohana in Gujarat, whom Cohen (1984: 69) describes as 'at best former Rajputs on the fringe of Hindu society'; and the Kanbis, 'an old, well entrenched, landed Sudra caste of agriculturists' (70) who effected upward mobility through entering the Vallabhite Vaishnava community. Pinch in his study of the Ramanandis (one of the four Vaishnava *sampradayas*) has similarly noted that the early-nineteenth-century ethnographic accounts of religious denominations in eastern UP by Francis Buchanan show clearly the upward social mobility brought about by acceptance into the Vaishnava fold. Firstly, 'Buchanan's remarks on religious practice in the Gangetic core, together with comments by other observers through the nineteenth century, indicate that Vaishnava gurus (and Ramanandis in particular) pursued a far more aggressive program of social and religious reform in comparison with their Dasnami and Nanakpanthi counterparts. Consequently, Vaishnava bairagis were drawn from the entire varna spectrum and included not only brahmans but many shudras' (Pinch 1996: 38). Secondly, these Bairagis encouraged their lay followers to adhere to a rigid moral code and a strict regimen. 'Describing Vaishnavas as "everywhere the most strict," Buchanan noted that "some few of them here [Bihar and Patna] will neither pray nor even show common civility to any god but those of his own sect." The emphasis on a pure life applied as well to daily diet: "All the Hindus, brahmans or sudra, of the sect of Vishnu, are remarkably strict in eating, reject altogether rice cleaned by boiling, all parched grains, and animal food." By contrast, Buchanan observed that "all the Sudras, except those of the sect of Vishnu, drink avowedly"' (ibid.: 38–9).

path was open to all. However, jati rules continued to be observed in qualified form: in fact information on the jati of the follower was scrupulously documented in the *vartas*. But even those regarded as entirely inauspicious and marginal could be integrated into the community by Acharyaji's mediation and gain a privileged place within it. When initiating a follower from one of the lower castes, Acharyaji would ask the question: how will you carry out the *seva* ritual in your environment? The devotee-to-be is inevitably reassuring that he will distance himself from non-Vaishnavas, as also from other varieties of Vaishnavas.

Initiation into the *sampradaya*, with its scrupulous attention to details of personal purity and morality, then, clearly signified upward mobility for the clean Sudra castes. The founder of a new *sampradaya* had to have something new to offer, and this ensured a radical flexibility, at least in the early stages of community formation of this particular path to the Lord. Acharyaji was certainly aware of shastric norms. But it was against these that he explicitly set up new norms which, he claimed, were based on practice, and which he knew to be radical in their departure from the old. What was regarded as orthodoxy or custom, *ved aur lok*, at that time was invoked negatively time and again.

The devotee could share his or her life in *seva*, which formed the kernel of human existence, only with those who were similarly disposed. If family members dissented or even went so far as to oppose the initiation, and the new way of life which followed upon it, some kind of separation was called for, often within the house. This sometimes meant that the devotee would have to separate his or her kitchen from that of the rest of the family, if the family could not be persuaded to follow the same path or if Acharyaji declared that they were not *daivi jivas*. Acharyaji did not tolerate even the barest suggestion of asceticism, and clearly this has to be understood as part of his determined opposition to the practice of certain *nirguna sampradayas*. The family setting was important for the community. However, the family in its turn had to be amenable to integration within the greater social unit which was the community.

The figure of Vallabha in the *vartas* comes across, then, not so much as the learned pandit and theologian as much as the popular, charismatic teacher to be observed in his manifold dealings with his disciples.[14] Acharyaji often accosts them on the many journeys that he makes. At the beginning of the compendium we are told that he thrice made the *prithvi parikrama*, circumambulation of the world. Considering the arduousness of the routes that led to the great pilgrim centres, we find Acharyaji setting out on these long journeys surprisingly often, either to Dvarika, Puri, or, in one instance, to the South. As other sources specify, in all Acharyaji spent nineteen years, from the founding of the *sampradaya* in 1493 to 1512, roaming the subcontinent.

The *vartas* remain somewhat ambiguous as to the nature of Acharyaji's connection with Jaganathdham and Dvarika, the two great pan-Vaishnava pilgrimage centres. He is often to be found in one of these centres, attracting new followers and, surely in some measure, deriving his authority from the charisma radiating from the deities there. In some of the tales the devotees are made to realize that he is not only mediator to the Lord but in fact identical with him. Thus the *varta* of Gopaldas Bamsvare, Khatri, relates how Gopaldas wins over two influential devotees by revealing to them that Acharyaji is in fact Ranchorji himself: '*Arel mem Sriranchorji pragat bhaye hai*' (168). Sriranchorji has manifested himself in Arel and he

---

[14] Vallabha was a scholar and a learned exegete of traditional texts. In this sense, he was more 'acharya' then 'guru'. The two terms have been used interchangeably in the Sanskrit tradition, almost as synonyms, but there is a connotational difference which has continued to be operative as well. As Minoru Hara has shown, the acharya is a specialist of particular fields of knowledge, which he mediates to his pupil over a period of time. Built into the relationship is respect and distance, though intellectual difference of opinion is, in principle, possible. In later classical tradition, guru also came to be used for teacher, though the term continued to mean respected elders as well. The guru–disciple bond becomes more emotional than intellectual and calls for the recognition of his absolute obedience by the disciple. Hara's distinctions seem then to be turned upside down in our case. Though Vallabha's designation is acharya in fact, in the hagiographical compendia at least he functions more as a guru. He has himself a highly emotional relationship to the lord as well as to his disciples and he mediates between the two in an entirely intimate, albeit authoritarian, manner. In this respect, Vallabha as *saguna* guru seems very close indeed to the gurus of the *nirguna sampradayas*.

talks and holds converse with all. And indeed Acharyaji obliges these devotees by appearing as Ranchorji, divining and resolving all their secret doubts. In other episodes, which take place either in Dvarika or on the way to it, Ranchorji is demoted to the status of a slightly subsidiary manifestation. The case of the Lord in Puri is similar. In the *varta* of the two brothers Jagannath Joshi and Narhari Joshi, sent by their mother to Arel to become disciples of Acharyaji, we hear that he himself has, in fact, left for Purushottampuri to obtain *darsan* of Sri Jagannathji. For fear of their mother the brothers follow Acharyaji to Puri. When they find him, he asks in all innocence—have you already been to the temple? The brothers obligingly run there, to find Acharyaji standing next to the deity. Has he taken another route to the temple and overtaken them, they wonder. They run back to him, to find him seated as they had left him. The two brothers pray to him: '*ham ajnani haim, jo sandeh kiyo, apu saksat purusottam ho*' (188), we are ignorant to have harboured doubt. You yourself are Purushottam. The guru is represented as omnipresent and closely associated, if not identical, with the great Vaishnava deities: he is capable of divining thoughts, forecasting events, and performing any number of miracles almost casually. And this happens early in the tradition, since this information is offered by the *varta* text, not the *Bhav prakash*.

But it is not Acharyaji's ability to perform miracles which is highlighted in the *vartas*; nor that of his followers, who seem to imbibe, as casually, the same capacity from him. Acharyaji's power is not to be confused with mere *siddhis* or magic of lower varieties. The *vartas* take pains to establish his distance from this kind of wonder-working and the devotees are, in fact, positively discouraged from interfering in the way of the world by performing any sort of miracle. For one thing, miracles disturb the normal run of things because they put more emphasis on worldly gains; for another, they mean that either Thakurji or Acharyaji or even both exert themselves on the devotee's behalf.[15] Therefore, restraint is to be exercised.

---

[15] See for instance the tales of Padmanabhdas and Tripurdas (151). Both devotees are made to realize that giving in to the temptation to perform miracles has meant that Thakurji had to labour on their behalf.

Acharyaji's primary task in the *vartas* is to attract and hold followers. He comes across as wise, tolerant, compassionate, full of *vatsalya*, himself a living representation and model for the central form of relating to the child Krishna. He comes to stand for compassion towards the downtrodden, for people in the extremes of sorrow, but most of all for people looking for the truth. To these he opens the way for authentic religious experience.

He is to be seen at dawn, bathing on the banks of a holy river, or in the evening, discoursing. It is here that he encounters souls in distress, crouching in various postures of despair. Often it is his voice, expounding on tales from the *Bhagavatapurana*, which attracts their attention and they come to him for succour. He does not seek out the affluent and the powerful, though they are welcome too. The *vartas*, it can hardly be emphasized enough, revolve around the lives of the marginalized and the oppressed, offering them the possibility of entering into their own intense, at times highly whimsical, relationship with the Lord. *Seva*, it is true, had its own ritual, but even here the code laid down by Acharyaji himself could be transcended if it was dictated by *priti*, love of the Lord. The present scholarly view—which ascribes elite following and Brahmanical manipulation to all *saguna sampradayas*—obviously falls victim to the stereotypes it creates.

It is from the humblest people that this community of the elect is chosen. Often they are nameless, for, as the *Bhav prakash* tells us, the devotees were often people with rustic names which the teachers did not see fit to hold fast for posterity: 'Now here and there Gokulnathji has not preserved the names. For the parents kept the names, some were called Phakira, others Ghasita. Of such Vaishnavas Sri Gokulnathji does not say the name. Therefore the names of sundry Vaishnavas have not been disclosed' (252). These are common, everyday people who rise to special status by the grace of Acharyaji and Thakurji. It is to these everyday lives that I now turn, in order to review how the compendium represents the constitution of the first community as bound together by the working of the guru.[16]

---

[16] I have chosen to focus on the lives of humble devotees rather than the eight famous poets of the *sampradaya*, known as the *ashtachhap*, or eight seals,

Laying Down the Path and Demarcating It

The *vartas* show Acharyaji at his most skilful, blending visionary power and compassion with a stern demarcation of his community from bordering or encroaching belief systems. Acharyaji sees the many Bairagis and Jogis, whose specific provenance is often left unspecified, as so many charlatans who haunt the very places he himself frequents—riverbanks and pilgrimage sites. He spares no effort to dislocate their authority and, where possible, demolish it. This is a feature common to all gurus of the period, irrespective of *nirguna* or *saguna* calling. No authority outside their own is allowed to hold its ground, not even in matters as trivial as those which call for the help of a soothsayer.[17]

---

some of whose *vartas* have been translated and analysed by Richard Barz (1976, 1992, 1994). The eight poets have been pressed into service as a special group within the two compendia. For the possible appropriation of Surdas, the best known of the eight, by the Vallabhite community, see Hawley 1983.

[17] This is a typical feature of all such accounts, as Simon Digby has remarked in connection with the Sikh hagiographical literature of the period, which could be characterized as firmly *nirguna* in provenance: 'Those who write about the harmony of syncretistic movements in medieval India should perhaps reflect that the number of anecdotes in medieval hagiography depicting the universal kindness and benevolence of religious leaders is small compared to the quantity of those depicting their formidable powers, their triumphs over their rivals and the awful consequences of their wrath.' Digby 1970: 306. The tale of Damodardas Sambhalvare, Khatri of Kannauj, one of Acharyaji's most devoted followers, illustrates well how Acharyaji disposes of the authority of others in matters connected with his followers: many a time when Acharyaji would alight upon his house, Damodardas would serve him by pressing his feet. Once he was asked to wish for something he had always wanted, but he said he had no wishes. Thereupon Acharyaji bade him ask his wife. She said all she wanted was a son. Acharyaji assured her that this wish would be fulfilled. Acharyaji left for Jatipura. She was soon with child. But this is when she committed a fatal mistake. Along with the wives of other *smartas*, she ran to a soothsayer (Dakotia) to ask about the sex of the child and was told it would be a boy. After some time, when Acharyaji came to Kannauj, and Damodardas made to touch his feet, Acharyaji said, don't touch me. '*Tokom anyasraya bhayau hai*', you have sought refuge with another (33). Damodardas pleaded innocence; whereupon he was told to ask his wife, who duly enlightened him. Then

The authority generated by places of pilgrimage, by ritual, asceticism, even traditional Sanskritic learning,[18] is displaced, if not entirely denied. But the *vartas* leave us in no doubt that Acharyaji considers the paths promising *mukti*, redemption, fitting only for those who choose to be satisfied with lower states of being. If *mukti* has any standing at all, it is made quite clear that it is a decidedly inferior state than that of bhakti. In fact the principle of maya, which sees the world as illusory, is vigorously disputed. It stands in direct opposition to *pushti*, which comes about in *this* world and *within* family and community. *Mayavad*, as Shankara's theological edifice is disparagingly called, is a blind alley for those who have once begun to tread the path of bhakti and *vairagya*. The kind of detachment which shrugs off responsibility towards others and makes for arrogance can be no other than the way of the errant. Thus it is that *mayavad* and the cluster of concepts surrounding it, including *vairagya*, detachment and the asceticism which it calls for, and *maryadamarg*,

---

Acharyaji pronounced his awful curse: a son would be born to them, but he would become a mleccha. So strong was the wife's wish to remain within the fold that she in fact asked her mother to take away the son the moment he was born. And so he was raised at his grandmother's home. When Damodardas died of old age, the wife put all his goods in a boat and sent it to Acharyaji in Arel, so that the son, who had indeed become a *turak* (a Muslim), could not possess it. She would depend forthwith on the succour of the other Vaishnavas. In short, seeking advice from an authority other than Acharyaji brought destitution and loneliness upon a woman who had once set her heart on becoming a mother.

[18] There is the tale of the boy Bula Misra from Lahore, who was so dim-witted that no amount of teaching could drill knowledge into him. In despair he attempted suicide by drowning in the river Ganga, at a remote site a little outside Kashi. But Sarasvati refused to become incriminated in this enterprise and came to his rescue, granting him boundless knowledge of the Shastras. He became a pandit of stature, but, even with Sarasvati to back him, he could not defeat Acharyaji. It was only when he sought refuge with him that he became a true pandit (264–5). But he was not allowed to partake of the fruit of this pleasure and take up residence in Kashi as an acharya of note. He was sent back home, like all devotees before him, to waiting parents, to take up family life again. So much for the worth of Sanskritic learning.

which is associated with *smarta* ritual and the Brahmans specializing in it, are seen as being in stark opposition to bhakti.[19]

In order to understand the nature of these polemics—i.e. the authorities Acharyaji seeks to dispel in order to establish his own—it is imperative that we recognize the nature of the relationship of this *sampradaya* to what it views as orthodoxy. The other imperative is to identify clearly the terms of reference within which Acharyaji and his followers operate: *daivi jiv, seva, mahaprasad, sanubhavata janana, bhagavadvarta*. Though they exist within banal, everyday reality, this reality is now shot through with the new ecstasy of being in communion with the Lord. This makes for the special tone of the text. While the everyday speech in which the tales are related grant it a quality of easy accessibility, the intense emotion and spiritual power radiated by Acharyaji raises these episodes to the level of the extraordinary and even the lyrical. The tales need to be told and heard in their entirety if we are to appreciate the nature of the world they delineate.

The following *vartas* offer vivid sketches of lives, lost and errant, which regain their footing by the grace of Acharyaji. In the first of these we have the tale of an adolescent in crisis.

The story, as related in the *Bhav prakash*, is that of Ramdas Samchora of Rajnagar or Ahmedabad. From early youth he showed signs of *vairagya*, disinclination for pleasures of the world. When he was 9 years old his parents married him to an 8-year-old girl. But he was attached to no one, conversed with no one. His parents had him taught much, but he learnt nothing. One day, he was sitting on the banks of a tank in Rajnagar. A *teli* or oil-presser came by with his ox carts to give his oxen water. One of the animals drank the water and fell down dead. The oil-presser began to cry. The ten-year-old said, why don't you take hold of him and raise him? The oil-presser said, how will it rise now, it has no life. Then, just like the young Siddhartha, the little boy asked, does everyone die, just like him? The oil-presser said, this is how it comes about, it is only a question

---

[19] See Glasenapp 1934 and Barz 1976/1992 for the delineation of Vallabha's theological edifice.

of a day here or there. Hearing this, Ramdas ran from that place. In a few days he reached Dvarika and took darshan of Ranchorji. Here, Acharyaji was to be found, relating tales from the *Subodhini*. And it came to Ramdas's mind that he wanted to stay with Acharyaji for a while and listen to the *katha*. He thought it would be to his good if he could serve him. And so it came about that he became his follower.

It is here that the *varta* makes itself felt. Acharyaji initiated him and gave him a *svarupa*. But it was Acharyaji's way, once bhakti had gained firm root in the disciple, to send him back home, even if it wrenched him to do so. Ramdas had a wife, herself a creature of god, *daivi jiv*, who pined at home for him; and he had parents. For the deliverance of their souls, it was necessary that Ramdas go back.

Ramdas does go back, but his parents are dead, his wife is at her parents' place. She joins him but Ramdas does not accept her and, in two or three days, he sets forth alone on a journey to Dvarika. She follows him, eats his leftovers, but he throws stones at her. And then Ranchorji begins to speak to him: why did you marry her? You are a follower of Acharyaji, so accept her. He makes the first overtures, and upon reaching Dvarika she receives her first initiation. Acharyaji comes by and seals the bond. It is not seemly, Ramdas thinks, to wander through the world with her. We should stay at one place and sing of the Lord. And so it comes about.

The commentary which frames the actual tale serves to make the hearer realize that *vairagya* was a trait that Ramdas had been literally born with. But this did not equip him with the means to resolve the dilemmas of existence. He had merely to witness one incident of life's impermanence to lose all sense of direction. He could, of course, have become a Bairagi or a Jogi. Instead, he was so fortunate as to win Acharyaji's favour and be early awarded a *svarupa*. But Acharyaji did not allow him to stay away from his own social world and sent him back to take up his rightful position within it. However, left to his own devices, Ramdas once again set off for Dvarika. His leanings seemed incorrigibly non-familial, but Acharyaji remained ever vigilant. He caused Ranchorji to follow him and made him realize that devotion to Thakurji took place *within* the world, and with his wife at his side. Both had a duty towards the other Vaishnavas, *saguna* or not. Interestingly enough, at no stage in this tale is there any mention of a temple or any obligation to serve the Lord in Dvarika. The emphasis is upon service to the *svarupa* granted him, and to the community.

Thus also the story, as related by the *Bhav prakash*, of two Khatri brothers: Ananddas and Visvambhardas from Prayag also tended to *vairagya* from early youth. They refused to marry, ran away from their home to Chitrakut, and had to be brought back by a remorseful father. Once, they were sitting on the banks of the Yamuna, mourning the eternal passages of birth and rebirth and seeing themselves condemned to being born again without ever having recognized the Lord. And so overwrought were they with the sorrow of their fate, that they beat their heads and cried out until they lost all consciousness. They lay there the night, upon the sand. It was then that Thakurji approached Acharyaji and said: two boys lie on the sand on the other bank of the Yamuna. They are in great agony over me. Present yourself to them and accept (*angikar*) them into the fold. And so they were initiated—but they were sent back home: 'And mother and father were both filled with great happiness. The sons were at home; if they had not been found, then what would have happened?' (249).

As the *varta* tells us, the brothers spent the rest of their lives in *bhagavadvarta*, stretching the storytelling hours so long that one would drop off to sleep while the other talked on. Then, in order to bring the story to fruition, Thakurji himself—who had begun early to let them experience his self (*sanubhavata janana*)—would step in to punctuate the story with his listener's 'yes' (*humkari bharna*) to prevent the flow being inauspiciously interrupted: 'And so from childhood onwards, the two brothers knew not the ways of *lok*, custom, and of *ved*, ritual, and the agony and sorrow of *samsara* could not prevail' (249). Thakurji needs the services of Acharyaji in order to save the two brothers from their own detachment and award them access to his *seva*, though once again, this is to take place within the world and within the framework of family life. Vallabha's opposition to ascetic orders and the itenerant life was decisive and firm.

Since *seva* itself was a domestic rite, the *svarupa* became a privileged member of the family, to be fed, clothed, laid to rest with more care, love, and respect than anyone else. For the marginalized and the isolated, *seva* became a means of integration into the community.[20] Acharyaji even goes so far as to tolerate the relationship of a devotee to a prostitute, commending this for raising the spiritual status both of the devotee and the fallen woman. The *varta* relates the tale: Once, when Sriacharyaji arrived in Kara, the Vaishnavas said to him: Maharaj, Madhodas, has kept a prostitute. Acharyaji asked, Well Madhodas, have you kept a prostitute? Madhodas said: My mind is intensely attached to her. This is why I have kept her. In this manner, Acharyaji put the question to him thrice. And all three times Madhodas said to him, Maharaj, my mind is intensely attached to her. This is why I have kept her. Then Acharyaji maintained a long silence. Upon this the Vaishnavas said to Acharyaji: Mahaprabhu, maharaj, your honour has been preserved until now. He will only be rid of her once you have spoken to him. Have you said nothing to him? Acharyaji resolved their doubts by saying: Do not be anxious. His mind is intensely attached to her, so how long will it take for Thakurji to turn it? And Gadadhardas has given his blessing to him, so that his devotion to Hari will be firm, such is Madhodas. Then all the Vaishnavas were satisfied and they were silent a long while. After this Madhodas's mind turned, and so he put the prostitute far from him. He adopted the way and dignity of the Vaishnavas and he became a good Vaishnava (92).

The *varta* offers the bare skeleton of this story; but the *Bhav prakash* goes on to provide much vivid detail as well as moral and social comment. Further, it carries the tale into Gosaimji time and spins the tale of the prostitute into an almost autonomous narrative. The words *veshya duri kini* are interpreted to mean that the prostitute, *veshya*, was told that she was a *sakhi*, friend, companion to Gosaimji. Thus, she is said to have waited for him for all of fifteen years, existing only on dry bread. When he arrived, she asked to be

---

[20] See Dalmia (2001) for a discussion of the special place awarded to women in the devotional community.

accepted into the fold. Gosaimji's reaction was curt: we do not make *veshya*s into our *sevak*s, devotees. Thereupon she took to a hunger strike. On the ninth day of his visit, as he was making preparations to depart, the *veshya* came into his presence, supported on the arms of two people. She said, Maharaj, today is the ninth day. Without food and water, my *pran*, life's breath, will leave if you do not accept me. Gosaimji knew then that she had been purified and he carried out the ceremonies of initiation. Not only this, he gave her a small *svarupa*, Lalji, for worship and care. The Vaishnavas admonished him: teach her the way of *seva*. Thus performing *seva*, it came about that her menstruation set in. Then the Vaishnavas forbade her to touch water, etc. for four days. But her love was so immense that she could not bear to forgo *seva*, and she simply carried it out. The other Vaishnavas ceased all communication with her. After some days Gosaimji arrived once again in Kara, and the Vaishnavas complained to him. When questioned by him the *veshya*'s reply was direct and straightforward: Maharaj, I have had as many worldly masters as the hairs on my body. It was because of you that they could be discarded. Now, through your grace, I have acquired an unworldly master. How can I live without him for four whole days? . . . I'll do as you say. Gosaimji saw that Thakurji was pleased with her, so he said: Continue doing as you have until now. And thus resolving her doubts, he sent her home: Hurry, Thakurji will be waiting for you. He told the other Vaishnavas that she was to be allowed to do as she did. She must not be admonished. But her case was a special one and he expressly charged the other Vaishnavas to desist from following her ways (93).

Another story, of an old woman, poor and inauspicious in her widowhood, whom Acharyaji endows with the most privileged form of *seva*, presents him at his most compassionate and nurturing. The *Bhav prakash* introduces this tale of a nameless Brahman from Arel who was married at 9 years of age to a sickly man. When she was 45 years old, her husband took ill and died. (It is hinted that she had a difficult life, tending a sickly husband who left her no progeny.) This Brahmani had never experienced worldly happiness and comfort at home. When she was left alone, her thoughts turned to the service of the Lord, and, living as she did at home, she thought she would become a follower of Acharyaji. Saying, I have spent all my life in the service of my worldly master, now he is dead, I seek refuge with you, she began to cry. Acharyaji had compassion for her. He not only imparted the name to her, on the next day he gave her a *svarupa* that had been given to him by a Brahman from the South who had departed to Kashi to take *samnyasa*. Being awarded a *svarupa* was a great privilege, and it was jealously watched by the other Vaishnavas. Not only did the Brahmani at once enter into the very heart of *seva*, Thakurji began to favour her almost at once with *sanubhavata*, that is, she began to hold the most intimate communion with him. This Brahmani was most guileless and simple in her ways and had no wealth or goods. She would place an earthen vessel before the Lord; her abode was narrow and tiny, the same room housing at once the kitchen, the temple, and the material for Thakurji's *seva*. She understood little of *achara*, proper ritual conduct, and her eyesight was poor. But she would serve with great love and it was this which kept Thakurji happy. She made do with those of her husband's former clients that were sent her. The Vaishnavas began to mutter amongst themselves. Why has Acharyaji favoured her with *bhagavadseva*? If he had bestowed this upon us, we would have performed the appropriate service. One day, the Vaishnavas could hold themselves back no longer; they went to Acharyaji and lodged a complaint. Acharyaji said, it is not ritual conduct, sacrificial act or wealth which makes me happy, it is *priti*, love of Thakurji, that I need, and it is of this quality that the Brahmani has plenty. Therefore, Thakurji acquiesces to whatever the Brahmani manages to do. Then the Vaishnavas fell silent. After having performed his evening prayer to Yamuna, Acharyaji betook himself in the direction of the Brahmani's house. The Vaishnavas said, Maharaj, you can give her your darshan and see for yourself what kind of *seva* she performs. She was busy preparing the evening meal and took no heed of Acharyaji's coming. The Brahmani was dim of vision and so she could not see much. She would make a *roti*, daub it with *ghi*, Thakurji would pick it up and partake of it. She would fumble for the *roti* and not find it. Then she would say, either the cats or the mice have taken it. She would bang the floor and make another *roti*. Then Acharyaji told her, Thakurji has partaken of it, not cats and mice. It is your great good fortune. The Brahmani said, it is because of you that Thakurji has partaken of it. But Acharyaji said, whatever you do will agree with Thakurji and please him. And afterwards he told the Vaishnavas, it is affection that Thakurji hungers for and he is pleased with the Brahmani (150–1).

The nameless Brahmani, apparently without being aware of her immensely privileged status, exists on terms of easy familiarity with the Lord, watched over and protected by Acharyaji. Her poverty is no barrier to the Lord granting her *sanubhavata*, nor is her widowed state. *Smarta* ritual or *maryadamarg* would have denied her, as also the prostitute, participation in auspicious ritual, but the path of bhakti opens up the possibility of new ritual relationships which create their own laws. Remarkably, while both women refer to the devotion they gave their worldly masters or Lords, the *veshya* speaks unashamedly of them in the plural. It is from the shortcomings experienced in these relationships that the women, in fact, draw their right to serve Thakurji and shower him with the whimsy and ecstasy of their devotion. However, their inclusion in the community and their erratic behaviour are not accepted without protest. Not only do the other Vaishnavas watch jealously over the privileges granted these poor, polluted women, they are quick to point out transgressions. In both cases, however, the gurus concerned make special concessions for the women's extraordinary devotion; and in the widow's case we see Thakurji himself validating her behaviour. Clearly, Thakurji and Acharyaji prescribe no absolutely binding path for devotion to the Lord.

Thus it is that people entangled in some form of woe or despair, adolescents in crisis, those looking for answers in life, widows, prostitutes, and Sudras, all find refuge at the feet of Acharyaji. However, lest the Vaishnava community seem to exist in idyllic and splendid isolation, we need to take note of the stern bounds within which Acharyaji cordons it off. The greatest emphasis is laid on keeping a clear distance from those who in fact seem the nearest. Thus, the lines demarcating Pushtimarg and other Vaishnava traditions— *maryadamargi* Vaishnavas as they are called in the *vartas*—are the most resolutely drawn. The sacred texts can be shared, but there are differences in interpretation and there is always the issue of ritual authority. Acharyaji can endow this on Brahman or non-Brahman alike, depending on ability and talent. And then jati hierarchies cease to function.

In the tale of Mukunddas Sahaniya, Kayasth of Malwa country, these issues are dealt with in some detail. The *Bhav prakash* introduces the two brothers, Dinkardas and Mukunddas, who stayed with Acharyaji and learnt the ways of the *marg*. But they did not receive a *svarupa*, only a letter of *brahmasambandha* which they were to serve. Their women were not *daivi*, therefore there was to be no commensality with them. Mukunddas had received *charanamrta* from Acharyaji, therefore he knew all the *sastras*, *vedas*, and *puranas* by heart. The *varta* comes in here with the information that Mukunddas composed beautiful verses, including a *Mukundsagar*. This was a compilation of *padas* which contained and explicated the twelfth *skandha* of the *Bhagavatapurana*. The Brahmans and pandits of Ujjain would come to him and say, come, we shall narrate the *Bhagavatapurana* to you.[21] But Mukunddas always said that he would listen to them only when he had the leisure. And so, many days passed. Once, they caught him playing the game of *chaupar*. And they said, you have leisure to play *chaupar*, but not to listen to the *Bhagavata*. But as they were not *margiya* Brahmans, he could not hear the *katha* from them (129). The *Bhav prakash* enters at this stage into a long exposition of why this is so: The fruit to be gained from *maryadamarg* is *mukti*, redemption, whereas in Pushtimarg, it is *ekangi pushtibhakti*, which could only be gained by seeking refuge with Acharyaji, so that all kinds of *ananda*, joy, connected with Acharyaji entered the heart. It could only take firm root in the heart if godly discourse could be heard from the mouths of the Vaishnavas of the Vallabhakula. If one listened with love to another, then it was to be regarded as *anyasraya*, seeking refuge of another: 'tatem anyamargiya som na

---

[21] This was obviously an attempt by *smarta* Vaishnavas to either dismantle and reduce his claims to being a talented poet and exegete, or subsume him within their own context.

bhagavaddharam ki bat puchani na apni kahni' (130). Therefore one was neither to ask of matters connected with *Bhagavaddharma* from those following another path, nor speak of one's own.

The *varta* takes up the tale here. There was an eclipse of the sun and Mukunddas was standing in the river invoking the Lord, when the pandit from Ujjain chanced upon him again. And this time he did not let go till Mukunddas relented and held discourse. He embarked upon an exegesis of a *sloka* from the *Bhagavatapurana*. Day became night and day again. The people of the village came to bathe in the river. Will you now be done with the meaning of this shloka? And Mukunddas said, it shall take a full six months. Then that pandit was quite exhausted. He said, the Lord has endowed you with this ability. What can a *jiva* know of it? And he acknowledged defeat. If at times he came again to put a question to him, Mukunddas found so many faults with the question that the pandit gave up coming (131).

Mukunddas obviously disobeys the injunctions of Acharyaji when he holds forth on the *Bhagavata* to one of alien belief. It is not quite clear whether he is at all interested in mediating his knowledge and insight of the text to the pandit, or whether he wishes merely to take care of the pandit's pretensions once and for all. The pandit does allow himself to be convinced of his prowess, and it is this which is portrayed as exemplary, as also his firm refusal to enter into the world of their discourse. The *Bhav prakash* warns clearly: 'There is no impurity greater than *anyasraya*, seeking refuge of another. Just as a woman's entire *dharma* leaves her if she abandons her own husband to seek another, similarly a Vaishnava's *dharma* is destroyed if he indulges in taking refuge of another. This is the *siddhanta* illustrated by the *varta*' (34–5). The tale is important also as illustration of the fact that even a text as sacred as the *Bhagavatapurana* cannot be considered sacred in and of itself. Taken by itself it generates no knowledge, radiates no authority. It needs training and authorization by Acharyaji, and later by those of his *kula*, for the exponent to gain the insight to interpret it for himself and to others. And as we have seen, this authority is not restricted to Brahmans. It can be granted to a Kayasth who happens to be a gifted poet. He can then be further gifted by Acharyaji so that he comes to possess the linguistic skills and vast reading needed to interpret an intricate poetic text in a manner which might put learned Brahmans to shame.

Demarcating the path was obviously a tricky task in a period where so many similar, if not overlapping, belief systems competed for the allegiance of presumably the same classes of people. The *vartas*, which so precisely delineated the authority of Acharyaji in all its ramifications and illustrated his teachings as operative in the tiny details of daily life, were themselves early raised to canonic status, not to be imparted to the unworthy even within the community.

The immense power generated by the *vartas* is illustrated in the story of Purushottam Joshi, Samchora Brahman from Gujarat, who visited Krishna, the son of Padmaraval Bhatt, in Ujjain. Purushottam Joshi would indulge in relating *bhagavadvarta*, tales of the godly, secretly at night to his wife, for he thought that Krishna Bhatt was not yet worthy of it. Four days passed and Krishna knew that they discoursed thus. When they were about to depart and Purushottam Josi already sat astride his horse, Krishna Bhatt held his horse from the one side and himself launched forth in *bhagavadvarta*. He did this in such a way that Purushottam Joshi lost all consciousness of being and was so engrossed in *rasa* that he made to alight from the horse. But he continued on his journey and Krishna Bhatt accompanied him to Gokul and they discoursed thus all the way. He lost all sense of time and did not know when they had accomplished the first stage of their journey. When he realized this, Purushottam Joshi pulled himself together, but *bhagavadvarta ka aves utaryo nahim*, the ecstasy of *Bhagavadvarta* would not wear off (180). And so he also began to talk to Krishna Bhatt, and night and day they indulged in this pastime, and so they reached Gokul where Gosaimji (for it is already a later period and we do not hear Acharyaji's voice in this tale) put Purushottam Joshi's mind at rest regarding the worthiness of Krishna Bhatt.

Thus it is that while tales of community-formation shape the *vartas*, the compendium in its turn acquires the function of further forming and perpetuating the community. This makes for the canonic status of the *vartas*, raising them to a level above that of the *Bhagavatapurana* and even of the *Subodhini*, Acharyaji's own commentary on the *purana*. The *Bhagavatapurana* remains central, but it is superseded, at least in their own representation, by the *vartas*, which had clearly originated as oral texts composed in everyday speech.

The main if not the sole authoritative instance in the tales is the charismatic person of Acharyaji. His authority and his sometimes idiosyncratic choices supersede the power of the deities in the well-known Vaishnava temples, as have seen, and of the well-known Vaishnava scriptures. It is he who selects his chief disciples, recognizing and consolidating their godly destiny, it is he who then also proceeds to form and shape the community of the elect, validating one mode of worship over another, correcting and guiding. His own special brand of bhakti, the ecstatic recognition of the Lord, the communion with him, and the lifestyles associated with this form of devotion, all remain centrally connected to his person.

Doubtlessly, the *vartas*, in that they set up models, idealize. Yet we must take note of what it is that they idealize. It is the poor and the lowly who are accorded such importance in the tales they tell. And the guru of this *saguna sampradaya* comes across primarily not only as an acharya but as a popular teacher, mingling with the common folk. He has knowledge of Sanskrit texts, of the classical schools of philosophy, of the *Dharmasastras*, and of *smarta* ritual. But he does not derive his authority from any of these venerable instances. In fact, he uses his knowledge of these to show up the hollowness of the traditions that they enshrine and to distance himself from them. His authority, which derives much more from his own peculiar experience of and communion with the Lord, overrides that of pilgrimage centres and temple images—as we saw in the tales of the Khatri brothers who rushed to Puri and Ramdas Samchora who hovered near Dvarika. As acharya and guru, he confidently overrules *varna* hierarchies. He allows Mukunddas Sahaniya, a Kayasth, to offer an exegesis of the *Bhagavatapurana* so powerful that it shames a Brahman into silence. He communicates with those whom he finds most in need of his message, regardless of their *varna* allegiance. He comes to their rescue in crises familiar to most healers, as with the Khatri brothers, and holds public discourse in terms which reach the unlettered and the simple, as well as the learned and the reclusive. He explicitly questions and defies *ved aur lok*, the norms laid down by the *Dharmasastras* and by custom. In fact, he rejects Brahmanic ritual, coining his own simple form of worship. He allows the marginalized and the despised, such as the poor Brahman widow and the prostitute, to practice this form of worship and allows for the most idiosyncratic modifications of even the simple ritual he prescribes if they are performed with love. In fact, it is the reciprocal and easy familiarity of the women with the Lord that, according to him, puts them above the rest of the community. And he proceeds to protect these women in all the deviations they unwittingly practice, from the wrath of the righteous in the community.

As I hope to have shown in this essay, we need to question the stereotypes set up both by later *sampradaya* tradition and taken over by contemporary scholarship, which would set forth the rather simplistic and partisan view of *saguna* and *nirguna* traditions as polar opposites, both theologically and socially. If there is one clear difference from the *nirguna*, it lies in the stress laid by Vallabha and his successors on family and communitarian formations and the need to practice, as far as possible, the new forms of worship within these. Apart from this, Vallabha and the *saguna* traditions of the day are as keen as *nirguna* to set themselves off from *smarta* ritual. They award as much importance to the figure of the acharya, and offer as direct and unmediated access to the Lord. Many of the features they stress present little difference from those preached by the great *nirguna* gurus. In fact, the analysis of both clusters of tradition calls for a finer differentiation and possibly much more sociological data before we as scholars are able, in our turn, to overcome and transcend sectarian prejudices. In short, we need to assess both the similarities and differences more carefully. At the least, it seems risky to conflate movements—laying such great stress on their particularity—with the many others, within and without the *saguna* and *nirguna* clusters, though today they seem similarly configured.

Many questions remain to be asked, then, before we can satisfactorily locate these movements in their respective socio-religious and political constellations through the five centuries of their existence. Minute attention to the aesthetic details of *seva*, as also the hereditary authority invested in members of his family, the misuse of power which reached the zenith of notoriety in the Maharaja Libel Case of 1862, have done much to shape the nineteenth-century image of the *sampradaya*. But these developments need in their turn to be regarded historically so that we do not lose sight of their beginnings. The later opulence of Vallabha's *sampradaya* has effectively blocked access to its initially radical message, as also its relative social flexibility. When did Vallabha's *sampradaya* become more exclusive and opulent? In what ways did it relate to others in the *chatuhsampradaya*? Was this only a strategic alliance, which agreed to take no cognizance of difference at one level while at others observing the strictest segregation? What of the many Vaishnavas who belonged to the drifting mass of people that visited temples and holy sites of particular *sampradayas* but as easily drifted to others? There are obviously no simple answers.

The end of the eighteenth century and the beginning of the nineteenth saw the construction of the neo-traditional framework with a renewed importance of *Dharmasastras* and *varnnashramadharma*, within which the colonial regime chose to operate. The nationalist endeavours were to create their own balances and imbalances. There were certain pan-Indian alignments, Sanskritizing moves. But this did not necessarily only lead to the formation and domination of elite groups, which in any case were constituted differently over the centuries.

Modern Hinduism, which operates both with monotheistic and Vedantic monistic claims, has seen fit to melt entirely the differences between the *nirguna* and *saguna sampradaya* clusters, and of these again to the *smarta* orthodoxy of their day. The balance it seems to have achieved is fraught with tensions of a kind which still need to be adequately assessed. But the way even thus far has been stony, and there have obviously been many intermediary stages. The original egalitarianism, which, as I hope to have shown, once made for the great popularity and success of Vallabha's *sampradaya*, could at later stages look for other channels to realize itself. There could be other schisms and alliances. If the Vaishnava *sampradayas*, by and large, once offered means to middling and lower-middle jatis to rise in status, then it is entirely possible that these very jatis, in a changed political constellation, might seek the support of the still lower to come into power.[22]

How is socio-religious power to be shared with others, with the post-Independence state, if we in fact choose to look at it in these terms alone? Even the absolute authority of the guru, though it might seem to point the way to state authoritarianism and right-wing Hinduism, could as well stand in the way of it. Thus, though it may be possible to trace certain tendencies in present-day Hinduism back into the Vedic period, can present political developments be similarly projected into beginnings. Can Hindutva be read backwards?

References

Barz, Richard, 1976/1992. *The Bhakti Sect of Vallabhacharya*. Delhi: Munshiram Manoharlal.

———, 1992. 'Krishnadas Adhikari: An Irascible Devotee's Approach to the Divine', in *Bhakti Studies*, ed. G.M. Bailey and I. Kesarcodi-Watson. Delhi: Sterling Publishers.

———, 1994. 'The Chaurasi Vaishnavan ki Varta', in *According to Tradition. Hagiographical Writing in India*, ed. Winand Callewaert and Rupert Snell. Wiesbaden: Harrassowitz.

Burghart, Richard, 1978. 'The Founding of the Ramanandi Sect', *Ethnohistory* 25: 122–39.

---

[22] As Pinch points out in connection with the social aspirations of the Ramanandis in the earlier part of this century, upward mobility emanating from claims to be both Vaishnava and *kshatriya* could mean 'two socio-religiously related but distinct cultural processes; for radical Ramanandis, Vaishnavism entailed a philosophical stance against all forms of elitism, social or religious for Yadavs, Kurmis, Kushvahas and many other "reformed ksatriyas" Vaishnavism provided the discursive and historical frame for a new, elite status that drew on a hierarchical world. In this sense, though the ideological poles of this study stand in rigid opposition, both represented reasonable and compelling options for the millions of ordinary people long stigmatized by the term shudra.' Pinch 1996: 140.

Bynum, Caroline Walker, 1987. *Holy Feast and Holy Fast: The Religious Significance of Food to Medieval Women.* Berkeley & Los Angeles: University of California Press.

Callewaert, Winand, and Rupert Snell, eds, 1994. *According to Tradition. Hagiographical Writing in India.* Wiesbaden: Harrassowitz.

Chandra, Satish, 1996. 'Historical Background to the Rise of the Bhakti Movement', in *Historiography, Religion and State in Medieval India*, 110–31. Delhi: Har Anand Publications.

Cohen, Richard J., 1984. Sectarian Vaishnavism: The Vallabha Sampradaya', in *Identity and Division in Cults and Sects in South Asia*, ed. Peter Gaeffke and David A. Utz. Proceedings of South Asia Seminar, 1980–1. Philadelphia: Department of South Asia Regional Studies, University of Pennsylvania.

Dalmia, Vasudha, 2001.'Women, Duty and Sanctified Space in a Vaishnava Hagiography of the Seventeenth Century', in *Constructions hagiographiques en Inde: entre mythe et histoire*, ed. Françoise Mallison. Paris: École Pratique des Hautes Études, IVè Section—Sciences historiques et philologiques, Serie II: Hautes Études Orientales.

Dube, Lalta Prasad, 1968. *Hindi bhakta-varta sahitya.* Dehradun: Sahitya Sadan.

Digby, Simon, 1970. 'Review of *Guru Nanak and the Sikh Religion* by W.H. McLeod', *The Indian Economic and Social History Review* 7.2: 301–13.

Glasenapp, Helmuth von, 1934. Die Lehre Vallabhacaryas. *Zeitschrift fur Indologie und Iranistik* 9.3: 268–330.

Gold, Daniel, 1987. *The Lord as Guru. Hindi Sants in the Northern Indian Tradition.* New York, Oxford: Oxford University Press.

Hara, Minoru, 1979. 'Hindu Concepts of Teacher: Sanskrit Guru and Acharya' in *Sanskrit and Indian Studies in Honour of Daniel H.H. Ingalls*, ed. M. Nagatomi, B.K. Matilal, J.M. Masson, and E.C. Dimock, Jr. Dordrecht: D. Reidel.

Hawley, John Stratton, 1983. 'The Sectarian Logic of the Sur Das ki Varta', in *Bhakti in Current Research, 1979–1982*, ed. Monika Thiel-Horstmann. Berlin: Dietrich Reimer.

Lorenzen, David, ed., 1995. *Bhakti Religion in North India: Community Identity and Political Action.* Albany: State University of New York Press.

Mulji, Karsandas, 1865. *History of the Sect of the Maharajas, Or Vallabhacharyas in Western India.* London: Trubner & Co.

Parikh, Dvarikadas, ed., 1971. *Chaurasi Vaishnavan ki varta (tin janma ki lila bhavana vali)*. Mathura: Sri Bajrang Pustakalay.

Pinch, William R., 1996. *Peasants and Monks in British India*. Berkeley and Los Angeles: University of California Press.

Tandan, Hariharnath, 1960. *Varta sahitya. Ek brhat adhyayan*. Aligarh: Bharat Prakashan Mandir.

7

Women, Duty, and Sanctified Space in a Vaishnava Hagiography of the Seventeenth Century

THE DYNAMIC RELIGIOUS MOVEMENTS OF KRISHNA-devotion which, as I have tried to show in the previous essay in this volume, constitutively determined the practice and self-perception of modern Hinduism in North India, came into being in the fifteenth century, in the last decades of the Delhi Sultanate. They developed with great vigour and verve till well into the eighteenth century, right through the reign of the great Mughal emperors. It was in the immediate vicinity of one of their capitals, Agra, that these movements sought their roots and spread their branches, to exercise decisive influence through the whole of the northern part of the country, from Gujarat to Bengal. The central focus of these fast-spreading communities was the fervent personal devotional relationship to the pastoral deity Krishna, henceforth to be experienced as an actual presence by visualizing and participating in the episodes which had once been enacted in these spots, that is, in the Braj countryside adjacent to Agra.

The lifespans of the founders of the two most prominent movements, Chaitanya (1476–1533) and Vallabha (1478–1530), were almost coterminous.[1] The new devotional traditions they established

---

[1] There has been some speculation regarding the social and political constellations which made possible the remarkable spread of these devotional movements, but a subcontinental survey and analysis has yet to be attempted. A preliminary overall thesis was offered by Satish Chandra in his Introduction

were life-affirming, emotional-ecstatic, and, in the case of Vallabha, explicitly family-oriented. New space was granted to women in the theology and mythology of these communities. Whereas the Chaitanya *sampradaya* (religious community) celebrated the erotic relationship of the beautiful cow-maid Radha to Krishna, Vallabha emphasized the parental relationship to the child Krishna. Here, tenderness and nurture played a central role. The *bhavabhakti* or emotional devotion practised was given a theoretical basis or legitimation, when in the middle of the sixteenth century classical Sanskrit aesthetic theory was radically reformulated by the followers of Chaitanya to express and contain the devotional experience centred on the relationship of the devotee to his or her god. According to the new classification, this relationship could be fourfold and embody the *bhava* (emotional attitude) of servant, friend, parent, or lover in respect to the deity. It was, however, left to Vallabha's successors to adapt and develop the devotional aesthetics to a temple ritual, called *seva* (service), refined and carried out on so lavish a scale that it could compete with any royal court. The *seva* was practised in modified form for the domestic cult. It was within the framework of this domestic *seva* that the devotee, if s/he were so favoured, could develop his or her relationship with the deity.

The theological space granted to women in the relationship to the deity, whether as mother or beloved, corresponded in some measure to the actual space permitted in the lives of devotees, specially women, to evolve this relationship.[2] There was a certain egalitarianism, both in the matter of caste, as also the position of women in respect to

---

to Savitri Chandra 'Shobha' (Chandra 1983), in response to earlier suggestions by Irfan Habib. The theological and philosophical basis for regarding these movements as in any way homogeneous has been questioned in Sharma 1987. To my knowledge, there have been no detailed studies of the historical configurations which enabled and propped up these movements in what is today the Hindi heartland. For Gujarat, Cohen 1984 made some succinct suggestions. More work is available on Bengal. Early attempts were made by Raychaudhuri 1953 and De 1961/1986, to be followed many decades later by Eaton 1993.

[2] Surprisingly little research has been devoted to the social and literary lives of the women devotees and poets of the period. Exceptions are Chandra 1983,

their men. However, it needs to be borne in mind that this space and the egalitarianism are not to be measured by present standards, but by the givens of Indian society in that age, for they always remained within the devotional framework and the hierarchies which came with it: that is, they were always subject to the absolute authority emanating from the preceptor.

In the following, I shall consider the early hagiographic prose narratives, called *Vartas*, of the *sampradaya* founded by Vallabha, as evidence of the remarkable latitude granted to women in order to enable them to follow the devotional path. These narratives refute a myth which gained ground in the British colonial period, namely that it was in order to preserve the honour of their women that, in the so-called Muslim era, Hindus had become particularly rigid in relation to their women. The women were then supposed to have become increasingly suppressed and secluded. As the propagators of the myth were to come to see it, it was as a result of this fear, that is, in order to preserve their honour and safeguard themselves from molestation by the Muslim rulers of the country, that it became common practice for women to burn on the pyres of their dead husbands.

The *Vartas*—extended narrative prose in Brajbhasha, the language of the region—relating the religious biographies of the devotees, were to form a major literary contribution to the newly resurgent vernacular prose literature.[3] The popular narrative genre, *bata* or *varta*, loosely translatable as 'tale', which was taken over and transformed for this purpose, consisted originally of incidents strung together for entertainment and/or didactic purposes. The *varta* was now endowed with an expressly theological-didactic purpose. In the course of the sixteenth century, the tales of devotees who had had the good fortune to be initiated by the first two preceptors of the Vallabha community were collected, ordered, and enriched with a

---

a pioneering attempt to approach the theme; Sangari 1991 is a brilliant analysis of the life and poetry of Mirabai; and Mukta 1994 explores the ideological and social relevance of Mirabai's life and songs as kept alive in the Dalit communities of Rajasthan and Gujarat today.

[3] *Varta* will refer to the hagiographical compilations of the Vallabha *sampradaya*, whereas *varta* with a lower case 'v' will refer to the genre as such.

commentary. There are thus two major *vartas* or hagiographic compilations. The first comprises a series of *prasangas* or episodes in the lives of 84 followers of Vallabha. The second is a collection of the lives of the 252, that is, 3 x 84, followers of his son Vitthala.[4] In the following, I shall concentrate on the first compilation, the *Chaurasi Vaishnavan ki varta*, or the tales of the 84 Vaishnavas, of which a good edition based on the manuscripts of 1695 and 1721 is fortunately available.[5] Vallabha is here referred to as Acharyaji or preceptor, the devotees are called Vaishnavas, or followers of Vishnu, of whom Krishna is regarded as the chief manifestation.

The *Vartas* offer us a view of the religious community in the very process of defining itself. Apart from seeking to attract new followers, a central concern of the tales is to propagate new means of forging the fellowship of Vaishnavas and of setting up the new codes of conduct which are to mark off its members from others. The attributes which are highlighted and commended are often *loka-aura veda-virudha*, contrary to popular and Vedic norms, as the *vartas* themselves are at pains to emphasize. In the interest of the *bhaktimarga*, the way of devotion, however, the preceptor and his immediate followers exhibit few scruples while overstepping what they regard as the stifling and constraining bounds of *maryadamarga*, the way of custom.

The *Vartas* proper are brief, forceful; a lively style of oral transmission is retained throughout. The *prasanga* (individual episode), two or three of which are strung together to form a single *varta*, begins directly with the relation of the events which serve to establish the didactic point. If the main characters are often left nameless, they are never faceless, for they express views and emotions which characterize them definitively. Since the texts are concise, the short

---

[4] Tandan (1960) remains the most comprehensive account of the *varta* literature produced by the Vallabha Sampradaya. Barz in his monograph on the *sampradaya* (1976) and later essay (1992) has devoted attention to the four famous poet-followers of Vallabha, accounts of whose lives are contained in the first *Varta* compendium. His essay (1994) is a more general survey of the hagiographic approach of the *sampradaya*.

[5] The reference is to the 1971 edition by Dvarikadasa Parikha. In the following, all page references are to this edition. The two long extracts in translation in the second half of this essay are also based on Parikha's text.

sentences make for a fast pace, descriptions are kept to a minimum; the action is related in a few words. The dialogue form adopted makes for the dramatization of the scene and the exchange between the main protagonists is devised so as to focus upon the central concern. The *prasangas* can then be considered scenic sequences, depicting dramatic highlights. As befitting drama, there is attention to detail, which is not amassed but brought into play where necessary. Finally—a point made clearly by the tale itself—there is practically no sententiousness in the main text. The commentary serves to explicate the model being set up, but it is never verbose or too learned to lose sight of the point to be made. The *Vartas*, then, treat questions concerning the ultimate values in life as propounded in the community and the course to be followed in critical life situations.

In order to appreciate the radicalism of the new movements in granting the space that they do to women, we shall turn to a short delineation of the position traditionally assigned to women in the Sanskrit treatises on religious and civil law. It must be emphasized at the outset that these are prescriptive texts which do not necessarily indicate the actual conditions of women at any given point in time. However, as prescriptive texts, they did—and have continued to—set the norms which were expected to be followed. The *Manusmrti* (Institutes of Manu), compiled in the first centuries of the Christian era and one of the most prestigious texts of the legal canon to this day (it was translated early by British colonial legislators) will thus be quoted extensively.

I cite first the maxim demanding the absolute fidelity and commitment of the wife to the husband, both in this life and the hereafter. For, at no time in her life was a woman to consider herself independent.

> 5.147. By a girl, by a young woman, or even by an aged one, nothing must be done independently, even in her own house.

> 148. In childhood a female must be a subject to her father, in youth to her husband, when her lord is dead to her sons; a woman must never be independent.[6]

[6] Citations of the *Manusmrti* are from the translation by Georg Buhler (1886/1970).

Second, there was to be complete subordination in all matters and expressly so when it came to religious concerns:

> 155. No sacrifice, no vow, no fast must be performed by women apart (from their husbands); if a wife obeys her husband, she will for that (reason alone) be exalted in heaven.

Her husband was to be her god and her salvational goal, and by serving him, she would attain the highest stage in afterlife. Dire punishment was to be her lot if she transgressed the laws of chastity during his lifetime or after.

> 164. By violating her duty towards her husband, a wife is disgraced in this world (after death) she enters the womb of a jackal, and is tormented by diseases (the punishment of her sin).

All religious literature, mythological, legal, and narrative, was at pains to emphasize the duties of a wife and her unflinching devotion to her husband.[7] Not content with negative exhortations, the literature also valorized the faithful wife, who was endowed with extraordinary powers, she was greatly celebrated. Tales galore were told to illustrate the supernatural powers of a virtuous wife (*pativrata*), who could stop the sun in its course in order to save the life of her husband or with one glance cause a man with evil designs to fall dead at her feet. The zenith of wifely devotion was the ultimate act of sacrifice, self-immolation on the funeral pyre of her dead husband, this practice later came to be known as *sati*. No contemporary prescriptive texts, especially as operative in northern India, have come down to us.[8]

---

[7] Cf. Kane 1974: chapter XI: Mutual Rights and Duties of Husband and Wife, 2/l: 556ff.; and chapter XV: *Sati*, for the treatment of this rite in the *Dharmashastras*.

[8] An exception is the Sanskrit treatise *Stridharmapaddhati, or, Guide to the Religious Status and Duties of Women*, written by Tryambakayajvan, a pandit in the eighteenth-century Maratha court of Thanjavur (Tanjore) in South India. The treatise has been paraphrased and commented upon extensively by Julia Leslie (1989). Though the work makes extensive use of stories and illustrations from the epics and the Puranas, Tryambakayajvan's rigid codifications of the laws pertaining to women is, according to Leslie, not of the puranic mould, which would allow women a measure of autonomy in matters relating to bhakti

However, prescriptions of this kind can be inferred from the polemics that the *Vartas* themselves indulge in.

The *Vartas* deliberately set up new norms, in defiance and explicit revocation of *veda aura loka*, the Vedic and commonly prevalent norms. Their own, they claim, were based on practice which they knew to be radical in its departure from the old: thus the paradigmatic nature of the tales told. In these tales the rights and duties of the good spouse were reinterpreted and in some cases dissolved altogether, but, since the framework in which this dissolution could take place was religious and pious, it was not left to the free will or caprice of the individual to take what course he or she pleased but, in all cases, made subject to a higher commitment.[9] The kind of emotional relationship demanded of the devotee, the complete identification with the needs of the Lord, the surrender of his or her own personality, was a task that women were considered more suited to perform. They thereby gained a special position of grace and authority even in regard to the preceptor. Before we proceed to analyse individual life-stories, we need to consider the family setting of the devotees from the perspective of the religious community.

In a newly forming community, an essential precondition was family solidarity in the matter of loyalty to Acharyaji, the preceptor. The new initiate was expected to win over his or her spouse, if possible parents, and certainly children. If this solidarity was not forthcoming, then the initiate announced that he or she would not drink water from the hands of the family members and began to cook his or her own meals separately. Thus, while living under the same roof, a symbolic separation was put in place to maintain and demonstrate difference. It was while dealing with such cases that the *Vartas* demonstrated a certain egalitarianism in respect to men and women.

If a partner was not *anukula*, agreeably disposed, i.e. if he or she was not actively inclined to participate in the devotional life, a

---

and *moksha* (Leslie 1989: 258–9). In general, the work follows the restrictive code of the later *Dharmashastras*, and in doing so more than confirms the tenets of Manu cited above. It goes further, however, when it exalts the practice of self-immolation, which had found no mention in Manu.

[9] See Sangari 1993 for reflections on the notion of women's agency.

separation could become desirable. When appealed to, Acharyaji supported the separation, but saw to it that this came about fairly, that for instance the wife was given enough means to maintain herself (98). However, if a man was not willing to follow the devotional path, as for instance in the case of *dharma ka virodhi pati* (186) 'the husband who was an opponent *of dharma*', the wife was simply asked to wait before she take initiation. Acharyaji announced, and it was made to seem as if it was no more than a coincidence, that the thus disinclined husband would not live long. Once he passed away, and Acharyaji was in the position of being able to forecast the exact time, the woman would be free to follow the devotional path.

The prime object in the life of the individual was to achieve intimacy with the Lord and it was this which made for social acceptability within the community. Men and women, alone, married, widowed, or abandoned, gained orientation in life and a respected place within the community once they acquired access to the devotional path. With a safe foothold on the destined route, the dreaded state of widowhood itself could lose its most awful aspects. However, it was not the familial stand as such which was discouraged. On the contrary, Acharyaji explicitly condemned renouncers and renunciation itself as a means of attaining salvation. Renunciation might lead to *mukti*, redemption, but *mukti* in this scheme of things was considered a lower stage than *bhakti*, devotion. The question, then, was one of maintaining bonds, but in such a manner that the primary bond, that between the deity and the devotee, was supported and confirmed. Thus, conversely, if it came about that a man so single-mindedly followed his devotional instinct, that he wanted to do away with all worldly attachments, and therefore refused to take cognizance of his wife, even though she was not only devoted to him but willing to follow the *bhaktimarga* as well, then Thakurji himself intervened, remonstrated with his devotee, and brought about a reconciliation between husband and wife (206).

In the following two tales we are witness to two situations in which fidelity and self-sacrifice are the issues. What decision-making scope do the women have? I shall quote from the main *Varta* text, which enters directly into the action, without any introduction of the protagonists, who are nevertheless vividly delineated.

The first tale deals with the wife of the Brahman Krishnadasa (370). Here, forging and maintaining the communal life of the Vaishnavas is put forth as the primary concern, which is to be given priority even over the obligations of the marital bond.

Varta 75, prasanga 1: Once, ten to fifteen Vaishnavas collected and set off to obtain *darsana*, benedictory view, of Acharyaji, the preceptor, at Arail. So they made a halt at Krishnadasa's place. On that day, there was no grain and no groceries at Krishnadasa's place and Krishnadasa himself was not at home. The woman prostrated herself in front of the Vaishnavas and bid them come into the house. Afterwards she fell into a reverie, there is nothing at home and he himself is not at home. The Vaishnavas must be hungry, what should I do about that? There was a trader in the village. Noting that she was a beauty, the trader obstructed her way now and then. 'If you would come to my house one night, you could take what you like.' Then the woman thought, I shall go to that trader. So she came to his shop and said: I shall come one night to you. I need grain and groceries. The trader was most pleased and gave her what she asked for. Then the woman brought the groceries home. She bathed, cooked, placed *bhoga*, sacrificial offering, before the Lord and offered *mahaprasada*, the consecrated food, to the Vaishnavas. She fed the cows with what was left over. For herself she took nothing. Later in the evening, Krishnadasa came home with grain and groceries. He was pleased to see the Vaishnavas and met them all. Afterwards he asked them, when did you come? Then the Vaishnavas said, we came at noontime. Then Krishnadasa asked the wife, the Vaishnavas must be hungry, take the grain and cook it quickly. The woman said, they have taken the consecrated food, don't worry. Then Krishnadasa said, how could the Vaishnavas have taken anything, there was nothing in the house. Then the woman told him what had come about. Then he prostrated himself before the woman and said, you are blessed, you have preserved my *dharma*, moral obligations ...

Later, when evening fell, Krishnadasa said to his wife, you've arranged a tryst with that trader. So he will be keeping watch for you. Our wish was fulfilled with his groceries, our *dharma* was preserved, now we should see that his wish is fulfilled. Bathe and beautify yourself. Then the woman bathed herself with ointment, put kohl on her eyes, the mark on her forehead, vermilion in the parting of her hair and scarlet colour on the soles of her feet. Then she prepared to leave. This was in the rainy season, the clouds burst and there was a storm. Then Krishnadasa said, the path has become muddy, your feet will collect mud. It won't look good if the scarlet of your feet comes off. It will disturb that trader's *mana*, frame of mind. So climb on my shoulder and I'll take you to his shop. Then he took her to the shop and came home. The woman called out to the trader, open the door. The trader came happily, water-vessel in hand. He said, wash your muddy feet. That woman said, my feet are good, dry and clean. The trader said, there is much mud on the way. How did your feet remain clean. Then the woman said: what business is it of yours to ask why my feet are clean. Do what you are supposed to do. Then the trader said, tell me truly, why did your feet stay clean in this rain? The woman said, my husband brought me to your shop on his shoulders. The trader said, have you spoken truly? Why did your husband bring you to my place? You never spoke to me otherwise. And then you said of your own accord, one night you would come. You said this and took grain and groceries. You didn't ask for any money. So tell me the reason for all this. Then the woman said, the Vaishnavas came to my place, five to ten *gurubhais*, fellow-disciples of my *guru*, and there was nothing at home. So I thought, of what use is this body. It isn't good that the Vaishnavas are hungry. That's why I took the grain for them. So my husband was pleased with you and brought me to your place. Hence have no fear in your mind. When he heard this, the trader began to curse this birth. And said, you, man and wife, are blessed. Then he prostrated himself at her feet and said, you are my *dharma ki bahan*, you have acquired the rights of my sister, forgive my failing. Then he gave her a new *sari* to wear and accompanied her to her house.

The moral of the story: serving fellow Vaishnavas is of more moment that marital fidelity, which is thus depicted as no absolute value in and of itself. Since the tale has to do with the woman's predicament, her perceptions, reflections and decisions, the action is unfolded from her perspective and articulates her observations. The focus is upon her and the camera moves with her, so to speak, following her from her own house through the muddy path to the trader's dwelling and then back to her house.

The second *Varta* to be considered here is somewhat more spectacular. It relates the tale of the good wife or sati (199), who is to immolate herself with her dead husband. The tale is related in order to make the point that the span of life granted to a human being is to be used primarily to attain the state of bhakti or devotion. The episode is embedded in the story of a devotee by the name of Rana Vyasa. In the preceding *prasangas*, Rana Vyasa has been himself shown to realize, slowly and painfully, that self-mortification, pride in asceticism, and the willingness to take one's own life are meaningless gestures, when it comes to realizing the ultimate truths in life. The woman in the tale is referred to simply as the Rajputani,[10] that is, as belonging to the Rajput or warrior caste, amongst whom the custom of widow self-immolation had long, though always only sporadically, been prevalent.

Varta 32, prasanga 2: Once when Rana Vyasa and Jagannatha Josh had bathed in the river Sarasvat and had just sat down to perform their *sandhya* ritual, a Rajputani whose husband had died came there to commit *sati*. Then Jagannatha Josh asked Rana Vyasa, those who commit *sati*, in

---

[10] The *Varta* uses the term Rajputan rather than the more usual Rajputani or Rajputni.

what form are they incarnated (hereafter)? Rana Vyasa shook his head and said: in vain do they burn their human body alongside a ghost. If such a beautiful body were to apply itself to the worship of the lord, then it could be saved. She burns herself with a ghost. So this birth is spent in vain. Thus he shook his head and spoke. At this moment, the Rajputani's eye fell on him. As she saw him shake his head, her *sati*, resolve, fell off. Then the Rajputani said to the people who were with her: I shall not commit *sati*. My resolve has fallen off. Then the people there said to her, we won't allow you inside the house (again). We will burn you right here. Then the Rajputani said, I won't come home. Make me a hut on the bank of this river, I shall live here. And if you burn me by force, then my death will fall at your head. And she cursed them thus. The next day, when Rana Vyasa and Jagannatha Josh went to bathe in the river Sarasvat, that Rajputani asked him, why did you shake your head yesterday when you saw me? Then Rana Vyasa said to the Rajputani, oh we were talking about many things amongst ourselves and laughing. Where will it get you to know about it? The Rajputani, said, why do you conceal it from me? You shook your head while you talked, so my resolve fell off and I did not burn myself. Therefore tell me the truth now. Tell me what my *kartavya*, duty, is and I shall follow it. You saved me from burning in the fire, so have the grace to tell me about it. In such manner, the Rajputani continued to insist strongly. Then Rana Vyasa said, we said amongst ourselves that even though she has received the best of incarnations in the human form, she burns herself with a ghost. A body which has not chosen to remember his name deserves to be castigated. It is utterly corrupt.

Then this Rajputani said, now I seek refuge with you. I shall sing *bhajanas*, devotional songs, and remember the Lord's name just as you tell me to, so that my hereafter improves. Therefore grant me grace. Then Rana Vyasa said, presently you are in *sutaka*, state of ritual impurity. Come when it wears off and I shall instruct you. Then that Rajputani prostrated herself and went into her hut. Then the pain of separation (from the Lord) grew and the hours stretched into an age. When will the *sutaka* be removed, when will Rana Vyasa instruct me, so that I can remember the Lord's name and devote myself to Him . . .

As depicted in the *Varta*, the Rajputani is not a silent victim of her fate. She has both a voice and the ability to act. If at first it is the men who watch her and shake their heads, she is also shown as watchful. Once her gaze is registered in the tale, the focus shifts to document her perspective. The tale proceeds to recreate her experience. She perceives, takes a stand, and makes decisions which she actually carries out at great peril to herself. All the religious texts which make reference to it view self-immolation as the ultimate sacrificial gesture of the *pativrata* or virtuous wife. A woman thus resolved to perform this sacrifice can virtually not retrace her step, for the family, deprived of this ostentatious show of virtue, stands to lose face socially. This well-nigh impossible task of surviving a refusal to perform the sacrifice at the very last moment is here shown as being entirely feasible. She is banished to a hut outside the settlement, but she can gain space and status in the new devotional community. A woman who would be considered an outcast is here declared to be a *daivi jiva*, a godly being, who gains rather than loses in prestige, for the ultimate moral of the tale is that each life has its own goal, that the husband is in fact not a woman's lord and that her life is valuable as human life. To be born in human form is to have the possibility of achieving the bhakti which the soul craves for through many births. To put an end to it by abruptly terminating a lifespan, which is to be regarded as a means of achieving the state of bhakti, is a senseless and vicious gesture.

The new devotional movements were to radically reformulate the role assigned to women and the status awarded to the practice of self-immolation, which later came to be known almost exclusively as sati.[11]

---

[11] Even the later Vaishnava *sampradaya*, founded by Svami Narayana (1780–1829), seems largely to have maintained the sanctified space reserved for women who devoted themselves to Krishna. The Gujarati *Satiigita* (1823), by Muktananda (b. 1757), a member of the *sampradaya*, follows, as Mallison in the introduction to her translation of the text points out (1973: 26), the Puranas rather than the *Dharmashastras* in its general attitude towards women. However, in setting forth the older radical views, while incorporating them into, by comparison, a more conservative Puranic mould, certain double attitudes came to coexist in unresolved tension. Thus, while maintaining that a married woman worship her husband as her only god and follow only the religious observances permitted by him, the work also advises that a woman abandon her husband should he not be a devotee of Krishna. Similarly, while

A woman's life, just as a man's, was intrinsically valuable as human life, it could be directed to achieve the highest of spiritual goals, and it was this which made for her moral worth. Her husband was neither her ultimate god nor guide. Within the dynamic framework of Krishna bhakti it was possible and desirable for a woman to seek to establish a relationship to her own god.

However, if this were to be seen as the last word on the issue, it would serve to do little more than simply tilt the balance of power a little more in favour of women. But release from the bond of absolute fidelity to the husband could have several possible consequences. Given the position of power which the Gosvamis of the *sampradaya* came to enjoy, which found expression in their claim to be living incarnations of Krishna, the thus released sexuality of women could also lead to other forms of exploitation, it could expose them to abuse of another kind. That this happened often enough to culminate in the scandal of the Maharaja Libel Case in the 1860s is then certainly an aspect which cannot be ignored (cf. Mulji 1865). The other, which also needs to be taken into account considering the heated debate around the issue of sati in the second quarter of the nineteenth century and through the 1980s,[12] is that the devotional movements of the sixteenth and seventeenth centuries established powerful alternative traditions regarding the status of women, socially and within the family. When trying to establish the role of women in Hindu society, past and present, it needs to be remembered then, that the later *Dharmashastras*, which are quoted time and

---

endorsing the self-immolation of widows, the work clearly states that it was only for those who did not seek moksha. In and of itself, ascetic widowhood was so exalted a state that it could serve as model not only for all non-widowed women but for all such who had rejected marriage in favour of a life devoted to Krishna. Thus, in the final event, religious observance was to be freed from authoritative direction by the husband. The real contradiction lay however in the double allegiance of the married woman to two lords, her husband as well as Krishna. I am grateful to Françoise Mallison for clarifying these points.

[12] There is, in the meantime, a vast literature on the topic. For a discussion of the religiosity of the rite, which formed a central concern of the debates and led to legislation in 1829, see Dalmia 1992.

again to establish the validity of the practice of sati in ancient and medieval India, are but one source of tradition. There are other textual traditions which need to be taken into account as well.

References

Barz, Richard, 1976/1992. *The Bhakti Sect of Vallabhacarya*. Delhi: Munshiram Manoharlal.

———, 1992. 'Krsnadasa Adhikar: An Irascible Devotee's Approach to the Divine', in *Bhakti Studies*, ed. G.M. Bailey and I. Kesarcodi Watson. Delhi: Sterling Publishers.

———, 1994. 'The Caurasi Vaishnavan ki Varta', in *According to Tradition. Hagiographical Writing in India*, ed. Winand Callewaert and Rupert Snell. Wiesbaden: Otto Harrassowitz, 1994.

Callewaert, Winand and Rupert Snell, eds, 1994. *According to Tradition. Hagiographical Writing in India*. Wiesbaden: Otto Harrassowitz.

Cauras Vaishnavanan ki varta (tina janma ki lila bhavana vali), ed. Dvarikadasa Parikha. 1971. Mathura: Sri Bajranga Pustakalaya.

Chandra, Savitri, 'Shobha'. 1983. *Social Life and Concepts in Medieval Hindi Bhakti Poetry*. Delhi: Chandrayan Publications.

Cohen, Richard J. 1984. 'Sectarian Vaishnavism: The Vallabha Sampradaya', in *Identity and Division in Cults and Sects in South Asia*, ed. Peter Gaeffke and David A. Utz. Proceedings of South Asia Seminar, 1980–1. Philadelphia: Department of South Asia Regional Studies, University of Pennsylvania.

Dalmia-Luderitz, Vasudha, 1992. 'Sati as a Religious Rite. Parliamentary Papers on Widow Immolation, 1821–30'. *Economic and Political Weekly*, 25 January.

De, Sushil Kumar, 1961/1986. *Early History of the Vaishnava Faith and Movement in Bengal. From Sanskrit and Bengali Sources*. Calcutta: Firma KLM.

Eaton, Richard Maxwell, 1993. *The Rise of Islam and the Bengal Frontier 1204–1760*. Berkeley: University of California Press.

Kane, P.V. 1974. *History of Dharmasastra (Ancient and Medieval Religious and Civil Law)*, vol. II, part I. Poona: Bhandarkar Oriental Research Institute.

Leslie, Julia, 1989. *The Perfect Wife*. Delhi: Oxford University Press.

Manu, 1886/1970. *The Laws of Manu*, translated with extracts from seven commentaries by G. Buhler. *The Sacred Books of the East*, ed. Max Müller, vol. 25. Delhi: Motilal Banarsidass.

Mulji, Karsandas, 1865. *History of the Sect of the Maharajas, or Vallabhacharyas in Western India.* London: Trubner & Co.

Mukta, Parita, 1994. *Upholding the Common Life. The Community of Mirabai.* Delhi: Oxford University Press.

Muktananda, 1973. *L'Epouse Ideale. La Satii-Gita de Muktananda*, traduite du Gujarati par Françoise Mallison. Paris: Institut de Civilisation Indienne.

Raychaudhuri, Tapankumar, 1953. *Bengal under Akbar and Jahangir. An Introductory Study in Social History.* Calcutta: A. Mukerjee and Company.

Sangari, Kumkum, 1991. *Mirabai and the Spiritual Economy of Bhakti.* Occasional Papers on History and Society. 2nd Series, no. 28. Delhi: Nehru Memorial Museum and Library (published also in *Economic and Political Weekly*, 7 and 14 July 14 1990).

———, 1993. 'Consent, Agency and the Rhetorics of Incitement', *Economic and Political Weekly*, 28/18, 1 May.

Sharma, Krishna, 1987. *Bhakti and the Bhakti Movement: A New Perspective. A Study in the History of Ideas.* Delhi: Munshiram Manoharlal.

Tandan, Hariharnath, 1960. *Varta sahitya. Eka brhat adhyayana.* Aligarh: Bharata Prakasana Mandira.

8

The Sixth *Gaddi* of the Vallabha *Sampradaya*

Narrative Structure and Authority in a *Varta* of the Nineteenth Century

In his book *Benares. The Sacred City of the Hindus: An Account of Benares in Ancient and Modern Times*, published in 1868, M.A. Sherring of the London Missionary Society was to record with a mixture of pride and indignation:

> Since the country has come into our hands, a great Impetus has been given to the erection of temples, and to the manufacture of idols, in Northern India. In Benares, temples have multiplied at a prodigious rate: and this rate at the present moment, is, I believe, rather increasing than diminishing. Judged merely by its external appearances, Hinduism was never so flourishing as it is now. With general prosperity and universal peace, and with a Government based on neutral principles, and largely tolerant of the national religious systems, Hinduism, under the leadership of men of the old school—princes, pandits, banyas (tradespeople), and priests—is making extraordinary efforts to maintain its position against the new doctrines of European civilization and religion, which they now begin to recognize as formidable opponents.[1]

Though it is doubtful that increased temple-building had only to do with Indian recognition of European civilization and religion as

[1] Sherring 1868: 38.

formidable opponents, Sherring was surely an acute observer of the sheer fact of temple accumulation around him.

The burgeoning of Hindu politico-religious activity can be traced back to a period well before the establishment of British political and military power on the subcontinent. Mughal decline saw the rise of the Marathas, who operated under a Hindu banner. Renewed activity in the Rajput states also testified to the existence of a nascent consciousness of the historical and pan-Indian dimensions of a new awareness of being 'Hindu'. Jai Singh II of Jaipur (1688–1748) made considerable efforts to unify the different Vaishnava *sampradayas* under common doctrinaire principles, and to make them establish links with Vedic ritual as well as with the Vedanta philosophy of Shankara and Ramanuja. This was accompanied by a renewed awareness of the varna system as the organizing principle of Hindu society. These characteristics, albeit with shifts of emphasis, were to remain constitutive of those movements in nineteenth-century British India which came to represent what in retrospect has generally been designated by the collective term 'neo-Hinduism'.

In Banaras the process Sherring describes had also been set in motion during the late Mughal period, largely under the Marathas, whose power expanded and intensified. They were concerned with rescuing the three holy places of the Hindus (*tristhali*)—Prayag, Gaya, and Kashi. In the second half of the eighteenth century, they built the city's ghats, so characteristic a part of the Banaras riverfront today. Not all their enterprises were to be so successful, for they vainly planned the rebuilding of temples on ancient sites where, in the meanwhile, mosques stood.

The building of ghats and temples took place not only at the initiative of rulers and princes. Merchants and landowners, who had come to power and made money under the aegis of the British, participated substantially in the process. Thus, if on the one hand the interest in reclaiming and occupying symbolically significant holy sites goes back to pre-colonial times, it prospers under the newer power constellations in the British period as well.

By the end of the eighteenth century Banaras had established its position as one of the most important trading and banking centres in North India.² The city's commercial aristocracy consisted of the Naupatti Mahajans, bankers who rose to prominence in the troubled period before the final collapse of the Awadh *navabi* and the formal takeover of the province by the East India Company.³ They were called Naupatti because they had settled in a newly cleared tract of land which was to become the centre of the city's commercial life. They had much political influence, having been instrumental in the installation of a Hindu raja in place of the Muslim military commander Mir Rustam Ali—who had been appointed by the Nawab of Awadh and had served also as the revenue and administrative head of the region. The interests of the Naupatti Mahajans were closely linked, though not always identical, with those of the raja and the Company.

I

It is instructive to look at the genesis of Gopal Mandir in Banaras, which was to be recognized as the sixth seat or *gaddi* of the Vallabha *sampradaya* and which grew and prospered in the period Sherring speaks of. The history of its rise to power and status is documented in the hagiographical Brajbhasha tract *Mukundrayji ki varta* (first published in book form in 1923).⁴ This, apart from supplying much information on the devotional ritual in Nathdvara and the elaborate attention paid to maintaining aesthetic harmony in the celebration of divine love, also records the influence of the newer configurations of power and their links with older traditional structures. The *varta* also provides clear indications of patterns that were to become characteristic of Hinduism in the nineteenth century.

---

² Cf. Motichandra 1985: chapter 8, *Banaras ke mahajan*, 313–30; Bayly 1978: 181–2.
³ There are various stories associated with the rise and formation of this group of banker-merchants. Motichandra 1985: 410–12 provides a list of their names as available in a contemporary document.
⁴ The full title of the work is *Srimukundrayji ki varta tatha Srigopallalji ki varta*. I am grateful to Dr Kalyan Krishna of the Banaras Hindu University for drawing my attention to the *varta* and to Professor Anand Krishna for elucidating many aspects which would otherwise have remained closed to me.

Gopal Mandir, a complex which was to assume grander proportions later, had been established by the rebel Raja Chait Singh in 1777. Though an illegitimate claimant to the throne, he had initially enjoyed the support of the British and was by all accounts a popular ruler enthused by temple-building. But the temple only came into prominence through the services of the charismatic Girdharji Maharaj, who traced his genealogy back through six generations to Yadunath, the youngest of the six sons of Vitthal, that is, nine generations removed from Vallabha himself. The names of this illustrious lineage have been preserved for posterity.[5] Girdharji was born in 1791 in Banaras and educated there, becoming known there for his high learning and piety. He had studied the Vedas and Vedangas, so that, apart from knowledge of the *seva paddhati*—the rituals of his own *sampradaya*—he had the advantage of being well versed in traditional schools of philosophy and ritual. This was to help him to establish linkages between the rituals of his own *sampradaya* and what was commonly accepted as Vedic. He left behind several learned works and commentaries, in Sanskrit as well as in Brajbhasha. The two best known, both composed in Sanskrit, are *Suddhadvaitamarkandeya*, an exposition of the philosophical-theological tenets of the *sampradaya*, and *Srutirahasya*, a work which grapples with the thematic complex concerned with Vallabha's manifestation in human incarnation (*manava vigraha*).

Girdharji served Gopallalji in Banaras, the deity worshipped by his family, but he was fascinated and attracted by the much greater ritual wealth and grandeur of Nathdvara and spent long periods there. On the strength of his high learning he persuaded Damodarji Maharaj of Nathdvara to part with a *svarupa* of Srinathji. The image, Mukundrayji, though not one of the *saptasvarupa*, was reputed to have been one of the two additional images originally in the possession of Vallabhacharya himself. Girdharji paid a handsome sum for the image, as the *varta* testifies that he also paid a large

---

[5] See Tandan 1960: 395 for an account of the distribution of the *svarupas* amongst the sons of Vitthal. For Girdharji's genealogy, see the article by Madhav Sarma in *Gosvami Srigiridharji maharaj dvishatabdi mahotsav smarika*, 1990: 11.

amount for the haveli of one Jairamdas in the Chaukhamba area of the city, in the midst of the residential quarters of the Naupatti Mahajans. He did this to enlarge the temple site of Gopal Mandir, as befitted the status of the hallowed image he had purchased. In 1827 Mukundrayji travelled with much pomp from Nathdvara to Banaras, in a great train of attendants and *bhaktas*, accompanied for protection on the way by *chaprasis* kindly provided by the British resident in Udaipur. On the outskirts of Banaras, Mukundrayji was received by Harakhchand Agraval, a leading Naupatti Mahajan. Harakhchand saw to immediate arrangements for the deity and contributed substantially to the funding and maintenance of the temple complex, which was ready two years later, in 1829.

The temple took up all the splendid ritual and festivity of Nathdvara, supported by the devotion and participation of the great commercial families of the area. The *padas* of the *ashtachhap* poets were sung in the temple, the Braj countryside was transported to Kashi. Harakhchand's grandson, the famous poet Harishchandra, was to commemorate the occasion in verse some decades later '*Kashi mem gokul kari dinho*' and '*Brindavan ko anubhav kashi pragati dikhayo*'.[6]

The revival of the Pushtimarg in the Braj area itself had taken place only in the late eighteenth century, largely at the initiative of one Purushottam (b. 1748). The movement was to receive further impetus in the course of the nineteenth century: some of the deities that had fled the Braj country in the reign of Aurangzeb and been settled in Rajasthan and Gujarat came back to occupy their more traditional seats in Braj.[7] Yet even amidst the general movement, Girdharji's removal of a deity from Nathdvara, the stronghold of the *sampradaya*, to an entirely new scenario in Banaras was a novel venture. Though Vallabhacharya himself had lived in Banaras, as also Vitthal for certain periods, the intervening period had seen little *sampradaya* activity. It was due entirely to the efforts and energy of Girdharji that the Pushtimarg once again gained prestige in the area. It is reported that, during his lifetime, the merchants of the

[6] *Bharatendu samagra*: 'Srigirdharji ki badhai', 'Uttarardhabhaktmal', pp. 146 and 70.
[7] Entwistle 1987: 221–4.

surrounding bazaars agreed to pay to the temple five and a quarter annas out of every hundred rupees of their business transactions, and, though this practice was not so stringent after Girdharji's death, some continued with it at least till the beginning of the twentieth century.[8] It is further recorded that the most cordial mutual relations were obtained with the Vishvanath temple, the central institute of the city, and that on the festive occasions of that temple, in deference to the majesty of the deity, Girdharji sent offerings made by Mukundrayji, who then also donned the costume appropriate to the occasion.[9] Girdharji's activities were not confined to Banaras alone but extended also to the other cities of the East, even as far away as Hyderabad.[10]

It was by no means 'the men of the old school alone', as Sherring claimed, who were behind the resurgence of pious activity, but an interlinkage of newer structures of power with the old, however fervently they chose to invoke tradition.

II

Here I shall briefly recount and analyse the narrative structure of the Brajbhasha tract known as *Mukundrayji ki varta* in order to consider the machinations which made possible the establishment

---

[8] Radhakrishnadas 1904: 18.

[9] Raykrishnadas 1976: 10 notes that the *prasadi mala*, flower garland of Mukundrayji was sent every day to Vishvanath, who showed his regard to the deity by wearing it. On *vaikuntha chaturdashi* he even donned a *tulasi mala*. On *shiva ratri* Mukundrayji in his turn wore a *baghambari chimt ka bana*, an attire which resembled a tiger skin. In Kashi there is no getting past Vishvanath. The *Chaurasi vaishnavan ki varta* narrates the deeds of Seth Puroshottamdas of Kashi, who was so staunch a Vaishnava that he offered no obeisance elsewhere. Bisheshvar (Vishvanath) appeared to him in a dream and asked him, since he did not bother to maintain neighbourly ties (*gamw ko nato*), to at least let him partake of the *mahaprasad* that the Seth offered to his deity. One consequence of his resulting gratification at being so honoured was that Bisheshvar attended henceforth to the safety of the pious Seth and appointed Kal Bhairav himself as his personal watchman (62–3).

[10] Cf. Madhav Sarma in *Gosvami Srigiridharji maharaj dvishatabdi mahotsav smarika*, 1990: 13.

of the sixth *gaddi* of the *sampradaya*. The date of the composition of the *varta* has not been recorded. To judge by the style, and the detailed, precise, and intimate knowledge of Girdharji's actions and reactions that the narrator betrays, it seems likely that it was put to paper during Girdharji's own lifetime, and that in fact large stretches of it were dictated by him. It is possible that, during the course of the nineteenth century, handwritten copies, as is customary among pious Vaishnavas, were in circulation, for the *varta* is mentioned by writers at the turn of the nineteenth century.[11] It was published in Banaras in 1923, only to become unavailable shortly afterwards, and it was as late as 1984, at the time of a grand celebration of the *chhappanbhog* in Gopal Mandir, that it was reprinted again.

The chief protagonists of the narrative are Damodarji II of Nathdvara, known more familiarly as Dauji Maharaj, who lived from 1797 to 1826, and Girdharji Maharaj of Kashi, who lived from 1791 to 1840.

Dauji reigned during a period of political peace and financial prosperity, so that it was possible to erect buildings, cultivate the arts, and celebrate festivals with great fantasy and enthusiasm. He is reported to have spent the year 1821 performing a *duhera manorath*, i.e. commemorating each festival twice, so that the year consisted of uninterrupted revelry.[12] It was during his time that the festival of the seven *svarupas* was first celebrated with much pomp. James Tod, renowned for *The Annals and Antiquities of Rajasthan*, has left a description of Dauji which, in fact, complements the account of the *Varta*:

> The present pontiff is about thirty years of age. He is of a benign aspect, with much dignity of demeanour: courteous, yet exacting the homage due to his high calling: meek as becomes the priest of Govinda, but with the finished manners of one accustomed to the first society. His features are finely moulded, and his complexion good. He is about the middle size, though as he rises to no mortal, I could not exactly judge his height... In times of danger, like some of his prototypes in the dark ages of Europe, he poised the lance, and found it more effective than

[11] Radhakrishnadas 1904: 18.
[12] Cf. Ambalal 1987: 64–8.

spiritual anathemas, against those who would first adore the god and then plunder him . . . He rode the finest mares in the country; laid aside his pontificals for the quilted *dagla*, and was summoned to matins by the kettledrum instead of the bell and cymbal.[13]

It is this regal gesture and authority, but innocence regarding matters of ritual symbol and theology, which we meet again in the *varta*. And it is this regal posture which is preserved in the many fine paintings of the time, influenced by the courtly style of Kotah.[14]

After Dauji's early death, his widow Laksmibahuji, who was a sister of Girdharji's own spouse, assumed the powers traditionally due to the dowager and became thereby the object of much attention and cajoling.

Girdharji Maharaj of Kashi (Kashivare, as he was known in Nathdvara) was by all accounts an aesthete of powerful presence. His tasteful *shringaras*, adornment of the deity, created models which were remembered and preserved for posterity in the paintings of the period.[15] It is reported that in Nathdvara he often dressed as Yashoda, the mother of Krishna, draping his shawl like a sari over his head, as an expression of his devotion to the child-god. 'It is said, that to identify better with Yashoda, he allowed his hair to grow long like an Indian woman. One day, however, he failed to attend the *seva* in time, having taken too long to wash and comb his long hair. This pained him, and to atone for this, he had his long hair shaved.'[16]

Mukundrayji ki varta is divided into thirteen *vartas*, or *prasangas*, of unequal length. The narrative begins in Nathdvara with

[13] Tod 1920: 642–3.

[14] Ibid.: 66–7.

[15] Ambalal includes the painting depicting *Chandrama ka Shrngar* in his selection (111). I quote from his description of the *shringar*: 'The Moon and moonlight provide the inspiration for this *shringara*. Srinathji wears a shimmering *gherdar vagha* of silver brocade. Over his *pagha*, a *dohra katra*, double plume, is ornamented with a single pearl at each of its two ends. The *pichhvai* is deep blue and has a tiny crescent-shaped new moon of silver suspended at its top centre' (154).

[16] Ibid.: 154.

Girdharji's ascent to prominence and it ends, as is fitting, in Kashi. Though conceived of as a pious tract, it is much more in the nature of a confidential state document, moving almost entirely within the inner circles, the *bhitariyas* of the temple, and records their dealings. The power configurations earlier alluded to—the prince, the merchants, and the British—are present at strategic points in the narrative, though their mention in the *varta* is often brief.

The narrative is structured as follows:

1–3	the establishment of Girdharji's authority in Nathdvara
4	Girdharji asks for the *svarupa*
5	Interlude, journeys, negotiations, death of Dauji
6–7	Girdharji cajoles Bahuji into fulfilling his wish
8	establishment of the temple for his own *svarupa* in Nathdvara
9–10	departure preparations and negotiations
11	the journey to Kashi
12–13	the installation of the *svarupa* in Kashi

Certain aspects make the Varta strikingly demonstrate trends characteristic of the period. First, to display his learning, Girdharji chooses to emphasize the correspondence of Pushtimarg *seva* to Vedic sacrificial ritual. He does this by the time-honoured convention of establishing a link which serves at once to enhance authority while maintaining the adequacy, if not superiority, of the practice of his own *sampradaya* (*varta* 1–2).

Second, establishing links of this kind becomes, in fact, the source of Girdharji's own authority, the means by which he is able to manipulate his way through the intricate power structures operating within the temple. The description of scenes in which he finally pushes his way forward is remarkable for its clear appraisal of the situation and its minute registration of detail (*varta* 4).

Finally, it is only towards the tail end of the *varta*, when it is not of much consequence and no more crucial for the establishment of authority (though certainly for its perpetuation), that there is some direct experience of the deity, an experience so characteristic of the older *vartas*, when the *alaukika*, miraculous workings of the deity become apprehensible to a wider circle of *bhaktas* (*varta* 11).

1–3. The establishment of Girdharji's authority in Nathdvara

1. In 1822 Girdharji witnesses the festival of the seven *svarupas* celebrated by Dauji. He is morose, he thinks: 'My ancestor has no name in the house of Srinathji.' He begins to display his monumental knowledge of the practices of the *sampradaya*, correcting minute details of Srinathji's dress, pointing out the significance of ritual objects in his vicinity: so much so that the narrator protests his inability to record all these discussions, some of which he considers to be of a nature too esoteric to be thus disclosed.

2. The second *prasanga* is a continuation of just this kind of exposition, the symbolic significance of rituals and observances, explicated at times on the basis of personal associations but moving always within a familiar theological system, so that those around him obviously have no problem respecting his explanations. The narrator, as the invisible presence at the side of Girdharji, speaks almost with his voice. The usual narrative device consists of Dauji first putting a question, thereby giving Girdharji the opportunity to elaborate. Typical, for instance, is the following discourse:

> Annakuta is the *yajna* of the Pushtimarg. This has been revealed at great length by Srigosaimji [a reference to Vitthalnath, the founder of *seva* in the *sampradaya*]. This is the reason why, in the compilation *Namaratna*, Srigosaimji has the name *govardhanardrimakhakrta*, 'made by the sacrifice of the Govardhana mountain'. Hence he is called *yajna makha*, for he revealed the *yajna* of Govardhana. The following are the items required for [Vedic] *yajna*. A *yajna vedi* or sacrificial ground, the installation of fire, *yupa*, stakes, *mandapa*, a pavilion, *godan*, the presentation of a cow, *balidan*, a gift to the deity, the invocation of all the gods, the recitation of the Vedas, the devotion of the god usually worshipped, the cleansing ablution, the feeding of Brahmans, and other such are the items needed in a *yajna*. The following is the *yajna* of the Pushtimarg. It differs from *maryadamarg*, or the customary way. Just as in *yajna* there is the *vedi*, so here there is the *navcaukiya*, the *simhasan*, or the lion-throne. Just as there are lines engirdling all four sides of the *vedi*, here there are the three steps on all four sides of the *simhasan*, which are for the *bhavas*: *satva*, *rajas* and *tamas*. Then a fire receptacle

is required on the *vedi*, so here Thakurji, the lord himself, is enthroned. And what of the fire? Why, that is the mouth of Bhagvan. *Mukhato jayate vahni*. Fire emanates from the mouth. From this pronouncement it holds that where Bhagvan himself thrones, what need of fire? And in *yajna* stakes are installed. Call the pillars stakes, by way of which *svarga* is obtained. Here there are the four pillars of the *chandova*, canopy. These are the four posts. For Pushtimarg awards all four, *dharma, artha, kama, moksa*. And just as in *yajna* there is the pavilion, so here, above the throne, there is the canopy. In the canopy there are nine colours, so here, if one views them separately, there are the nine varieties of *bhaktas* and it is their *bhavas* which bear blossom. Just as in the canopy there are nine colours, so there are separate altars for the three kinds of *yajna* fire, *ahavaniya, garhapatiya* and *daksaniya*, so here the Lord himself resides and thus the separate altars have no function. And if there is the presentation of cows, here there is the play of cows. On the day of *hatadi*, or the divine market stall, the ears (of the cows) are awakened (they are made aware) so that on the day of Govardhan-worship they can be made to play. To give is subject to the will of the masters, here the *bhaktas* have hidden wishes. And the hidden *rasa* is attained when it is caused to be revealed, hence there is the play of cows here, both when the ears are awakened and when there is Govardhan-worship. And in *yajna* there is the cleansing ablution, so here Govardhan is washed. Why? Because here there is no difference between the worshipper and the worshipped. You are the worshipped in the form of Govardhan, and as Purushottam, you are the worshipper (7).[17]

A mixture of Vedic *yajna* and later *puja* ritual is contrasted and equated with the great festivals of the *sampradaya*, Govardhan Puja and Annakuta. Girdharji has displayed all the scholastic splendour of his learning with great dexterity.

3. There is a *shastrartha*, dispute, with Anantacharya, a follower of Ramanuja, who has humiliated the learned in the court of Udaipur, and has come to Nathdvara with similar intentions. He

[17] Vallabhacharya recognized the Vedas as the highest authority. However, the equating of Vedic sacrifice with *pushtimarg seva*, which had developed independently of it, serves to underline the heightened significance of the Vedic ritual as legitimizing ritual practice at this juncture. I am grateful to Catharina Kiehnle for helping me to elucidate the passage translated.

cannot outwit Girdharji, who caps his discourse with a volley of quotations from the *shastras* on the significance of the *tulsimala*, which Anantacharya has until now disdained to wear. From now on Girdharji is established as an authority in Nathdvara, and if Dauji has doubts, he turns to Girdharji.

4. *Girdharji asks for the* svarupa

4. He has finally acquired the position to risk the venture and ask for a *svarupa*. Apart from providing a fascinating glimpse of the kind of internal operations behind the benign *jhamki* of Srinathji the *varta* also gives us an impression of the battle of wills that now ensues regarding the question of authority and subversion of authority within the temple community. The following is a description typical for its minute observation of emotional action and reaction:

> In this manner, after he had examined him in all kinds of ways, it entered the mind of Sri Dauji Maharaj, that it was from him alone (Girdharji) that he would receive the *gopalamantra*. He resolved this in his mind. Then one day he said, what I ask of you now, tell me instantly, without first consulting books and compilations. Then Girdharji Maharaj said, I have the blessings of the feet of my guru, Sri Dvarikanathji Maharaj. He had asked me something one day, and I replied instantly, so he had been most delighted, and had blessed me, saying that if anyone queries you regarding the *shastras*, then you will respond with a thousand answers. When he heard this, Sri Dauji Maharaj was most delighted. After this, on the tenth day of the bright half of Magha, *samwat* 1879, on the day of the lunar eclipse, acclaiming it as a solemn occasion, he thought of receiving the *gopalamantra* from him. Upon this, some near relative said to Sri Dauji Maharaj, it is not proper to take the *gopalamantra* from him. If you have to take the *gopalamantra*, then it has been the tradition to take it from one's own self. Besides you have your own blood relatives, take it from them. But he did not agree to this. So the near relative went to Sri Dadiji Maharaj (the revered grandmother) and said that it is not proper to take the *gopalamantra* from him. So Sri Kamalabahuji sent for Sri Dadiji Maharaj and said this. She explained it to him in many different ways. But it would refuse to enter his mind. Then in the name of twenty-one of the Vallabha family, a missive was

placed before Srinathji. And the reply authorized Sri Girdharji Maharaj. Then he received the *gopalamantra* on the day of the eclipse. Then Sri Dauji Maharaj asked, what should I give you as *gurudaksina*. Upon this Sri Dadiji Maharaj observed, he will only take something *alaukika* (otherworldly) as *daksina*, he won't take *laukika* (worldly substance). When they heard this, all the near relatives became very silent. After some time had passed, he inquired again, what is this *alaukika* substance. Then Sri Girdharji Maharaj said, if I were to ask for it, you would not be able to part with it. Then Sri Dadiji Maharaj said, ask and I will give. Then he said, my ancestor had no name in the house of Srinathji. For my ancestor did not claim a *thakurji*. So let me have a single *svarupa* of the *thakurjis* who reside by the side of Srinathji. (15–16)

Dauji offers some resistance and puts forward theological arguments as to the impossibility of granting this wish. He is easily outwitted. Then Dauji asks him to keep the matter quiet; he will do the needful sometime when Dadiji is away. For he knows, and he says this with some anger, that Girdharji will not let go of him until this is done. So Girdharji decides to observe silence for a while.

Dadiji does leave town and Dauji is forced, for the present, to part with a *venu*, a flute of Srinathji, in order to represent his presence in Kashi and to provide protective company for the *svarupa*, which will follow one day, and for which, he is pressed into signing a document. Girdharji offers an unspecified amount of gold, which Dauji does not refuse.

He leaves the city and spends some time with the army of Maharaj Daulat Rao Sindhia. It is probable that he gets financial and political support from the Maratha chief, though there is no explicit mention of this. However, once back in Kashi, he is able to buy the haveli of Jairamdas Pansari for twice its value.

5. *Interlude, journeys, death of Dauji*

5. The fifth *prasanga* is a brief account of various journeys. There is much movement. Dauji goes to Calcutta, he stops on the way in Banaras, but Girdharji is himself on the move. Dauji expires in the Braj country. Shortly afterwards his widow, Laksmibahuji, summons Girdharji to Nathdvara. On the way Girdharji stops at

several key places, meets various personages of royal blood, allays their doubts and performs *seva*.

6–7. *Cajoling Bahuji into fulfilling his wish*

6. Bahuji is pleased with him in several ways, and is similarly pressed into signing a document. Like her late husband, she also allows him the right to perform several kinds of *seva*. In return, though she is a mere woman, she receives the *gopalamantra* from him.
7. Girdharji manages to secure a temple in the precincts of the Srinathji complex for his own *svarupa*. There is much festivity, but that night there is a pitched battle between his people and mixed Hindu–Muslim troops led by a Bhatt, who is not further identified. Girdharji has a vision of Srinathji himself, coming to his rescue with a *chakra*. It is as if seeing him the hostile troops flee. After some more negotiations, and the offer of further gifts, he finally manages to carry off both the tiny *svarupas* in triumph to the new temple. The *varta* records his immense gratification at being able to celebrate the ceremony of *rajbhog* with his own *svarupa*.

8. *Establishment of the temple for his own* svarupa

8. The eighth *prasanga* is an account of a riotous celebration of Annakuta and Govardhan Puja, with detailed descriptions of ritual, costume, and delicacies prepared for the delectation of Srinathji. Mukundrayji has come into his own.

9–10. *Departure preparations and negotiations*

9. Girdharji, after having spent a year thus in Nathdvara, prepares to depart. He asks for the traditional regalia (*pracin abharan*) of his own *svarupa*. Further Mukundrayji now possesses the hereditary retainers that a *svarupa* requires, all twenty-two of them (their names and their duties are inventoried). Girdharji meanwhile performs the most prestigious *sevas* in the temple. He is also gaining in stature as a prospective *tilakayat*. For the first time, a dream, important in the repertoire of the religiously

THE SIXTH GADDI OF THE VALLABHA SAMPRADAYA

empowered, is reported. Navnitapriyaji, the second most important image in the temple, chooses to communicate with him thus.

10. Once the question of departure comes up, and the problem of safety on the way, it is inevitable that the British come into play. The Adhikari of the temple asks the British Resident in Udaipur for protection and is graciously provided with a *chaprasi* (peon), and *farman* (letter of authorization). As regards finances, a banker is applied to, who only parts with cash after a *hundi* (promissory note) is put forward: this is from Lala Radhakrishnadas of Kashi, whose reliability as a pious Vaishnava is further confirmed by the Adhikari.

There is some commotion, once it is to be decided who will accompany the procession to Kashi. The retainers, one and all, refuse, for they are afraid that there will be violence (*upadrav*) when Mukundrayji actually leaves the temple premises.

11. *The journey to Kashi*

11. Bahuji Maharaj comes to the rescue and issues firm orders that all the necessary personnel must assemble. She threatens that if due respect is not shown to Girdharji, offenders will not be allowed to re-enter the village of Nathdvara. The train now consists of 600 armed soldiers, Hindus and Mlecchas, 23 wagons, big and small, 54 *moti ka bel* (?), 2 carpenters, 1 washerman, and 1 tailor. The journey commences each day after *rajbhoj*. It is like a bridal party. Musical instruments are procured on the way. They fear attack from a party of Bhil marauders, but by the grace of Mukundrayji, the attack is warded off and a real bridal party looted instead. In one of the overnight camps, the British Resident and the Rana of Kheda come to pay their respects. Several wonders, small and big, are recorded: Mukundrayji is flowering into a full-fledged deity, with his own choice taste and caprices. Thus for instance:

There was a tank on the way, where there was a huge tree. We rested the palanquin there in the shade of the afternoon. Suddenly a *nat* [acrobat] appeared, in order to perform a *tamasha* [show]. He sent word to the Maharaj. But Maharaj said it would cause delay. Give him something and send him off. So we gave him something and sent him away. Meanwhile, we prepared to leave. As the palanquin was lifted, it became heavy. Mukundrayji was pouting, just as a child who insists upon seeing a *tamasha*. The palanquin would not be lifted. So Maharaj-ji asked, what is going on. He thought: he wants to see the *nat* perform. So the *nat* was summoned straightaway and was made to perform. So there was quite a *tamasha*, and afterwards he was well rewarded. Only after the *nat* departed could the palanquin be lifted. He performed many such *balalilas* on the way. How far can one write it down? (33)

Thus an incident typical of Vaishnava *vartas*, the personal experience of the deity, occurs towards the end of the narrative. Once they reach the vicinity of Kashi, the city's fabulously wealthy banker Harakhchand is summoned and told to make preparations for the reception in the city.

12–13. The installation of the svarupa *in Kashi*

12. There is a brief account of the arrival in Kashi, with Harakhchand heading the reception, the colourful procession through town, the elephants, the guns, the soldiers, the gaily attired Vaishnava *jan*, the singing women, the shower of rupees, the rituals, till finally Mukundrayji arrives in the house of Girdharji.
13. Finally all three, Srinathji's *venu*, Mukundrayji, and the older image Gopallalji receive *rajbhoj* together. A dream incident has already warned Girdharji's mother into taking care that a *dhvaja* (banner) is installed over the sanctum (*nij mandir*). Asked by a banker *bhakta* about what kind of bhakti, devotional attitude, he would prescribe, Girdharji lays down that Gopallal is to be served with *pitr bhava* (paternal devotion) and Mukundrayji with *pati bhava* (marital devotion). The elaborate devotional ritual in the temple is carried out faithfully and the deity thus fully installed.

Thus, of the thirteen *vartas*, three are concerned with Girdharji demonstrating his prowess in Nathdvara, the fourth involves a testing of his lately gained power, the fifth is a bare account of strategic manoeuvres and, with the death of Dauji, a temporary power vacuum. The sixth and seventh *vartas* are further exercises of power, this time with Laksmibahuji, the eighth records the final triumph over opposing forces in Nathdvara, and the establishment of his own temple. The ninth and tenth show the process of extraction of the deity from the intricate weave of the temple complex. Only in the eleventh is there some record of the impact of the deity Mukundrayji, whose *varta* it ostensibly is. The last two *vartas*, the twelfth and the thirteenth, repeat the festive ritual of Nathdvara in Kashi, coming full circle, as it were.

III

I will attempt a preliminary comparison between this nineteenth-century *varta* and the mainstream *varta* literature of the Vallabha *sampradaya*, in that I consider the perspective and the ambience of the *vartas* as well as their overall direction. Inevitably, the generalizations involve some simplification.

Apart from the *vartas*, contained in the well-known collections *Chaurasi Vaishnavan ki varta* and *Do sau bavan Vaishnavan ki varta*, which focus on the exemplary lives of single *bhaktas*, and concern themselves with some aspects either of their original moment of conviction by Acharyaji or Gosaimji, or other edifying incidents in their lives, there are *vartas* which are in the nature of more general accounts. These are narrations of the evolution and consolidation of the faith along with the history of the Vallabha clan, which are centrally connected with this development. As a prototype of this last variety, I take the *Srinathji prakatya ki varta*, which chronicles and elucidates the history of the *sampradaya* from its very inception— the manifestation of Srinathji, the flight from the persecution by Aurangzeb—to the settlement, under the protection of the Rana of Udaipur, in the village in the Vindhya hills known henceforth as Nathdvara.[18] Here, as in our Varta, there are negotiations and

---

[18] See Tandan 1960 for detailed information on the first two mentioned *vartas*, and Barz 1976 for his useful introduction. Vaudeville's analysis (1980) of *Srinathji prakatya ki varta* remains exemplary.

journeys, yet the whole consists of short episodes and the perspective changes constantly. The listener moves from person to person and from landscape to landscape, but, most important of all, the deity can communicate directly with the people of Braj and, primarily through the medium of dreams, ask that his own needs and caprices be attended to, which he can reward generously and in very concrete ways. He can also intervene directly in their lives and perform miracles. It is simple in language and is directed primarily towards the faithful. Though the Gosvamis, as patriarchs, have dealings with the highest political personages, the tone remains colloquial, didactic, and edifying. In his study of the *varta* literature Hariharnath Tandan has noted as typical characteristics of the older *vartas*: 'There is as much variety in the subject matter of the *varta* as there is in the various portrayals (*charitra*). No difference has been made with regard to caste and rank, male–female, high–low, rich–poor, and if one were to count, then people of ordinary rank will be found in larger numbers. From this point of view, the *varta* literature is a thing of ordinary folk, and is connected to the literature of the people.'[19]

By contrast, our *varta* moves almost entirely in the world of the Gosvamis, within their orbit of power: they have no need of dealing with the lowly, and there is no mention of them apart from their function as retainers. Srinathji in so far as there is any need to consult him, communicates directly with the Gosvamis. His presence is confined to *nij mandir* (the inner sanctum): the Braj countryside is symbolically represented by the temple complex itself. The negotiations are confined to figures of power, the language is correspondingly measured, and none come up for explicit criticism. Even the Bhattji who leads the armed attack is neither located for us in the temple hierarchy nor further mentioned. In fact, people are only mentioned when they react to Girdharji's moves. Similarly, the machinations of the others are registered and recorded only if they affect Girdharji. The perspective is thus almost entirely confined to that of Girdharji himself. The camera moves along with him, so to speak, viewing the surroundings almost entirely from his angle of

[19] Tandan 1960: 53.

vision, in terms of his particular need of the moment, and focusing on the persons he has dealings with.

The need of political and financial protection involves delicate negotiations with the Marathas, and with the princes of the adjoining Rajput states ruling under the aegis of the British. And all-important is the patronage of the merchants who make maintenance of the establishment in Banaras possible. Their interests in the link are apparent—apart from the prestige attached, and the opportunity to gain public approval for their largesse and piety, there is the solidarity which is generated within their own community, and which is commemorated with each festivity in the temple. It is no coincidence that Girdharji buys a haveli and establishes himself in the midst of the residential and commercial area of the Naupatti Mahajans, Lala Radhakrishnadas's support is available at a decisive juncture, which makes the move out of Nathdvara possible, Harakhchand finances the festivities to welcome the deity in Banaras and organizes the further maintenance of the temple complex. These classes of people are present in the older *vartas*, but as so many *bhaktas* amongst the *bhaktas*, and they tend to speak and are spoken of in the same familiar idiom as the people. If they do not comply with the wishes of the deity, they are often shown as humbled for some didactic end. In *Mukundrayji ki varta* they are present as part of a power constellation, which provides the givens of the situation; apart from offering their power and wealth as part of their devotion, they are not themselves affected by the deity in any noticeable way.

The means of establishing authority, as Girdharji so ably demonstrates, is the knowledge of the most minute details of ritual and ornamentation, a science that has become so rarefied and at times so pedantic that the practitioners themselves display perplexity when asked to explain the significance of a precise sequence. When this knowledge is blessed with the appropriate genealogical connections, for Girdharji is a descendant of Yadunath, it is still possible to influence and extend the prevailing hierarchies. The hagiography here becomes an account of sacral power and the authority this bestows. This is in sharp contrast to the source of authority in the older *vartas*, where it is also possible to wield power and receive due acknowledgement from the community if there has been direct experience of the deity, whether in person or in a dream.

The only concession that is made to the general *varta* style is towards the end, in the eleventh *varta*, when Mukundrayji assumes the characteristics of the whimsical child god who would buy certain items and reject others. This does indeed establish a link, however tenuous, to the vast corpus of Vaishnava *varta* literature, well known to the pious.

Mukundrayji ki varta is essentially a document of the nineteenth century which, amongst other notable features in the attempt to establish the elaborate series of equations with Vedic sacrifice, testifies to an awareness of the need to establish links with an authoritative canon. This points to the developments later in the century, when Hinduism consolidated itself increasingly by various integrative devices, one of the most effective being that of providing the overall umbrage of the Vedas, in order to absorb traditions and *sampradayas*, which both differed and overlapped. On the whole, with *Mukundrayji ki varta* we have moved a long way from the pious tracts that comprise the early *vartas*. Our *Varta* has all the restraint and the diplomacy of a confidential state document, a recitation of the machinations and manoeuvres of Girdharji Maharaj, who caters for and reflects the concerns of newer constellations of power, namely the 'princes, pandits, banyas and priests' invoked in Sherring's book—some of a vintage newer than they would care to acknowledge—operating in tandem with older institutions of power.

References

Ambalal, Amit, 1987. *Krishna as Shrinathji. Rajasthani Paintings from Nathdvara.* Ahmedabad: Mapin Publishing.

Barz, Richard, 1976. *The Bhakti Sect of Vallabhacharya,* Faridabad: Thomson Press.

Bayly, C.A., 1978. 'Indian Merchants in a Traditional Setting: Benares 1780–1830', in *The Imperial Impact: Studies in the Economic History of Africa and India,* ed. Clive Dewey and A.G. Hopkins. London: Institute of Commonwealth Studies.

———, 1981, 'From Ritual to Ceremony: Death Ritual and Society in Hindu North India since 1600', in *Mirrors of Mortality: Studies in*

the Social History of Death, ed. Joachim Whaley. London: Europa Publications.
Chaurasi Vaishnavan ki varta, ed. Dvarikadas Parikh. *Samvat* 2027. Mathura: Sri Govardhan Granthmala Karyalay.
Entwistle, A.W., 1987. *Braj. Centre of Krishna Pilgrimage.* Groningen: Egbert Forsten.
Glasenapp, Helmuth von, 1934. 'Die Lehre Vallabhacaryas', *Zeitschrift fur Indologie und Iranistik*, 9, 3, 268–30.
Gosvami-Srigiridharji maharaj dvishatabdi mahotsav smarika, 1990. Ed. Lakshmi Shankar Vyas. Varanasi: Bharatnarayan Gupt Sudhadvatta Japa-yajna Samiti.
Harishchandra, 1987. *Bharatendu samagra*: 'Srigirdharji ki badhai', 'Uttarardhabhaktmal', pp. 146 and 70. Ed. Hemant Sarma. Varanasi: Hindi Pracharak Samsthan.
Motichandra, 1962. *Kashi ka itihas*. 2nd ed. Varanasi: Vishvavidyalay Prakashan.
Radhakrishnadas, 1904. *Bharatendu babu harishcandra ka jivan carit*. Repr. Lucknow: Hindi Samiti, Uttar Pradesh Shasan, 1976.
Raykrishnadas, 1976. 'Bharatendu samsmaran 1', *Dharmayug*, 29 August, 10–12.
Sherring, M.A., 1868. *Benares. The Sacred City of the Hindus: An Account of Benares in Ancient and Modern Times.* Repr. Delhi: B.R. Publishing Corporation, 1975.
Srimukundrayji ki varta tatha Srigopallaji ki varta (first pub. *samvat* 1980). Ed. Pandit Ramnathji Shastri. Varanasi: Ramdas Agraval, *samvat* 2041.
Tandan, Hariharnath, 1960. *Varta sahitya, ek vrhat adhyayan*. Aligarh: Bharat Prakashan Mandir.
Thiel Horstmann, Monika, 1990. 'Jai Singh II (1688–1745) Hinduherrscher in einer Wendezeit', Antrittsvorlesung, Universitat Bamberg 19. February.
Tod, James, 1920. *Annals and Antiquities of Rajasthan, or, the Central and Western Rajput States of India*, 3 vols, ed. with an Introduction by William Crooke. Repr. Delhi: Motilal Banarasidass, 1971.
Vaudeville, Charlotte, 1980. 'The Govardhan Myth in Northern India', *Indo-Iranian Journal* 22, 1–45.

9

The Modernity of Tradition

Harishchandra of Banaras and the Defence of Hindu Dharma

CENTRAL TO THE RITUAL OF MOST *SAMPRADAYAS*, THE communities which were to collectively subsume themselves under the category 'Hindu' in the course of the nineteenth century, was the traditional practice of *murtipuja*, or image-worship. When Hinduism as a whole came under siege, it was this practice which most often and consistently came under attack, initially from Christian missionaries, but then increasingly also from the leaders of newer trends within Hinduism—for if Hinduism was to claim a 'modern' status, this was the tradition which first needed to be discontinued or justified in a way which did justice to the needs of the times. This did indeed begin to happen by the end of the nineteenth century. It was no longer left largely to the pandits, regarded as wholly traditional, to defend the practice. There was a wider-based move to re-establish tradition, for which the term 'modernization' seems wholly appropriate, if modernization is understood as an operation which entails a process of alteration and improvement of what is basically an older and already existing institution or system in order to accord better with contemporary conditions.[1] The revalidation—which I see as one central response

[1] This is less a definition of the term than an attempt to circumscribe its actual usage. Cf. Williams 1983: 208–9.

in the debate with the missionaries and with the newer formations which claimed to speak for all of Hinduism—came from Kashi, which regarded itself as the centre of authority for all matters regarding religion and surely also 'tradition' in the widest sense. The person who best exemplified this old/new tradition was Harishchandra (1850–85), the city's prime literary figure, educationist, publicist, and patron of the arts, well ensconced within the ranks of the city's merchant aristocracy.

In matters of religion, Harishchandra spoke as a follower of Vallabhacharya, as a Vaishnava, and as a Hindu. The strategies which he deployed in making his representations were determined in part by the nature of the challenge issued but also by considerations as to how the different *sampradayas* which together came to constitute modern Sanatana Dharma could be represented as a cohesive whole. *Murtipuja* remained a pivotal issue in this debate, which of necessity centred around the valorization of tradition. I shall follow the debate around this single strand since, both in attacking as well as in justifying this immemorial practice, the issues concerned crystallized most clearly.

There is no need to re-establish that *murtipuja* had come under vicious attack from Christian missionaries. It was one of their favourite means of demolishing the claims of Hinduism as they understood it. However, to briefly recall the tone of the invective, I will quote one example from Banaras in the second half of the century.

The Benares Institute had originally been established in 1861 by 'English-speaking native gentlemen', as they designated themselves, to exchange information and views for which there was no other collective forum. The issues varied: the fruits of Orientalist research, knowledge of antiquity, social reform, education, literature, philosophy, and the arts. Harishchandra himself became a member early on. The Institute's activities had been substantially expanded in 1864: not only were Europeans permitted membership for the first time, they were also allowed to take over much of the organizational activity. It was here that a lecture was delivered in defence of Hinduism and specially of image-worship, printed anonymously in 1867 under the pen-name 'A Hindoo'. It occasioned an indignant response by

James Kennedy, who summarily brushed aside all that the lecturer could offer by way of defence:

> 'A Hindoo' rests his main defence of Hindooism on its being a symbolical and representative religion. Here we are on a ground where we can see each other, and where the questions between us can be brought to an issue. That can be neither symbolised nor represented, which is incapable of being conceived in any degree. There is then an objective reality in religion, which can be in some measure brought within the reach of our minds, and to the realisation of which we are helped by symbol and representation. In order to this end being secured it is indispensable that the symbol be such as at once to make more plain and impressive the object symbolised. The symbol must be simple, directly suggestive of the object, and worthy of it. If the symbol be complicated, laden with details, unsuggestive of the object, and mean in its features, it obscures and degrades what it proposes to explain and adorn. Far better to have no symbols at all, than unintelligible or unworthy symbols.
>
> ... Our Hindoo friends, you must allow us, if we speak the truth, to express our thorough conviction ... We have seen the weary traveller bow down before some rudely carved stone, and we have wondered what he could find in it to raise his heart to God. We have seen the sick and sorrowful, imploring relief from the gods they supposed to dwell in these stony forms. We have been in some of your most sacred temples, and have there seen the images, which from day to day receive the homage of thousands. We cannot think that any of yourselves will maintain, that tried by the standard of human taste these images are beautiful, or suggestive of intellectual and moral qualities. The beauty and unearthly grandeur, which the Greek sculptors succeeded in imparting to their statues, have been beyond the reach of your artists, doubtless in great degree because they have been beyond the reach of your Pundits.
>
> 'A Hindoo' says, 'It is not the image that we worship as the Supreme Being, but the omnipresent Spirit that pervades the image as he pervades the whole universe.'
>
> We suppose this defence is as old as image-worship itself. To such worship there has always been a strong tendency, and yet it appears so absurd, that thoughtful and intelligent men must find something to explain it away. Whatever plausible argument may be advanced for image-worship, we believe if history teaches anything, it teaches, that such worship materialises and debases the human mind, gives most

unworthy views of God, and in the case of the vast majority leads to a fetishism, which in principle is identical with that of the most barbarous tribes. Till India rises above this idolatry, she will never have her proper place in the world. The enlightened among you would be much better engaged in denouncing it, than in bolstering it up with worn out and sophisticated arguments.[2]

If the grounds for the rejection of image-worship were on the one hand aesthetic and moral ('rudely carved stone', 'materialises and debases the mind', 'unworthy'), on the other hand reason ('thoughtful and intelligent men') clearly spoke against the practice. Characteristic was the patronizing tone against the intellectual pretensions of those who had newly mastered English and sought to wield the weapons of the enlightened.

The missionary stance was widely registered. However, since the missionaries stood entirely and uncompromisingly outside the Hindu theological system and condemned it as altogether untenable, it was not with them that the defenders of tradition carried out their debate but with those within the Hindu fold who seemed to adopt a missionary attitude, and it was here that issues concerning the constitution of canonical authority and the legitimation of tradition were thrashed out. For our purposes, the frame of reference is provided most conveniently by the writings of Rammohun Roy, who was not only one of the earliest in the field but who also enunciated the issues concerned most clearly. Four instances were to crystallize as determining this debate.

First, there was the question of scriptural authority, for as Rammohun had specified as early as 1817: 'The validity of theological controversy chiefly depends upon Scriptural authority, but when no authority is offered, the public may judge how far its credibility should extend.'[3] Scriptural authority for Rammohun meant the Vedas as interpreted by the Upanishads and Upanishadic thought as developed by Vedanta philosophers, foremost among them Shankara. Since the Upanishads were authoritative, there was no effort to account for the

[2] Kennedy 1874: 198–201.
[3] Roy 1817: 101–26.

many gods of the Vedas, which were then also seen as propagating monotheism; Rammohun made no distinction between monism and monotheism. Polytheism for Rammohun was propagated by later texts such as the Puranas and the Tantras:

> Are all these peculiar gods the great Brahmu, or do you call only one of them so? In either case your opinion is unfounded. For if each is to be regarded as the supreme Brahmu, then the assertions of the Vedas are false, which speak everywhere of one Brahmu only. And to admit many independent Brahmus, would be also contrary to reason; for if there are five or ten independent Brahmus, then it must be granted that each of them is possessed of the power of creating, preserving and destroying . . . to consider only one of them as Brahmu is contrary to the Shasters and to reason; for as the Poorans speak of one fictitious personage which they call Brahmu, thus they speak in other places of several other fictitious personages which they likewise call Brahmu; now to consider a fiction which occurs in one place of a book, as truth, and not to consider that a fiction which occurs in other places of the same book, is altogether inconsistent. (69)[4]

The second issue, then, was that of the validity of later scriptural tradition. Rammohun rejected the Puranas vigorously. He was caustic about worshippers of Vishnu, and even more so about the ecstatic religion of Chaitanya:

> It is said, both in the Poorans and Tantras, that when Vyasa was dishonoured in Kashee (Benares), he was enraged, and endeavoured to build a Kashee to be called after his name. From that time he began to write various falsehoods in the Poorans, in order to deprive the Shasters of Sheeva of their authority, and to injure his great reputation . . . It

---

[4] This and the following citations from Rammohun Roy stem from his *Dialogue between a Theist and an Idolater* which was printed under a pseudonym and appeared first in 1820, both in a Bengali version and an English translation under his own name. It was widely discussed and the Bengali version was reprinted several times, right up to the middle of the nineteenth century. An abridged version was published by the Tattvabodhini Sabha in 1846, to be reprinted again in 1866. The views propagated in the tract were thus to remain long in circulation. Page references are to Stephen N. Hay's edition (Calcutta, 1963).

THE MODERNITY OF TRADITION

is singular too, that the devotees of Vishnoo never bring forward proofs of their religious systems from the universally renowned ten Oopnishads, the Vedas, the Vedanta, the Nyay and other four Darshans, and the celebrated eighteen Shmreetes of Manoo and others, and the very celebrated Mahabharat, because these contain nothing of their Joogalbhajan and the two brethren. Moreover, in order to establish their system, they bring forward false assertions from those Poorans and Tantras, whose real design cannot be discovered and which are not renowned in the world, and which are also without commentaries. But learned men will never embrace a system which does not agree with the celebrated Shasters. (116–17)

The third issue was the validity of the tradition established by the forefathers in ritual and social conduct. Rammohun rejected them for their changeability and inconsistency, in fact on the same grounds as he rejected the Puranas. He accused his contemporaries of wilfulness: rather than selecting those practices of their forefathers which could genuinely exercise a model contemporary function, they chose to follow those that suited them:

That is very strange, that you drag forward the name of your forefathers, in order to defend your playing with images, whereas in all other matters, whether secular, or spiritual, you pay very little regard to their manner of life. We know, there are thousands among you, whose forefathers were devoted to the practice of meritorious works, and to the study of the sacred sciences; whereas they themselves, in perfect opposition to the habits of their forefathers, give themselves altogether up to worldly pursuits, and are serving foreigners; and if any make his fortune among them, he is spoken of as the chief of the family ... Some whose forefathers were devotees of the female deities, or Bamacharees, are become devotees of Vishnoo, or rather followers of Choitanya. On the other hand, many whose forefathers were devotees of Vishnoo, are now devoted to the worship of female deities ... Many whose forefathers made merchandise with their daughters, in consequence of their having become rich, marry now their daughters to Cooleens (Brahmins of the highest cast), whereby they ennoble their family. You see accordingly, that in every other respect you deviate from the customs of your forefathers; only if you are exhorted to worship the supreme God, you defend yourselves with the name of your forefathers as with a shield ... 'Why do you not practise the worship of Brahmu, which is enforced in all the Shasters, though it has been neglected by your forefathers? Namely, why do you neglect the worship of Brahmu, which is commanded every where in the Vedas, Poorans, Shmreetees, and Tantras, and waste your time in worshipping idols?' (88– 9)

Further, not only had these forebears constantly changed their allegiance to deities, they had at various periods chosen to consider a variety of ancient personages as sages. Rammohun, then, polemicized against the heterogeneity of tradition, for he saw the manifold strands of it negating each other:

> Thus persons of different sects consider different men as pious. But the religious sentiments of these pious men belonging to different sects are very much at variance with each other. Now must we indeed consider all these as pious men, and embrace their discordant sentiments? Or must we regulate our conduct with respect to religion according to the Shasters? The truth is, to the name of pious men the following are entitled: Manoo, Jagyabalkya, Bashisht'ha, Gotam, Vyasa, and similar men; these approved only the worship of the supreme God, as I have shown before. (91)

Fourth, there was the role of reason, which at least in the later Hindi literature was often represented as *buddhi*, as the criterion for determining the validity of tradition. Rammohun frequently evoked the testimony of 'reason' as the final instance in discounting traditional ritual and worship:

> But what can be more melancholy than that children of men, to whom God has given the power of judging what is good and evil, right and wrong, if they are asked, why they give themselves up to such a line of conduct, whereby they make themselves the laughing-stock in this world, and do themselves exceedingly great injury in that which is to come, viz., why they consider as spiritual worship, and practise accordingly such things as these: snapping their fingers on the mouth . . . striking each other at certain festivals, and singing exceedingly disgusting and obscene songs; and why they reproach God by describing him as guilty of theft, deceit, voluptuousness, anger, covetousness, and similar crimes, should not be able to assign any reason for their conduct, but should only answer, like such sheep and camels and other unreasonable beasts. 'Our forefathers did so, and therefore we do likewise.' (94–5)

It was reason which accounted for the credibility of men in the modern world, and it was its lack that made them the general laughing stock. In effect, then, all that could be considered as constituting tradition as a continuum, that is, later scriptural texts and the practice of the forefathers, was rejected as anachronistic. All that came after the Vedas, which constituted the first and foremost canonical authority, had to be carefully screened and scrutinized by reason.

A similarly severe stand regarding developments in later tradition was taken by the Arya Samaj, which was equally rigorous in its rejection of image-worship, though the language used by Dayanand Sarasvati was stronger and more abusive. Of the many reasons which Dayanand gave for discarding idol-worship, one was that it was a sign of 'mutually antagonistic beliefs and practices' which 'create bad blood in the country and lead it to its ruin.'[5] Dayanand, then, also saw heterogeneity as so many deviations from a singular authority constituted by the Veda. Like the missionaries, he was censorious of the multiple Hindu gods. Krishna fared especially ill at his hands, but the followers of Vallabhacharya had it doubly difficult. Their elaborate *seva* was nothing if not the most refined form of image-worship centred on a celebration of the pranks of this most rakish of deities. As his biographer has recorded, Dayanand himself considered the neo-Vedantins, as he called them, and the Vallabhacharyas to be his two chief opponents.[6] He had written two pamphlets against them, apart from attacking them ferociously, as was his wont, in his *Satyarth Prakash* (Light of Truth).[7] In chapter 11, 'On an Examination of the Different Religions Prevailing in Aryavarta (India)', he devoted considerable space to the malpractice and beliefs of the Vallabhacharyas, though he began with a round condemnation of the Vaishnavas as a whole, who, he proclaimed, were worse than the Shaktas and the Shaivas since they did not believe in the teachings of the Vedas.[8]

[5] Dayanand 1883/1984: 380.
[6] Jordens 1978: 101.
[7] First published in Hindi in 1875, rev. edn. 1883. I have cited from the 1984 reprint of the nineteenth-century English translation.
[8] Ibid.: 365.

Dayanand dissected and dismembered the *Bhagavata Purana* in his characteristically authoritative manner, discredited the traditions of the Shri Vaishnavas, finally to dwell at some length on the doings of the Gokul Gosains,[9] epitomes of lechery and greed of the utter decadence of the Vallabhacharyas. He had of course the countrywide reverberations of the Maharaja Libel Case to support his accusations: 'It is worth remembering', he admonished, 'that this sect was founded in falsehood and hypocrisy.'[10] In short, the later scriptures, gurus, pandits, and forefathers had no place in *satyartha* (religious truth).

In Banaras the response to the challenge issued by the Arya Samaj was taken up amongst others by the Dharma Sabha, which had been organized by the Maharaja of Banaras in the late 1860s. The Sabha considered itself expert in all ritual matters. It consisted of pandits whose authoritative knowledge of the various Shastras was widely recognized in the city, but also of other notables, the executive secretary of the Sabha being none other than Harishchandra. In the early 1870s Harishchandra extended his authority in religious matters by means of the tracts he published and the journals he edited; *Kavivacansudha* and the later *Harishchandrachandrika* quickly established a powerful reputation in the Hindi-speaking region. In these journals he published his translations of Sanskrit devotional texts, of the *Shandilya* and *Narada-bhakti sutras*, besides taking a public stand on a number of religious issues. He also drew his authority from the association that he founded and headed, the Tadiya Samaj (1873), which propagated theological and social solidarity amongst the various Vaishnava *sampradayas*. The three features which crystallized in his writings and activities were: (1) Vaishnava monotheism as the most ancient and authentic strand of the long tradition which constituted Sanatana Dharma; (2) Devotional *bhakti* as the overarching principle which could subsume all deviating traditions, since *jnana* or *buddhi* played only a subsidiary role in the relationship to and realization of God; and finally (3) Image-worship as a central feature of Vaishnava bhakti and as forming the one common denominator for all manner of Hindu *sampradayas*.

[9] Ibid.: 450–60.
[10] Ibid.: 451.

The continuous debate called for by the challenge issued by the missionaries and the Arya Samaj was to lead to a consolidation of the conviction that the devotion to a single, personally accessible, and iconically represented god was a central feature of Sanatana Dharma. For what he considered the overruling importance of Vaishnava monotheism in determining this tradition, Harishchandra found the support not only of Orientalists, such as Albrecht Weber and Monier Williams in the evidence they gleaned from the older literature in Sanskrit, but also of officials-turned-antiquarians. These included men such as George Grierson and F.S. Growse, known for the similar representations they found in the later devotional literature in the vernacular, which they considered as hovering near the kind of monotheism the missionaries proclaimed as characteristic of Christianity. However, image-worship was to remain the one essentially distinguishing factor, from both the Arya and Brahmo Samaj, as well as from Christianity. Nearer home, Harishchandra had the writings of Rajendralal Mitra as indigenous Orientalist and secretary of the Asiatic Society actively to advocate the antiquity and authenticity of Vaishnava monotheism as the only true religion of the Hindus.

The emphasis on image-worship had many implications. For one, it allowed immense diversity once the principle underlying its legitimation was granted, since the arguments which were to be brought forward in its favour were based on the longevity of the practice, the place given to it in the post-Vedic scripture, and the respect thus due to it rather than any one theological tradition. If the personal god could be worshipped as an image, the diversity became irrelevant; it was merely one of several ways, which all pointed to the one god.

The debate with Dayanand Sarasvati centred on this issue and was of long standing in Kashi. Several accounts of the famous *shastrartha* which set the discussion in motion are available. For us, the one in circulation among the pandits themselves is the most relevant, since it represents their perception of the event.[11] It took place in the

---

[11] The debate was documented and printed in the contemporary Sanskrit monthly journal *Pratnakampranandini*, on the basis of which a Hindi tract

autumn of 1869 in the Anandbagh of the Raja of Amethi and was presided over by the *Kashi naresh* (the Maharaja of Banaras) and his head pandit, Taracharan Tarkaratna Bhattacharya. In effect it was an extended version of the conventions of the Dharma Sabha. There were several pandits, but two had been specially appointed to accost the challenge: one was Swami Visuddhanand Sarasvati and the other the equally well known and erudite Bal Shastri. Harishchandra, attended by his younger brother, also graced the occasion, alongside other notables. The line of argument as presented by the pandits is important for understanding the traditional response to such a challenge, since it is also part of the process of the evolution of Harishchandra's own thinking. The debate centred around *murtipuja*. The question, as posed at the outset by Dayanand, was whether it had been legitimized by the Vedas. Dayanand maintained that only that which was found in the Vedas was to be considered authentic. Pandit Taracharan was the first to put the question of whether there was any passage in the Veda, or for that matter in the Srutis and the *Manusmrti*—which formed a part of the Vedic canon for the Swami—which denied the status of the Smrtis, Puranas, and Itihasa, in short, whether the Vedas themselves expressly denied the validity

---

entitled *Sachcha Kashi shashtrartha* by Mathuraprasad Diksit was published in 1916 and reprinted in 1969 and 1972. It is the account based on this tract which is available in Upadhyaya 1985: pt II, 37–42. Jordens 1978: 68 sums up the Arya Samaj version: 'The available records of the proceedings, one by the Swami himself and the other by a Bengal pandit, show that Dayanand kept the attacks of his opponents at bay with great self-assurance and competence. He had a constant struggle to bring the pandits back to the precise topic, "that idol worship is or is not taught in the scriptures", and no pandit managed to produce conclusive proof for their side. Then the end came quite suddenly. One pandit read a text to the Swami, who did not recognize the passage and asked to inspect the manuscript. He was handed the leaflet and started to examine it in silence. As he was doing so, the pandits rose in unison and declared the Swami defeated . . . There is no doubt that the sudden closure of the debate and the proclamation of Dayanand as the loser was a mischievous act on the part of the pandits, who could not afford to come out the losers in that citadel of orthodoxy.'

of later tradition, for only then could all that followed be considered *vedaviruddha* (contrary to the Vedas). To this Dayanand said all that which was not in the Vedas was *vedaviruddha*. Taracharan could only respond rather sardonically with another question which was to remain unanswered: *Yah ved ka kathan hai athava srimanji ka kathan hai?* ('Is this the pronouncement of the Veda or that of your esteemed self?')

The issue was the recognition of later tradition as germinating in the old, thus legitimizing it. Were the Puranas, as also later philosophy, including Vedanta, to be recognized as authoritative or not? Dayanand was cornered into admitting that the *nirakara* Brahman of the Vedantins comprised the knowledge of the Vedas, and their mutual knowledge of each other. This admission could be shown to lead to several contradictions, if one took either Vedantic philosophy or the Vedas seriously and expected each to be consistent in itself. The learning of the pandits, their tricks and turns in argument, were not to be easily matched, and by a series of steps Dayanand was reduced to silence. He lost, but his was a forceful personality which was not going to be silenced. The Kashi pandits were subjected to repeated confrontations with his way of thinking. This also led to the crystallization of the Sanatana standpoint with regard to the key issues mentioned above.

Harishchandra published a tract entitled *Dushanmalika* (Garland of Censure) in the following year (1870) which strung together sixty-four counterarguments, formulated as a series of tripping questions.[12] The fifty-ninth and sixtieth questioned the legitimacy of only choosing to recognize some strands of *parampara* (tradition) while discounting the rest on the evidence of *buddhi* alone:

> 59. Say what evidence there is and what argument can be brought forward in support [of the claim] that all the books of the Veda

[12] The full title of the tract was *Murtipujan ka nishedh karnevale Dayanand prabhavit logom ke gale ki dushanmalika*: 'a garland of censure for the neck of the likes of Dayanand and all such who negate image-worship'. The full text of the tract is available in Brajratnadas 1954: 689–98. The translation of this and other Hindi quotations that follow is my own.

and all their mantras are still the same as those which emanated from Ishvara and that since such an age their form has not changed and that they have retained the rishis' very same syllables and that no one has since interpolated mantras of their own making.

60. If you were to say that they have been handed down by *parampara* [tradition], then in the case of the Vedas, tradition is to be decisive, but the image-worship which has [also] been handed down by tradition is not similarly to be recognized. What kind of evidence is that and if you were to say, by virtue of our own *buddhi* we recognise that these are the very same Vedas, then what evidence is there that your *buddhi* is in order and what argument to support it?

Harishchandra was clearly putting forward the same arguments as those which had come up during the great *shastrartha*. If tradition sanctified and was itself the prime evidence, what made it possible for the Arya Samaj to reject such a central strand of it as *murtipuja*? When it came to the precise transmission of the Vedas, it was accepted as self-evident that tradition had preserved the exact and unchanged order of words as issuing from the mouth of the rishis; but when it came to other traditionally handed-down practice such as *murtipuja*, extraneous factors, such as the operations of *buddhi*, were also brought to bear on the issue of whether this was to be recognized as tradition at all. Such a procedure nullified, in effect, the very concept of tradition.

The violent rejection of image-worship, issued as a persistent challenge to the *Sanatanadharm avalambi*, continued to provoke a constant a denial of it. As late as 1876, when Harishchandra had fairly evolved his position, an editorial in the *Kavivacansudha* could be entitled *Murti puja kya pap hai*? (Is image-worship a sin?').[13] The piece had obviously been provoked by the presence of the Swami in Kashi, who had convened a public meeting in the house of Syed Ahmad Khan, where the 'enlightened' of the city had obviously considered it worth their while to show their faces—as the same issue of the journal reported. The main arguments in favour of the

---

[13] *Kavivacansudha*, vol. 7, no. 44, 10 July 1876.

practice of image-worship were, first, its longevity: *jo murtipuja pap hai, to anadikal se aj tak jo log inmem hue unki kya gati hui?* (If image-worship is a sin, what of people who have practised it from time immemorial?). To abandon the ways of the *pita-pitamah* (forefathers) led inevitably to atheism. Second, the author argued, the operations of *buddhi* were fickle. Only Ishvara (God) himself could know what the essential features of dharma were; for the rest, what was known as dharma or adharma was what man himself had devised according to the dictates of his own nature, associates, country, time, and *buddhi*. What he considered worth following in one period could change entirely in the next, for *buddhi*, when it came to the essential matters of religion, ultimately deflected away from faith. It followed therefore that

> to believe in Ishvara on the strength of *buddhi* alone is folly. Ishvara is *alaukika*, beyond this world, and *buddhi* is of this world, therefore Ishvara can be no subject for consideration by *buddhi* . . .
>
> But believers alone recognize that Ishvara is the highest deity to be worshipped by man, and that he is accessible by means of love and that he is far removed from deceit; truth, kindliness, purity are his natural law, just as falsity and violence are opposed to this. Therefore, our statement is directed only towards those who are themselves believers. We ask, how can people such as Dayanand ever have access to Ishvara, people who are filled with the arrogance of their own dharma, whom no one has ever seen, not even in a dream, with their eyes filled with the tears of ecstatic love, but who have only been seen fighting, falling into a rage, raving right and left and always entangled in the rights and wrongs of argument.[14]

Clearly opposed to the claims arrogated by *buddhi*, to the truth which maintained its stand by the strength of argument alone, was the higher and purer truth of devotional, even ecstatic, love. This was the third and strongest argument for *murtipuja*: it was bhakti which sanctified it. On the one hand, then, *parampara* was being held up as legitimation, since wilful change, even if it figured as god's own will, could only lead astray. On the other hand, it was the *jnana* and

[14] Ibid.

bhakti opposition being transferred into the contemporary context, with *buddhi* or reason now standing in for *jnana*. The writer of the editorial then went on to ask how it could ever come about that Ishvara would not accept the devotion of those who chose to see and worship him in a specific form, if they did so with an innocent heart and with intense devotion. For one thing was certain, that all *upasana* (worship) had a single direction, and all the forms it took were occasioned by time, place, and differing *samskaras*, the social as well as the inherited psychic patterns of perception and behaviour. Could one then maintain that image-worship was sinful? It was much rather a virtue, since it caused those with the coarsest of minds to devote themselves to worship. This was a stand, then, which allowed for a plurality of traditions functioning on the single principle of devotion.

This position on image-worship was repeated in debates with the Brahmo Samaj, though the occasions when these occurred were rare since the influence of the Samaj in the North West Provinces remained marginal. The Brahmos tended to be subsumed under the collective term 'enlightened', which implied intellectual subservience to the British, the rejection of all traditionally sanctioned practice, and which, as we have seen, was more a term of abuse than any form of recognition.

But the Brahmos had to be put into their place as well, so they also came up for censure. In a dream, communicated in the form of a letter in the *Kavivacansudha* in 1877 and signed *ek arya hiteshi* (a well-wisher of Aryas), who to judge by the style and content was none other than Harishchandra, the 'enlightened' were taken to task.[15] The dream consisted of a dialogue, held between a *nishacar* (evil night-walker or spirit) who stemmed from Bihar (there had been some influential Brahmos there) and a Kshatriya, whose main qualification was that he annihilated evil spirits of all kinds. The *nishacar* was an enlightened gentleman who had no caste affiliations, since he neither recognized caste nor the authority of *shastriya yukti*, that is, the pronouncements of the Upanishads and the Puranas. The

---

[15] *Kavivacansudha*, vol. 8, no. 22, 2 April 1877.

Kshatriya was bitter in his castigation of the utter arrogance of this creed:

> What would you know of the essence of the Vedas, Puranas and image-worship? You only needed to learn a little English to don the turban of all the sciences of the world and to become so enlightened that you could proceed to censure the ways of your father, grandfather and great grandfather (who were thousands of times cleverer and more learned than you). You who attach the tail of wisdom to your behind, have you paid heed that men of other faith, that is, the Christians and the Muslims, continue to believe in the pronouncements of their prophets?

As against this, the Kshatriya claimed the *ved-puran-vihit arya dharma* as his *mat* (faith) and proudly asserted that image-worship, if carried out faithfully, led to *jnana*, which in turn led to bhakti. He recommended, rather pragmatically, that the *nishacar* subscribe to the journal *Kavivacansudha*; further that he study the commentary to the *Bhaktisutra* as written by Harishchandra, who was then praised in the most exalted terms, as patron and the guardian of Brahmins and cows, as versed in the most diverse forms of erudition, as knowledgeable in matters of dharma, in fact as the protector of *arya dharma*. The Kshatriya's most impassioned plea was reserved for the cause of tradition: that one should stick to the dharma of one's birth, and remain true to one's own country and customs, for *apne parampara, dharma, riti, vyavahar ki ninda karna kumati ka kam hai* (to condemn one's own tradition, dharma, customs, behaviour is a sign of ill judgement). Unmoved, the *nishacar* could respond that the Kalanki Avatar (the stained/defamed incarnation: a mischievous word play on Kalki, the incarnation of Vishnu who is to manifest himself at the end of Kaliyuga) had already taken incarnation and wandered the breadth of Bharatvarsh (India), proclaiming in loud tones: 'Do not worship idols, do not heed the Puranas.' The author wished, in disclosing this dream, to protect his countrymen from falling into the snare of Kalanki and thereby losing their foothold on the securely accessible path to Vaikuntha.[16]

---

[16] The reference to Kalanki could be a covert dig at Keshabchandra Sen who, from 1871, had begun increasingly to affect a prophet-like stance. He

I have cited this popular rather than learned response at such length because I believe it was this broad-based position which was to mould the face of modern Hinduism, rather than the iconoclasm of more radical formations such as the Brahmo and Arya Samaj, which served rather as catalysing agents. Confirmed in this rebuttal were all the traditional instances which Rammohun Roy had initially challenged. The Vedas found bare mention as sacral literature; *parampara* could not be seen as terminating with the Vedas, to be authorized and reinvoked centuries later by self-made prophets. The later traditions, specially the Puranas, were considered the legitimate offspring of the Vedic canon and worthy of being cited as equally authoritative; hence the formulation, *ved-puran-vihit-arya-dharm*, a *murtipuja* as propagated in the Puranas, in its very plurality pointed to the fact that the several approaches, if performed with bhakti led to the one personal God. The bearers of this parampara were the pita-*pitamah*, whose practice retained model function and was not to be questioned by the operations of something as fickle as *buddhi*. This could only operate in the sphere of *samajniti* (social mores), which did need change and adjustment from time to time, which task, in the present age, when the rulers were of an alien culture, could not be performed as of old by rulers and their priests and had to be seen to by the people themselves.[17] But the long tradition of Hindu dharma needed no such arbitrary intervention. This *parampara* by its very nature could not date, since it set itself forth and so maintained itself anew constantly. Thus the tradition possessed a modernity which

---

genuinely believed that the Samaj and the particular movement that he led were in the nature of a special dispensation of Providence and that all he said and did was to be regarded as the furtherance of divine command. Keshabchandra publicized his views freely, and the resistance which was bound to arise within his own ranks became equally a matter for public debate. See Sastri 1974: 169f. It was to assume dramatic proportions in 1879–80 when the New Dispensation was officially proclaimed and the schism with the Brahmo Samaj was finalized. Keshabchandra made a public appearance in the guise of a prophet, complete with his twelve apostles.

[17] Brajratnadas 1954: 900.

could not only retain itself in the present world, but also take care of the country's ills.

This process of legitimation can well be described as modernization if we return to the premise we set out with, that is, 'modernization' as an operation which entails a process of alteration and improvement of what is basically an older and already existing institution or system in order to accord better with contemporary conditions. In some ways, the position—iconic, monotheistic, devotional—worked out by Harishchandra and his contemporaries could be seen as pointing in a most sinister fashion to the kind of climaxing—iconic, monotheistic, devotional, political—which we have witnessed in the Ramjanmabhumi agitation, with the difference that today there seems to be no debate within Hindutva as to the validity of *murtipuja* and members of the Arya Samaj join in the effort to resurrect a temple and instal a *murti*. The plurality of voices which once clamoured in debate seems to have subsided. The question which remains to be asked, then, is: What has changed in the course of the century that lies between us and Harishchandra to make heterogeneity seem a threat so overwhelming that it has become necessary to pit Hindu dharma against those projected as the wholly Other, the Muslims? Is it in order to enforce the kind of homogeneity which conspicuously did not characterize the broad-based popular conceptualizations of the nineteenth century?

References

Brajratnadas, ed., 1954. *Bhartendu granthavali: tisra bhag*. Banaras.

Dayanand Saraswati, 1883. *Light of Truth*, trans. Chiranjiva Bharadwaja. Delhi: Sarvadeshik Arya Pratinidhi Sabha, rpnt 1984.

Jordens, J.T.L., 1978. *Dayanand Saraswati: His Life and Ideas*. Delhi: Oxford University Press.

Kennedy, James, 1874. *Christianity and the Religions of India*. Mirzapore: Orphan Schools Press.

Roy, Rammohun, 1817. *A Second Defence of the Monotheistical System of the Vedas in Reply to an Apology for the Present State of Hindoo Worship*, in Rammohun Roy, *The English Works of Raja Rammohun Roy*. Allahabad, 1906; New York: AMS Press, 1978.

Sastri, Sivanath, 1974. *History of the Brahmo Samaj*. Calcutta, 1911–12; rpt. Sadharan Brahmo Samaj, 1974.
Upadhyaya, Baldev, 1985. *Kashi ki panditya parampara*. Banaras.
Williams, Raymond, 1983. *Keywords: A Vocabulary of Culture and Society*. Oxford: Oxford University Press.

PART III

The Hindi Novel
Nineteenth-Century Beginnings

10

A Novel Moment in Hindi

Pariksha Guru

FEW WOULD DISPUTE THAT THE NOVEL, AS THE NEW and prestigious narrative genre in the literatures of India, was born in the nineteenth century. Though one model for it was obviously derived from the novel in English, the question which needs to be asked again when analysing and evaluating early specimens of the genre is whether it is adequate to use exclusively Western prototypes as criteria. As Todorov points out, genre is firstly 'a certain model of style to which the author refers, even if he wishes to violate it; in the second (case), it is a certain horizon of expectations, i.e. a set of pre-existing rules which orient the reader's understanding and allow him to receive it and appreciate the text.'[1] These are a range of genres: together they form a system within any given period and they can only be defined by their mutual relations. The novel in its new Indian setting could be none other than a mixed genre. As we shall see, several models of style were explicitly invoked by its exponents, who could do nothing other than claim to satisfy certain older expectations while introducing the new. In order to grasp and evaluate the significance of the new expectations, it then becomes vital to understand in what way they continue to remain embedded in the old. To measure the early novel by the grade of realism achieved

---

[1] Todorov 1974: 958.

in character, plot, or setting is obviously to reduce the multiplicity of traditions which go into its making to a single 'realistic' model from the West.[2] Here, I will review an early prose narrative in Hindi in order to trace what the author explicitly sets out to do, and what evaluative categories he proposes, as also to distinguish the literary traditions which he cites as having gone into its making.

Though a variety of prose narratives had been experimented with by the last decades of the nineteenth century,[3] including some incipient novels, *Pariksha Guru* (The Tutelage of Trial, 1882) is considered the first novel of note in Hindi. However, after awarding the work this distinction, literary histories tend to dispose of its actual achievements in a few summary remarks.[4] Yet, if one is alive to the tensions of the period, the novel turns out to be not only of historical interest but also makes for lively and absorbing reading. The author, Shrinivasdas (1851–88), belonged to a respected merchant family of Delhi.[5] The second of three sons, he was educated at home in Hindi and Urdu, had some Persian and Sanskrit, and was widely read in English. He succeeded his father as the agent of a well-known *kothi* based in Mathura. He was a public figure of some note, the Panjab Government having asked him to occupy the posts of both Municipal Commissioner and Honorary Magistrate of Delhi. By all accounts, he was urbane, courteous, and successful, devoting the time he could spare from his business to literary pursuit. He wrote

---

[2] In connection with this discussion, see also Walker 1988 and Schamoni 1992.

[3] Mukherjee 1985 remains the most comprehensive single attempt to size up the history of the novel as it evolved in the Indian languages. For early novel writing in modern Hindi literature, see McGregor 1970 and Dalmia 1997: 291–300.

[4] Thus, for instance, Ramchandra Shukla's pioneering work devotes all of ten lines to a description of the work: Shukla 1947: 4730. Trivedi, in his short analysis (1993: 211f.) is one of the few critics to point out that this didactic tale is also lively.

[5] See Brajratnadas 1950: 45–57 for more biographical details on the author. Also the essay by Kalsi (1992: 772f) some of whose propositions, however, I would want to see qualified, as noted below.

articles, four plays of varying quality alongside the single novel, and edited his own journal, *Sadadarsh*, for a short period—it was later assimilated into *Kavivacansudha*, the journal edited by his close friend and literary mentor Bharatendu Harishchandra.

In *Pariksha Guru* Shrinivasdas depicts the Delhi merchant milieu, the old-time *sahukari* that he knew so well, in its contact and skirmishes with the new fashions and learning from the West. In his highly informative essay, Kalsi has maintained that the novel 'draws its subject matter from the extravagant lifestyles of the traditional Hindu elites, the rich Hindu bankers and traders, rather than the peculiar traits of the middle class as is generally assumed by Hindi scholars.'[6] He also remarks that '(n)ineteenth century Hindi authors used the medium of the novel chiefly to counteract western influence on Indian society. Their primary concern was not the portrayal of middle class life as such, but the preservation, regeneration and veneration of old Hindu cultural values as against the threat of western influence.'[7] Here I diverge from Kalsi's astute discussion and argue that there is no unqualified East–West encounter in the novel which simply allows the East to emerge triumphant. It is the extravagant lifestyle of a wealthy and immaturely westernized youth rather than Hindu bankers in general that the novelist exposes to severe critique. Set up as a model against this extravagance are the new middle-class values as lived and represented by Brajkishor, the lawyer. He is the new professional man who yet continues to revere the good in the older lifestyle. Thus, traditional Indian values are to be perpetuated only with due modification, while Western influence is to be critically absorbed. There is a careful separation of the chaff from the grain.

Though Shrinivasdas himself apparently moved with assurance in both worlds, the unreflecting imposition of the new upon the old, as he pointed out repeatedly in the course of the work, made for tensions and uncertainties. The duality of the traditions at work, even the need to operate with both, was reflected in the very terminology

[6] Kalsi 1992: 763.
[7] Ibid.: 768.

he used in presenting the book to his readers. In the Hindi subtitle he denoted the work as a worldly tale (*samsari varta*), that is, as setting forth the familiar generic tradition of *varta*, albeit in a decidedly worldly vein. In the English dedication, he emphasized the novelty, describing the venture as 'my humble attempt at novel writing'. The longer Hindi dedication (*nivedan*) made it additionally clear that it was to be a book written in an entirely new style. This implied, the writer clarified, that the narrative would not be sequentially ordered (*silsilevar*), that is, it would begin without an introduction of characters. The tale would contain a portrait (*citra*) of an imaginary gentleman (*kalpit rais*) of Delhi. In order to make the portrayal more natural (*svabhavik*), special attention would be paid to everyday speech (*sadharan bolchal*). The writer would not always clarify who it was that spoke; only when the need arose would this be indicated. With the introduction of these new devices the reader, it was implied, would be a direct and unmediated witness to events as they were imagined to be actually taking place. Thus, a new realism. The writer further explained the introduction of paragraphs and syntactical marks, specifying the function of inverted commas, as also of commas, colons, semicolons, interrogation and exclamations marks, parentheses and full stops. In short, all of the new signs directing the reader how to read the text. The whole mode of presentation would then be novel and would, at least initially, seem alien to the reader. But before venturing to comment on the work, the reader was asked to go through *all* of it.[8] The very necessity of these lengthy explications makes it clear that in some respects, the reader's expectations had to be created before they could be fulfilled. The new genre was then voicing and fulfilling what were perceived to be the new needs of the times and it was this which made the business of novel-writing in modern Hindi an affair more of changing perceptions than the sheer appropriation of a prestigious literary genre from Europe.

In this connection I should like to turn to an issue which I can only touch upon here, and which I hope to elaborate upon subsequently, that is, the new gender roles and the sexual division of labour of

---

[8] Citations are from the Collected Edition of Shrinivasdas' work (1964: 153–5). All further references to the text are by page numbers.

which the novel as a genre became one of the prime literary bearers, in that it offered ample space for the renegotiations involved, in direct depiction of character and action which could hold fast the tiniest of details, in actual encounter, and in the narrator's own comments and interpretations.[9] *Pariksha Guru* takes up and complements the theme which had first been set forth in novel form by Pandit Gauridatta (1836–1905) in his *Devrani jethani ki kahani* (The Tale of the Younger and Older Sisters-in-law) which had appeared in 1870 and is often considered the first venture in novel-writing in Hindi. The work is only forty-eight pages long and tells of the fate of a merchant family in Meerut, struggling to keep up with the times. They acquire a younger daughter-in-law who can read and write in Nagari and an older one who is rustic and uncouth in all her ways. The fortunes of the family are shown to be in the hands of the women of the house. If they are wise, thrifty, and foresighted, they help their men to prosperity and bear sons whom they alone can equip to meet the needs of the day. As Pandit Gauridatta specifies in his preface, the work is written in a new way (*naye rangdhang se*). It is in the language of women as spoken in the families of Banias (merchants) of the region. It has further the advantage of revealing (1) what the Banias do in times of birth, marriage, death, and the like; (2) the differences between literate and illiterate women; (3) how boys are reared and ought to be; (4) women's work and the kind appropriate for them; (5) the damage illiterate women cause when they perform household tasks and the advantage of literate women performing the same task.[10] Pandit Gauridatta has the same claim to realism as Shrinivasdas, though in setting out to describe the manners and customs of Banias, he offers an even more explicitly ethnological approach: his account of things, he says, is written as it actually takes place in the homes of business folk. There is not a hair's

---

[9] For the persistent recurrence of the good-woman theme in the early novel literature in the Indian languages, see Mukherjee 1985: 23ff. For an account of the Urdu novel on the theme, Nazir Ahmad's *Mirat al-urus* (The Bride's Mirror, 1869) which was soon to attain wide popularity, see Naim 1984: 300–2; for gender roles in the early Kannada novel, Paddikal 1993: 230–2. For a more sustained discussion of these new gender roles, see Sangari 1991.

[10] I cite here from Gopal Ray's edition of the work (1966: 1f.).

breadth of difference between the two, he assures us. It is, then, not only the language which is new, it is also the mode of perception and the prescription of new gender roles, which are in this tale depicted in altercation with the old. We need also to keep in mind that this tale was written as an entry in a prize competition and thus sought the approval not only of a new readership but of an English jury as well.[11]

However, in considering the formal aspirations of *Pariksha Guru* it needs to remembered that the new reader was also the old reader, therefore certain older expectations were carried over into the new.[12] This was reflected in the fact that the new novel referred to two narrative traditions in its title, the religious-didactic tradition of the *varta* as also the worldly-secular of the novel, contained in the modifying adjective *samsari*. But it also invoked as its models works as various as the Mahabharata, the Gulistan, *Stribodh* (Instruction for Women: one of the many manuals for women in circulation at the time), the novels of Oliver Goldsmith, the essays of Lord Bacon, and the *Spectator*—the eighteenth-century moral weekly in English (156). A further important model was the collection of *niti-katha* or didactic tales which was not explicitly referred to but frequently cited, the *Hitopadesha*.[13] Could these models be blended and fused?

The *niti* or didactic tales, with the pragmatic, this-worldly morality of the *Panchatantra* and *Hitopadesha*, offered fruitful possibilities of combination with the kind of moral observation, social realism, and character portrayal presented in the essays of the English moral

---

[11] For details of the prize offered by the educational authorities, see Kalsi 1992: 765.

[12] We apprehend texts, as Jameson 1986: 9 has pointed out, 'through sedimented layers of previous interpretations, or—if the text is brand-new—through the sedimented reading habits and categories developed by those inherited interpretative traditions.'

[13] The *Hitopadesha* was one of the earliest Sanskrit works to be published in translation by the Fort William College. Translated by Lallujilal into Brajbhasha, it appeared in 1806 under the telling title: *Rajniti, or, Tales Exhibiting the Civil and Military Policy of the Hindus*. It was to see several reprints. For bibliographic details, see Krishnacarya 1966: 5f.

weekly and the writings of Goldsmith.[14] Both traditions took full account of the primacy of worldly happiness and success. The *niti* tales took an inherently dark view of human nature and tended to see much if not all of human action as motivated largely by want, greed, lust, and pride. It was possible to reach any goal, good or bad, depending on the viability of the ruse (*upaya*) employed. To offset this vision of the survival of the fittest or shrewdest, the compendia also carried tales, fewer in number and lower in credibility, which saw virtue rewarded, and which operated with the character of the true friend and the true retainer. Whatever the final outcome, the tales were concerned with relationships, with reflections on the reliability and constancy of friends and dependants. Nothing or nobody could be taken at face value, the nature (*svabhava*) of each, particularly of friends, was to be tested. One of the key concepts in the *Hitopadesha* was *pariksha* (trial).[15]

It is no coincidence that the term *pariksha* is not only a part of the title of our novel, it forms the keynote of the work. Only *pariksha* can test the true nature of an object, only *pariksha* can lay bare the true *svabhava* of a person and of friendship, and only severe *pariksha* can teach a long-deserved lesson and make a person see the error of his ways.[16] We could, if we so chose, see *Pariksha Guru* as the modern version of the frame story of the *Hitopadesha*. Just as the unlettered sons of the king of Pataliputra, who live a life of luxury and waste, need lessons in the ways of politics and men, so Madanmohan, the

---

[14] On the importance of the *niti-katha* in the early literature in modern Marathi, see Raeside 1970. Blackburn 1996: 8 has noted the importance of tales from the *Panchatantra* in Tamil literature of the early modern period. The work was brought into a 'respectable' prose translation by Tantavarayar Mutaliyar, an influential Tamil Pandit at the College of Fort William, in 1826. It enjoyed much popularity so there were several reprints. Its subversive qualities and tricky morality, however, inevitably also inspired later official British disapproval (ibid.: 13ff.).

[15] As the work specifies right in the beginning (1949: 19): one should examine the *svabhava* of all men rather than (any) further qualities.

[16] Thus the various uses and explications of the term on pp. 158, 186, 187, 194, 225, 362, 391.

hero of our tale, needs to be taught the error of his ways, though less so by the telling of tales than by actual trial. The king's lament with regard to his sons could as well be applied to Madanmohan: 'Youth, wealth, power and ignorance lead to misfortune, if one has just one of these. What is there to say if all four are there.'[17] But in *Pariksha Guru* other models are superimposed upon the didactic *niti* tale. The realistic but on the whole dark view of human nature coexists with the idealized characters: the perfect friend, the ideal wife, and the sentimentality upheld by novels such as Goldsmith's *Vicar of Wakefield* (1766). There results then a fusion of narrative traditions to create a third—a hybrid—form, where neither can be considered to be fully reproduced. First, the main difference from the *niti* tales lies in the sustained narrative which operates within a larger socio-political framework than what a short tale could offer. The protagonists are seen as at least partly created by their environment and by their education to become in their turn the bearers not only of their own destiny but also that of the new collective, the nation. Second, new roles and gender models are being created. The new merchant and the new professional man, who together go into the making of the emergent middle class, are delineated anew and offered explicitly as role models for the new man. The role foreseen for the perfect wife is as clearly delineated, if only briefly touched upon. The idealized characters play thus a more prominent role than they do in the *niti* tales. The third difference lies in the more detailed working out of the notion of character, which now has space to evolve, to contain contradictions but also to allow for change. Mechanical turns and twists of the plot remain no longer necessary to generate action; the interaction of characters can provide enough momentum. There thus need be no sudden surprises which bring about the final resolution of the crisis. In *Pariksha Guru* this resolution comes about due to the foresight of the true friend, who works with his knowledge of the character of man and is thus in a position to anticipate and steer events.

The tensions are provided by one point of view or evaluation, generated by the changes in the social environment, being opposed

[17] *Hitopadesha* 1949: 3.

to another. It is these tensions which offer opportunities for long moral deliberations. What are the oppositions?

The old ways (*purani chal*) are represented by the father of the protagonist, Madanmohan. He was a merchant of the old school, unostentatious, thrifty, quick on the uptake, recognizing and making full use of the trends in the market and thus through wisdom and caution making big money out of little. He lived frugally, without pomp and show; he had few, but trustworthy, retainers. He knew only Hindi. In many ways admirable, his grasp of the social and political situation proved inadequate to meet the needs of the day. For one thing, like others of his generation, he believed the progress of the country was the concern of statesmen alone. He thought only in terms of his own interests and community. However, he was aware of the need to educate his son differently. But since his horizon was limited, he picked the wrong teachers. They taught the young man not only Hindi, English, and Persian, but also the ways of pleasure and, it is hinted, corruption. Madanmohan grew up indolent, and after his father's death was a law unto himself. He adopted the new ways (*nayi chal*). What did his English learning bring him? False imitation (*jhuthi naqal*) of the English. He furnished his house in the most extravagant and latest style. He kept a variety of new carriages for his conveyance and a stall full of the most fancy breed of horses. He subscribed to a number of journals but read them only for the advertisements of new goods from the West. Gullible, innocent, swayed to and fro constantly, foolhardy but not evil of intent, he attracted a host of hangers-on and flatterers who schemed and plotted for his favour in the best style of the *niti* tales.

The alternative to *purani chal* could then not be *nayi chal* but *sacci sahukari* (true merchanthood). One of the frequent visitors to Madanmohan's house is Brajkishor, the young lawyer, who knows the old ways and holds them in esteem but sees the need for change. He knew how to make right use of the new institutions, in his case, the court of law. A successful mediator between the old and the new, he represents the new ideal of the professional man, who views progress as a matter not only of personal but national responsibility.[18] As he

---

[18] See Appendix below for the character sketch of Lala Brajkishor.

points out, all the conditions and materials required for the progress of the country were present in Hindusthan, *hath hilaye bina apne ap gras mukh mem nahim jata* (199; a morsel of food does not reach the mouth unless the hand is made to move). Thus the new generation needs to take note of the situation in the country in order to remedy it. As Brajkishor maintains:

> People who study, do so in order to join [government] service, they abandon the professional occupation of their forefathers. As for those who discuss matters regarding the progress of the country, their aims are not genuine, they make a lot of noise about small things. But they do not pay the attention they ought to the progress of learning, the propagation of machines, new ways to increase the produce of the land and profit in commerce so that the losses in the country can be made good.[19]

When the final catastrophe breaks upon Madanmohan—when his sins catch up with him, his creditors bear down upon him, and he is declared insolvent—the question that Brajkishor poses is not a psychological one but the larger social and political one: 'If Indians today have become addicted to the imitation of the English, then instead of indulging in the imitation of meaningless things, like eating habits and so on, why don't they imitate their genuinely good qualities? Why don't they adopt their views concerning the welfare of the country, craftsmanship and commerce?'[20] The fate of the individual has come to be tied up with larger issues. I would submit that it is this widened perspective, this awareness of the individual placed in the larger context—social, historical, and political—that makes for the necessity of the single narrative framework provided

---

[19] *Jo log parhte haim ve apnem* [sic] *bap dadom ka rozgar chorkar keval naukari ke liye parthe haim aur jo despnnati ke hetu carca karte haim unka laksa accha nahim hai ve thothi batom par bahut halla macate haim parantu vidya ki unnati, kalom ke pracar, prthvi ki paidavar barhanem* [sic] *ki nai, nai yukti aur labhdayak vyapar adi avasyak batom par jaisa cahiye dhyan nahim dete jisse apane yaham ka ghata pur aho* (201).

[20] *Hindusthaniyom ko aj har bat maim* [sic] *angrezom ki naqal karne ka caska par raha hai to vah bhojan adi nirarthak batom ki naqal karnem* [sic] *ke badle unke sacce sadgunom ki naqal kyom nahim karte? desopkari, kargari aur vyapar adi maim unka drstant kyom nahim lete?* (330).

by the novel and for the legitimacy of this new genre. It is in this new context that the *svabhava* of men now has to be probed, to undergo *pariksha*. Thus it is not only Madanmohan but whole ways of life, the old as well as the hastily adopted new, which have to stand the test of the present. The conflict can be said to be between the falsely new and the genuinely new. This does not imply that the old is to be rejected; rather, it is to be modified with changed circumstances.

Though relatively little space is reserved in *Pariksha Guru* for Madanmohan's wife—the lone woman to play a role in the tale—her appearance is vital to the structure of the novel. Without the good wife (*pativrata*) the new way of life would be incomplete; it would tell only half the story. The new merchant and the professional man both need their other half to manage the increasingly cordoned-off domestic space which complements the public sphere. *Pariksha Guru* does not thematize the oppositions between the old ways and the new in the private sphere. These had been thrashed out in *Devrani jethani ki kahani*, which had thrust into the background the elder sister-in-law, rustic, uncouth and wasteful in her ways. In our novel she is present, so to speak, in her absence; it is she whom the perfect wife replaces. However, Madanmohan's wife is a more cultivated version of the younger sister-in-law. She has stepped straight out of *Stribodh*, as it were. The courtesans Madanmohan and his friends visit find bare mention. There is no hint in the new genre of the wily women of the didactic tales, as shrewd and quick on the uptake as their men.[21]

What of the narrative structure of the work? How does the tale propel itself forward? In spite of the fact that it is conceived of as a single and rounded narrative, the forty-one chapters which comprise the whole have an instalment character, retaining this feature of the weekly journal. The chapters are kept short, as befits a weekly column, an average of seven printed pages. Every once in a while, while winding up a chapter, the writer begs to be excused that a certain topic cannot be set forth for lack of space. They have headings reminiscent of the thematic concerns of the *niti* tales but also of the

---

[21] See Appendix for the character sketch of Madanmohan's wife.

moral essay, such as *sangati ka phal* (the fruits of company), *mitra milap* (the meeting of friends), *sacci priti* (true affection), and so on.[22] Apart from these moral reflections, there are scenic sequences consisting less of description than of dialogue, a trait inherited from traditional narrative genres meant for oral delivery, such as the *dastan* and the *varta*. The language is bright, colloquial. Even when moralizing, myriad tales can be related to illustrate a point and profuse citations from motley sources marshalled to support it. It is here that the chapters tend to assume the character of an essay.

With the first chapter, we enter the tale directly, without any preambles. The scene of the first encounter is represented, symbolically enough, by an English merchant shop, offering fancy fripperies at exorbitant prices. The two English commercial men who have to do with Madanmohan are depicted as self-seeking and exploitative, aware of the advantages they enjoy in the British Raj. As per programme, we see the characters in action first and become acquainted with their modes of thinking in chapters reserved entirely for the presentation of arguments and counterarguments on moral and social issues. Brajkishor presents the enlightened view, propagating new ways which have been mediated and moderated, while Madanmohan and his friends persist in supporting new fashions and crave instant satisfaction. It is their *kathametat* (how so this), in the style of the *Hitopadesha*, which prompts Brajkishor to prose on and on at times.[23] It is only once we have come to know them, that we are offered lively character sketches. Chapter 9, for instance, is entitled *Sabhasad* (courtiers). Here we are offered a view of the gallery of rogues, colourful and unscrupulous in the best style of the old *niti* tales, but presented with a new awareness of psychology and observation of idiosyncratic detail. It is their vivacious comment and conversation which makes for the realism of the work and breathes life into it. They are the scum which has been thrown up by the

---

[22] On the significance of the moral essay in this early period of Hindi literature, see Dalmia 1997: 260–7.

[23] See Appendix for an instance of a homily as framed and enlivened by the impertinent comments of the friends.

churning of the new with the old. They are clerks, middlemen, the newly forming lower-middle class, half educated and needy, with a smattering of knowledge about the new ways, with little chance of rising in their own profession. Once again it is all a question of *upaya*, of ruse, when it comes to gaining one's own ends.

The two main manipulators, Munshi Chunnilal and Master Shimbhudayal, had been trained to operate in the new institutions, the court of law and the Anglo-Vernacular school respectively. Chunnilal had worked formerly for Brajkishor, assisting him in court. He was thrown out of work when Brajkishor found him cheating his clients left and right. He then attached himself to Madanmohan. As the narrator admits with some reverence, he was a living incarnation of Iago. He was quick to recognize the weaknesses of other people and of course he knew Madanmohan's *svabhava* thoroughly. He knew that Madanmohan liked to keep high officials happy, that he was inordinately fond of bodily pleasure, and endlessly intrigued by the idea of making much money at little expense. However, Madanmohan had little real inkling either of how to make money or keep it. Thus, Chunnilal had ample opportunity to plunder and loot.

Master Shimbhudayal had originally been employed as an English teacher for the young Madanmohan. He had entertained the young man with Shakespeare's *Twelfth Night* and *Much Ado about Nothing*, with Ben Jonson's *Every Man in his Humour*, Swift's *Drapier's Letters, Gulliver's Travels*, and *Tale of a Tub*, and tricked him out of small articles, such as a watch, a walking stick, and handkerchiefs. When Madanmohan grew a little older, he had quickly inducted him into the erotic literature of all the languages at his command, while taking great care to keep these doings secret from Madanmohan's father. Initially, he had trouble with Chunnilal but the two managed to adjust to each other's needs and *garam lohe ki tarah apas maim mil gaye* (were soldered together like two bits of heated iron).

The rest of the courtiers are quickly described. They schemed together for their own ends. There were frequent clashes of interest, but though they lost no opportunity to do each other in, they also had to make some allowances for each other. There were also two single, small-time operators, belonging to the *purani chal*. Pandit

Purushottamdas had been going in and out of the house since Madanmohan was young. He made a good income from his work as astrologer, but his was a nature racked by envy, and if there was one thing he could not bear, it was seeing others prosper. To tear apart other people's character was his favourite pastime and he took genuine delight in seeing others suffer, doing his best to trip them when he could. But he had little knowledge of the new, was slow of thought, and no match for the other two. He suffered them to make fun of him if it kept Madanmohan amused. In fact, he was their plaything, a pigeon with clipped wings.

Hakim Ahmad Husain, doctor to Madanmohan, was an out-and-out coward. He did everything to please Madanmohan, going so far as to prescribe the desired instead of the required medicine. He belonged to the variety of people who do not eat for fear of indigestion and undertake no business for fear of loss. In all his doings he preferred the *purani chal*.

Finally, there was Babu Baijnath, an employee of the East Indian Railway Company. He had good knowledge of English and was well acquainted with the enlightened thought of Europe, but his self-interest covered all his better qualities and he did not think to act for the public weal in accordance with his learning. In this respect he was like an elephant—the teeth he ate with were other than the ones which he put on show. He had a good income, but he remained dissatisfied with it. He had so managed to impress Madanmohan that the latter considered him the wisest and the most reliable of his friends.

There is an almost inadvertent gaiety in the mode of the courtiers' operations and counter-operations, with Madanmohan fluttering helplessly between them, torn between his own caprices and the interests of his courtiers.

But things could hardly remain suspended in this state of eternal pleasure-seeking. Amongst all of these hangers-on there was also one Harkishor. It was a clash of his character with the rest which was to bring about the final catastrophe. He was strong-willed and seemed to be hard-working, but he only expended labour as long as he found things going his own way. His was an impatient nature which made only a surface study of men and events. He liked hobnobbing with the rich but friendship with him was not free of fear, for once angered, he could prove dangerous. He took little care to appease the others, who watched his movements jealously. His well-meaning labours being twice rejected by Madanmohan, he felt compelled to ask for the money owed to him. The hangers-on managed the situation so that he was thrown out of the house. He promptly took revenge and spread the rumour of Madanmohan's impending insolvency. The narrator devotes a lively chapter or two to these doings. As a result, the establishment was thrown asunder like a house of cards and Madanmohan found himself in a debtor's prison.

In this hour of need the only real friend, it turns out, is Brajkishor. Though temporarily alienated from Madanmohan, he has kept watch over the affairs of his friend. However, he has not been totally idealized, in the manner of Mr Burchell in Goldsmith's *Vicar of Wakefield*, nor is he quite so omnipresent. Madanmohan admits that his legal profession had made him worthy and self-righteous, that he tends to talk on and on, and this critique is presented as his own insight rather than the narrator's ironic comment. Brajkishor manages to free Madanmohan from the clutches of his debtors, clear his name, and reinstall himself in his former position of power—a sadder and a wiser man. However, it needs also to be noted, that for all his love of virtue, it is characteristic of the pleasure that the novelist himself takes in his roguish figures, and perhaps a mark of his particular brand of realism, that they are allowed to slip off unpunished. They fail to live up to the expectations one can have of genuine friends and unabashedly choose to melt into thin air in Madanmohan's gravest hour of need.[24]

Characteristic of the social reform agenda of the novel and its documentary tone is that, once he has seen the error of his ways,

---

[24] In recording the multiplicity of voices and the socially diverse speech of his era, Shrinivasdas' work, I would submit, lives up wonderfully to what Bakhtin (1981: 411) sees as characteristic of the novel as genre. According to him, 'the novel must represent all the social and ideological voices of its era, that is, all the era's languages that have any claim to being significant; the novel

Madanmohan himself asks that his tale be written down so that others benefit from it.

> 'The suffering that ought to have fallen upon me on account of my folly has done falling on me. I can see no advantage in sparing myself falsely now. For the sake of all these people I would like the whole account to be printed and made public', Lala Madanmohan said.
>
> 'Is there need of it? Those who want to learn will find the world full of moral treatises', said Lala Brajkishor, thinking over the matter in relation to his own person.
>
> 'There is no need to be ashamed of things which are true. I want with all my heart that once my faults become public, people have their eyes opened by seeing their [ill] consequences. I shall relate for you to put down in your account all that I talked about with all those that I talked to', said Lala Madanmohan enthusiastically.

This primacy of social concern and correction, as Ramvilas Sharma has pointed out, directly sires the didactic-realistic tradition which is set forth in the early novels of Premchand.[25] To measure these either by the Western criteria of realism or by the mores of the didactic fable alone is obviously to emphasize one tradition at the cost of another and to miss entirely the new in the Indian literary landscape which has come into being in the process, that is, the expression of bourgeois realism by way of modifying the *niti* tale.

References

Bakhtin, M.M., 1981. *The Dialogic Imagination. Four Essays*, ed. Michael Holquist, transl. Caryl Emerson and Michael Holquist. Austin: University of Texas Press.

Blackburn, S., 1996. 'To Create a New Vernacular: The Cultural Politics of Narrative in Nineteenth-century Tamil'. Paper presented at the 14th European Conference on Modern South Asian Studies, Copenhagen, 21–24 August.

---

must be a microcosm of heteroglossia [social diversity of speech types].' For an exceptionally lucid exposition of Bakhtin's principles, see Pechey 1986: 1–6ff.

[25] Sharma 1975: 93–9.

Brajratnadas, 1950. *Bharatendu-mandal*. Banaras: Shri Kamalmani-granthmala-karyalay.
Dalmia, V., 1997. *The Nationalization of Hindu Traditions. Bharatendu Harischandra and Nineteenth-century Banaras*. Delhi: Oxford University Press.
Gauridatta, 1966. *Devrani jethani ki kahani*. Patna: Granth Niketan. (First published 1870.)
Goldsmith, Oliver, 1966. *The Vicar of Wakefield*. In *Collected Works of Oliver Goldsmith*, ed. A. Friedman, vol. IV. Oxford: Clarendon Press.
Hitopadesha, 1949. Bombay: Nirnaya Sagar Mudranalay.
Jameson, F., 1986. *The Political Unconscious. Narrative as a Socially Symbolic Act*. London: Methuen.
Kalsi, A.S., 1992. '*Pariksaguru* (1882): The First Hindi Novel and the Hindu Elite', *Modern Asian Studies*, vol. 26, no. 4.
Krsnacarya, 1966. *Hindi ke adimudrit granth*. Banaras: Bhartiya Jnanpith.
McGregor, R.S., 1970. 'The Rise of Standard Hindi and Early Hindi Prose Fiction'. In T.W. Clark, ed., *The Novel in India: Birth and Development*. London: George Allen and Unwin.
———, 1974. *Hindi Literature of the Nineteenth and Early Twentieth Centuries*. (*A History of Indian Literature*, ed. J. Gonda, vol. 8, fasc. 2.) Wiesbaden: Harrassowitz.
Mukherjee, M., 1985. *Realism and Reality. The Novel and Society in India*. Delhi: Oxford University Press.
Naim, C.M., 1984. 'Prize-winning Adab: A Study of Five Urdu Books Written in Response to the Allahabad Government Gazette Notification'. In B.D. Metcalf, ed., *Moral Conduct and Authority. The Place of Adab in South Asian Islam*. Berkeley: University of California Press.
Padikkal, Sh., 1993. 'Inventing Modernity: The Emergence of the Novel in India'. In T. Niranjana, P. Sudhir, and V. Dhareshwar, eds, *Interrogating Modernity: Culture and Colonialism in India*. Calcutta: Seagull.
Pechey, G., 1986. 'Bakhtin, Marxism and Post-structuralism'. In F. Barker, P. Hulme, M. Iversen, D. Loxley, eds, *Literature, Politics and Theory*. Papers from the Essex Conference 1976–84. London/New York: Methuen.
Raeside, I.M.P., 1970. 'Early Prose Fiction in Marathi'. In T.W. Clark, ed., *The Novel in India, its Birth and Development*. London: George Allen and Unwin.
Sangari, K., 1991. 'Relating Histories: Definitions of Literacy, Literature, Gender in Early Nineteenth Century Calcutta and England'. In

S. Joshi, ed., *Rethinking English. Essays in Literature, Language and History*. Delhi: Trianka.

Schamoni, W., 1992. *Literature and Modernization in Japan. The Changing Geography of Literary Genres 1850–1890*. Oxford: St Antony's College (Richard Storry Memorial Lecture, no. 4).

Sharma, R., 1975. *Bharatendu-yug aur hindi bhasa ki vikas-parampara*. Delhi: Rajkamal.

Shrinivasdas, 1964. *Shrinivas granthtavali*, ed. Shrikrsnalal. Banaras: Nagaripracarini Sabha.

Shukla, R., 1947. *Hindi sahitya ka itihas*. Banaras: Nagaripracarini Sabha. (First published 1930.)

Todorov, I., 1974. 'Literary Genres'. In Th.A. Sebeok, ed., *Current Trends in Linguistics*, vol. 12. The Hague: Mouton.

Trivedi, H., 1993. *Colonial Transactions. English Literature and India*. Calcutta: Papyrus.

Walker, J.A., 1988. 'On the Applicability of the Term "Novel" to Modern Non-western Long Fiction'. In *Yearbook of Comparative and General Literature*, vol. 37.

Appendix

Character Sketch of Brajkishor

Lala Brajkishor is the son of poor parents but his character is honest, careful and simple. Though he is young of age, he has great experience. He does what he says. A great deal about him has already been said in the book so it is not necessary to say anything particular about him. Yet it is impossible to resist saying that he is a choice product of God's creation. He is a lawyer but he does not side falsely with his clients. He does not take fraudulent cases and does not load on work beyond his capacity. He takes fitting care of the cases that he does take on. And often he prosecutes cases for the poor who have been unjustly persecuted. The high officials and citizens have great regard for him . . . Lala Brajkishor has no desire to indulge in worldly pleasure and he sees money as necessary only to take care of worldly tasks. For this reason he has, with toil and with dharma, generated enough money for these worldly tasks; he spends the rest of his time in the pursuit of knowledge and the welfare of the country.

For him there is true merit in helping those of the poor who really cannot make a living, or are ailing and have no money for their treatment or no one to take care of them. He sees his true dharma in giving education or teaching some handicraft to enable livelihood to those children who have not reached understanding and whose parents cannot do anything from lack of knowledge or means. He sees his true dharma in spreading discussion of useful knowledge, in having good books translated from other languages or having them written anew and propagated in the country, in giving encouragement to the true well-wishers of the country and to able men and in making known machines, the cultivation of land and other truly patriotic things . . . (301–4)

Character Sketch of Madanmohan's wife

With regard to her husband, Madanmohan's wife was truly affectionate, well-wishing, a companion in pleasure and pain and obedient, and in the beginning Madanmohan also held her in great affection. But when he began to keep the company of friends such as Chunnilal and Shimbhudayal, he caught the addiction to dance and music and went into raptures over the false airs and graces of the courtesans . . . His poor, simple, able wife began to seem rustic to him. For a while things were kept secret, but how can there be pleasure in the flower of love after a worm has entered it? . . . Madanmohan's wife has not even learnt how to be angry with her husband. Madanmohan is a god in her eyes. She forgets all her pain when she sees his face and she turns a blind eye to his biggest faults. Madanmohan does not think of her for days, but she lives only to see him. She sees her life as being not for herself but for him alone, he is the master of her life [*pranpati*]. . . With very little expense she has seen to such good arrangements in the house that Madanmohan does not have to expend the least labour at home. When she has leisure, she does not sit idly, gossiping about other people and chattering about jewels and jewellery, she practices reading and writing, embroidery and drawing pictures etc. . . . The children are very small but while playing she teaches them the basic moral principles and unawares, by increasing their knowledge of things, she slowly stimulates their own natural capacity to increase their knowledge. But she does not burden their minds, there is no hindrance to their freedom to indulge in innocent play and laughter. (291–4)

Instance of an Homily as Framed and Enlivened by the Impertinent Comments of Friends

'What work do the rich have besides living in luxury?' Master Shimbhudayal said. Pandit Purushottamdas said, 'It is said in the *Hitopadesha*, the king indulges in enjoyment, the minister always takes care of work. If something goes wrong in the business of the state, blame attaches to the minister.'

'Yes, that's the ways of the rich here, but their way is distinct from the rest of the world. What is considered appropriate for them is considered inappropriate for the rest of the world. Each word of theirs sends their listeners into raptures. Nothing they say is considered to be without ingenuity. The rich here do not consider it inappropriate to do any of the things that everyone knows to be bad, which even the most lowly would be ashamed to do, which even the most dissolute would shrink from making public. They neither worry before launching into any deed nor do they think of its consequences. The wealthy here consider themselves to be the lords of Lakshmi herself but this is not the law of God; he has created the poor and the rich as equals in his creation.' Lala Brajkishor began to speak. 'The man who breaks God's law will surely be punished for this wrong. The people who indulge in pleasure and enjoyment don't belabour their minds and bodies. Firstly, because of their own inattention, their splendour will not continue to remain with them and if it does, in accordance with the law of nature, their minds and bodies will become successively weak and useless.' . . . 'But excessive labour also brings about fatigue', Babu Baijnath said. (183–5)

11

Generic Questions
Bharatendu Harishchandra and Women's Issues

TWO CONCERNS HAVE MOVED THE PRESENT INQUIRY.[1] The first has to do with the representation of gender in the wide range of literary genres in modern Hindi in the latter half of the nineteenth century. We have now come to accept that the main thrust of the new narrative literature of this period was the division of lived spheres into the public and the private, the male and the female, thereby creating new forms of patriarchy. In the introduction to their seminal work on South Asian women's studies, Sangari and Vaid have pointed to what has come to be considered typical for this period:

> A new kind of segregation is imposed on women, whose identity is now to be defined in opposition to women from lower economic strata. This process is not dissimilar to the one which pushed the middle class woman into the seclusion of the private sphere as a mark of class status and superiority (among other things) in Victorian England. It is also at the

---

[1] This essay has benefited from the comments and critique of friends and listeners in Berkeley, Cambridge, Paris, Seattle, and Urbana-Champagne. Stuart Blackburn and Francesca Orsini have further submitted it to a close reading and offered many helpful suggestions.

same time implicated in a new formation of the home as the insulated private sphere which is to be free from even temporary challenges to male authority.[2]

While accepting and working with these propositions, the time may now have come to build upon and refine them. I shall attempt to show here that, even while the new grids of private and public, male and female, were coming into being, there existed already, or came into existence simultaneously, challenges to these newly constituted spheres, some in genres *reproduced*, some in genres *introduced* (to use terms employed by Francesca Orsini).

The second concern, which overlaps with the first, has to do with gender differentiation in the work of Bharatendu Harishchandra of Banaras (1850–85), a major figure in the formation of modern Hindi literature. Committed as he was to both tradition and renewal, a writer who was part of the old elite yet straining out of the mores which bound it, what position did Bharatendu take on the woman question within the various genres in which he wrote? It seems possible to extract a clear agenda, coeval with the one outlined by Sangari and Vaid, if we concentrate entirely on the example of a particular genre—the literary journal *Balabodhini*—in which he explicitly addresses women. But, as we shall see, he deals in ways that contradict these very propositions when writing in other literary modes. The exclusions in one seem to become the focus in others. Does a particular literary genre, then, make possible a particular kind of discourse? Do the newer, more prestigious genres supersede the more traditional?

Harishchandra is considered by many as the progenitor of modern Hindi literature. He is also best remembered for his creative use and propagation of modern Hindi as a literary vehicle, and for an incredible ability to attract and encourage writing talent within his vast coterie of friends and correspondents. He enjoyed a particularly privileged position in Banaras, belonging as he did to the city's commercial aristocracy, the Naupatti Mahajans—bankers who rose to prominence in the eighteenth century. Just as his father before

---

[2] Sangari and Vaid 1989: 11–12.

him, Harishchandra played a leading role in the cultural life of the city. There are accounts of gatherings of poets and musical evenings which he organized. He was on terms of easy friendship with the maharaja, and it is said that Harishchandra contributed greatly to the expansion of the Ramlila of Ramnagar by devising the dialogues of the *lila*. He was an honorary magistrate of the city until his voluntary resignation, and he was in contact not only with local British officials and Orientalists but also with the Asiatic Society of Bengal in Calcutta. We know that he kept track of their publications, including the lectures and essays published in the august *Asiatick Researches* by major British Orientalists, and that he knew and corresponded with the society's secretary, Rajendralal Mitra, a venerable scholar and ardent Vaishnava. All this was in addition to the societies and school he founded, and the three journals he edited. What Harishchandra had to say about the woman question in the decades when it was the most heatedly debated topic would therefore obviously carry the weight of cultural and social authority.

The 1870s saw the height of Harishchandra's publicizing activity and his standing as a centrally important public figure in the North West Provinces. His two literary journals, *Kavivachansudha* (1868–85) and *Harishchandra's Magazine,* which was later renamed *Harishchandrachandrika* (1873–85), were to become legendary in their own time. In these he dealt at regular intervals with social-reform debates of the time. I have written at length on these journals in my monograph on Harishchandra, dealing only briefly there with, and reserving for more detailed treatment here, the women's journal *Balabodhini* which he edited from 1874 to 1877. As the first woman's journal in Hindi, this occupies a place of special importance in literary history.[3] Turning to the files of this journal after engaging with the liveliness and wit of the other two journals (which were appearing at the same time, and which went on much longer) is a

---

[3] See Dalmia 1997. Only a few copies of *Balabodhini* were printed, as was usual within such early ventures, and there were numerous gaps in the files. I was able, after the completion of my book in 1997, to supplement and almost complete the files with the issues a friend in Banaras had most generously made available to me, along with those in the India Office Library, London.

sobering experience. The tone is almost consistently puritanical and restrictive; it preaches and patronizes, and this despite its editorship under one of the most innovative writers of the period. Whichever way the matter is turned, a critical reading of *Balabodhini* adds little insight to the work already done in the last few decades on women's journals in nineteenth-century India.[4]

Balabodhini was, all the same, a pioneering venture in Hindi. It seemed to have had a sufficiently clear agenda which called for a reorganization of domestic space and a reinvention of patriarchal authority. It was almost entirely Victorian in its orientation, with a consequent redefinition of the role of the woman primarily as housewife and mother. Yet the very clarity of this agenda begs for deeper engagement with the issues it raises. It seems so unlikely that Harishchandra should be propagating Victorian notions of domestic and public propriety in a manner as indiscriminately as *Balabodhini* suggests, when read in isolation. Harishchandra, we know for a fact, never had a simple or straightforward acceptance of tradition; on the contrary he had a complex relationship with it whereby, despite his desire to modernize, he refused to discard it in its entirety. His effort was to modernize even while revalidating certain strands of tradition, for which purpose he could and did invoke a variety of authoritative instances. Apart from various Sanskrit sources, he turned to contemporary resources, such as work by folklorists in Europe which unearthed local traditions.[5] And indeed, on further investigation and reflection, I also found that contesting configurations emerged if Harishchandra's other literary works pertaining to women were taken into account. In what follows, then, I shall discuss, in addition to *Balabodhini*, two powerful projections of women's voices by Harishchandra, namely a religio-erotic play, and a short social-reform novel. The questions I shall seek to answer will have to do both with literary genres and with gender roles as represented in them. In what

---

[4] By, amongst others, Meredith Borthwick on Bengali, and by Gail Minault on Urdu journals for women.

[5] See Dalmia 2001 for a more detailed discussion of the theme.

relationship do a traditional allegorical play and a popular novel stand to this writer's journal? Do these continue to exist in their respective realms, unaffected by the other, or do they trespass on each other's territory? Do they validate or invalidate one another? And finally, in what ways are the discourses in these three related genres, as practised by Harishchandra, deployed to bring about, reinforce, or challenge social power relations?

I shall review, then, *Balabodhini* (1874–7), the entirely new genre of a journal for women which seems to be preaching a new segregation of spheres for men and women; second, *Chandravali* (1876), a traditional *raslila* type of dramatic composition, erotic-devotional, but written primarily in modern Hindi rather than in Brajbhasha; and finally, *Kulin Kanya athava Purnaprakash aur Chandraprabha* (A Girl of Good Family, or Purnaprakash and Chandraprabha, 1882), a love story, but also a daring social-reform novel which alternates between intimate and denunciatory tones. In short, we shall look at three works: the journal, emancipatory/oppressive, and intent on separating the spheres now defined as exclusively male and female; the play, erotic/androgynous, almost melting male and female into each other; and the story/novel, romantic, entirely heterosexual, fiercely opposing prevailing social norms.

Before we proceed to analysis, however, I should like to add a caveat: Harishchandra was not the sole author of the works mentioned above. Several authors wrote for *Balabodhini*, and its editor had another collaborator in many of his literary projects, namely Mallika, the young Bengali woman who had lived under his protection since he was twenty-three (some say since he was fifteen). We know next to nothing about her early life, she was possibly a child widow. She was obviously well educated and cultured. She appears in his literary works as 'Chandrika', the young moon. *Harischandra's Magazine* was renamed *Harishchandrachandrika* after her, so it can be safely assumed that she was a literary partner in this enterprise, as well as in many others. There is, for example, constant play on her name in many of his literary creations. He included thirty-six Bengali verses composed by her—love poems sometimes addressed to Krishna and often including the authorial signature 'Chandrika'—in *Prem Tarang* (1877), a collection of his own poems.[6] As a woman of letters she seems, in her poems at least, to be perpetuating the tradition of poetry-writing cultivated by many courtesans and public women. In her prose writings, however, she seems explicitly to advocate the new domestic ideals of the middle-class mistress of the house, adept housekeeper but also literate and cultivated companion and mother, the *bhadra mahila*, in fact, of Bengali novels and short stories. She was probably a coauthor of various articles in *Balabodhini*, and she most certainly wrote the short novel *Kulin Kanya athava Purnaprakash aur Chandraprabha*, published under Harishchandra's name.

We shall need, then, not only to go beyond a single project but also the notion of a single author, even though I shall continue for the most part to refer to Harishchandra as the author. Though the works do not stem from his pen alone—in some cases he seems only to have lent his name and authority to them—I consider them part of a single literary project and public persona, for it was thus that they were presented to the reading public. While analysing the contradictions thrown up by these three works, then, I shall be concerned not so much with Harishchandra's own peculiar psychology, nor with the problems of dual authorship, but with the larger social and literary orientations as represented by the collective operating under his name.

Balabodhini, a slender journal of ten pages, was a monthly which first appeared in January 1874.[7] It managed to survive a little more than three years. No information is available on the number of copies

---

[6] This first appeared in the *Kavivachansudha* on 9 April 1877, to be later published by Mallikchandra and Company, a press Harishchandra co-founded with Mallika. The text is to be found in Harishchandra 1935/1946: 177–220, where it appears in the third impression of the above press (no date is appended to this information).

[7] Calcutta and Bombay, as Presidency towns, had already acquired a head start in the field: here women's journals, invariably connected with reformers and reformist movements, had begun to come out by mid century. In Bengal, the most well-known journal was *Bamabodhini Patrika*, which came out in 1863 and continued until 1906. It was managed by Kailashkamini Dutt and edited by her husband Umesh Chunder Dutt; both were ardent Brahmos. In

printed, although it is known that a hundred copies were bought by the government. When this patronage stopped, the journal came to an abrupt halt, ceasing publication in February 1878. In spite of its later reputation, we need to note that its readership, at the best of times, could only have been scanty.[8] Harishchandra's regard for the venture and his sense of loss when it had to be discontinued is documented in a letter he wrote to Chintamani Dharphale who, in 1878, was the proprietor and editor of *Kavivachansudha*, the journal into which *Balabodhini* was now assimilated:

> My sorrow that the journal did not run [for long] is beyond words. If it is the way of the world to love a poison plant only because one has planted it oneself, as also a bad son who one nurtured in one's own lap, how much more this ambrosial creeper, this child one loved more than one's life? Government has stopped subscribing to it from this new year. The reason for this is my Hindi, which has always disturbed the hearts of my opponents. It is true, the mighty have no eyes, they only have ears. Otherwise Hindi would not have come to this pass.[9]

Harishchandra's distinct voice is most urgently heard in the first issue of the journal. Speaking in the first person—as a public figure, social reformer, and nationalist—he introduces the journal as a 'younger sister' of prospective women readers, a sister who will now presume to mix and mingle with them.[10] They are asked to listen attentively to this newcomer, even if the advice given does not appeal to them.

Bombay, the Gujarati *Stri Bodh* came out in 1857. It was to have an even longer lifespan than *Bamabodhini*: the last preserved issues of *Stri Bodh* are from 1950. Marathi was a late arrival in the field. The first periodical for women, *Subodh Patrika*, started by Moro Vitthal Walvekar, member of the Prarthana Samaj, was to come out in 1877. Cf. O'Hanlon 1994: 15. Tamil had a women's journal in 1860, though this was short-lived. See Borthwick 1984 on *Bamabodhini*, with an extensive analysis of the issues treated by the journal; on women's journals in Bengal, see also Bannerji 1991. On *Stri Bodh*, see the excellent article, Shukla 1991; on Urdu journals for women, see Minault 1998.

[8] With the exception of a single issue in the first year and the fourth and last year, the files of the journal are now almost complete.

[9] Cited in Sahay (1905), 1975: 74f.

[10] As Sangari points out, 'the use of women's voices "feminized" the genre.

The humble tones of the address are belied by the enormity of the task this younger sister sets out to shoulder: 'If you pay attention to my childish stammer, then I shall plead with the Almighty that the women of my Hindustan become literate and share equally in the destinies of their men.'[11] Clearly, the 'equality' being called for here is ambiguous. It is men who have to realize the state of affairs in the country and take steps to remedy it, thus granting women some measure of participation in their lives. The nationalist tone of this piece is further confirmed by the rousing essay which follows, entitled simply 'Stri', woman. 'Bharatvarsh' is unhappy, we are told. It is thus, and sometimes as 'Bharatkhand', that India is referred to, and not as 'Hindustan', which could, since it is a word of Persian origin, have a Muslim ring. Bharatvarsh has been attacked repeatedly by enemies, its wealth and knowledge have been destroyed. This has cast such dark shadows that Hindus are not able to discern the real value of women, the priceless jewels within their own homes. Women have been kept ignorant, they have not received their fair share of knowledge: this is the biggest cause of misery among Hindus. Knowledge has no currency in Hindu households, not even in the loftiest among them: in fact it often finds more favour in the houses of the lowly. The importance of literate and well-informed mothers cannot be overemphasized.

Another piece in the same issue, entitled 'Shilavati' (The Woman of Good Conduct), depicts the life of a virtuous wife. This rather conventional article contains a little treatise, ostensibly written by Shilavati, on the present state of the women of Bharatkhand. This rather awkward double-authorship device is perhaps introduced to attribute the ensuing opinions that follow to a respected woman, and thereby endow them with yet more authority. The treatise sets out to prove that egalitarianism in the treatment of the sexes had once existed in the country:

The male projection of pedagogic women and women's consenting voices preceded any writing by women in this genre; in later decades it would either powerfully undercut the voices of dissenting women or shade into women's own consenting voices.' Sangari 1999: 343.

[11] Harishchandra 1874–7: 1/1, January 1874.

> Formerly, daughters and sons had the same status, and all their activities were the same . . . Even though the Lord has given women and men an equal part in the origin and sustenance of his creation, and there are many tasks in the world which only we can perform, we do not know why minds have been so twisted that people lose heart the moment they hear we poor creatures have been born . . . Fathers never love their daughters, nor make any effort to educate their daughters—because they think the moment they are educated they will become independent.[12]

The essay continues in the same rousing tones to defend the cause of women's education. It covers well-traversed ground in maintaining that mothers are the best instructors for their sons, but it also goes further, proclaiming that women were always active in various fields of knowledge and that there were many famous women poets, past as well as contemporary.

The language of these pieces has the lively flow of Harishchandra's pen. It carries colloquialisms within a lightly Sanskritized idiom. In subsequent issues, this standard is sustained only in some of the pieces: the rest relapse into a dull monotone or even substandard language. In fact the very next issue, of February/March 1874, carries a notice to the effect that the editor of the paper is not in good health, that his illness is such that he must desist from reading and writing. In retrospect, this piece of news can be seen as the harbinger of a singular change of tone. The essays, dialogues, and short or serialized disquisitions that follow seem intent on portraying and proclaiming the need for the utter subservience of a good wife to her husband, in contrast with the notions of equality so clearly articulated in the first issue. There are no editorials now, no reader participation, no actual news coverage. There are no articles by women. Though women are addressed directly in the various educative ventures which form the mainstay of the journal, they are more often than not regarded as coarse and uneducated, rustic in habit and belief. The attempt is to urbanize, modernize, and make the housewife and mother a domestic key to the social well-being of the nuclear family.

---

[12] Ibid.

Since the education of women was considered a male responsibility,[13] it is not surprising that nineteenth-century women's journals were both edited by men and contained articles largely written by them. This male editorship probably accounted for the extremely controlled, even censored, nature of the subject matter offered, a central feature of *Balabodhini*, as of other women's journals of the period. There are no non-didactic tales, no novels, no jokes, no anecdotes. *Balabodhini* contributes its share to the creation of the new domestic model, to which end are offered the many *charitra* (portraits) of ideal women, both Indian, such as Savitri, and foreign, such as Joan of Arc. These traditional models in fact depict new gender roles—those engendered by the planned domestic economy and the need for an educated and educating mother. The writers, however, for all their emancipatory rhetoric, seem more intent on establishing the authority of the male head of the household than working out any notion of equality. When any of these famous figures steps out of the bounds of the domestic or defies male authority, she is firmly put back in her place. Joan of Arc is roundly berated—the writer is one Bihari Chaube—for trying to do more than she or any other women could have achieved under the circumstances: 'Too much daring, and powers too wonderful, bear bad fruit. And it is well nigh impossible that all this can be true of women who falsely imitate armless goddesses and play at being Bhavani. And the girls who begin to believe in such should refrain from doing so. Women should, instead, devotedly worship the husbands in their own homes.'[14]

Shiva's consort, Sati, is similarly taken to task for disobeying her good husband and misbehaving by insisting on going to her father's

---

[13] For instance, the *Kulinstri Kirtti* (1894), a missionary manual for women of good families. In the concluding piece, entitled *Hindustan ki striyom ke liye shiksha*, the author points out that though the women of Hind have many admirable qualities, they have many lamentable traits as well, all of which can be traced to lack of knowledge, for they have received no instruction: therefore the real fault lies at the door of men, *jinhom ne unhem vidya nahim parhai* (who never imparted learning to women: 146). The manual then goes on to praise the eagerness for learning demonstrated by *some* women.

[14] Harishchandra 1874–7: 3/6, 42.

house despite his reservations. Her story is introduced with this stern admonition: 'The woman's highest dharma in the world is to obey her husband's orders and her highest good also resides therein. The woman who does not recognise this dharma suffers intense pain in the end, and not only does she suffer from such disobedience but members of both clans [hers and her husband's] are overtaken by calamity. We excerpt the tale of sati from *Srimadbhagavata* as illustration of this.'[15] The censorship is such that the conventional Brajbhasha verse, which was printed so extensively in Harishchandra's other journals, is here absent, being obviously considered too erotic. The devotional frame in which it was often ensconced did not make it any the less threatening. The gendered description of *shringara*, or the erotic mode, even in devotional guise, was not meant to be a shared experience.[16] Such verses could lead a woman's thoughts away from her husband: 'O woman of good understanding [*sumati*], women of good [Kulin] families behave in such a way that, never mind song, not even a word from them reaches the ear of another. For such women singing is wicked, for ornamentation of sound, eroticism, the union or parting of a couple—all these make the mind turn astray . . . and it is also inappropriate for a woman to practice the singing of devotional songs [*bhajans*], for such discourse is shameless . . .'[17] Since bhajans were poetic compositions designed to be sung, they carried a sensual dimension which made them thoroughly undesirable in the new household setting. They might release erotic energies and were therefore to be strongly discouraged. This certainly seems one explanation for the absence of religious and other popular verse in the journal. There is only one long poem by Harishchandra which welcomes the Prince of Wales to India, and more specifically to Banaras.[18] (Since this is a political poem, it can presumably do no harm to the women who read it.)

By and large, the songs, stories, and performative genres associated with women of the lower classes were banned from women's

[15] Ibid.: 1/6, June 1874.
[16] This is a point I owe to Francesca Orsini.
[17] Harishchandra 1874–7: 2/8, August 1874.
[18] Ibid.: 3/6, June 1876.

quarters in the more respectable classes. There is, then, consistent discouragement to the singing of popular songs and bhajans, as well as socializing with other women and going to fairs and markets.[19] Women are warned again and again to stay away from public places: 'O woman of good understanding [*sumati*], it is entirely inappropriate for you to go to fairs and shows and other crowded places, for all kinds of people come there and no private (*ekant*) spot is available for women.'[20] Congregations on riverbanks and other such public places during ritual occasions can only lead to some variety of shameless conduct. In fact, religious ritual and practice, as creating possibly autonomous spheres for women, are treated with almost the disapproval expected from Christian missionaries. In a short skit entitled 'Lavali–Malati Samvad' (The Dialogue between Lovely and Malati), where two women converse with each other, fasting is categorically discouraged: it is seen as a sign of the lack of education. It is Lavali with her Western name (Lovely) who offers these emancipated views about women who indulge in excessive fasting: 'They fast up to four days in the week. This causes the parents-in-law discomfort, the mother- or sister-in-law has to do the cooking, sometimes the elder brother-in-law or his wife have to take over, but she lies around fasting; we don't observe these customs in our village.'[21] Lavali cites a Sanskrit verse from Parashara,[22] which is translated into Hindi so as to leave absolutely no room for doubt about its contents: a woman who fasts while her husband is still

---

[19] As Sangari points out: 'near universal attempt of these texts to erase earlier (or at least existing) forms of women's sociability and reciprocity under the signs of idleness and gossip . . . corrupting effects of women's conversations . . . resistance to domestic labour and marital relationships.' Sangari 1999: 339–40.

[20] Harishchandra 1874–7: 2/8, August 1875.

[21] Ibid.: 1/5, May 1874.

[22] *Parasharasmrti*, the work attributed to Parashara, from which the author quotes, is a late compendium on the rules of conduct, law and custom, with a clearly conservative stance on matters pertaining to women. P.V. Kane, in his *History of the Dharmashastra*, dates it in some period between the first and fifth centuries of the Christian era. See Kane 1969: 1/1 464.

alive contributes to the diminishment of his life, and she herself goes straight to hell. The women also agree that 'Our highest god is our husband. We gain in the life beyond by serving him, not by ritual bathing and other observances and image worship.'[23]

As laid out in this piece, the most important fasts connected with prayers for the long life of the husband can indeed be observed, but nothing beyond that. There is no article on religion, nor any retelling of mythological tales. In fact religion plays practically no role in the advice dealt out to women. When Rama and Sita make an appearance in a skit entitled 'Prempathik' (The Wayfarers of Love), they do so in an almost secular context. Their conversation limits itself to the description of seasons and the beauties of nature. The author—possibly Harishchandra in collaboration with Mallika— takes obvious inspiration from Tulsidas' *Ramcharitmanas* for this seasonal description. There is no erotic tension between the two divine lovers. When Sita protests that the heat and dust of the forest do not matter to her as long as she follows him, Rama indulges in excessive praise of her housewifely virtue:

> Beloved, when you say such things, my eyes fill with tears and my throat constricts. Praise be the clan in which daughters such as you are born, and the clan into which you marry. Earth itself rests on such virtue; your moral conduct and character will set an example and be a model for other women. Your name will shine like the sun and the moon till the end of time. It is true that being happy only in the happiness of the husband is the dharma of a virtuous wife. We are proud of a housewife such as you.[24]

Sita herself proceeds to point out the joys of rural life to her husband in what sounds suspiciously like urban middle-class rhapsodizing about the joys of life in the country: 'And where there is the shade of some dense tree, the wayfarers pause to rest from their labour, some take their bundle, others their arm, for a pillow to lie down to sleep, some talk of stray matters. They buy small things to take some

---

[23] Harishchandra 1874–7: 1/5, May 1874.
[24] Ibid.: 2/1, January 1875.

nourishment from the shops set up under a little shade; some sit in the direction of the breeze to cool their bodies.'[25] The countryside recedes to picture-book dimensions. The middle-class woman, withdrawn from any participation in the productive process and with limited property rights, is being confined, in whatever state of enlightenment, within the walls of the middle-class home and then made to take an almost textbook peep at the rest of the world.[26] Her attire, as a later piece lays out in no unclear terms, should proclaim her new status, at once privileged, puritanical, and restricted: 'The clothes a woman wears should be of the kind that will entirely veil her bodily parts and not be such that the several parts appear separate. Clothes etc. are worn only so that the bodily parts remain hidden . . .'[27]

All this advice is contained in an innocuous series which runs under general titles such as 'Shishupalan' (childcare), 'Balaprabodh' (the young girls' guide), 'Stricharcha' (conduct code for women), 'Garbhinicharya' (the pregnant woman's manual), 'Gurusarini' (digest of weights and measures consisting of verse to be memorized and taught to the young), and 'Arthaniti va Arthashastra' (the economics of landownership). These articles and series contain practical advice to the housewife and mother regarding the new hygiene, medical care, and the newly emerging middle-class social code. If there is additional information regarding matters political and economic, it is imparted with the specific intention of educating women to become the future instructors of sons. The long serialization of a play as political as Vishakhadatta's Sanskrit *Mudrarakshasa* in Hindi translation in *Balabodhini* bears clear testimony to this intent.

Of further importance in our context is the fact that in the many columns filled with good advice regarding the duties of the

---

[25] Ibid.: 2/1, January 1875.

[26] A later skit carries the information that the time is an autumn morning, the place on the banks of the Godavari. Rama and Sita climb down the bank, carrying *jalpaan*, eatables. It almost sounds like a picnic. There follows a conversation about matters relating to the household of Dasharatha, and once again there is some landscape description. Ibid.: 2/11, November 1875.

[27] Ibid.: 3/1, January 1876.

housewife, as also in the little skits and sketches illustrating them, there is no discussion of social reform, though the question of reform revolved largely around the status of women in society. It was a major preoccupation of the editors of the vernacular papers when addressing the larger general public, and Harishchandra himself had participated fully in this exercise in his two major journals.[28] Some consensus around these issues obviously formed a vital constituent of the self-perception of the emergent middle class. Yet, though the editors of women's journals were themselves reformers, and included Harishchandra, the issues contested so vehemently in the period—from sati and widow remarriage to polygamy—were largely missing from the pages of women's journals.[29] Women were not expected to participate in the debate, let alone determine the resolution of the issues at stake. It is not surprising, then, that the little skit on the fate of Sulochana, the wife of Ravana's son Meghanada, exalts sati rather than questions it.[30]

By and large, the journal's issues focused on useful knowledge with little or no attempt at amusement. No genre considered entertaining was deemed fit for women, no new entertainment genre was evolved for them. The lively editor of the two other journals—irreverent, colloquial, curious, and amusing—was here conspicuous by his absence. Most of the pieces in the journal seem to have been written by less-well-known men from the provinces, the works themselves often barely disguised translations and adaptations passed off as their own and possibly published as independent booklets elsewhere. The last three issues contain one instalment each of serializations, lengthy stretches of *Mudrarakshasa*, advice to the pregnant, and a long botanical article. It is not surprising that the journal ceased publication abruptly with the February issue of the fourth year.[31]

---

[28] See the discussion of Harishchandra's essays pleading for social reform, with focus on the woman's question, in Dalmia 1997: 316–22.

[29] Pointed out in Shukla 1991: 65.

[30] Harishchandra 1874–7: 1/8, August 1874.

[31] The December 1876 (3/12) issue consists in its entirety of a long instalment of the translation of the Sanskrit play *Mudrarakshasa*. The January 1876 (4/1) continues a long serialization 'Garbh' (conception), from the

Harishchandra was obviously compiling and editing the journal as a public responsibility, with no great verve or new insight. Though much of the subject matter in the journal stood in polar opposition to the traditional model of the wife and mother (we need only think of the discouragement to practise religious ritual and the hostility to the social world of the extended family), the venture itself seems to have been an obligation no public man of letters of the period could afford to ignore, so compulsive were its demands.[32] Mallika may have participated in the writing of the skits, but their didactic tones do not betray the liveliness of her pen—not as we know it from other works. As such it remained a novel venture in the Hindi world, clearly and determinedly participating in the definition of new spaces. The husband/father was set up as head of a nuclear household, at this stage as a projected model, with a rigid codification of the subservient role of the housewife/mother, and the domestic labour which was to be entirely her lot.

Androgyny and Desire

Nevertheless, in the middle of this very period, i.e. the mid 1870s, Harishchandra was busy writing another work concerned with the very matter banned out of existence in the journal. This was a full-length erotic-devotional play, with a woman, Chandravali, at its centre, a *gopi* who loved Krishna with wild abandon. The play was cast in the mould of the Raslila, a traditional genre, the roots of which can be traced back to Braj country from the fifteenth to the sixteenth centuries and to the many Krishna cults which sprang up around this period and congregated there.[33] The Raslila genre had a

---

November issue (3/11) of the year before and begins yet another series, this time botanical (*Udbhij*). The last issue of the journal that we possess, February 1877 (4/2), then predictably consists of an instalment of *Udbhij*.

[32] Thus also the venture by Sayyid Ahmad Khan of Delhi. His shortlived journal for women, *Akhbar un-Nissa*, was founded in Delhi in 1887. No trace of this remains, apart from its name. Cf. Minault 1998: 107.

[33] See Hein (1972) and Hawley (1992) for more information on the origin and evolution of this form.

clearly religious-ritual framework and consisted of the re-enactment of episodes from the childhood and youth of the pastoral god in his miraculous pranks and amatory dalliances. The lila had originally been enacted by adult actors, though later these were replaced by child actors who came to be regarded as representatives of the deities for the duration of the play. An important role was played by the narrator, who relates the tale and adds comments, knitting together the various parts of the play, i.e. the short dialogues, the devotional songs, and the dances. By the nineteenth century the Raslila had crystallized into a highly conventional form within a clear ritual framework. Harishchandra was later to describe the form as *bhrashta*, or corrupt, in his long treatise on the history and aesthetics of the modern Indian and more specifically Hindi drama.[34] However, he considered the form vital enough to recreate it in a new, more realistic, mode as part of his long-term agenda of creating a corpus of plays in modern Hindi.

The plot of the play continues to correspond, however, to the typical *Nikunjlila*, the largest class of *lilas*.[35] Chandravali, along with Lalita, has a place of some importance in the pantheon of the Vallabha *sampradaya*, one of the major devotional communities which came into existence in the late fifteenth century in the Braj region. In Nathdvara in Rajasthan, where the main temple of the community came to be located, Chandravali's birthday is celebrated two days before Radha's, on *bhadra shukla sashthami*.[36] Harishchandra was almost certainly acquainted with Rupa Gosvami's sixteenth-century Sanskrit play *Vidagdhamadhava*, wherein Chandravali in her love for Krishna becomes Radha's chief rival.[37] Chandravali in our play signs her love-letter by drawing the symbol of the sickle-moon, a signature Harishchandra was himself known to use on his official stationery,

---

[34] By Harishchandra's own estimation, the *raslila* was to be considered *bhrashta* (corrupt), *jis mem natakta shesa nahin rah gayi hai* (wherein no dramatic quality has survived)—as against the classical Sanskrit dramatic forms—in his essay 'Natak', in Harishchandra (1950), 1975: 1014.

[35] Cf. Hein 1972: 163–78.

[36] Cf. Vairagi 1977: 43.

[37] Cf. Wulff 1982.

since it included Chandrika, Mallika's pen-name in her poems. This would indicate the inclusion, if not actual participation, of Mallika in the composition of this venture as well.

In this re-creation, *Chandravali* retained the religious colouring of Raslila, but a number of conventions were dropped or modified and new ones introduced. The form was clearly being reconstituted so as to better answer the needs of the modern stage and presumably cater to an audience not consisting only of a congregation of devotees. The body of the narrative was no longer loosely strung together, it was cut up into scenes on the basis of the locale of the action. The narrator becomes superfluous in this reorganization and was consequently dropped. There was a backdrop, i.e. a more realistic setting, presumably on a proscenium stage with curtains. There were clear-cut stage directions for adult actors, possibly female impersonators in the case of the women, whose movements, body language, and costumes, even those of the allegorical characters, were described in a manner more realistic than hitherto. But there was obviously also the need to Sanskritize, in order to finally elevate the form and locate it within the great tradition. Thus, there was selective use of the conventions of Sanskrit drama.[38]

The language of the play was no longer Brajbhasha, but racy, colloquial Hindi, though Braj was retained for the verse, since it was the canonical language of the Vallabha *sampradaya*. Braj was also used by Krishna and the three allegorical figures. Chandravali, however, only spoke Braj when talking to them, yet she always reverted to Hindi when talking with her friends, and most of all in her soliloquies. She was obviously more realistically presented and more personalized than the rest. The new prose writing of the period was self-consciously and deliberately in Hindi rather than in Braj, which was fast acquiring a more local, if not dialect, character. To be more 'realistic' and reach out to a wider audience would mean the use of modern Hindi rather than Braj in the central body of the play. A great deal of this new realism came via the commercial Parsi stage, since this was the one model of the modern which was accessible on

---

[38] For a detailed discussion of this point, see Dalmia-Luderitz 1992.

stage rather than on paper. As has been pointed out, characters in the Parsi theatre thought about themselves, soliloquized, speculated about their actions, and about the spaces that they inhabited and the relationships that they enacted. This is the mode adopted by Chandravali in the play. Both her language and the melodramatic mode that she adopts, as we will see below, seem directly modelled on the Parsi theatre.[39]

The body of the play consists of four short *amkas*, or acts, in Hindi prose, interspersed with Brajbhasha verse. It is framed within the conventions of classical Sanskrit drama, in marked departure from the conventional *raslila*, which has no such preliminaries. The play begins with a *prastavana* (prologue), which serves primarily to introduce the playwright. Asked by the *pariparshvika* (assistant manager) why the play of a newcomer has been chosen for performance, the *sutradhara*, or director of the play, explains:

> parama premanidhi rasika bara, ati adara guna khana
> jaga jana ranjana ashu kavi, ko haricanda samana.
>
> (Abode of love, best of all the *rasika*s, a mine of virtue worthy of the highest respect, who in the world can equal Harishchandra as spontaneous poet, when it comes to delighting people.)

The playwright is then speaking as a *rasika*, a connoisseur, to his audience, but also as a *new* dramatist, who is modernizing even as he sets forth the traditional.

The manager and his assistant vacate the stage to make way for Shukadeva. The *vishkambhaka* (introductory scene) consists of a dialogue between Shukadeva and Narada, the two heavenly *bhaktas*, who still view the love of the *gopis* as more elevated than theirs. Of these *gopis*, Chandravali has attained the most advanced state of love. Though, for reasons of love, Radha has split herself into two and in a sense is also Chandravali, it is she who prevents the union of the two lovers. The two bhaktas, caught in the remembrance of the idyllic Braj countryside, unable to bear the pain of separation, need only to hear the sound of the flute to rush away to witness the lila.

[39] Kapur 2004.

By using these introductory devices, the play is effectively set within a context, whereby Chandravali's love is not to be mistaken for earthly passion but to be seen rather as the most elevated form of bhakti. At the same time, though not setting out to do so, in making the setting and the language more realistic, the poet is providing models which cannot but have a bearing on earthly lovers. There is a new individuation and psychologization in the presentation of the figures of the play, particularly of Chandravali, and an egalitarianism in the love relationship between woman and man, almost androgynous in their melting into each other. The whole range of emotions possible within the state of separation is depicted in the body of the play. Noteworthy in our context is the extreme eroticism of the entirely earthly desire of Chandravali for her lover, as his for her. In the second *amka*, Chandravali's long soliloquy is interrupted by the Devi of the forest, and by Sandhya and Varsha, personifications of evening and rain respectively, who tease and provoke her out of her wits. Gay, mischievous, and mournful, the scene rushes through a whole variety of moods: Chandravali runs to trees to ask them of Krishna, mistakes the moon for the sun, night for day, herself for Krishna, and runs finally into the dark of the forest to falter and lose her way. It is in this wild passion verging on madness that there are clear resonances of Ophelia in her madness, of the psychologization of Shakespearean drama as presented in all its excess by the much-derided but highly influential Parsi stage. Thus Chandravali in the following soliloquy:

> (recollects her state) Alas, I was so forlorn that I called night day. Whom did I seek? Oh woe, what must have the three friends said about my state? Oh, it was the moon which has hidden itself behind the clouds. Oh, the murderess is the rainy season, I had forgotten. There is no seeing the way in this darkness, where shall I tread and how shall I reach home? Look, O beloved, all that appeared enticing on the way to the tryst now seems terrifying. Oh, the forest which seemed so benevolent now seems so frightening. Oh look, everything is there, only you are not. (Tears flow from her eyes) Beloved, where have you gone? Why have you abandoned me?

She despairs and faints, to be rescued by the three, the Devi of the forest, and by Sandhya and Varsha, who have, after all, kept track of her. Harishchandra's lively use of Hindi, teasing, provocative, wild, melancholy, and tragic by turns, makes for a new realism in the self-analysis of the despairing Chandravali:

> O lord, to whom should I confide these desires, to whom should I reveal my ecstasy? Beloved, the night is short and there is much to be played out. Minuscule my life though boundless my enthusiasm. There seems to be no place here for one as smitten as me. The days and night go by in weeping. No one asks about my well-being, for no one in this world looks at the heart, they look only at external things. Oh, I've become useless, derided by friend and foe. I left everyone and resorted to you alone, but you've made things come to this pass. Oh, to whom should I belong, whose face should I behold, if I'm to go on living? Beloved, after I'm gone, you won't find another quite like me . . . You make me furious and I feel like saying many things. Enough, I shall curse you now . . . Liar, liar, liar.

This is a woman who speaks of a physical passion which disturbs her social relations and makes for an immense loneliness. Krishna comes to her finally, disguised as a beautiful *yogini*, a woman ascetic. This is a traditional enough device. Of particular note in this modern setting, however, is his self-representation, as well as the form in which he reveals his love. There is nothing to distinguish him in his passion and abandon from Chandravali herself. In fact, the play constantly evokes the androgynous nature of the *sakhya bhava*, the companionate mode of relating to the Lord, making possible the interchangeability of gender, since both seem to be inherent in both lovers. Chandravali identifies herself as Krishna when, in her lovelorn state, she is asked who she is. Krishna appears as a yogini, beautiful even in disguise and radiating such profound resemblance that Chandravali is instantly drawn to her. The *yogini* sings a Lavani, a song in semi-classical mode:

sanchi jogin piya bin biyogin nari

Only a woman pining for her beloved is a true yogini.

There is play on the word '*jogin*', woman ascetic, and '*biyogin*', any woman parted from her beloved and yearning for his presence, whereby religious and erotic love become indistinguishable. Any woman seeking the presence of her lover can be sublimated as being a true *yogini*. There is a further tantalizing element. This presentation of erotic longing is being sung by a man in the guise of a female ascetic to his beloved, who recognizes the male within the female, so to speak. The expression of desire is not gendered, at best it is androgynous. Chandravali is led to muse:

> (to herself) Oh, oh, how her song pierces my heart. Her words have an indescribably strange power on my heart. But perhaps it is my heart which is becoming more vulnerable. Oh, oh, her voice is exactly like that of my beloved. (Controlling her tears with an effort) Let me make her sing a little more. (Loud) Joginji, if it is not too much trouble, may I ask you to sing on (saying this she sometimes looks at her with affection and sometimes bows her head, lost in thought).

And she is both immensely attracted and tortured by the possibility that the *yogini* could be Krishna. In the final act, Krishna in fact confirms that she is within him, as he is within her. The whole is then once more sublimated to the religious level, as Chandravali, rather than Krishna, pronounces the *bharatavakya*, the closing aphorism of the play:

> *yaha ratnadipa hariprema ka sada prakashita rahe*
>
> May the jewel-lamp of the love of Hari keep the world forever lit.

This is the successful incorporation of the traditional *raslila* into the literary canon which Harishchandra was in the process of establishing. In a fast urbanizing and modernizing society, the *raslila* was beginning to acquire the status of a folk form.[40] By creating drama in modern Hindi, Harishchandra was appropriating two models, the folk *raslila* and classical Sanskrit drama, the latter providing the initiatory and other structural conventions, thereby raising the whole to a new classical status. Inasmuch as the form he now created was to be considered modern, though it derived its status from the classical,

---

[40] This estimation corresponds to H.H. Wilson's categorization of these forms as of 'inferior description' in the introductory essay to his influential *Select Specimens of the Theatre of the Hindus*. Wilson 1835: xv.

he was at appropriate moments also free to introduce newer stage conventions and innovate in myriad ways.

I have discussed the issue of dramatic convention at some length in order to demonstrate that Harishchandra is indulging in something more than a merely repetitive exercise in piety. He is modernizing the form, making it stageworthy in a new urban context. He innovates most of all in the use of Hindi, a language which was only then beginning to achieve literary status and flexibility. Brajbhasha, with its explicitly devotional/liturgical register, is inserted within this more secular linguistic frame. However, the devotional-erotic focus, with its fluid gender boundaries, remains intact. It is no wonder that there is a decided shift in the critical evaluation of the play. If earlier-twentieth-century critics tended to magnify the qualities of the play,[41] a later more puritanical age reacted with some discomfort and made efforts to marginalize it, for the play ill befitted the image of a poet who had been canonized as the father of modern secular Hindi literature.[42]

If it is not explicitly addressed to women, may we assume that the play has any bearing on the woman question? At no point in the preliminaries or the concluding scene does Harishchandra speak of the Hindu *nari* (woman). Yet the very fact that, in spite of its traditional theme, the play is offered as a modern composition with all the conventions of the modern stage would suggest that it could not be relegated to the religious sphere alone. There seems to be a clear refusal in the play to separate the spheres of women and men; and the treatment of the two lovers, as I have tried to show above, is decidedly androgynous.[43] By and large, this kind of poetry,

---

[41] Sahay 1975: 183–8; Brajratnadas 1962: 161–2; Varshneya 1974: 93–4. As Varshneya also points out, in addition to the conventions of Sanskrit drama, Harishchandra seems also to have made a successful attempt to maintain here the three unities of Western drama.

[42] Thus, for instance, the discomfiture of Sharma 1984: 114 and the relatively distanced interpretation by Taneja 1976: 74–80, who views the play as lacking in internal and external conflict and the erotic element as disturbing the dramatic quality of the play.

[43] Ashis Nandy speaks of there being a greater tolerance for androgyny

drama, and art form, depicting the various aspects of *shringara* (the erotic mode), when also legitimated as representing overtly religious experience, made possible male and female cohabitation, and a shared sexual and emotional space which was not always differentiated along gender lines. Though this religious experience was seen as a primarily male preserve, it was also accessible to women, especially if they had managed to achieve high religious standing—as had the great sixteenth-century devotional figure Mira. Thus, theoretically, this form represented male and female subjectivity, and not just the appropriation of women's voices. It could still be argued, however, that, shared or not, this was sublimated religious and/or aesthetic experience which was not meant to be reproduced in the domestic realm. As a purely sensuous experience, at this level, it remained the preserve of men of means, accessible in extra-marital relationships. For women, the experience could only become possible if they were courtesans or dangerously transgressive lovers. Therefore, in this period of increasing puritanism, this religious-erotic territory remained barred to respectable women. Yet, couched in religious terms, it existed as an at least theoretically legitimate space for shared sensuous experience, and it could be claimed as such by a later age.

Toppling Patriarchy

In 1882, towards the end of his short life, Harishchandra published under his name yet another work focusing on women, the novel entitled *Kulin Kanya, athava Chandraprabha aur Purnaprakash*. The genre was very slowly coming into circulation in modern Hindi: the creation of the novel in Hindi, begun in the 1860s, continued to be an arduous process. Most of the early ventures were written in response to the need for textbooks in the modern languages. Colonial educational authorities often offered small cash awards for such attempts. British patronage being considered prestigious and

---

in India, though his treatment of the theme is disappointingly brief. Nandy 1983: 36.

the cash incentive most welcome,[44] there was a strong pedagogical impetus behind such works, which by and large validated and reinforced the positions taken up in journals such as *Balabodhini*. Literary histories dutifully record the titles and authors of these novels but dwell at greater length on the better-known novelists of the twentieth century.

However, there is another genealogy of the novel, a more popular and pliable one, which has largely been ignored by literary historiography. It seems to have come directly through Bengali, where under the penship of Bankimchandra the novel had developed into a sophisticated form of entertainment as well as education. Harishchandra's novel, as written by Mallika, was born of this lineage. It had a direct, racy style and it plunged straight into the narrative without preamble. The plot was clearly delineated, the character sketches short, the action swiftly related.

Mallika translated from the Bengali or re-created three short novels, of which *Kulin Kanya* is supposed to have been the first, probably written around 1880. It was included in an anthology of Hindi works, *Bhasha Sar* (The Essence of Language,1884); though it was offered as a translation, the Bengali original has not been traced. Most critics agree that it was the re-creation of a story taken from Bengali, enriched by several minor characters of Mallika's own invention, and embellished with local detail—for it is set in Hindi- and Urdu-speaking Lucknow.[45] Clearly, Mallika added much that

[44] See Kalsi 1992 for a discussion of the prizes awarded, and Dalmia 1998 for the pedagogy of the early novel in Hindi.

[45] Ray 1968 offers the most reliable information on Mallika's publications. Three works are attributed to her. The first is *Radharani* (the original is a short romance by Bankimchandra, 1877), translated and published as by '*kisi pati-prana abala*' (a helpless woman, the life-breath of her husband) in 1883 (Banaras: Mallik Chandra and Co.) The second is *Saundaryamayi*, yet another translation from the Bengali, published under her own name in 1887 and printed by Amar Yantralaya in Banaras. Finally, *Chandraprabha aur Purvaprakash, Upanyas*, published by the Khadagvilas Press under Harishchandra's name in 1888 (not 1889 as Ray maintains), as the title page of the copy available in the India Office Library clearly proclaims. The same press brought out another edition in 1921. There is also an undated edition of

was her own to the novel; we have two fragments of novels similar in design, tone, and intention, which though not published in her lifetime further confirm her style and authorship.[46] They deal with romantic love, of its impossibility, and the many taboos surrounding the social interaction of young men and women. *Kulin Kanya* remains a work which can be considered twice-filtered: it appears under Harishchandra's name and in the guise of a translation, though here again we are told that Harishchandra participated in it to the extent that he corrected the Bengali idiom which laced Mallika's Hindi. Later tradition has been quite clear in its verdict that this novel was primarily the work of Mallika.

Kulin Kanya is a brilliant early piece. It consists of eleven short, crisply constructed chapters. They are crowned by quotations from the most venerable works, from Vaishnava scriptures, Nanddas, Tulsidas, and from Brajbhasha poets of standing such as Biharilal. They endow the work with literary respectability. The narrative falters somewhat at the beginning since it is not always able to organize the information to be conveyed, and is sometimes awkward in its introduction of characters. But once the line or two of necessary information is out of the way, the pace picks up. There is a spontaneous, easy use of language, quick exchange of dialogue, and unselfconscious description of feelings which never becomes mawkish. The language is lightly Sanskritic, reminiscent of Bankim, while the dialogue is in a more colloquial Hindi.[47]

---

the work published by the Hari Prakash Yantralaya in Banaras. According to Ray, Brajratnadas, the poet's grandson, maintained that the work was originally written in 1880, its language having been corrected and improved by the poet. However, this remains speculative.

[46] Another manuscript in what is believed to be her handwriting and her Bengali-inflected Hindi was found almost a century later. See the article by Bate Krishna and Girish Chandra in *Saptahik Hindustan* (17 September 1989) for further information on this work (which seems to be combined from two unfinished works) as well as long excerpts from it published under the title *Kumudini*.

[47] On Bankim's language, see the translators' introduction to his *The Poison Tree: Three Novellas* (1996: il).

The tale seems typical of its times and is told quickly. Chandraprabha is the daughter of a Kulin Kanyakubja Brahman, four times married.[48] One wife bore him a son and a daughter, one wife only a daughter, and the other two remained barren. He lived with the wife who had borne the son and the daughter. The wife Gunamanjari who had only a daughter, named Chandraprabha, lived with her brother in Lucknow. Chandraprabha is of marriageable age now, but it is not easy to find a groom of her father's caste-standing. She has fallen in love with a young man, Purnaprakash, who studies in Lucknow's Canning College, and he with her. The two observe each other as he goes in and out of his sister's house nextdoor. Chandraprabha's father is indifferent to her fate. This is clearly an ill-fated romance, since Purnaprakash is a Brahman of lower-caste status. It is the mother who feels deeply for her daughter and guesses what preoccupies her. Whatever the gender of the original author of the novel, the Hindi re-creation is written almost entirely from the perspective of the women. The first chapter depicts a tender scene between mother and daughter, for it is this relationship which forms the focus of the novel.[49] Chandraprabha is perched on a window overlooking the neighbour's house. The mother takes her weeping daughter's chin in her hand and says: 'You'll gain nothing by worrying. Who can wipe away what the unknown has ordained for you?'

However, after initial discouragement, the mother does arrange to have her daughter marry the young man of her choice. The father has been asked to take a hand in the matter of finding a suitable groom but has remained inactive for a long period. Once the marriage is arranged, however, he turns up at the last minute with a prospective

---

[48] In the latter half of the nineteenth century there was an intense debate around the practice of polygamy, indulged in by the high-standing Kulin Brahmans of Bengal. The many young women they married, since suitable bridegrooms of the same caste were a rarity, lived a life of want and scarcity. Apart from anything else, there was always the danger of early widowhood for several women at once if one such husband died.

[49] Bankim's *Radharani*, which Mallika was also to translate, begins with a focus on a mother–daughter relationship, this time a dying mother tended to by her devoted daughter.

groom of his choice, an elderly man of the right caste standing. The father has also arranged to pay a suitable dowry for her. The mother exchanges sharp words with her husband and shows them the door. But the husband has a last resort, which is to threaten and then actually proceed to fast unto death. And such is the awful force of the sin which visits those who have caused a Brahman's death that the mother is forced to give in. But while her husband and the elderly bridegroom wait outside the women's quarters for the marriage to be performed, inside the two young lovers are united in lawful wedlock in a ritually binding wedding ceremony. The father and the elderly groom-in-waiting pronounce the most awful curses, whereupon Chandraprabha's maternal uncle, who has shown great emotional concern for his sister and niece, throws the two intruders out as unceremoniously as they themselves had burst upon the scene.

Though the predicament of the mother, abandoned since early youth, and of the two lovers of unequal caste status seeking union, is typical of its times, the course that the tale itself takes is not. Chandraprabha longs for a happiness that cannot appropriately be granted. The best way to take care of her needs would have been to have her die a tragic death of some sort. She could thus gain the reader's sympathy, and provide emotional release while disturbing no norms.[50] But the dynamism and quick pace of the novel have been propelling the narrative in another direction. The women are daring and impertinent. Their conversations and their manoeuvres provide a novel perspective. They mercilessly expose the wiles of the father and the elderly bridegroom.

The mother, Gunamanjari, is the main agent of change. Her reflections and action provide the focus:

> Gunamanjari grew most anxious. Her daughter's happiness was her happiness, and in her unhappiness lay her unhappiness. Her worry grew as she saw her daughter grow thin. She was filled with remorse when she thought of how she had sent Purna away. Many a time she got up to write to him, then felt helpless. She has sent him off once, with what

---

[50] I am grateful to Paula Richman for remarking upon this. Bankim's transgressive women characters are rewarded by one kind of death or another.

face can she call him back again? After three months had passed in this state, she could hold herself back no longer.

She wrote a letter to Purna, saying the marriage had been fixed, and all they awaited was his arrival. Even if Chandraprabha's father was to bring a groom as good-looking as Kamadeva and as learned as Brihaspati, and even if he were of the highest clan, Gunamanjari would give Chandraprabha's hand to him alone.

Gunamanjari wrote to him thinking that if she could not make Chandraprabha happy in her own lifetime, what in fact would she have achieved in her life? The compulsions of *kaulinya* (good birth) made her live the life of a widow in spite of her husband's existence; she would not let her dear daughter suffer such torture.

And this, as we have seen, is just what she does proceed to do, hampered by all the obstacles her husband puts in her way. Throughout the narrative, in fact, there is a clear resistance to autocratic men. When, in a heated exchange, her husband asks her what she lacks, what needs she could possibly have, living as comfortably as she does, she bursts out, 'What am I unhappy about, what do I lack? My only unhappiness is that neither you nor I die.' Faced with such resistance, he thinks of beating her into acquiescence, but he cannot do this, the narrator points out wryly, because he finds himself in her natal home. So he has to descend to argument and ruse. And in the midst of all this, he and the elderly groom indulge in the pettiest of bickering about the exact price of the bride. At the final moment of disclosure, when the two men discover what has taken place inside the women's quarters and break into the most vile verbal abuse, it is the maternal uncle who censures them: 'Get out of the house. You use words bigger than your mouth can hold. On such an auspicious day, you utter such inauspicious words.'

Once again, the work has no explicit agenda, nationalist or otherwise, though obviously the theme of social reform does underlie the narrative, dealing as it does with the polygamous excesses of Kulin Brahmans.[51] However, there is no rhetoric regarding the state, fallen

---

[51] The Hari Prakash Press copy does further qualify the title as follows: *Kulin vivah sambandhi ek chhoti si akhyayika* (A short tale regarding Kulin marriages), indicating that a reformatory agenda was inherent in the narrative.

or otherwise, of the Hindu woman. In fact, there is no mention of any of the newer institutions of authority—save on one rather telling occasion: when the prospective groom and the father discover that they have been tricked, the disgruntled bridegroom calls out to the colonial authorities, the Magistrate Sahib and Company Bahadur, for help and intervention. We may be overinterpreting if we understand this as an indictment of colonial institutions which backed the newly reinforced patriarchal order. Yet this is the sole invocation of any colonial institutional authority. But, whether it sets out to propagate social reform or not, the novel remains a strong statement of women's desires, needs, bonding, and defiance, and it comes from the pen of a woman who neither knew conventional domestic life nor the need to break out of it, though she may have once had to suffer the consequences of its restrictive codes.

In Retrospect

Gender roles as propagated in the late nineteenth century could by no means be considered fixed, even at the prescriptive level. The counter-thrusts continued to exert power and attract. *Chandravali* was considered a powerful work and Mallika's novels were reprinted well into the 1920s. Thus, the androgyny of Chandravali and the fierce defiance of the women in the novel coexisted with the new puritanical code laid down by *Balabodhini*.

For all the importance of these concurrent voices, I would not want to suggest that the explicit agenda of the journal need not be accepted at face value. It is true that most of its contents stemmed from pens other than Harishchandra's. But equally clear, though projected only as a model at this stage, the journal's stern codification of woman's domestic role and the division of space into public and private would soon gather more force and be taken as a grid by myriad social institutions. This grid continued to be maintained and propagated by conduct books pouring in from the West, translated or adapted by missionaries and civil servants and supplemented by their own pamphleteering. As a genre, the woman's journal continued to generate and reflect normative expectations.

What has posterity chosen to remember, what has found approval, and what perpetuation? In fact, all three works discussed above have been largely forgotten or ignored. Even *Balabodhini* seems to have been too early for its times. It finds dutiful and honourable mention in all biographies of Harishchandra, but there has been no further engagement with its contents or format. Hindi journals for women only found perpetuation at the turn of the century, when the message was propagated in less ponderous ways.[52] As for *Chandravali*, opinions, as we saw above, were divided. If earlier, more traditionalist, critics claimed high literary status for it, later critics were embarrassed by its eroticism and excessive emotion. And *Kulin Kanya*, though apparently popular in its time, was all but forgotten. It was certainly not considered a part of Harishchandra's standard collected works. Mallika herself has not found mention as one of the earliest women writers in Hindi.

As far as the modern Hindi literary canon is concerned, the *raslila* suffered perhaps the greatest eclipse, since it so obviously belonged to a premodern realm. Its very egalitarianism, its explicit address of women's sensuality and sexuality, would surface several decades later in the literature produced by women writers. I am thinking of the erotic-mystical poems of Mahadevi Varma in the 1930s, which occupied an almost religious-philosophical realm, since this was the one area considered legitimate for the articulation of such experience.

Though the combative tones of *Kulin Kanya* would seem to belong almost entirely to the realm of fantasy, the very existence of such attitudes shows that they could, at the very least, create these realms in fiction. It has been maintained that the behaviour of characters in novels is code-oriented and they tend to animate rather than expand the code.[53] The romantic attachment which goes hand in hand with initiating, establishing, and maintaining companionate marriage and the new nuclear family may well be the code which animates

---

[52] See Talwar (1989) for a discussion of women's journals in the first decades of the twentieth century.

[53] See Luhmann 1986: 11.

this early venture, and in this it can be seen as merely extending the code that the journal propagates. Yet it does push the boundaries of the acceptable while doing so, not only in that caste rigidities are seen as less binding, but in that it so fiercely indicts patriarchal autocracy. While Harishchandra and Mallika, as authors, seem here to be primarily involved in filling out the details of companionate marriage, with its suggestion of shared emotional, erotic, and mental experience, they also support the notion of the mutual choice of marriage partner, which is surely a vital element of companionate marriage as well. Even giving this kind of support means entering dangerous territory, however, for if the choice is to be mutual, female as well as male, it violates the kind of patriarchy that family life, as projected in the journal, represents. Therefore, the journal and novel, while overlapping in their goal of setting up a nuclear family, in this respect clearly part company. Further, in the novel it does not merely remain a question of men seeking to reform a male-managed social set-up; rather, the women are agitating for reform and taking steps to bring it about. In this early novel, the possibility of all agency being concentrated in the hands of the mother, and of close bonding between mother and daughter, becomes a reality. Such possibilities would recede radically in the following decades. As Premchand would show in his immensely powerful and popular novels of the first quarter of the next century, in *Sevasadan* (1916) and *Nirmala* (1926), the mother–daughter relationship would be the worst affected by the new patriarchal order and the renewed importance of dowry.[54] Mothers would often be the first to push daughters out of the house into unsuitable matches with elderly bridegrooms for material considerations. Female subjectivity, erotic as well as reformist, would continue to be held in severe check through the literature of the early twentieth century by male writers, a hegemony internalized by women writers. It would be the 'tradition' created by the new patriarchies, the amalgamation of the old and the new, and

---

[54] See Plummer (1999): 'Dowry and Personal Property in the Lives of Women in Colonial India: The Novels of Premchand', M.A. thesis, University of California, Berkeley.

their 'victimization' of women which would be relentlessly depicted and exposed in the prose literature of the following decades: journals, novel, and ultimately the short story.

The three works considered here suggest contesting stances which, though addressing related issues, would remain in their separate spheres for many decades. As a genre, the novel would perhaps finally emerge as being best able to carry the concerns of the three works discussed here. But in the late nineteenth century they would remain confined to different genres, representing the coexisting but unresolved needs of the times. It is as such that they would be represented in the works of Harishchandra, who in his short but intensely creative life would contain in his works the whole range of social possibilities, presenting with great eloquence and vigour the new puritanical mould, the devotional–erotic framed anew, and early feminist protest—with each of these excluding the possibility of the other.

References

Bannerji, Himani, 1991. 'Fashioning a Self: Educational Proposals for and by Women in Popular Magazines in Colonial Bengal'. *Economic and Political Weekly*, 26 October.

Bate, Krishna and Girishchandra Chaudhari, 1989. 'Mallika: Bharatendu ki dharmagrhita.' *Saptahik Hindustan*, 17 September.

Borthwick, Meredith, 1984. *The Changing Role of Women in Bengal 1849–1905*. Princeton: Princeton University Press.

Brajratnadas (1935), 1962. *Bharatendu Harishchandra*. Allahabad: Hindustani Ekedami.

Chatterjee, Bankimchandra, 1887. *Bankim Samagra. Collected Novels of Bankim Chandra.* (Hindi), ed. Nihal Chandra Varma. Banaras: Pracharak Granthavali Yojana.

———, 1996. *The Poison Tree: Three Novellas*. Translated by Marian Madden and S.N. Mukherjee. Delhi: Penguin Books.

Chaudhari, Girishchandra. 1986. 'Bharatendu ki Preyasi'. *Saptahik Hindustan*, 28 September.

Dalmia, Vasudha, 1997. *The Nationalization of Hindu Traditions: Bharatendu Harishchandra and Nineteenth-century Banaras*. Delhi: Oxford University Press.

———, 1998. 'A Novel Moment in Hindi: Pariksha Guru', in *Narrative Strategies: Essays on South Asian Literature and Film*, ed. Vasudha Dalmia and Theo Damsteegt. Leiden: CNWS, and Delhi: Oxford University Press.

———, 2001. 'Vernacular Histories in Late Nineteenth-Century Banaras: Folklore, Puranas and the New Antiquarianism'. *Indian Economic and Social History Review*, sp. issue: *The Dilemma of the Indian Intellectual, 18th to 20th Centuries*, ed. Nita Kumar, 37/3.

Dalmia-Luderitz, Vasudha, 1992. 'A National Theatre for the Hindus. Harishchandra of Banaras and the Classical Traditions in Late Nineteenth-Century India', in *Literature, Language and the Media in India*, ed. Mariola Offredi. Delhi: Manohar.

Harishchandra, 1874–7. *Balabodhini* 1.1, 1.2/3, 1.4.–1.6 (January, February/March, April–June 1874), 1.8.–1.10 (August–October 1874); 2.1.–2.12 (January–December 1875); 3.1.–3.12 (January 1876–December 1876); 4.1.–4.2 (January–February 1877).

——— (1884), 1888. *Chandraprabha aur Purnaprakash. Upanyas*. Patna: Khadgavilas Press, Bankipur.

——— (1935), 1946. *Bharatendu Granthavali. Dusra Bhag* (*Granthavali* II), ed. Brajratnadas. Banaras: Nagari Pracharini Sabha.

——— (1950), 1975. *Bharatendu Granthavali. Pahla Khand* (*Granthavali* I), ed. Shivprasad Mishra 'Rudra' Kashikeya. 2nd rev. ed. Banaras: Nagari Pracharini Sabha.

Hawley, John Stratton (1981), 1992. *At Play with Krishna: Pilgrimage Dance Dramas from Brindavan*. Delhi: Motilal Banarsidass.

Hein, Norvin, 1972. *The Miracle Plays of Mathura*. Delhi: Oxford University Press.

Kalsi, A.S., 1992. 'Pariksaguru (1882): The First Hindi Novel and the Hindu Elite'. *Modern Asian Studies*, 26/4.

Kapur, Anuradha, 2004. 'Impersonation, Narration, Desire, and the Parsi Theatre', in *India's Literary History: Essays on the Nineteenth Century*, ed. Stuart Blackburn and Vasudha Dalmia. New Delhi: Permanent Black.

Kane, P.V., 1969. *History of Dharmashastra. Ancient and Medieval Religious and Civil Law in India*, 1/1. Poona: Bhandarkar Oriental Research Institute.

Luhmann, Niklas (1982), 1986. *Love as Passion: The Codification of Intimacy*. Trans. from the German by Jeremy Gaines and Doris L. Jones. Stanford: Stanford University Press.

Mallika, 1989. 'Kumudini'. *Saptahik Hindustan*, 17 September.

Minault, Gail, 1998. *Secluded Scholars: Women's Education and Muslim Social Reform in Colonial India*. Delhi: Oxford University Press.

Nandy, Ashis, 1983. *The Intimate Enemy: Loss and Recovery of Self under Colonialism*. Delhi: Oxford University Press.

Plummer, Christopher E., 1999. 'Dowry and Personal Property in the Lives of Women in Colonial India: The Novels of Premchand'. Master's thesis, University of California, Berkeley.

Ray, Gopal, 1968. *Upanyas Kosh. Khand Ek*. 1870–1917. Patna: Granth Niketan.

Sahay, Shivnandan (1905), 1975. *Harishchandra*. Reprint. Lucknow: Hindi Samiti, Uttar Pradesh Shasan.

Sangari, Kumkum, 1999. *Politics of the Possible. Essays on Gender, History, Narrative, Colonialism*. Delhi: Tulika.

——— and Sudesh Vaid, eds, 1989. *Recasting Women: Essays in Colonial History*. Delhi: Kali for Women.

Sharma, Ramvilas (1953), 1984. *Bharatendu Harishchandra aur Hindi Navjagaran ki Samasyaem*. Rev. ed. Delhi: Rajkamal Prakashan.

Shukla, Sonal, 1991. 'Cultivating Minds: Nineteenth Century Gujarati Women's Journals'. *Economic and Political Weekly*, 26 October.

Talwar, Vir Bharat, 1989. 'Feminist Consciousness in Women's Journals in Hindi: 1910–20', in Kumkum Sangari and Sudesh Vaid, ed. *Recasting Women. Essays in Colonial History*. Delhi: Kali for Women, 1989.

Taneja, Satyendrakumar, 1976. *Natakkar Bharatendu ki Rangparikalpana*. Delhi: Bharati Bhasha Prakashan.

Varshneya, Lakshmisagar (1948), 1974. *Bharatendu Harishchandra*. Allahabad: Sahitya Bhavan.

Vairagi Prabhudas, 1977. *Shrinathdvara ka Sanskrit Itihas*. Aligarh: Bharat Prakashan Mandir.

White, Cynthia L. (1970), 1971. *Women's Magazines: 1693–8*. London: Michael Joseph.

Wilson, Horace Hayman, 1835. *Select Specimens of the Theatre of the Hindus*, translated from the Original Sanskrit, vol. I. London: Parbury, Allen, & Co.

Wulff, Donna Marie, 1982. 'A Sanskrit Portrait: Radha in the Plays of Rupa Gosvami', in *The Divine Consort: Radha and the Goddesses of India*, ed. J.S. Hawley and D.M. Wulff. Berkeley: Berkeley Religious Studies Series, 1982.

12

Pilgrimage, Fairs, and the Secularization of Space in Modern Hindi Narrative Discourses

Introduction

PILGRIMAGE SITES AND PATHWAYS HAVE FOR SO LONG been regarded as integral to the geography of the subcontinent that, in mustering proof of India's nationhood, it was these that Mahatma Gandhi brought forward as evidence. As he saw it, they marked and linked India as a culturally cohesive territory long before the notion of India as nation became current. And certainly there is no dearth of material to support the importance of pilgrimage places from at least the early medieval period. Sanskrit digests compiled from the twelfth century onwards have systematized the information related to pilgrimage, the legends which have grown around the sites, and the rituals which structure the pilgrim's journey.[1] Religion and religious experience may have changed in the

---

[1] This essay was written as a tribute to Monika Boehm-Tettelbach, who straddles both worlds, the religious and the secular, with such ease.
The earliest digest on the stages and duties of a pious life as ordained by the Shastras, the *Krtya-kalpataru*, was compiled by Bhatta Laksmidhara in the late-eleventh or early-twelfth century. Of its fourteen parts, the eighth was entirely devoted to pilgrimage. See P.V. Kane 1973, the modern-day digest, which

process of modernization, but in no way could they be said to have receded in the meantime. Print culture would, in fact, only intensify the production of literature on the pilgrimage experience, whether in extolling the features of the sites concerned in brightly covered booklets and pamphlets, or in relating and expanding on the myths connected to them. However, another sphere also ushered in by print culture—modern literary genres in Indian languages—seems to have removed and relegated religion to another realm. Even while taking note of religious experience, these genres chose rather to regard—and at times even to explore—religion as part of the human dilemma rather than a (salvific or otherwise) resolution to it. This is a vast topic, which awaits further exploration. In an attempt to open the discussion, this essay will focus on a small segment of this literature, that of the incipient novel and the short story in modern Hindi, on the cusp of the modern as it were, and its handling of the pilgrimage experience.

How do we set up some kind of a grid for this experience in terms that allow for the juxtaposition of modern narrative discourse with it? There is vast rural participation in pilgrimage, to sites near and far.[2] Given the popular nature of pilgrimage, and the freedom of practice that this has entailed, no manual can encompass or indeed determine the range that is available and possible. However, the digest makers and ritual specialists were dealing with just such issues of heterogeneity, and the conceptual tools they evolved over time, which were widely disseminated subsequently, have heuristic

---

comprises all older ones, for detailed accounts of this and other later important digests. Crook 1918 and Bharati 1963 offer brief and useful surveys of the sites and motives of pilgrimage on the subcontinent, with their respective modes of—at times sweeping—generalization.

[2] Bharati speaks of the 'ruralization' of Hindu religious practice in the early medieval period, 'through its partial absorption into local and Non-Brahminical cults' (1963: 137). I find this concept of the absorption of Brahminism into rural landscapes, rather than Brahminical appropriation of local cults, useful since it allows for an understanding of a range of practices, which in fact remained unaffected by Brahminical concepts and rituals.

value in enterprises such as that undertaken here. It is thus that we turn to P.V. Kane, the most distinguished modern digest maker, who has devoted a generous section to pilgrimage in his monumental *History of Dharmasastras*, compiling the information gleaned from the medieval compendia to document the myths as also the rituals comprising pilgrimage.[3] The pilgrim's journey can thus be roughly divided into three ritual moments. It begins with the resolution or *samkalpa* at a given point in time. The ritual which accompanies the firming of this resolution provides an occasion to begin with the austerities—fasting, sexual abstinence—as mental and physical preparation for the hardships of the journey or the yatra itself. This second and most extensive phase is marked by the demands it makes of the pilgrim: the more arduous the mode of travel, the more meritorious its gains. The third stage consists of the rituals to be performed at the culminating point of the journey, the dip or *snan* in the holy river or the glimpse or darshan of the deity at the holy site, be it temple or cave. In the matter of gauging the experience of the pilgrimage, however, Kane's prescriptive measures help us little, as little as the vast pilgrimage literature at the sites themselves, with its promises of the merit to be gained and the bliss to be attained by undertaking such yatras.

Of the range of representations possible, with the literature extolling the sites (*mahatmya* in Sanskrit and Hindi) at one end and the modern fictional at the other end, the halfway ground could well be marked by the anthropological, which seeks to recover the pilgrim's experience. Iravati Karve's (1962) now classic account of her pilgrimage to Pandharpur most effectively marks the key moments of pilgrimage as a religious act for us today and provides the best possible foil for the discussion of narrative fiction that follows. The yatra to Pandharpur has a defined collective form:

> The pilgrimage starts from Alandi where Dnyasheshwar died voluntarily at age twenty two in the presence of hundreds of people. The silver image of his feet are [*sic*.] taken every year in a palanquin to Pandharpur so as to reach the town the day before the first Ashadhi Ekadashi, the eleventh

---

[3] The chapter on *Tirthayatra* in Kane 1973: 552–84.

day of the waxing moon in June–July. Simultaneously, different 'saints' born between the fourteenth and seventeenth century and belonging to this cult also start—that is, their foot-images start—for this pilgrimage from different parts of Maharashtra. Each palanquin is accompanied by pilgrims.[4]

The pilgrimage is then not only the lonely act of an individual at some random moment in time, but a shared experience, a rite of passage with definite stages. We can additionally resort to Turner's reading of the three phases of the rites of passage as providing yet another analytical perspective to the three stages we have identified above. These three phases, which correspond only in some measure to Karve's, are (1) separation, (2) margin or liminal, Latin for 'threshold', and (3) aggregation. Separation comprises symbolic behaviour signifying the detachment of the individual or group either from a fixed point in the social structure, and/or from a set of cultural conditions. This would be the moment of embarking on the pilgrimage, rather than *samkalpa* itself. The second or 'liminal' period sets in with the yatra, when the ritual subject or the passenger passes through a cultural realm that has few or none of the attributes of the past or coming state, while in the third or final phase—of reaggregation or reincorporation—the passage is consummated and the ritual subject, individual or corporate, is in a relatively stable state once more and, by virtue of this, has rights and obligations *vis-à-vis* others, of a clearly defined type.[5] The second or liminal phase, that of yatra itself, will be of particular interest in the reading of both Karve's account and later fiction, for it is on this stage that they primarily focus.

Karve communicates her *samkalpa*, or the first phase, which leads her to detach herself from the familiar and the known, very briefly. Neither her father's family nor her husband's had been members of the Varkari cult, she tells us, therefore she had not yet participated in it. When she decided to embark on the pilgrimage, she took

---

[4] Karve 1962: 14.

[5] See 'Liminality and Communitas', in Turner (1969), 1995. Subsequent citations from Turner are from this work, unless otherwise indicated.

no notebook and no pen with her, pushing back the scholarly, as it were, in order to participate as fully as possible in the collective experience.

The temporal and spatial sequence while on the way to Pandharpur is re-enacted according to a collectively evolved rhythm, which the pilgrims know from hearsay, from repeated enactment of the yatra or indeed from observing each other:

> Tai bent down and took up the dust on the road. God's saints were passing today on this road. The dust under their feet was sacred. I too dipped my finger in the dust and put it to my forehead. The ritual was followed every day. We joined our own group. The *mridang* drum gave the rhythm, the vina lute strummed the time, the men with two small *tal* cymbals tied to a string around their necks marked time and sang one of the multitude of sectarian songs composed since the thirteenth century.

> The quality of compassion is to love—
> To love without thought of return—
> As a mother loves her child.[6]

During this liminal phase the pilgrim becomes part of a social order that is familiar and yet unfamiliar, and of a time scheme which is both of now and of another time, as the sectarian songs composed since the thirteenth century signal: 'It removes him from one type of time to another. He is no longer involved in that combination of historical and social structural time which constitutes the social process in his rural or urban home community, but kinetically re-enacts the temporal sequences made sacred and permanent by the succession of events in the lives of incarnate gods, saints, gurus, prophets, and martyrs.'[7] A 'simultaneity of past and future in an instantaneous present', close to Walter Benjamin's understanding of messianic time,[8] though so intriguingly linked to a sense of history in Karve's case, as she recalls the moment of composition of the songs, which carries for her a sense of tradition in measurable and measured time. The austerities, the hardships, and the suffering are a necessary

---

[6] Karve 1962: 15.
[7] Turner 1969: 207.
[8] Anderson (1983), 1991: 24.

component of this phase, which is one of vulnerability and internal as well as external transition and change: 'As we proceeded on our way, the hot sun burnt our faces and left everyone looking tired and parched. The daily toil left everyone exhausted, all complained about aching feet and legs, but hardly anybody protested about the work. The older women were very lovingly looked after. The hard work and cheerful attitude of the women always surprised me.'[9] Though there is a clear sense of caste and class—the hierarchies which determine the order of the procession and the spaces occupied during the nightly halts—the road does bring a kind of levelling and contact otherwise excluded from daily social intercourse. If I may belabour the term once more, a sense of *communitas*, which 'is almost everywhere held to be sacred or holy', is engendered, which is, however, 'made evident or accessible, so to speak, only through its juxtaposition to, or hybridisation with, aspects of social structure.'[10] 'There were hundreds of professional beggars and poor people. They ate whatever people gave them, spread their mat wherever they found room, and walked with the palanquin. They suffered if it rained.'[11] Accidents befall people on the way, there is also discord, they are exposed to each other's pain, they recall the misery and loneliness of their lives, but 'If anyone used bad language or became angry, others would say, "You must not do that while we are on the way to Pandhari", and the offender would be ashamed and fall silent. I saw this several times.'[12]

And then there is the vast panorama of this surge of humanity stopping for a rest in the fields and spreading out across them in moments which level out difference in social status:

> In the early afternoon, thousands of people would stop at a roadside brook, and the moving scene would become stationary for a time. The first thing everybody did at a halt was to dry the clothes which had been washed at the early morning bath. Then all the fields would be carpeted

[9] Karve 1962: 16.
[10] Turner 1969: 127 and 128.
[11] Karve 1962: 17.
[12] Ibid.: 21.

by the coloured saris spread out to dry. Blue smoke and reddish flames rose from hundreds of fires in the noon air. From the morning till the evening, one's ears were ringing with sound of the cymbals and drums and the devotional verses of Tukaram, Dnyaneshwar, Eknath, Namdev, and other poet-saints.[13]

Though Karve so wonderfully conveys the liminality of the experience, the in-between of temporal and social structure, and the sense of *communitas*, at the final and culminating moment she detaches herself from the group.

> That was the last day on the road. By evening the companions of all those days would part. Each one would go to his or her place of residence. I had an uneasy feeling—my eyes were filling again and again.
>
> Haushi had told me, 'The last bit of the plateau is called, Weeping Plateau.'
>
> 'But why?'
>
> 'Oh, you have got to cry when you walk there.'
>
> All around me, people were saying good-bye to each other. I could find no words—I could only nod to the companions in my *dindi* to say good-bye and start on ahead. Then came the entrance gate to the town. But somehow I was feeling restless. I could not see Him, who had been there, sometimes in the *dindi*, sometimes ahead of us, sometimes under a tree, and sometimes near the well. When I turned round, I saw His back and He was marching away in the opposite direction. 'Why, Dark One, are You leaving too? Are You not coming into Pandharpur?' He smiled and shook his head. 'Where are you off to?' Without a word, he merely waved His arm and began to walk fast. The black ploughed fields and the sky full of heavy clouds soon engulfed that delicate dark figure with the blanket on his shoulder. And I stepped inside the gates of Pandharpur with streaming eyes, weary legs, and a heavy heart.[14]

Karve's sporadic and elusive encounters with the Dark One occur *during* the journey, rather than at its end. For her, then, it is not Pandharpur and the experience of the formalized darshan which appear to be the 'source of healing and renewal'. The primary experience of the pilgrimage, it is suggested, takes place *with* and *through* the pilgrims. It is their fervour, their belief, their collective

[13] Ibid.: 18.
[14] Ibid.: 29.

bringing alive of tradition that make the encounter with the Dark One a possibility. Both the first and the last stage, the *samkalpa* and the darshan, virtually disappear to make way for the middle one, the yatra which comes to comprehend the entire experience.

New Perspectives and Prescriptives

Early experiments in narrative prose in modern Hindi continue to be concerned with the act of pilgrimage. It is not as if the world of the social actors in the cities and towns of North India changes so rapidly that a section of society becomes unconcerned with religious observance. What does seem to change, however, is the perspective of the writers, who see themselves as active participants in the process of societal modernization. They often have a reformative agenda, to which even those stemming from professedly traditional quarters seem to subscribe. Though they continue to deal with religious and social custom as it prevails, it is to question and modify it rather than move within it. They participate in what McKeon has called 'continuity and discontinuity'; what marks discontinuity is a radical 'perspectival change'.[15] In treating of experience formerly seen in ritual terms, our authors relegate the experience of the spiritual to its own realm, moving through the world in 'horizontal-secular, transverse time',[16] which is no longer ordained and regulated by any divine instance. Pilgrimage narratives when transposed to modern genres, then, reflect another kind of transition, another kind of liminality, as the actors cross into new social worlds, and new states of being, when 'all that is solid melts into air.'

With these perspectival changes in mind we turn to the work of Shraddharam Phillauri (1837–81), whose novel *Bhagyavati* (1877) is regarded as one of the first in Hindi, and Rajendrabala Ghosh (1882–1949), better known as Bang Mahila, one of the first to write short stories in Hindi. Both writers describe the experience of the *Kumbh Parva*, better known as the Kumbh Mela. Phillauri embeds the Kumbh experience in his novel, as one of a series of cautionary

---

[15] McKeon (1987) 2002: xiv, xvi.
[16] Anderson (1983), 1991: 37.

tales, whereas Bang Mahila centres the story, *Kumbh mem choti bahu* (1906), on the experience.[17] They focus on the material dangers to which the pilgrim is exposed, rather than on ritual aspects, which they seem to take as a frame, without further need to refer to it or, indeed, to spiritual pitfalls or gains. And the moral of their stories bypasses even the notion of the spiritual, which is neither questioned nor addressed.[18]

The Kumbh Mela is the largest and most spectacular fair on the subcontinent. It may be helpful to briefly recall its main features, so that we can relate the details in the two narratives to them. The mela is celebrated in a twelve-year cycle by rotation at four sites: at Haridvar on the Ganges; Prayag/Allahabad on the *sangam* or confluence of the Ganges and Yamuna; Nasik on the Godavari; and Ujjain on the Sipra. The first two are the most important sites for the mela, which lasts for a whole month, though particular days are considered specially auspicious for a dip in the holy waters: the *purnima* or full moon of Chaitra for Haridvar and the *amavasya* or new moon day of Magh and Bhadrapad for Prayag.[19] The Kumbh Parva,

---

[17] Rajendrabala translated the story, originally written by her mother Niradavasini Devi in Bengali, into Hindi. It was published in the prestigious journal *Sarasvati*.

[18] As Lambert-Hurley has shown in her introduction to an early Urdu account of a Hajj by Nawab Sikandar Begum of Bhopal (2007; first published in English translation in 1870), there is little interest at this stage in modernist explorations of notions of the self. Apparently written in response to the prompting of the translator (the wife of the British Agent in Bhopal), Sikandar Begum penned an account more social-historical than in any explicit way concerned with recounting the ritual or indeed the personal spiritual aspect of the journey, which took several months. Lambert-Hurley quotes an essay by Barbara Metcalf which deals with late-twentieth-century Urdu accounts of pilgrimage, which more vividly convey the modern sense of immediacy of experience ('less about the Haji than the Hajj'). The essay, Metcalf 1990, is presently not available to me. I am grateful to Ritu Menon for drawing my attention to Sikandar Begum's account.

[19] Bathing in rivers is extolled as a purifying act even in the Vedas, and Kane devotes a considerable section to these passages. Whatever their individual origin, the sites and their merits first find extensive treatment in the Puranas

by all accounts, first came into being as a congregation of ascetics, whose ceremonial remains its most spectacular and central feature. In fact, the very origin of the Haridvar Kumbh, which is supposed to have been the first to evolve, is linked to Naga ascetics. There is evidence of their existence at least from the Mughal period, but if on the basis of their own genealogies their foundation is to be followed back in time, then their origin could be pushed as far back as the twelfth century.[20] Other ascetic orders apparently soon followed suit and descended in large numbers to the banks of the rivers. They made their way to the river in ceremonial procession on important bathing days. The primary ritual transactions of these orders, such as their initiation rites, and all other organizational business such as the election of their main office-holders, takes place there. There used to be much violent scuffling on matters of precedence in the procession, so that the officers of the British colonial state stepped in to establish order. They determined the sequence in which the orders proceeded to the river and posted their own state apparatus there to control not only the milling crowds but also the sprawling township of tents and makeshift enclosures housing the pilgrims and the teeming entertainment and consumer market. How and in what ways will our narratives take note of such details?

Pandit Shraddharam Phillauri, the author of the early Hindi novel *Bhagyavati*, was introduced to the heated religious debates of late-nineteenth-century Punjab, between Hindus, Sikhs, Muslims, and Christians of various hues, in the years that he worked for an American Presbyterian missionary whom he was helping with the translation of the Bible and the Quran. Within a matter of years, he

---

and the digests, which further systematize them. Given this trajectory, it can occasion no surprise that the Kumbh Mela finds no mention in Vedic or indeed Puranic literature and that its origin is shrouded in legend. See Bonazzoli 1977 and Dubey 1987 for extensive discussion of the evolution of the Kumbh Mela; Bonazzoli for the analysis of the Puranic material, as also of the later digests on the Prayag Kumbh Mela, and Dubey for a survey of all Kumbh Melas, with additional information from Persian chronicles, travel reports, and gazetteers.

[20] Dubey 1987: 129.

came to distance himself entirely from the work of the mission as also from the Arya Samaj, which was gaining such rapid ground in the Punjab—though both would have left an imprint on him—to become a full-time preacher of Vaishnava Hinduism.[21] He would go on to found his own Sanskrit schools. We have here then an author who was fully cognizant of the trend of the times but did a complete about-turn to become part of a 'traditional' religious formation. But he was no less a modernizer for that and he chose to write his work for women in a modern genre.

Bhagyavati was a work of its times; it was full of episodes that illustrated some useful maxim. The narrative was conjoined and held together by the figure of Bhagyavati herself. A model daughter-in-law, educated, fully informed about the rapid social changes under way—Indo-British law, Western medicine (inoculation), hygiene, pregnancy, and childcare—and always pre-armed with a volley of good advice, she was placed in a Brahmin household in Banaras. Her radical views had initially made her so unpopular in her new family that she had been ejected from the household. But her exemplary conduct and readiness to come to their rescue when needed made not only for her eventual return but also for a general acceptance of her leadership role. Soon after her reintegration in the family she was blessed with a son. And the grateful father-in-law decided to embark on a pilgrimage to Haridvar. Bhagyavati participated fully in its organization, though her earlier conduct indicated an all-round impatience with ritual and 'superstition', particularly that connected with ascetics, whom she tended to dismiss summarily as charlatans, and whose splendid outfits in Haridvar she would castigate as being unworthy of men of God.[22]

---

[21] More extensive information on Phillauri's activities as a Vaishnava missionary can be found in Jones 1998. I cite from the 1973 edition of *Bhagyavati*. All translations from the Hindi are mine.

[22] Once Bhagyavati has taken the ritual bath on the fortieth day after the birth of the son, the mother-in-law offers her a welter of charms and bracelets to put around not only the boy's neck and wrists but also around her own. She says: 'Oh Bahu, one of these is from Baba Gomitigiriji, and another has come from Baba Bhaironath Jogi. This thread I have got from a Mahantji and this

PILGRIMAGE, FAIRS, AND THE SECULARIZATION   297

They journey from Banaras not to the nearby Allahabad/Prayag but to Haridvar, nearer and better known to the author, who hailed from Punjab. Though trains have already appeared on the horizon as a possibility, the family opts for the older mode of travel, and the narration conveys the distance, ardour, and danger of the journey with knowledge and insight. The three stages of pilgrimage are clearly delineated. However, what is entirely missing is the spiritual–sacred aspect of such an enterprise. Though the account is almost ethnographic in its detailed description of the material preparations for the journey, there are no descriptions of any spiritual observances in preparation or indeed of the sites concerned.

What follows is concerned primarily with the dangers of the yatra, as it is now exclusively called. The women travel in the covered wagon, the father-in-law in the palanquin, Manohar, called Shastriji, Bhagyavati's husband, on horseback, and the Brahmin cook on foot. The cook goes ahead, sets up the camp, buys supplies from the *modi* (grocer), and prepares the meals. It is when they reach Prayag that they find themselves part of a vast sea of humanity, surging towards Haridvar, and inevitably they mingle with others. The sense of community is restricted to the immediate family in spite of the fact that the oxen cart becomes one of a long procession of vehicles as they near their destination. But at the very onset, Bhagyavati has warned her family to be on guard: there will be many an *uchakka* (scoundrel or conman) who will be on the lookout for spoils. The journey acquires the character of one primarily concerned with warding off danger to property and person.

These dangers are described with some relish and at some length. The *uchakkas* are ever on the lookout for spoils and the gullible Brahmin cook can only be trusted up to a point. They need to be ever watchful, a task most capably performed by Bhagyavati, if they are to survive. There are several such occasions, for their tents are

---

has been given by Pandit Rudramainji. All of Kashi regards him as a *siddha*, he knows the *mantra-shastra* so well. So here, take them all and tie them on respectfully. Thanks to them, the boy will remain protected.' Phillauri (1877), 1973: 81.

clearly those of the wealthy and powerful: a set of *uchakkas* makes friends with the family but most of all with the cook. They detect that he resents Bhagyavati because she is so controlling. The cook is persuaded to grind certain seeds which, once he mixes them in their food, will put the whole family in his power. They are the narcotic *dhatura* (thorn-apple) seeds, as Bhagyavati will later discover. But the family will be so doped that the crooks will make off with all their movable goods, the oxen, and the smaller of the mules. Bhagyavati has the habit of burying the bundle of money and jewellery in a pit near their camp each night, so the family is not utterly destitute. The cook is suitably punished and promises to mend his ways. They have to be particularly watchful, she says, because on such a journey, *sabki vrtti tamoguni hoti hai* (everyone displays a tendency to lethargy). One does not eat or sleep at the right time; there is much stress. There is no mention of spiritual gain through the suffering inflicted on such a journey and the hardship borne. It is as if the family is moving through profane rather than sacred spaces, and it is a secular instance of authority, the police as the arm of law, that comes to the rescue when needed. There seems to be little need of any arm of God.

The crowds are a threatening and overwhelming presence; not even sections of it solidify into some community of faith. Bhagyavati herself gets lost towards the end of the journey. Barefoot, without money, armed only with her wits, she reproaches herself: God is punishing her in her pride. She is lucky enough to arrive at a temple, which turns out to be a girls' school, run by the local raja, who is liberal and generous. As soon as he hears of her learning, he has her escorted on to Haridvar, where she asks her companions to post a notice at every well-known dharmashala and Shiva temple between Kankhal and Haridvar, saying she, Bhagyavati, will wait for her family at the bridge on the Ganges Nahar. Her mother-in-law has been beside herself, but her father-in-law has known she will find a way to save herself. The reader does not need to wait for the message to be spelt out. Bhagyavati herself sums up the lesson that they all need to take back home with them: never wear jewellery at such a mela. If wearing earrings, cover your ears tight so that they are not

PILGRIMAGE, FAIRS, AND THE SECULARIZATION   299

pulled out along with the earrings. Moving about in such a crowd is a matter to be undertaken with great caution. Bhagyavati had watched a Marwari being knocked down by the crowd and then trampled to death. Take note of the particularities of your own camp (*dera*), so that you find your way back. Look out for being tricked when buying wares. Finally, and most of all, keep a lookout for fake holy men.

Once they reach their destination, Panditji asks his family: 'Well, now you have performed the Kumbh *snan* [holy dip] and the mela is about to be dispersed. What would you like to do now? Should we wait for the mela to disperse or you would like to leave now?' Bhagyavati's advice will not surprise us. They leave at once and after some days arrive safely in Kashi. The fruits of the journey, as the family communicates them to their neighbours, are tales of their ordeal and of Bhagyavati's foresight and wisdom. They are reintegrated into their community, in the happy knowledge of having seen more than their neighbours. If on the one hand the entire experience of such a journey and its various stages, the *samkalpa*, the vulnerability engendered by the yatra and its hardships, the culminating *snan*, and the reintegration into the community are intact, on the other hand what is missing is the ritual, spiritual/sacred character of the yatra and the sense of fulfilment that could emerge from it.

Bhagyavati is an early and straightforwardly prescriptive novel which cannot be accused of much subtlety of thought or indeed be seen as necessarily representative of what would follow. To enter into it in such detail could be regarded as questionable if the enterprise did not point in a direction which remains more or less constant: a faith often shaken but not engaged with at the level of faith. This engagement is now relegated to the explicitly religious sphere. Even if the writers of these early narratives do not belong to the great reform movements of the late nineteenth century—the Arya Samaj in North India and the Brahmo Samaj in Bengal with its all-India impact— the traditional religious communities to which they belong are also modernizing and it is these changed perspectives that the new literary genres reflect. People had always embarked on pilgrimages from a variety of motives; modernity may have made for further shifts in that, but what engages the writers discussed here is the rigour and danger of travel, and in later narratives, interiorities gone awry.

New Liminalities

It is the dangerous and threatening aspect of the enterprise which is foregrounded in *Kumbh mem chhoti bahu*, the short story published almost two decades later. Though the story could also be regarded as reformative in its agenda, it is grounded in a milieu that does not seek to be seen as other than traditional, even if some of its members have moved away from it, and it is told from the inside, as it were, from within the workaday world of domesticity, with its envies, solidarities, and banter. The tone is much more intimate than in *Bhagyavati*, and it is much more persuasive. The *chhoti bahu* (younger daughter-in-law) of the story is a misguided young woman, but she is also forlorn and vulnerable: the narrative tone shifts from ironic distance to an almost involuntary sympathy once tragedy overtakes her.

The reference now is to the Allahabad/Prayag Kumbh. Rajendrabala Ghosh was born in Banaras of highly literate and cultivated parents who had moved there from Bengal in 1858 and who would soon move to Mirzapur.[23] Her mother Niradavasini's family was from Calcutta, and mother and daughter would remain in close touch with writing from Bengal. Rajendrabala's parents allowed contact with the literary circle which met regularly in their house, amongst whom there were figures as illustrious as the young Ramchandra Shukla, the literary historian and critic. Though she wrote from behind the purdah observed in her family, her thoughts were progressive for her times and she was a spirited woman. She wrote under the pseudonym Bang Mahila and her stories—she was amongst the first to write them in Hindi—and essays on diverse topics were published in the best-known Hindi journals of the day, such as *Sarasvati*. She also translated her mother Niradavasini's short stories into Hindi, of which the story discussed here is one. Her writing was confined

---

[23] See Mody (2000) for extensive information on Bang Mahila's family and literary career. I cite from the standard edition (1988) of her works.

to a brief span of twelve years, from 1904 to 1916. At the death of her husband she chose to—or was constrained to—lead the secluded life of a widow and ceased to write entirely.

Kumbh mem chhoti bahu exhibits an awareness of time and space which has moved a considerable distance from the oxen-cart days of *Bhagyavati*. As Schivelbusch has noted in his study of railway travel, '(t)ransport technology is the material base of potentiality, and equally the material base of the traveler's space-time perception. If an essential element of a given socio-cultural space-time continuum undergoes change, this will affect the entire structure; our perception of space-time will also lose its accustomed orientation.'[24] The railways came to India in 1853, but just ten years later the railway tracks crisscrossing the subcontinent exceeded 2500 miles. The major pilgrim centres on the plains soon became part of the link: faith could not remain unaffected by these technologies. Large-scale pilgrimage traffic had existed before the coming of the railways and women were clearly a part of it. But with the coming of trains, it increased manifold along with fuller female participation. Easier travel would further blur the lines between pilgrimage and tourism and make instant decisions to travel more viable.[25]

Our story opens with a bird's-eye view of a domestic scene. It is a winter afternoon in Pandera, a village near Mirzapur, in the Brahmin household of Ramnarayan Mishra. The women are in the courtyard, the mother-in-law sits sunning herself, watching her grandchildren play, while her two *bahu*s prepare the evening meal. The younger of the *bahu*s is a restless creature. She has visited her paternal aunt the day before and heard them talk about their impending pilgrimage to the Kumbh Mela at Prayag. It is just a couple of days to *amavasya* and the new moon is particularly auspicious for bathing. Chhoti Bahu has one major worry: that she will be excluded from this exciting venture. The mela happens only every twelve years, so it will be a long time before it happens again, and she longs to go: 'Who knows who will be king then and who yogi? And if I die sometime in between, my heart's wish will remain locked in the heart.'

[24] Schivelbusch 1986: 44.
[25] Kerr 2001: 307.

It is the wilful insistence of a wayward individual, not particularly pious in intent, and it is not taken up by the family. The mother-in-law has been to Prayag once, but not to the mela. There is no question of Shivnarayan, her younger son, taking her there: 'He has studied English and become out and out Christian. All he does is cast our gods and ancestors to the furnace.'[26] And as for the father-in-law, he believes: 'with a pure mind, the Ganges can be found in the water vessel at home.' Here we have a mother-in-law who sympathizes with the wish, a father-in-law who sees no space for women in such ventures, and in Shivnarayan, a husband unable to prevent his wife from leaving. A straggling group is formed once Chhoti Bahu attaches herself to her aunt's family. No sense of community can be engendered in this case. This initial phase of preparation is much shortened by the possibility of quick train travel.

The scene at the railway station is still novel enough for most readers to warrant description. The narrator's second bird's-eye view affords us a glimpse of the multitudes and marketable goods on the move: 'There is a great crowd at the station, wherever you look only the craniums of people, and pile after pile of bundles, goods, packages.' Shivnarayan is not at home when they depart for the station. He comes rushing to bid his son goodbye and there is a heart-rending scene when little Lallu is torn away from his father's embrace. 'The whore of a train lets out a shrill whistle. And eating fire, drinking water, throwing smoke, the train hurtles on, as if illustrating the ephemeral nature of the world.' Absolute stillness descends now where there had just been so much noise and bustle. The train track and the relative silence of the train compartment are spaces which convey no sense of being propelled towards a ritual destination. Not only is distance contracted, time itself seems to shrink. We are in calendrical, clockable time. Chhoti Bahu remarks on how pleasant it is to be in the train, no hustling crowds as people had predicted in order to scare her. The pilgrimage has been compressed into a matter of hours, and the journey is over in no time. As Schivelbusch has noted, train schedules made for the necessity of standardizing

[26] Bang Mahila 1988: 47.

clock time globally in the late nineteenth century. To realize what this compression and marking of time by the clock changes for the pilgrim, we turn once more to Turner:

> A pilgrimage center, from the standpoint of the believing actor, also represents a threshold, a place and moment, 'in and out of time', and such an actor—as the evidence of my pilgrims attests, hopes to have there direct experience of the sacred, invisible, or supernatural order, either in the material aspect of miraculous healing or in the immaterial aspect of inward transformation of spirit or personality. As in the liminality of initiation rites, such an actor pilgrim is confronted by sequences of sacred objects and participates in symbolic activities which he believes are efficacious in changing his inner and, sometimes, hopefully, outer condition from sin to grace, or sickness to health. He hopes for miracles and transformations, either of soul or body.[27]

With the train speeding on, there is little sense of sequentiality of sacred objects, of increasing sacralization. The liminality and the vulnerability engendered by travel manifests itself only once they reach Prayag, still on the journey to their 'holy of holies', so to speak, before they can take the dip in the river. We are now afforded yet another bird's-eye view, that of the site of the fair. The narrator now offers us a perspective coloured by concerns nationalist rather than sacral. She describes the scene with gentle irony, seeing the vast community of pilgrims as part of the larger 'imagined community' which seeks to escape rather than confront the vast issues of poverty and hunger:

> It is *amavasya* today. An unforgettable vista is to be seen today on the banks of the Triveni at Prayagraj . . . O proud Hindu progeny, may your firm belief in Hindu dharma be ever praised! At a time when the votaries of other faiths snuggle under their quilts and are reluctant to expose even their faces to the cold, from that early hour till sunset, children, women and even the very old, happily, joyfully, take dips in waters colder than ice. Praise be the Hindu *jati*! Praise be Hindu family clans! This insignificant authoress bows down to touch your feet not once, not hundred, not thousand but tens of million times. O brother Hindu! You

[27] Turner 1974: 197.

have no other kind of strength left to you now, just the strength of your faith. May God allow your immense faith to remain unbroken, this can be the sole wish of your humble servant.

The sands on the banks of the three rivers have acquired a new life. With what joy the poor inhabitants of Bharat collect the fruits of their good deeds today. Some have clothes to cover themselves, some do not even have those. Some have food to fill their stomachs, some do not even have that. But at this moment in time, on this pure earth, they all enjoy happiness in the same measure.

Amongst this inestimable mass of humanity, can be seen a familiar figure, it is none other than our Chhoti Bahu, carrying her Lallu, and standing along with her cousin, aunt, and other relatives.[28]

With the value of faith so greatly diminished in view of the greater needs of the nation, what culminating moment can await us now? Will Chhoti Bahu be able to reach the waters? Just then all pandemonium breaks loose. An elephant runs amok. Shankarlal, the cousin, grabs hold of Lallu, but his old mother is knocked over and severely injured. He hands Lallu back to his mother. At that moment, the sadhus having had their dip, the police open the way to the river and now all mayhem really breaks loose, as the vast mass of humanity surges to reach the waters. Lallu and his mother are torn apart, both are knocked over, she cries out for her son, the crowd surges and Shankarlal loses sight of them. Later, after hours of despair and self-reproach—he will be blamed for not having taken care of mother and child because they were not his own immediate family—of searching through mounds of corpses, huts, the banks of the river, the police station, he hears that Chhoti Bahu is in the hospital. When they find her there, all she can do is cry for her son. Her husband has been informed, and he comes rushing to her bedside. I would like to briefly recall Turner's words regarding the reaggregation and integration of the ritual subject, once the liminal phase is over: 'The ritual subject, individual or corporate, is in a relatively stable state once more.' Chhoti Bahu remains forever stuck in the liminal: 'Oh unfortunate Chhoti Bahu! Not even a trace of your child is to be

[28] Bang Mahila 1988: 49–50.

found on this good earth. His tender body, soft as butter, has been ground to flour under the feet of a hundred thousand men.' Chhoti Bahu cries herself into a dead faint, and it looks as if she will follow her little son into the other world. A more inauspicious breaking up of the group which set off so gaily from the railway station can hardly be imagined, a pilgrimage more drained of meaning.

'Even if We don't have Faith Ourselves'

Two examples, from two well-known Hindi novels of the first part of the twentieth century, may serve to further our reflections on pilgrimage and the secularisation of space in the modern literary genres. In both, the central women protagonists turn to pilgrimage when at the end of their tether, the time-honoured cultural resource available for such moments. Premchand's second great novel, *Premashram* (Abode of Kindliness, 1922) focuses on the family of Gyanshankar and Premshankar, landowners with a family seat in Banaras. Gyanshankar, unscrupulous and ambitious, though married, woos Gayatri, who has been early widowed. She is fabulously rich, can afford to flaunt her modernity, and displays a surface fascination for religion, to which Gyanshankar, who ultimately becomes her lover, panders. When she finally becomes aware of his manipulations and machinations, she embarks on a life of austerity. Clad in white and barefoot, she seeks out the famous sites of pilgrimage—Haridvar, Rishikesh—and men in holy garb. Finding no solace in either, restless and wandering, she comes to a savage end, plunging down a ravine, at the bottom of which there are waters which open up mercifully to receive and hide her bones from posterity.[29] In Agyeya's *Nadi ke dvip* (Islands in the Stream, 1951), a novel published three decades later, a defiantly independent Rekha, almost recklessly modern in her ways, falls back on the same cultural habit when faced with a joyless future. She has been ill, and though divorce has just released her from an unhappy marriage, she sees no path back to Bhuvan whom she had loved. As she writes to him:

---

[29] Premchand 1922: 575.

And what now, Bhuvan? I feel restless. I won't stay on in Calcutta now. I've thought that I'll take my aunt and go off on a *tirtha-yatra*. Perhaps you'll laugh; you won't have seen any signs in me of the faith needed for a *tirtha-yatra*, and I can't say that aunt yearns for it either, that she depends on it in any way. Despite that, we may find some peace in travel and constant change of one scene for another, even if we don't have faith ourselves, we may derive consolation [*santvana*] from seeing others who have faith. We'll leave in a couple of days, starting in Puri and then going on South. It's February now and I think we'll manage to go through summer this way and get back in the monsoons.[30]

In Karve's anthropological narrative we saw a transfer of faith was possible for the span of the yatra itself, if not later, but it is no longer accessible to the conflicted, who seek a mode to exist in the modern world. But neither the faithful, nor the modern sages Aurobindo and Ramana Maharishi, whom she and her aunt meet, can afford Rekha the peace that she seeks. It is not religion, then, that disappears from the modern world: it remains a strong presence for most. The faithful continue to exist, but in modern fiction they retreat to the background as it were, either to a past that cannot be recovered, or to a sensibility that becomes equally elusive for the central figures in our novels.

In lieu of a conclusion, then, and switching to another genre, we turn to a poem by Arun Kolatkar from *Jejuri* published in 1973. In this evocative series of short poems, Kolatkar conveys both the depth of experience associated with Jejuri as a place of pilgrimage, a depth endowed to it by centuries of pilgrim travel and of faith carried to it, but also its remoteness and inaccessibility. The poem cited catches the moment not so much of the poet's flippant refusal to engage with faith but a sense of something hollowed out and meaningless. *Makarand*, the title of the poem, means 'nectar'. It is also the name of the poet's brother. Rather than face the flatness of ritual in the recesses of the temple, the poet chooses a moment of solitary reflection:

Take my shirt off
and go in there to do pooja?
No thanks.

[30] Agyeya (1951), 1971: 253.

Not me.
But you go right ahead
if that's what you want to do.
Give me the matchbox before you go
will you?
I will be out in the courtyard
where no one will mind if I smoke.

References

Agyeya (1951), 1971. *Nadi ke dvip*. Allahabad: Saraswati Press.
Anderson, Benedict (1983), 1991. *Imagined Communities: Reflections on the Origin and Spread of Nationalism*. London and New York: Verso.
Bang Mahila, 1988. *Bang Mahila Granthavali*. Sudhakar Pandey, ed., Benares: Nagari Pracharini Sabha.
Bharati, Agehananda, 1963. 'Pilgrimage in the Indian Tradition'. *History of Religions* 3.1 (Summer).
Bonazzoli, Giorgio, 1977. 'Prayag and its Kumbha Mela'. *Purana* 19.1 (January).
Casanova, Jose, 1994. *Public Religions in the Modern World*. Chicago and London: The University of Chicago Press.
Crook, W., 1918. 'Pilgrimage (Indian)', in James Hastings, ed. *Encyclopaedia of Religion and Ethics*. Edinburgh.
Dubey, D.P., 1987. 'Kumbh Mela: Origin and Historicity of Indian's Greatest Pilgrim Fair', in R.L. Singh and Rana P.B. Singh, eds, *Trends in the Geography of Pilgrimages: Homage to David E. Sopher*. Benares: The National Geographic Society of India, Benares Hindu University.
Gopal, Lallanji and D.P. Dubey, eds, 1990. *Pilgrimage Studies. Text and Context*. Allahabad: The Society of Pilgrimage Studies.
Jones, Kenneth W., 1998. 'Two *Sanatan Dharma* Leaders and Swami Vivekananda: A Comparison', in William Radice, ed., *Swami Vivekananda and the Modernization of Hinduism*. Delhi: Oxford University Press.
Kane, P.V., 1973. *History of Dharmasastra: Ancient and Medieval Religious and Civil Law*, vol. 4. Poona: Bhandarkar Oriental Research Institute.
Karve, Iravati, 1962. 'On the Road: A Maharashtrian Pilgrimage', *Journal of Asian Studies* 22.1 (November).
Kerr, Ian J., 2001. 'Reworking a Popular Religious Practice: The Effects of Railways on Pilgrimage in South Asia', in Ian J. Kerr, ed. *Railways in Modern India*. Delhi: Oxford University Press.

Kolatkar, Arun (1974), 2005. *Jejuri*, Introduction by Amit Chaudhuri. New York: New York Review of Books.

McKeon, Michael (1987), 2002. *The Origins of the English Novel 1600–1740*. Baltimore and London: The Johns Hopkins University Press.

Metcalf, Barbara, 1990. 'Pilgrimage Remembered: South Asian Accounts of the Hajj', in Dale F. Eickelmann and James Piscatori, eds, *Muslim Travellers: Pilgrimage, Migration, and the Religious Imagination*. London: Routledge.

Mody, Sujata, 2000. 'Writing the New Hindi Nari: Bang Mahila (1882–1949) and the World of Hindi Letters'. MA. thesis, University of California, Berkeley.

Nawab Sikandar Begum (1870), 2007. *A Princess's Pilgrimage* [Original title: *A Pilgrimage to Mecca*] trans., edited, and introduced by Willoughby-Osborne, and with an afterword by Siobhan Lambert-Hurley. Delhi: Women Unlimited.

Phillauri, Sraddharam (1877), 1973. *Bhagyavati*. Delhi: Sharada Prakashan.

Premchand, 1922. *Premashram*. Calcutta: Hindi Pustak Agency.

Schivelbusch, Wolfgang, 1986. *The Railway Journey: The Industrialization of Time and Space in the 19th Century*. Berkeley: University of California Press.

Turner, Victor (1969), 1995. *The Ritual Process: Structure and Anti-Structure*. New York: Aldine de Gruyter.

———, 1974. 'Pilgrimage as Social Processes', in Victor W. Turner, *Dramas, Fields and Metaphors: Symbolic Action in Human Society*. Ithaca and London: Cornell University Press.

13

The Locations of Hindi

IN TRACING THE VICISSITUDES OF MODERN HINDI, AS IT was and has come to be, Alok Rai accomplishes in his 130-page tract, *Hindi Nationalism*, the brilliant feat of traversing densely grown terrain that would, normally, need several volumes.[1] Beginning in the early nineteenth century, and handling dexterously the social, historical, political, cultural, and literary strands which go into making the intricate weave of a language, Rai addresses issues as complex and as vexed as: What was/is Hindi and where/when was Hindi. I shall briefly recount Rai's theses, blending in my own reflections and suggesting further areas of investigation. My focus will be on the role played by literary activity in the evolution of modern Hindi. This is what has endowed the language with political presence and status, and made possible its distancing from Urdu and Brajbhasha, both of which have come to be, at best, regarded as near relatives. Finally, I shall turn to the location of Hindi *vis-à-vis* English, a positioning Rai highlights throughout his tract.

After a brief introduction into the present politics of the language, a project of sorts which seeks to retrospectively and in all finality

---

[1] Rai 2000. I should like to specially thank Arindam Chakrabarty and Nandini Gooptu for their suggestions and insights when I presented some of the ideas outlined below earlier this year, in Hawai'i and Oxford respectively. I also thank Rashmi Sadana and Sujata Mody who have helped to further disentangle some knots, though many still remain tied.

distinguish Hindi from Urdu on the basis of script and religio-cultural allegiance, in the second chapter of his tract Rai discusses the significance of the name 'Hindi'. I share his belief that there was (though Rai says 'is') one common language of North India, a conglomerate of dialects and sub-dialects originally going by the denomination Hindi, and its variants (Hindui, Hindugi, Hinduhi, Hinduki, Hindavi), to mean the language of the people of Hind as against that of Turkistan and Faras. This language, written in the Perso-Arabic script and enriched with words from Persian and Arabic, was given literary recognition in the first half of the eighteenth century. It came to be known as Zuban-i-Urdu-i-mu'alla and was cultivated not so much as the language of Muslims but as the language of the elite of Delhi.[2] Varieties of this language, written in the Devanagari script, and officially regarded after the institution of Fort William College in Calcutta in 1800 by the East India Company as the language of the Hindus, were to be increasingly enriched with words from Sanskrit

---

[2] But even then it did not lose its Hindavi character. Aijaz Ahmad's 'In the Mirror of Urdu' makes some important points with regard to both script and vocabulary, generally used to ascribe a peculiarly Muslim character to the language: 'Urdu is doubtless written in a modified form of the Persian script, but so were several other languages of northern India including Sindhi and Brahui. No one has yet suggested that Sindhi, with its much higher proportion of Arabic words, or Brahui, a patently Dravidian language, is a special vehicle of this so-called Islamic consciousness. Nor does anyone doubt that the phonetics, the morphology, and the entire syntax of Urdu are derived from a Prakritic base.' On the issue of vocabulary, Ahmad goes on to cite Syed Ahmad Dehlavi as he set about to compile the *Farhang-e-Asafiya*, an Urdu dictionary, in the late nineteenth century. Syed Ahmad 'had no desire to sunder Urdu's relationship with Farsi, as is evident from the title of his dictionary. He estimates that roughly 75 per cent of the total stock of 55.000 Urdu words that he compiled in his dictionary are derived from Sanskrit and Prakrit, and that the entire stock of the base words of the language, without exception, are derived from these sources' (2000: 112–13). As Ahmad points out, Syed Ahmad, as a member of Delhi's aristocratic elite, had a clear bias towards Persian and Arabic. His estimate of the percentage of Prakritic words in Urdu should therefore be considered more conservative than not. The actual proportion of Prakritic words in everyday language would clearly be much higher.

and, one day, be standardized enough to be considered worthy, and indeed in need of, separate literary production. However, it was the common predecessor, the largely oral Hindi/Hindui/Hindavi, not excessively Sanskritized or Perso-Arabicized (if I may coin the term), that remained the substrate middle language. It is to this alone that Rai refers as Hindi without inverted commas. 'Hindi' and 'Urdu' within inverted commas refer to two identifiable styles or registers which, in the service of ulterior political agendas, have been 'sought to be hived off and infected with, on the one hand Sanskritic, and on the other, Perso-Arabic borrowings.'[3]

In Flux

Modern print Hindi, as we know it now, came into existence in the course of the nineteenth century. But even in the mid-nineteenth century it was still in flux and there was little awareness of its existence as the common spoken and written language of the Hindus alone. The awareness of its Hinduness could be said to have been almost imposed upon the populace by colonial intervention a good few decades before the Hindu elite themselves took up the cause of Hindu-Hindi. In 1846 James Ballantyne, the newly appointed principal of the Benares Sanskrit College, asked students to use Hindi in their written exercises.[4] The students showed no enthusiasm when asked to apply themselves to using the language of their own daily intercourse more correctly. Ballantyne pressed the most intelligent of the students into formulating the reasons for this apparent disregard for form. Their somewhat bewildered response shows clearly that the term 'Hindi' had little or no currency, at least in this part of North India:

[3] Rai 2000: 15.

[4] Ballantyne had written a grammar of Hindustani (*A Grammar of the Hindustani Language: followed by a series of grammatical exercises, etc.* London: Cox & Co., Edinburgh: Ballantyne and Co., 1838) and obviously participated in the belief that a language of the Hindus existed as an autonomous entity. For a detailed discussion of Ballantyne's contribution to the curriculum of the Benares Sanskrit College, see Dodson 2000.

> We do not clearly understand what you Europeans mean by the term Hindi, for there are hundreds of dialects all in our opinion equally entitled to the name and there is here no standard as there is in Sanskrit. If the purity of Hindi is to consist in its exclusion of Mussalman words, we shall require to study Persian and Arabic in order to ascertain which of the words we are in the habit of using every day is Arabic or Persian and which is Hindi. With our present knowledge we can tell that a word is Sanskrit or not Sanskrit, but if not Sanskrit it may be English or Portuguese instead of Hindi for anything we can tell . . . what you call Hindi will eventually merge in some future modification of the Urdu: nor do we see any great cause of regret in this prospect.[5]

Ballantyne was obviously pressing Sanskrit students to use 'pure' Hindi which excluded 'Mussalman' words and it was this that caused bewilderment. But even in the late nineteenth century, when the cause of Hindi had begun to acquire nationalist dimensions, Hindi with or without inverted commas was considered to be in flux. It was an idiom in need of both standardization and wider propagation. Bharatendu Harishchandra (1850–85), reverently referred to as the 'father of modern Hindi', and surely a partisan observer, was clear about this need. He made no attempt to disguise the fact that there could be no question yet of a standard language, or of Khari Boli as the one language spoken in the majority of the homes in the North West Provinces. As he specified in a short treatise entitled *Hindi bhasha* written in 1883/4 at the tail end of an intensely busy career writing in Hindi: 'Languages have three sections (*vibhag*), that is, the language spoken at home, the language of poetry, and written language. It cannot be ascertained what the language spoken in the homes of the North West Provinces is, since in the province of Delhi, as well as in other cities, no one speaks Hindi at home besides the Khatris and the Panchahi [western] Agravals, so much so that after every *kos* the language changes.'[6]

The Khatris and Agarwals had also brought Hindi to the east with them, that is, it was also spoken in Banaras, but here it was

---

[5] Nicholls 1907: 99, cited in Rai 2000: 65–6.
[6] Bharatendu Harishchandra 1890: 1.

an entirely alien idiom, for in most homes of Banaras and on the streets, a variety of dialects prevailed. As for the language of poetry, Harishchandra was quite definitive in his verdict, it was clearly Brajbhasha. Even this monopoly was not recognized by all, he ruefully admitted, Tulsidas had used Avadhi. When it came to the language of prose, that is, written or print language, he confessed that there was much disagreement. Some wanted a generous mixture of Urdu words, others insisted on Sanskrit words, but finally all ended up by writing according to their own taste and this was the reason why no language could be fixed upon as standard. In short, he seemed to be saying that Hindi did not yet exist as a standardized language, in either spoken or written form; or rather, that it existed in a variety of forms. He himself advocated the use of a simple, easily comprehensible language, which had not too much imported from Sanskrit but which clearly distinguished itself from Urdu.[7]

Hindi at the end of the nineteenth century had many battles to fight before it could claim full-fledged literary, social, and official status and finally distinguish itself from Urdu. It is these battles that Rai sets out to identify and delineate. His brief tract is divided into seven chapters of unequal length. The third and the fifth, 'The MacDonnell Moment' and 'The Heroic Agenda', are the most extensive; together they form almost half the tract. They analyse that interplay of colonial and nationalist politics which was to lead to the divisive policies which finally separated Hindi and Urdu. 'The MacDonnell Moment' concentrates more heavily on the colonial—

---

[7] Bhikharidas of Pratapgarh, near Allahabad, has noted the variations in the use of Brajbhasha in his *Kavya Niranaya* (1746), a poetic manual of some repute. He distinguishes two levels of Persian loan words in Brajbhasha. The first consists of mixed, colloquial terms, which he calls 'sahaj Parsi', the other level he calls 'jaman bhakha', an evidently distinctively Persianized style of language. He gives no indication of his own preference. The significance of the differences he notes, between the colloquial, that which was entirely integrated, and that which was difficult of understanding lies for us in the fact that it had existed for at least a century before Harishchandra's time. For a detailed discussion of the evolution of Brajbhasha usage and its importance for the development of modern print Hindi, see McGregor 2001b.

the official, missionary, and local. 'The Heroic Agenda' focuses on the indigenous elite enterprise of creating the national language via the standardization of the print/literary language and the formulation of the political agenda which went hand in hand with it.

Though the split was early cemented when two separate departments for Hindustani (which was to come to mean Urdu) and Hindui (later Hindi) were established at the College of Fort William in the early nineteenth century, the question whether the split was brought about by these means is likely to remain a matter of debate: there is evidence that there was a distinct awareness of 'Muslim' languages amongst the elite in Mughal India. According to Muzaffar Alam, Jamal-ud-Din, author of the *Farhang-i-Jahangiri*, the first comprehensive Persian lexicon, compiled during the reign of Akbar, dwelt at length on the point that Persian and Arabic were the languages of Islam.[8] That there had existed an awareness of difference cannot be denied. But it was not a distinction which was carried into the language of everyday use. And it certainly does not follow that this was a distinction which need have had any bearing in modern secular spoken and literary language. However, once the notion of Hindi and Urdu as two autonomous linguistic entities was set into motion, there was practically no looking back. Elsewhere I have written at length about the standardization of the language we know as Hindi today, by means of dictionaries and grammars. Produced in great profusion through the nineteenth century, they sought to encode the language so that it could clearly distinguish itself from Urdu, which had been subjected to a standardizing process much earlier.[9]

A second high point was reached in 1900, almost exactly a century after the institution of Fort William College, when Sir Anthony MacDonnell, Lt Governor of the North West Provinces and Oudh, officially promulgated that Hindi (written in the Nagari script) be recognized alongside Urdu as official court language. He did not speak of different scripts but of two different languages. The Kanpur plague epidemic measures lately undertaken by government had inspired

---

[8] Alam 1998: 329.
[9] Dalmia 1997: 146–221.

a resistance which had brought the two communities together. MacDonnell's order deliberately emphasized their difference. Rai suggests that MacDonell was making an explicitly political move; I would go further and see it as express collusion with the high-caste Hindu elite of the North West Provinces, which once again officially cemented the difference. And there was no question that there were differences in the meantime: 'Hindi' was rapidly Sanskritizing.

Rai contributes important new insights in 'Making a Difference', his fourth chapter, to the matter of this Sanskritization of Hindi in the late nineteenth century whereby the cursive Kaithi script (used by Kayasths) was ousted by the Bhabhni (or Brahmin) script. He notes the contribution of the Bengali intelligentsia to the process of Sanskritization as they increasingly occupied important bureaucratic posts in the North West Provinces. The high rate of illiteracy in the province (97 per cent) was a clear indication that the language question was one of power struggle between the elite rather than a matter of wide public concern.

It is in this regard—the mutual hardening of attitude between Hindiwallahs and Urduwallahs—that in his fifth chapter Rai offers one of the many insights that dot his tract. He points to the fact, almost entirely overlooked in contemporary discussions of the issue, that in trying to come to terms with the loss of cultural confidence *vis-à-vis* the British, the respective high-caste Hindu and Muslim elites reconstructed their histories very differently. For the Muslim elite in the second half of the nineteenth century, the cut-off point for the decline of Indian civilization was 1857. It was here and very recently that they saw the beginning of their downward slide. For the Hindu elite, there was less immediate 'tension and self-laceration'; they saw the present as sobering but also as the end of centuries of 'Muslim tyranny', a perspective which transformed 'the complex cultural process of the preceding centuries into nearly a whole millennium of defeat.'[10] However, this defeat, which was seen as being offset to some extent by the great devotional movements of the fifteenth and sixteenth centuries and the poetic corpus then produced, could be

---

[10] Rai 2000: 72.

followed by a rapid regeneration, a period of modernization whereby Hindus could come into their own. Thus the heroic agenda.

Standard Hindi was yet to become the language of widespread domestic use in the cities; it had little rural presence. But in the first decades of the twentieth century there had come to be widespread agreement amongst the propagators of Hindi that it was indeed being spoken (almost) everywhere in North India. Though barely three decades earlier Bharatendu had admitted quite candidly that this was absolutely not the case, Mahavirprasad Dwivedi (1864–1938), editor of the influential Hindi journal *Sarasvati*, felt little or no qualms in blithely proclaiming a truth which could at this stage be no more than a desideratum: 'This is our language, it is the language of our mothers, it is the language of our sisters, it is the language of our children.'[11] Dwivedi contributed to bringing about this state of affairs by his efforts to standardize literary usage by regulating syntax and orthography, dropping colloquialisms, and enriching language with conceptual terms drawn from the Sanskrit.

Khari Boli

While the matter of standardized Hindi prose was being thrashed out by Dwivedi and others in the pages of *Sarasvati*, a parallel effort was under way to produce a corpus of poetry which, in creating itself, created a language with clear Hindu nationalist aspirations. This effort both linked and distanced itself from the Brajbhasha devotional and erotic tradition. This particular process seems to have been set in motion by Ayodhya Prasad Khatri in 1887 with the publication of a polemical tract entitled *Khari boli ka padya* (Verse in Khari Boli). Rai focuses upon and discusses in some detail the ensuing controversy and debate. Khatri maintained in all seriousness, as if offering a novel insight, that Khari Boli was entirely capable of becoming the language of poetry which received the expected resistance from those still busy composing Brajbhasha verse. This insistence on the

---

[11] '*Hindi ki vartman avastha*' (The present state of Hindi, 1911), in Dwivedi (1911), 1965.

creation of Khari Boli verse was in some senses a deliberate strategy to oust the already existing poetry in the strand of Khari Boli written in the Perso-Arabic script, which was now cast to the exclusive lot of Urdu and viewed as alien by virtue of its script and subject matter. Writing poetry in Hindi then meant drawing upon Sanskrit yet more profusely. This was part of an older legacy in Brahminical culture which resorted to Sanskrit when it was necessary to emphasize and connect to this heritage.[12]

Even after the MacDonnell moment, then, the prefaces of the canonical works of early modern Hindi literature exhibit a great deal of anxiety about correct Hindi usage with a clear Sanskrit orientation. Thus 'Sanskrit is respected throughout Bharatvarsh. There is a plenitude of Sanskrit words in Bengali, Marathi, Gujarati, even in Tamil and Panjabi. If our Hindi language presents itself to the gentlemen of these provinces after it has absorbed a great many Sanskrit words, then they will respect it much more than common Hindi because it will be easier for them to read and comprehend it.' The writer is Ayodhya Singh Upadhyaya 'Hariaudh' (1865–1947) in the tract-like preface of the first large-scale poetic venture in this newly Sanskritized Hindi: his long narrative poem, entitled *Priya*

[12] McGregor has made this point in two important essays, 2001a and 2001b, citing various earlier Avadhi and Brajbhasha examples of this strategy of resorting to Sanskrit in order to enrich and raise the level of the poetic language. A very early instance is Damodara, a Brahmin, using an early form of Avadhi in his treatise *Uktivyakti prakarana* (c. 1150) to explain the grammar and usage of spoken Sanskrit to young Brahmin students. Damodara often substitutes a Sanskrit term even in the vernacular he is using in his explicatory narrative instead of the more current vernacular (thus 'vrishti' for 'baras'). McGregor goes onto cite a number of similar cases in the poetic idiom of Brajbhasha, especially as laid down in manuals. 'The tendency that this illustrates, for Sanskritised usage to emerge in contexts of involvement with Sanskritic culture, was to be fundamental to the formation of literary expression in Brajbhasha, Avadhi, and most Indian languages, down to, and notably in the case of modern Hindi.' McGregor 2001b: 205. I would suggest the substitution of the term 'Sanskritic culture' with 'Brahminical culture', since it more precisely pinpoints the groups involved, rather than the other, which may be understood to represent all of Hindudom.

Pravas (The Departure of the Beloved, 1914), for which Upadhyaya claims *mahakavya* or epic status. He uses the metrical conventions of Sanskrit rather than of Urdu or Brajbhasha, and he gives detailed technical reasons in his preface for doing so.

While it is not difficult to agree with Rai that Hindi sought to maintain a respectable distance from Brajbhasha verse in the first half of the twentieth century, the process seems to have been more complex. For, the very poets self-consciously distancing themselves from the older Braj tradition yet forged internal links with it by recasting its themes and concerns in a contemporary frame and idiom. Thus, *Priya Pravas*, for all its Sanskritic pedantry in the matter of verse, treats a theme beloved in the Braj devotional-literary canon. It is set in Braj country, in the period following Krishna's departure for Mathura. Krishna has sent his friend Uddhav to console the inhabitants of Braj, particularly the forlorn *gopis*. In the modern poem, it is no longer a question of highlighting the values of bhakti monotheism, as it was in Nandadas's famous Braj re-creation of the Bhagavata episode in the sixteenth century. It is social reform on a national scale which was now propagated in relating the deeds of Krishna and the heroic stance that Radha is finally persuaded to adopt.[13]

Poetry in this new Hindi then partially overcomes the anxieties created by its relatively late arrival on the literary scene by adapting and transforming the themes and concerns of Brajbhasha and Avadhi verse. We see this anxiety until well into the 1930s, while the thematics of poetic works in Braj and Avadhi continue to be appropriated and subjected to repeated reworkings in larger or smaller format. Krishna becomes a *mahapurush* or great man, rather than an incarnation of Vishnu, in *Priya Pravas*; Radha a social reformer. In Maithili Sharan Gupta's (1886–1964) epic poem *Saket* (another name for Ayodhya, 1932), the Rama story does not follow in Rama's footsteps, as in the older Ramayanas, but is related instead from the perspective of those who remain behind in Ayodhya when he goes into exile along with Sita and Lakshman. The narrative focuses specially on Urmila, the wife Lakshman leaves behind, and the intense sorrow

---

[13] For more on *Priya Pravas*, see McGregor 1998.

of their separation. Later poets continue to tussle with these themes and reformulate them. The iconoclastic Chayavadi poet Suryakant Tripathi Nirala (1897–1962) writes a poem, 'Tulsidas' (1938), on the great Avadhi devotee-poet to reflect his own philosophical and social concerns. Hindi poets are thus creating interval links with an earlier tradition by reoccupying the spaces they clear and relocating traditional themes in a secular setting.

On the one hand Brajbhasha and Avadhi literature, which was bracketed with it, have been firmly pushed back. They have come to be seen as period manifestations, poems of the 'Bhakti kal' or devotional period, products of a religious and cultural reawakening in the face of Muslim oppression. Bhakti kal is followed by 'Riti kal' or the period of courtly, 'mannered' verse, with its more problematic erotic verse in Brajbhasha. But fast upon its heels comes the dawn of a new age, the 'Adhunik' or modern period, with its nationalism and its push for social reform, which overcomes the morally dubious effects of courtly indulgence: thus the periodization of Hindi literature, undertaken by Ramchandra Shukla (1884–1949), the best-known literary historian of the period, in his magisterial *Hindi sahitya ka itihas* (History of Hindi Literature,1929). Muslims (with some exceptions) and what had come to represent Urdu literature have been firmly excluded from the canon Shukla sets up. From this point on, Urdu and Hindi literature establish entirely different trajectories.

It is in this period of intense nationalist fervour that Maithili Sharan Gupta writes his ponderous but nevertheless sonorous poetic work *Bharat Bharati* (1912) in Khari Boli, which explicitly lays out the history of the Hindu people from the golden break of dawn in the Vedic-Aryan period through later glories, the brief unhappy period of the Muslim occupation, the British interlude, which affords some peace and some security, but which nonetheless remains alien, to a future age where there could be yet another dawn. This work is both modelled on and written as an explicit rejoinder to the earlier Urdu work: Hali's *Musaddas* (1869), which performed a similar feat for the Indian Muslim elite.[14]

---

[14] For a detailed analysis of *Bharat Bharati*, see Orsini 2001: 192ff.

In his next chapter, 'Hindi Nationalism', Rai discusses the literature of Chhayavad, a nature mysticism current in the 1920s and 1930s, which draws upon the English Romantic poets and Tagore as much as upon Vedanta. Sumitranandan Pant (1900–1977), who came to represent the most stereotypical image of the Chhayavadi poet—with his flowing tresses, easy lyricism and ecstatic love of nature—asks once more in the famous preface to *Pallav* (Foliage, 1928), for the creation of a soft and tender language in poetry, and for the use of Sanskrit words directly imported rather than taken over in their Hindi or Braj forms, though now with great care and consideration for the sound quality of words and away from the ponderous rhythms of early nationalist poetry in Hindi. And, once again, Pant sees the need to discuss metre, style, and lexis at great length. After the 1930s these anxieties subside. Some battles, it seems, have been won.

Provisional Deference

By this time, Hindi has reclaimed territorial authority and seeks nationwide expansion on the basis of its Sanskritic vocabulary. K.C. Chattopadhyaya, president of the Hindi Sahitya Sammelan in 1949, proclaims: 'Pure Sanskrit words are used in the same form everywhere. Therefore only that language can be acceptable all over India which is rich in pure Sanskrit words.'[15] This also means a shrinking of its lexical reservoir, with increasing restriction on the use of words seen as colloquial or too explicitly 'Urdu'. However, a Hindi thus conserved turns out to pose more of a threat than a promise of national glory to the other languages of newly independent India. In the Constituent Assembly debates of 1949 the fanaticism of the Hindiwallahs destroys the prospect of Hindi as the sole national language of India. Nehru speaks up for Hindustani but he cannot prevail. The result is the compromise Munshi–Ayyangar formula of 1950: Hindi is to be the official language of the republic along with English. The matter would be reviewed in 1965. But the political situation in the country had changed radically by this time: there had been widespread and violent protests against Hindi, leading to the linguistic reorganization

---

[15] Rai 2000: 109.

of states in 1956. This reorganization ended what Rai calls the provisional deference to Hindi. With the introduction of the three-language formula, theoretically, formal equality was established between Hindi and the other Indian languages and schoolgoing children in the Hindi regions were required to learn another Indian language alongside English and Hindi. Thus, English, the associate official language, continued to remain dominant.

With the stiff and unbending policy followed by the relevant institutions which continued to Sanskritize and sanitize, school Hindi and official Hindi become almost dead languages. Krishna Kumar has written about the dissociation of this Hindi from the lived world of the generation of schoolchildren who have been condemned to learn it.[16] And in this respect Rai is surely right when he says: 'Hindi is a dwindled thing today.'[17]

But are there not many Hindis? More than the one which is officially sanctioned and propagated? Is this not where the hope for the future could lie? Do things not change, once even this official, sanitized Hindi, projected originally as the language of (high-caste) Hindus, comes to be imposed equally on educational institutions in the country and the city, on Hindus and non-Hindus alike, on high and low caste (as far as these last have access to it in the states where it is the official language of instruction)? Does not this very fact modify its high-caste Hindu character? Once hitherto excluded groups and communities, women, Muslims, and Dalits begin to write in it, do they not stretch and expand it beyond its Dwivedi–Shukla contours?

For, and Rai says this clearly and unmistakably a little earlier in his tract, 'Hindi offers valuable insights into the making of Hindutva, but it is not entirely to be confused with it.'[18] Just as Hindutva is not to be projected backwards, we need to note that official Hindi, for all the damage it caused and continues to cause, has not entirely determined what writers, poets, filmmakers, and television scriptwriters did and do with it. S.H. Vatsyayana Agyeya

---

[16] Kumar 1991.
[17] Rai 2000: 119.
[18] Ibid.: 93.

(1911–87), the pioneer modernist poet, novelist, and publicist, articulates the literary resistance to official Hindi:

> There is at least one language in the country which claims that nothing within it has changed since a thousand years. As if any such thing can ever happen. This claim is false, it is nonsensical, the concept of language at the base of this claim is itself a mistake; the assumptions regarding the evolution of language are false. This mistake (and if it is political fraud, then this is political fraud) is doing great harm to the language. Spread once with the intention of becoming a hindrance in the way of another, it is now obstructing the progress of its own language. If what it says is true, then language would have been a dead thing for a thousand years, would have died even before these thousand years: and if it is not true, then to insist upon it is to impoverish again a language already wrought and still being wrought.
>
> There has been such a tendency in Hindi, but no respected literary person has given it support or encouragement, this has been Hindi's great good luck and its strength . . . Whether my Hindi is the national language or not, whether it is made to serve as the opportunistic link in the life of the nation or not, it is first and foremost a language which is expanding. And because it is expanding, it changes continuously but has at the same time a form which is stable, authoritative and standard.[19]

Even as Agyeya acknowledges that there had been a necessary process of standardization, he makes clear that this was not intended to, and indeed has not served to, throttle all further growth. The question would then be: if 'high' literature had once played such a vital role in endowing Hindi with cultural presence and political status, and if indeed most modern and especially post-Independence writers have not followed the dictates of official Hindi—as Rai also points out but does not expand on—could there be some slim chance that they will once again play some role in the politics of language, though this time round in fighting the ossification of Hindi?

Contours Stretched

As a language which has acquired official status, Hindi is no longer territorially bound. In fact, even before it was declared one of the

[19] Agyeya 2000: 27–8.

official languages of the Indian Union, writers from non-Hindi-speaking provinces, most prominently from Punjab, had elected to write in Hindi for various cultural, socio-religious, and political reasons. After Independence this was increasingly the case.[20] Post-Independence literary Hindi, then, for all its Sanskritization, has expanded to encompass lifeworlds far removed from those it had allowed itself to recognize in its constricted beginnings. The influence of the Bombay film, which also absorbed filmmakers from different regions, specially after Independence, the livelihood film and television have provided for Hindi and Urdu writers and what this has meant for their literary and cultural horizons, are matters which remain to be explored in sufficient depth. Meanwhile it is clear that 'village' Hindi and the language of the various regions, which now belong to the Hindi belt, alongside 'Muslim' Hindi and 'Dalit' Hindi, have stretched the literary contours of the language.

To begin with 'village Hindi': in post-Independence Hindi literature there has been a significant increase in 'regional' expressions, admittedly embedded in a Khari Boli which has by now been solidly standardized. This was a process which set in most widely in the early 1950s and 1960s. Allied to the Nayi Kahani (New Story) movement of the period, with its focus on a new kind of urban realism, this was a movement, if indeed such autonomy can be claimed for it, which came to be called Anchalik (regional). The novels and short stories which constituted it made extensive use of regional speech in the dialogues of the protagonists. Thus, if Premchand in writing of the peasants of the United Provinces in the 1920s and 1930s in a sense translated their speech into 'high' Hindi, in this post-Independence writing from the provinces, the original speech of the region tended to be retained without any effort at translation. Phanishvarnath Renu (1921–77) one of the best-known Anchalik writers, retained the original Maithili speech of his characters, making no concession to the tastes of the urban Hindi reader in other provinces. So

---

[20] There are some parallels here with the post-Independence Hindi film scenario. Ravi Vasudevan has suggested that the Bombay film of the 1950s, in its relationship to Punjab and Bengal, be explored as 'constructing itself as a national space.' Vasudevan 1994: 111.

evocatively did he capture the rhythms of this speech and so sharply etched was his depiction of the politics of the region in the period immediately preceding and following Partition that his novel *Maila Anchal* (Soiled Border, 1954) became one of the most celebrated in modern Hindi literature. He set a veritable trend in the use of Anchalik speech which urban writers resented and resisted. Thus, Mohan Rakesh (1925–72), a prominent Nayi Kahani writer, was to protest:

> Some new story writers [*naye kahanikar*] are also very insistent about the use of regional/local words and idioms. This does not startle in a given story if certain effects are to be achieved. This is additionally desirable if the language is to be enriched in its expressiveness. But we should not forget that language is our medium and the success of the work is in the [total] effect it communicates. If language itself becomes a hindrance in communication, then it deals a blow to its own intentions. It is a different matter if an author is writing for a regional/local audience. Then compositions of this kind are appropriate. But there are so many regional dialects of Hindi, that it will be asking too much of the common reader if he is expected to understand a language loaded with words and idioms of any given local dialect merely because it has also been dubbed 'Hindi'. The kind of suspicion some people had about the use of Sanskrit words has now been extended to such regional words. Just as, previously, the common Hindi reader did not accept a language he found inaccessible, so he will be unable to accept this language. One major reason for this is that the language no longer remains natural. In the past several hundred years, Khari Boli has purified itself. It is praiseworthy if we further cleanse it, but not so that we lose all faith in its expressiveness. A while ago this kind of insistence on dialect appeared in the Irish novel. The result is obvious. Readers did not accept it.[21]

Muslim Writing in Hindi

As the popularity of a great deal of 'regional' writing outside the immediate region of its production showed, local speech was seen as indeed adding to expressiveness. By and large readers did accept

[21] Rakesh 1975: 36.

such 'regionality', though this did not mean that these words and expressions were integrated into standard Hindi.

There was another important development in the 1960s. With the decline of Urdu publishing and the inaccessibility of education in Urdu, a number of Muslim writers turned to publishing their works in the Nagari script. This practice had precedence. Premchand, in the early teens of the twentieth century, had for this reason turned initially to Hindi. This was not a matter of simple transcription, however; it also involved the use of expressions no longer so current in literary Hindi. For even if Muslim writers adapted the standard Hindi idiom, they naturally also used more Urdu words.[22] There were some amongst them who insisted on both their regionality and their (however secular) Muslim identity, such as Rahi Masoom Raza (1927–92). He makes a personal appearance in his *Adha Gaon* (Half the Village, 1966), a novel which he first sought to publish in Urdu. Since no suitable publishing outlet could be found for it, he transcribed it into Devanagari. It subsequently attained great fame as a major Hindi novel and won a Sahitya Akademi award. In some ways this is also the theme of the novel: the rescripting of identity, as Raza's words when he personally intervenes in the narrative to make clear:

> The Jana Sangh says that Muslims don't belong here. How could I have the audacity to say that this is untrue? But I feel compelled to say that I belong to Ghazipur. My bond with Ghazipur is unbroken. It is not only a village, it is my home. Home. This word exists in every dialect and language in the world and it is the most beautiful word in every dialect and language. And therefore I repeat my words. Because it is not only a village. It is my home. 'Because'—how strong the word is. There are thousands and thousands of such 'becauses' and there is no sword sharp enough to cut through this 'because'. And as long as this 'because' is alive, I, Sayyid Masoom Raza, will remain an inhabitant of Ghazipur,

---

[22] Ulrike Stark, in her Heidelberg dissertation published subsequently as a book (Stark 1995), has analysed at some length the shifts in vocabulary from more Urdu to less Urdu, less Sanskritic to more Sanskritic, that came about in Muslim writing in Hindi.

even if my grandfather belonged elsewhere. And I give no one the right to say to me, 'Rahi, you don't belong in Gangauli, so go, for instance, to Rae Bareli.' Why should I go, sahib? I will not go.[23]

Muslim writing in Hindi, then, cannot be regarded as a case of assimilation alone.[24] Hindi has to stretch lexically to include the very Urdu words it had sought to exclude, and in doing so, its literary horizon cannot but widen. Clearly, it is usurping a good part of the space Urdu had once occupied and this is both problematic and troubling. Yet it is a development which needs to be noted.

Dalit Writing

The caste barrier has been similarly broken by Dalit writing, though this was to happen only in the 1990s on any remarkable scale. Dalits had once played character roles; even in reform literature, they tended to be marginal. Dalit writing today is often expressly autobiographical. And even if it is a middle-class readership that Dalit writers seem to address, they provide novel perspectives which stretch the bounds of middle-class imaginations, as caste-Hindus are instructed in the ways of those who may be denominationally Hindu but whose religious and social practice follows its own codes. Omprakash

---

[23] Raza (1966), 1993: 290.

[24] Though there is great danger that it will be seen as such, as for instance in such seemingly liberal articles as the one by L.M. Singhvi in *The Hindustan Times* of 11 January 2001. On the one hand, Singhvi's propositions seem broad-minded and accommodating: 'I would like to make a plea for Urdu in the Devnagari script as a parallel provision, not as an exclusive alternative. We should popularize Urdu in the Devnagari script not to supplant the script in which it is conventionally written, but to widen the access of the people. Urdu literature ought to be made available in Devnagari with meanings and annotations in the footnotes. Hindi readers will then enjoy Urdu immensely. The reach of Urdu will expand.' But this broad-mindedness is coupled with the clear tendency to see the practice of language communalism as one-sided. The tone is patronizing: 'Friends of Urdu should avoid the trap of religious communalism. The future of Urdu's tryst with India lies in mutual affection with Hindi, instead of mindless opposition or alienated competition with Hindi. Vote-bank and communal politics will be counterproductive. A positive and

Valmiki offers detailed descriptions of the rituals observed in his community in his autobiographical *Joothan* (Polluted Leftovers):

> Everyone in our colony was Hindu in name, but they did not worship any Hindu gods or goddesses. On Janmashtami, Jaharpir or some *paun* was worshipped instead of Krishna. This, too, was not on the eighth day of the lunar fortnight, but on the ninth day, just before sunrise.
>
> Similarly, people do not worship Lakshmi on Dipavali; either piglets are sacrificed to *Mai Madaran* or else a *halva* is prepared. A *kadhai*, that is a feast of *halva-puri* is made . . .
>
> Even though I lived in such an environment, my faith in these gods and goddesses did not remain after I had matured, that is, after I was able to think for myself. I thought that these *bhagat-s* were charlatans.
>
> Whenever such *puchhas* took place in my home, I would either sit outside or wander about. This had been a habit of mine since childhood. My actions would often upset father. He would speak of maintaining our ancestors' religion, a religion that I could not even swallow. I did not argue with him, however, about these subjects; I would just keep my mouth shut and sit down. He would become irritated. He scolded me. In the end, he, too, would become annoyed and keep quiet. He would then ask me the same question over and over, 'Munshiji, you haven't become a Christian, have you?' I used to reassure him, 'No, I have not become a Christian.'
>
> Yet something akin to a rage would erupt in my mind, and it wanted to declare, 'But I am not a Hindu either.' If I were a Hindu, why do Hindus hate me so much, why are they so prejudiced against me? Why, with every word they utter, would they make me so conscious of the inferiority of my caste? This question also occurred to me, 'Is it necessary to be a Hindu in order to become a decent human being?' I have grown up witnessing the cruelty of Hindus, and I have endured it as well. Why have attitudes of caste-supremacy become a source of pride and why do they only strike at the weak? Why are Hindus so heartless and cruel to *dalits*?[25]

---

modern secular agenda for Urdu will give it due place in language academies, schools, and colleges, rather than being the preserve of madrasas, which are themselves awaiting modernization. Urdu can be a language of India's liberal ethos only if it rejects obscurantism and orthodoxy.'

[25] Valmiki 1997.

Once it has encompassed a plurality of regions, communities, and interiorities, can Hindi remain caste-Hindu and male? And I have not even begun to speak of women's writing, in some ways the most dynamic and innovative of all recent writing, which has opened up vast spaces unlit before. The poetry of Mahadevi Varma and the novels of Krishna Sobti, Geetanjali Shree, and Alka Saraogi most readily spring to mind. To discuss their work in any detail would ask for an essay of considerable length. I revert, then, once again to the conclusions of Rai's tract, which in the light of the above surely seem conclusive: 'this people's Hindi is truly a middle language, the easygoing vernacular of North India, born out of the necessities of intercourse between different peoples, communities and cultures, which were forced to rub together in the daily business of living over centuries. Like all real languages, it is a complex system of overlapping registers and dialects . . . polycommunal as well as multilingual in its sources.'[26] And if it were truly so, and if this flexible, polycommunal, and multilingual Hindi, which has expanded in a myriad ways to become a language *not* only of high-caste Hindus—though admittedly still dominated by them—were the Hindi taught in schools and colleges and used for official intercourse, we would surely have something more akin to a language claiming the status of the second official language of the Indian Union, if not the sole national language. But how can the policy change be effected?

Since this is not the case, it remains for us to answer the question: why is it no longer possible for literary practice to influence policy-making? Literary production once provided the very grounds and substance of the language which claimed political recognition for itself. What has changed? Can it now not provide impetus to the massive reorientation in official policy which is so urgently needed? In short, how can the gap itself be made narrower between the wealth and variety of literary production in Hindi and the political agenda which has frozen language into the kind of stasis which can only reproduce itself?

[26] Rai 2000: 103.

Lost Status

A change of direction now would have far-reaching consequences far beyond the linguistic, as Rai points out in the concluding pages of his tract. 'For Hindi, on the other hand, to resume its necessary national destiny, it would have to distance itself from those regional elites—not to put too fine a point on it, Hindi belt savarna—whose lust for "nationality" produced "Hindi" in the first place. Only thus could it hope to break free from a crippling cultural politics and regain its regional character and loyalties. Clearly, however, such a process would have consequences far beyond the matter of language per se.'[27] It would mean loss of control, of the power to include and exclude.

But in the meantime, Hindi has itself lost the social and cultural status and with that the literary status which it once seemed fated to enjoy. This status has been increasingly arrogated by English and the neo-colonial English-speaking elite. If once there were bilingual authors who deliberately chose to write in Hindi or the other Indian languages, such as Agyeya, and if once there were bilingual readers, the situation changed radically after the 1950s and 1960s. As Meenakshi Mukherjee pointed out, only in the decades after Independence did Indian writing in English proliferate to the extent that it has, creating and catering to its own readership.[28] Reading habits are set early and the separation of those who read English and those who read in the vernacular now tends to begin early. 'The two groups', as Krishna Kumar has shown,

> live in two different cultural worlds, with their own specific zones of knowledge and ignorance. Children attending the elite English-medium schools of Bangalore, for instance, express disdainful unfamiliarity if asked about the literature written in Kannada. Living in the same city, they stay aloof from the symbolic world of the culture in which the majority of the children live. This kind of isolation from the world of the vernacular is neither a coincidence nor simply an act of omission on the school's part: it is an integral aspect of these children's socialization. The

---

[27] Rai 2000: 120.
[28] Mukherjee 2000: 176.

academic and other components of the culture of the English-medium schools make English a conduit which links the child with the West, and especially with America, and with the global economy in which America has a dominant position.[29]

And that has meant not only alienation from the world of the majority, but also literary and cultural impoverishment. Writing in English means constant translation into the cultural world of English, where language registers are lost and a host of connotations and associations remain irreproducible. As Meenakshi Mukherjee puts the matter:

> the normal ground conditions of literary production—where a culture and its variations, a language and its dialects, centuries of oral traditions and written literature, all interact to create a new text—do not exist in the case of English. Take for example the case of Malayalam, which is not only the spoken and written language of the geographic area called Kerala with oral variations between different groups—the Nairs, Nambudiris, the Christians, the Mapillas, etc.—but also the language of films, both commercial and serious, its songs, folk tales, riddles, nonsense verse, nursery rhymes, proceedings of the Vidhan Sabha, slogans in processions, rhetoric of public speech, conversation on the football field, street-corner humour as well as of Kathakali and a long literary culture. A fictional text that is produced in this language today draws upon and echoes the reverberations of this layered plurality that surrounds and nurtures it.[30]

But mourning the loss incurred cannot reverse history. Alongside writing in Kannada there will be writing in English and in certain circles it will enjoy more prestige. It can also not be a question of denying the brilliance of a great deal of new writing in English. The question seems much more to be: to what extent can the worlds which seem to have separated, be made to meet again, to overlap again? Partha Chatterjee, who has written eloquently about the bilingual scholar operating as a full member in two different academic arenas,

---

[29] Kumar 1996: 70.
[30] Mukherjee 2000: 173.

has the uniquely advantageous position of being interpretive and critical in both [the Western academy and an intellectual arena shaped by a modern non-European language] . . . On the other hand, if struggling with the act of translation, whether in this arena or that, is the very stuff of what the bilingual intellectual does, then even in the knowledge that there must always remain a residue, a loss of meaning, one would still be entitled to the belief that translation is an act of transformation— changing not only that which is being translated but also that to which the translation is a contribution. And if, as would be the case with many bilinguals, the act of translation works in both directions, then one might be entitled to the further supposition that . . . one is contributing to the critical transformation of both.[31]

There may be a handful of bilingual scholars who could contribute to the critical transformation of both worlds, but if we were to operate with this analogy and ask: how many bilingual readers, who genuinely participate in both worlds, exist today, the answer may be more depressing than not. For Hindi to become Hindi without inverted commas, for it to participate in the world of the English elite and for the elite to participate in the creation and consumption of Hindi literature, a little more than 'less Sanskritization and more colloquialization' would have to come about. The educational hierarchies, the cultural competences, which so divide the worlds, which make for two different universes of literary production and dialogue,[32] would have to be entirely overhauled. For this to come about, the English and the Hindi elites would have to enter into a dialogue, into collaboration with one another. And take the many other spoken and written Hindis into account. What forces could impel them to do that?

Perhaps it is in this light, of mutual ignorance, disregard, and even hostility, that we have to see the Rushdie statement which so incensed the English-speaking Indian intelligentsia, who hurled back all kinds of insults at Rushdie, though they themselves (we ourselves) participate in the dichotomies which call forth such statements. In Rushdie's oft-quoted words I find uncanny echoes

---

[31] Chatterjee 1997: 284.
[32] Charted in Orsini 2002.

of earlier formulations: 'The prose writing—both fiction and non-fiction—created [in the fifty years after Independence] by Indian writers working in English, is proving to be stronger and a more important body of work than most of what has been produced in the 16 "official languages", during the same time: and indeed, this new, and still burgeoning, "Indo-Anglian" literature represents perhaps the most valuable contribution India has yet made to the world of books.'[33] Compare that with this:

> I have no knowledge of either Sanscrit or Arabic. But I have done what I could to form a correct estimate of their value. I have read translations of the most celebrated Arabic and Sanscrit works. I have conversed, both here and at home [England] with men distinguished by their proficiency in the Eastern tongues. I am quite ready to take the oriental learning at the valuation of the orientalists themselves. I have never found one among them who could deny that a single shelf of a good European library was worth the whole native literature of India and Arabia. The intrinsic superiority of the Western literature is indeed fully admitted by those members of the committee who support the oriental plan of education.[34]

Once people, Indian in blood and colour, but if not quite English then neo-colonial in tastes, in opinions, in morals, and in intellect, have been cast in this mould, can they, without resorting to 'Blut und Boden' ideologies, be transformed yet again? Can they, at the very least, become bilingual? It is the great merit of Alok Rai's erudite, passionate, and polemical tract that it has pinpointed these issues and reopened these debates.

References

Agyeya, S.H. Vatsyayana, 2000. *Kavi-man*, ed. Ila Dalmia-Koirala. Bikaner: Vagdevi Prakashan.

Ahmad, Aijaz, 2000. 'In the Mirror of Urdu: Recompositions of Nation and Community, 1947–65', in *Lineages of the Present: Ideology and Politics in Contemporary South Asia*. London: Verso.

---

[33] Rushdie 1997: x.
[34] *Selections from Educational Records* 109.

Alam, Muzaffar, 1998. 'The Pursuit of Persian: Language in Mughal Polities', *Modern Asian Studies*, 32/2: 317–49.

Bharatendu Harishchandra, 1883. *Hindi Bhasha*. Kashi: Khadgavilas Press.

Chatterjee, Partha, 1997. 'Talking about Modernity in Two Languages', in *A Possible India: Essays in Political Criticism*. Delhi: Oxford University Press.

Dalmia, Vasudha, 1997. *The Nationalization of Hindu Traditions*. New Delhi: Oxford University Press.

Dodson, Michael S., 2002. 'Re-Presented for the Pandits: James Ballantyne, Useful Knowledge, and Sanskrit Scholarship in Benares College during the Mid-Nineteenth Century', *Modern Asian Studies* 36/2: 257–98.

Dwivedi, Mahavirprasad (1911), 1995. '*Hindi ki vartman avastha*', in *Dwivedi Rachnavali*, vol. 1, ed. Bharat Yayavar. Delhi: Kitab Ghar.

'Hariaudh', Ayodhya Singh Upadhyaya (1914), 1966. *Priya Pravas*. Banaras: Hindi Sahitya Kutir.

Kumar, Krishna, 1991. *Political Agenda of Education: A Study of Colonialist and Nationalist Ideas*. Delhi: Sage Publications.

———, 1996. *Learning from Conflict*. Tracts for the Times 10. Delhi: Orient Longman.

McGregor, Stuart, 1998. 'Ayodhyasimh Upadhyay (1865–1947) and his *Priya Pravas*', in *Classics of Modern South Asian literature*, ed. Rupert Snell and I.M. Raeside. Wiesbaden: Harrassowitz.

———, 2001a. 'The Formation of Modern Hindi as Demonstrated in Early Hindi Dictionaries'. The 2000 Gonda Lecture. Amsterdam, Royal Netherlands Academy of Arts and Sciences.

———, 2001b. 'On the Evolution of Hindi as a Language of Literature', *South Asia Research* 21/2: 203–17.

Mukherjee, Meenakshi, 2000. *The Perishable Empire: Essays on Indian Writing in English*. Delhi: Oxford University Press.

Nicholls, George, 1907. *Sketch of the Rise and Progress of the Benares Pathshala or Sanskrit College, Now Forming the Sanskrit Department of the Sanskrit College* (written 1848). Allahabad: Government Press.

Orsini, Francesca, 2001. *The Hindi Public Sphere, 1920–1940: Language and Literature in the Age of Nationalism*. Delhi: Oxford University Press.

———, 2002. 'India in the Mirror of World Fiction', *New Left Review* 13, Jan./Feb.

Rai, Alok, 2000. *Hindi Nationalism*. Tracts for the Times 13. Delhi: Orient Longman.
Rakesh, Mohan, 1975. '*Hindi kathasahitya: Navin pravrittiyam*', in *Sahityik aur Samskritic Drishti*. Delhi: Radhakrishna Prakashan.
Raza, Rahi Masoom (1966), 1993. *Adha Gaon*. Delhi: Rajkamal.
Rushdie, Salman, 1997. Introduction, in *The Vintage Book of Indian Writing 1947–1997*. London: Vintage.
Selections from Educational Records, Part I, 1781–1839, 1920. Ed. H. Sharpe. Calcutta: Superintendent Government Printing, India, 1920.
Singhvi, L.M., 2001. 'Resurrect the Language', *The Hindustan Times*, 11 January.
Stark, Ulrike, 1995. *Tage der Unzufiedenheit: Identitaet und Gessehlschaftsbild in den Romanen muslimischer Hindischriftsteller (1965–1990)*. Stuttgart: Franz Steiner Verlag.
Valmiki, Omprakash, 1997. *Joothan*. Delhi: Radhakrishna.
Vasudevan, Ravi, 1994. 'Dislocations: The Cinematic Imagining of a New Society in 1950s India', *Oxford Literary Review*, Special Issue on India: Writing History, Culture, Post-Coloniality, 16: 1/2, ed. Ania Loomba and Suvir Kaul.

14

Hindi, Nation, and Community

THE BROAD-SCALE MOVEMENT WHICH BEGAN TO project Hindi as the language of the nation, centred in Banaras but with a growing network in other North Indian cities, began to gather force from the 1870s. Considering that Hindi was still in the process of finding its modern form, the claim of the movement's leaders was a tall one. In order to find its new feet, Hindi needed to overhaul its very base—syntactically, lexically, orthographically—and set about educating the readership it needed to legitimate itself. For the newly emerging professional classes in the cities of North India, as they sought to organize and orient themselves socially, culturally, and politically, and voice their grievances to those in power, the need to create a forum of some sort was urgent. It was from their ranks that the leaders, authors, and potential readers of modern Hindi emerged. Theirs was a call for a shared language of communication and a literature that could substantiate the claim to an autonomous cultural identity. That this process led increasingly to a clear-cut split between Hindi as the language of (North Indian) Hindus, and Urdu as that of Muslims, is a fact that has come to be widely recognized, though it continues to be contested by those who would rather see these languages as separate entities from their very origins, at whatever point in time these origins are placed. But no one, to my knowledge, contests the fact that Hindi and Urdu did come to figure as more or less autonomous entities by the beginning of the twentieth century. The present anthology charts this course of nation-formation and nationalism, and the inclusions, exclusions, and inner splits that accompanied these processes. It also makes apparent the shared ground between Hindi and Urdu that was and is as profound as the growing mutual antagonism.[1]

While delving into these issues, we need to remind ourselves of Hindi's present location, so as not to remain caught up in the past. The kind of colloquial Hindi used by the media has freed itself from the shackles of the Sanskritization which increased manifold in the years immediately following Independence. Hindi today has also opened up in a yet more staggering way to receive words from English: it seems no longer to be defining its status in an antagonistic relationship to the culture and politics represented by English through years of colonization. English is a global language and the language of India's urban elites. There is, therefore, a relentless give and take between Hindi and Indian English, and this works in both directions.[2] We need only to think of advertisements that so generously mix English and Hindi; it is a moot question whether they are in English with a mixture of Hindi or the other way around. This is the new Hindi, the language of the media, of newspapers, FM radio channels, and commercial TV, not to speak of the Bombay film. It is very powerful and seeks no stamp of approval from any authority.

Yet there is still a vast literary production which continues to use a more chaste Hindi. This Hindi may take in regional varieties of language-use, but it minimizes or avoids English expression. Poems, short stories, novels, and essays in this form of Hindi are read and written by young and old in the vast region known as the Hindi belt, and increasingly in the smaller towns rather than in the big metropolises. This literary Hindi is no longer defining itself against Urdu; it has contained it to a large extent. I use the word 'contained' in

---

[1] This essay was first published as one part of a two-part Introduction to an anthology of Urdu and Hindi nationalist writing: Shobna Nijhawan, ed., *Nationalism in the Vernacular: Hindi, Urdu, and the Literature of Indian Freedom* (Ranikhet: Permanent Black, 2010).

[2] A whole issue of the Hindi quarterly *Vak* (April–June 2007) considers the critical issues related to this new Hindi.

both its senses: the generous one, which opens up to receive words and works which would otherwise have been written in the Urdu script; but also in the sense of curbing Urdu's independent growth. So there are both aspects within this form of Hindi, positive as well as negative.

And finally, of course, there is still Sanskrit-infested official Hindi, fossilized but preserved in the wide network of governance. These are all forms of current Hindi, with whatever prefix we may choose to describe their register, and with whatever regard or lack of regard we choose to use or not use them.

Given this state of affairs, there has been criticism of historical studies that seem to relive—and, it is suggested, thus seek to revive—past disputes. Why constantly hark back to the antagonisms of the Hindi–Urdu divide?[3] Why go back to the history of the Hinduization of Hindi and its often narrow nationalist bent when Hindi seems to have outgrown—and, it is suggested, overcome—this stage? To accept this proposition, however, would mean deliberately overlooking the anti-Urdu stance which remains an inherently and durably troubling aspect of academic and institutional Hindi. It would mean shutting our eyes to the role that this Hindi can still play in the kind of exclusivist identity formation which would leave out, or at best subsume, Indian Muslims. We need then to recall the history of modern Hindi and its close association with nation-formation for many reasons: to provide a corrective to the present, to remember its shared ground with Urdu, and to recall that there was a period before the polarization when there was little or no conflict because there was less standardization and less politicization. It is equally necessary to remember the vast mobilizing role that Hindi has played in the nationalist struggle, when nationalism meant emancipation from the stranglehold not only of the British but that of native elites; to contest the view that Hindi could only be the Hindi of chauvinists who would use it to deny other claims; to recall the dynamism that allowed voices never heard before to be raised in a public sphere

---

[3] Thus, for instance, the polemics by Abhay Kumar Dube in the *Vak* issue cited above.

which, though monopolized by male upper castes/classes, could be radically challenged by peasants, women, Dalits. And finally, given that the English-speaking elites today regard Hindi—and for that matter the other Indian languages which have been demoted to 'regional languages'—as conservative and even regressive, we must remind ourselves that Hindi was a major *modernizing* force in the years before and indeed after Independence (regrettably, this anthology stops with 1947).

The process of nation-formation and modernization in the North, within what is today seen as the Hindi belt, was extremely rapid—it took place in a matter of eight decades or less. And this process was so successful in casting a veil over Hindi's initial, formative period, that the claims of its movers and shakers in the first half of the twentieth century regarding the age and venerable stature of the language have come to be accepted as commonplace. Given that the history of Hindi has come to be so closely entwined with the history of the nation, this is not surprising. Political and linguistic nationalism both suggest that the origins of motherland and mother tongue are so hoary that they are beyond dispute. The texts of the period we cover, however, clearly show the historical processes by which the nation was imagined, of its contours being mapped, its myths forged and recast to respond to contemporary political needs, and of these new 'truths' then finding their way into texts for children who must be made to grow into citizens of 'a once-proud nation'.

The range of tasks for the nation and national-language makers was immense: a vast vocabulary needed to be forged for scientific-philosophical discourse and for a literary canon flexible enough to deal with a range of issues in a range of registers. Some of the terminology sought was readily available in Sanskrit. But a great deal had to be coined anew if the emotive, affective power of the language was to expand, and if literature was to look not for past stature alone but also for wider and deeper communication—on matters that spanned the private and the public spheres, and about those excluded from the public sphere. Thus, we find ourselves dealing with contradictory trends. On the one hand there was steady Sanskritization in the effort to make of Hindi an intellectual vehicle of thought, as also of pan-Indian reach and—it was thought, given the shared Sanskrit origins of many regional languages—pan-Indian comprehensibility. On the other, there were movements to widen the notion of nation so as to include those that had been marginalized by the establishment world of caste-Hindus. It is in order to document this dual process that this anthology provides a selection not only from what would rapidly come to be regarded as canonical texts, but also from sources less well known today—from journals and tracts, and writers long forgotten.

In order to appreciate Hindi's rapid growth in the eight decades or so under consideration, we need to remind ourselves that, even in the mid-nineteenth century, what we know today as Hindi had barely begun to come into existence.[4] It has been often thought, in fact, that an awareness of the language's 'Hinduness' was almost thrust upon the populace by colonial intervention a good few decades before the Hindu elites of the North took up the cause of Hindu–Hindi. To cite an oft-quoted instance: in 1846 James Ballantyne, the newly appointed principal of the Benares Sanskrit College, asked students of the College to use Hindi in their written exercises.[5] The students, however, showed no enthusiasm when asked for greater effort in using the language of their daily intercourse. Ballantyne pressed the most intelligent students into formulating the reasons for this apparent indifference to their own language. The students' somewhat

---

[4] For accounts of the Hindi–Urdu divide and the growth of Hindi in the nineteenth century and thereafter, see King 1994; Dalmia 1997; and Rai 2000. For detailed documentation and analysis of the period of the greatest pre-Independence expansion of Hindi, see Orsini 2002.

[5] Ballantyne had written a grammar of Hindustani (*A Grammar of the Hindustani Language; followed by a series of Grammatical Exercises, etc.*, London: Cox & Co., Edinburgh: Ballantyne & Co., 1838) and obviously participated in the belief that a language of the Hindus existed as an autonomous entity. For a detailed discussion of Ballantyne's contribution to the curriculum of the Benares Sanskrit College, see Dodson 2002: 257–98.

bewildered response shows clearly that the term 'Hindi' had little or no currency, at least in this part of North India:

> We do not clearly understand what you Europeans mean by the term Hindi, for there are hundreds of dialects all in our opinion equally entitled to the name and there is here no standard as there is in Sanskrit. If the purity of Hindi is to consist in its exclusion of Musalman words, we shall require to study Persian and Arabic in order to ascertain which of the words we are in the habit of using every day, is Arabic or Persian and which is Hindi. With our present knowledge we can tell that a word is Sanskrit or not Sanskrit, but if not Sanskrit it may be English or Portuguese instead of Hindi for anything we can tell . . . what you call Hindi will eventually merge in some future modification of the Urdu: nor do we see any great cause of regret in this prospect.[6]

Ballantyne was obviously pressing his Sanskrit students to use 'pure' Hindi, which excluded 'Musalman' words, and it was this that caused bewilderment. Even in the late nineteenth century, when the cause of Hindi had begun to acquire nationalist dimensions, the language was considered to be in a relatively fluid state, in need both of standardization and wider propagation.

Bharatendu Harishchandra (1850–85), 'father of modern Hindi' and surely a partisan observer, made no attempt to disguise the fact that there could be no question yet of a standard language (Khari Boli) as the only language spoken in the majority of homes in the North West Provinces. As he specified in a short treatise entitled *Hindi Bhasha* (written in 1883–4, at the tail end of a prolific career of writing in Hindi): 'Languages have three sections [*vibhag*], that is, the language spoken at home, the language of poetry, and the written language. It cannot be ascertained what the language spoken in the homes of the North-West Provinces is, since in the province of Delhi, as well as in other cities, no one speaks Hindi at home besides the Khatris and the Panchahi [Western] Agravals, so much so that after every *kos* the language changes.'[7]

---

[6] Nicholls 1907: 99, as cited in Rai 2000: 65–6.
[7] Harishchandra 1883: 1.

As for the language of poetry, Harishchandra's verdict was quite decisive: it was Brajbhasha and sometimes Avadhi. When it came to the language of prose—that is, written or 'print' language—he confessed that there was much disagreement. Some wanted a generous mixture of Urdu words, others insisted on Sanskrit words, but finally all ended up writing according to their own taste. In short, he seemed to be saying that Hindi existed in a variety of forms. He himself advocated the use of a simple, easily comprehensible language which did not import too much from Sanskrit, but which clearly distinguished itself from Urdu.

These were matters that needed urgent attention and Harishchandra spared no eloquence when pushing for them. In his long verse address to an appreciative audience, *'Hindi ki Unnati par Vyakhyan'* (A Discourse on the Progress of Hindi, 1877), he outlined the agenda for modern Hindi as he envisioned it: better communication and thus more cohesiveness within the family; literate mothers who could begin to teach their sons at a very young age, fostering pride in their own cultural heritage; a systematic appropriation of Western knowledge via the translation of scientific and technical works; more newspapers and political consolidation, together making for the progress not only of Hindi and its community but of the nation:

> Look, look, Bharat's rising sun has lit up the east
> Rise, let the heart's lotus unfold, destroying the darkness of grief . . .
> Appropriate all the sciences, power, intelligence and knowledge
> Do away with mutual discord, unite, be the mine of all virtue.[8]

The turn of the twentieth century saw a range of institutions spring up to espouse the cause of Hindi. The youthful founders of what would become the most dynamic, and with time also the most august of these, the Nagari Pracharini Sabha (Society for the Propagation of Hindi, Banaras, 1893), radiated immense energy. The society developed manifold activities, many of which were modelled on the Asiatic Society of Bengal in Calcutta. Equipped with a library as early as

---

[8] Citations, unless noted otherwise, stem from this anthology.

in its fourth year, the Sabha's most important activity was the search for manuscripts in Hindi and Hindi-related languages. Its findings, enshrined in voluminous Search Reports, would provide the basis for the standard editions for the works of the major Brajbhasha, Avadhi, and modern Hindi poets and writers. The Sabha's research-oriented journal, the *Nagari Pracharini Patrika*, which began publication in 1896, would continue to appear for well over a century, first as a quarterly, from 1907 on as a monthly. The Sabha's dictionary project, which was the focus of the second decade of its activity, led to the publication of the eleven-volume *Hindi Shabda Sagar* (1929). Given the seminal importance of this dictionary in virtually constructing the lexical base of the language, it is perhaps not surprising that the first major history of Hindi literature, *Hindi Sahitya ka Itihas* by Ramchandra Shukla (1923–9, revised edition 1940), originated as the preface to this dictionary.

Shukla's history had been preceded by the work of the Mishra Bandhu (three brothers who lived between 1873 and 1951), whose singular enthusiasm for Hindi is a reminder that a great deal of this early work was the result of individual effort, often over a lifetime. It was personal devotion to the cause of Hindi that made for their astonishing output at a time when there was little by way of reference material. The brothers wrote several works of criticism, as well as fiction and poetry, but are remembered most of all for their pioneering literary history: *Mishrabandhu Vinod* (Delight of the Mishra Brothers, 1914), a magisterial three-volume survey of about 5000 poets, encapsulating a powerful response to colonial ideologies that decried India's literary backwardness.

The literary scene was also to expand from its nucleus in Banaras to include Allahabad, the new capital of the North West Provinces (later the United Provinces), with its concentration of university, colleges, law courts, and government offices. It was here that the dynamic and fast-expanding Indian Press launched its equally dynamic Hindi journal *Sarasvati* (1900). Mahavir Prasad Dwivedi (1864–1938), editor of the journal from 1903 to 1920, almost single-handedly helped to standardize Hindi and shape the course of Hindi literature. Though he is remembered today more as a stern critic and pedant, he had a vast and generous vision of literature, which included the sciences. He freely admitted the need to tap the wealth available in English and Sanskrit, not to say Bengali and Marathi. But most of all, he fostered a coterie of new writers who went on to create a substantial body of literature: poetry, essays, short stories, reviews, and reports from far corners of the world—from the USA in the West to Japan in the East. A Hindi reading public was fast coming into being.[9]

There was concurrent activity in other fields: education, and the growing political espousal of Hindi by nationalist leaders. The Arya Samaj, founded in 1875 by Dayanand Saraswati, made the earliest institutional efforts to propagate Hindi. The Samaj came to enjoy unprecedented popularity in the Punjab, providing as it did cultural and social orientation for the modernizing Hindu elites of a region in which religious identity was coming to matter, most of all when it came to jobs in the colonial administration. It was in the Punjab, in a non-Hindi-speaking environment, by virtue of its association with Hinduness, that Hindi, early championed by Dayanand, became an important discipline in schools and colleges.[10] It became a taught subject as early as 1876 in the Dayanand Anglo-Vedic College of Lahore (1876).[11] It was the medium of instruction in the famous Jullunder Women's School and College (1895) and came to be propagated yet more rigorously in the Gurukul Kangri (1900) established by the traditionalist wing of the Arya Samaj. This last measure was to give it an immense boost and much publicity, as various nationalist leaders, including Gandhi, were received in the Gurukul with much fanfare.[12]

---

[9] After the 1920s several important Hindi journals, some very medium-sized, began to appear from provincial towns such as Mirzapur, Etawah, Gorakhpur, Khandwa, Jabalpur, Indore, and Ajmer, connecting the local to the larger literary sphere. See Orsini 2002: 66.

[10] Jones 1976 (2006) remains the classic study of this period of Hinduization in Punjab.

[11] The Lahore College was the forerunner of a series of other such institutions across the Punjab and in several cities in the United Provinces: Kanpur, Dehra Dun, Banaras, Lucknow, Anup Shahar, Meerut. See Orsini 2002: 112.

[12] Fischer-Tiné 2003 is an important study in German of the Gurukul as a nationalist institution; it awaits translation into English.

These nationalist leaders were also to play their part on the forum offered by the Hindi Sahitya Sammelan in Allahabad (Association for Hindi Literature, 1910), which had grown out of the Nagari Pracharini Sabha.[13] From its inception, the Sammelan addressed the growing Hindi intelligentsia and Congress leaders such as Tilak and Gandhi, who were beginning to propagate Hindi as the national language. The first 'Conference of the National Language and National Script', organized in Lucknow in 1916 with the support of the Arya Samaj, welcomed as participants Gandhi, Annie Besant, Madan Mohan Malaviya, Swami Shraddhanand, and various other luminaries. Resolutions on the unity of the nation, Nagari as the national script, and Hindi as the national language, were passed with much enthusiasm. But right from the start, there were differences of opinion on the reasons for Hindi's qualification as the national language. Tilak (as also, in due course, the Sammelan) regarded Hindi as the language of the Hindus, which meant favouring a Sanskritized Hindi. Gandhi regarded Hindi as the language of the people and of village India, and as a force which opposed English rather than Urdu. He favoured a more colloquial idiom which he and others liked to call Hindustani: this was very different from the nineteenth-century British use of the term, which had denoted Urdu rather than Hindi. These very fundamental differences were to lead to a split between Gandhi and the Sammelan leadership a few decades later. But meanwhile the Congress session, held in Nagpur in 1920, was able to reach a compromise and declare Hindi-Hindustani the national language of India. All proceedings of the Congress were, as far as possible, to be held in the national language—a fraught proposition that aroused the immediate resentment of Muslim members.

But there was no denying that Hindi had gained in political importance, as a grassroots movement as much as one propagated through powerful institutions. Though Hindi literature came to be

---

[13] The following account is based on the information provided in Orsini 2002: 137. See Das Gupta 1970 for the role played by organizations such as the Nagari Pracharini Sabha and the Hindi Sahitya Sammelan in furthering the cause of Hindi on the national stage.

recognized as a university discipline only in the 1920s,[14] the need for teachers at all levels was growing rapidly. The Hindi Sahitya Sammelan played an important role in helping to create a body of instructors in Hindi literature. It also instituted examinations, initially only in UP and Bihar, but eventually all over India, which came to enjoy wide popularity and carry much prestige, offering as they did a convenient alternative to expensive and time-consuming university degrees.

The present anthology includes a sample of works by poets beloved of this first readership, which was learning, along with its creators, to appreciate the new configurations of language and power. Early-twentieth-century poets wrote then not only in Brajbhasha, which flowed more easily from their pens, but ventured into modern Hindi poetry and with that into new thematics: nature poetry, alongside patriotic and reformatory verse—but nature poetry, at this stage, also linked to the notion of national territory. Thus Shridhar Pathak (1860–1928) wrote extended poems on natural beauty, mapping geographically specific landscapes in words and phrases just being wrung out of Hindi's lexis. For one of his more popular poems, Pathak turned to Kashmir, with its Sanskritic as well as Mughal associations, invoking Srinagar and the Jhelum with much pride and emotion:

> All around, snowy mountain peaks, as if a crest of diamonds in a crown.
> The pure current of the river flows by, as if her maiden moon necklace.
> That diffused beauty of the blooming earth, of the wood and grove,
> Arose as if from the womb of the earth, a trove of jewels.
> That beauty of the snowy peaks, rivers, lakes, and woods, as a whole

---

[14] The Banaras Hindu University introduced Hindi as a university discipline in 1922, six years after its founding; the University of Allahabad in 1923; and the universities of Lucknow, Agra, etc. in 1926.

Pervades the sphere, graces the four directions,
As if the shape of a brilliant jewelled crown garland.
A necklace strung of priceless orbs and tied over the head of India.

—*Kashmir Kusum* (The Beauty of Kashmir, 1904)

If Pathak has receded in the memory of readers, much more enduring has been the reputation of Maithili Sharan Gupta (1886–1964), foremost of the coterie of poets formed by the editor of *Sarasvati*, and early awarded the title *rashtra kavi* (national poet) by an appreciative readership. Gupta's metrical schooling took place at home, by a traditionally trained bard who had been in the service of his wealthy father. His verse retained the rousing, ringing intonation of older heroic poetry, but new notions of history informed his view of the past. Poetry lovers and patriots would come to memorize and recite whole stanzas of his epic poem *Bharat Bharati* (1912). The poem recalled the glorious deeds of Aryans and mourned the subsequent periods of cultural downfall. The poem's anti-Muslim tones, however, spared the British, who were lauded for the progress and peace they had made possible. It ended with an inspiring vision of what was to come. The cast of these verses was carried over into Gupta's other works. Himself a Rama devotee, he wrote the widely lauded *Saket* (or Ayodhya, 1932) a modern rendition of the *Ramayana,* to reflect the fate of the family members left behind in Ayodhya once Rama went into exile. Gupta could take up epic themes and characters with similar ease—as for example Abhimanyu, one of the Pandu sons in the *Mahabharata*, whose ignoble killing became the focus of Gupta's second major work, *Jayadrath Vadha* (The Slaying of Jayadrath, 1910). The valiant young Abhimanyu was lured by Jayadrath into a battle formation where he was treacherously killed. Jayadrath's own slaying by Arjuna, leading the outnumbered Pandava forces, was the theme of the second half of this martial epic poem. Abhimanyu was a figure with whom the revolutionary youth of the nation could identify:

> Unarmed Abhimanyu surrounded by armed men:
> 'I just want what is fair and right, to have a weapon,
> Put a weapon in my hand, then show me your heroism.
> Then shall I see your resolve and earnestness.
> What, are you seven? Even if you were one hundred,

Still would I bring you to tears.
Acting on my hunger for battle, I would
Bring you instantly to eternal slumber.'

Past heroics were traced not only in myth but also in history—academic as well as popular—which entered modern Hindi literature alongside myth and legend, enlarging the frontiers of its reach and laying out verifiable contours of the past.

Popular history found many forms. The vast repertoire of plays, mythological and historical, supplied by the commercial Parsi or 'Company' theatre, were written in an idiom colloquial enough to be understood widely and claimed by both Urdu and Hindi when the need arose. The many offshoots of this theatre toured the length and breadth of the subcontinent through the first decades of the century. A more staid and Sanskritized Hindi was used in the historical plays of Jayshankar Prasad (1889–1937), a major poet and dramatist. Prasad's plays dealt with ancient Hindu history, turning to the early centuries of the common era and the Gupta period for cultural and political validation. The widely acclaimed historical novels of Vrindavanlal Varma (1889–1966), still to be found in paperback editions in railway station bookstalls, focused by contrast on the romance and heroism of the medieval period. Published from the late 1920s and rooted in the rugged landscape of Varma's beloved Bundelkhand, they related tales of Rajput glory. The painstakingly researched history that informed his novels was enriched by the dense folklore that pervaded a countryside dotted with stone forts and delicately ornate palaces, many of them in ruins. If many of these Rajput narratives carried the inevitable anti-Muslim tone, Varma's wildly popular *Jhansi ki Rani Lakshmi Bai* (1946), an invective against the treachery and greed of the British as much as a celebration of Lakshmibai, climaxed with the death of the Rani, fighting valiantly in the 1857 uprising, which was projected as the first war of Indian independence in the novel:

> Suddenly the Rani was struck in the stomach by one of the British riders. And though she turned around and killed him, blood began to seep out of her stomach. She immediately thought—'I am now going to lay the foundation for independence', and said to Raghunath, 'Do not let

the British defile my body' as she moved forward . . . The Rani was slicing through the British soldiers with her sword, and the resulting pandemonium gave Raghunath some time.

The light went out of her face. The sun had set. The light settled on the western horizon, and the fading rays of the sun spread into the sky. A stillness covered everything . . .

> Baba—'The light is immortal. Everything fades and yet the rising sun brightens everything again. The Rani is now immortal.'

It was this ethos, of pride in the motherland and its history and culture, which then percolated into children's literature and journals. Thus, *Kumari Darpan* (Mirror of the Maiden), edited by Rameshwari Nehru of Allahabad, when speaking of 'Bharat Dwellers' (February 1917), could proclaim in simple prose:

> The Aryans knew how to read and write and compose poetry. The Aryans have bequeathed us a vast anthology of mantras that is known as the Rig Veda. We know some of the issues of those early days from these mantras. Once the Aryans had established kingdoms they began to fight one another. The story of a massive battle between the two kings has been written up in a Sanskrit text; it is called the *Mahabharata*. The text was recited many years ago and continues to be recited. Another similar story is called the *Ramayana*.

The patriotism this called forth, to rise and respond to the challenges of the day—industrialization, the alleviation of poverty—can be seen in this brief excerpt from the journal *Khilauna* (Game):

> And look, we import more goods than most other countries, such as clothes, toys, alcohol and other things. We buy these things obsessively and send lakhs and crores of rupees out of the country. If we bought the same things from the factories in our country then our revenue would stay in the country and go to the people who live here. This money would alleviate their dire poverty . . . That is why we should only use things made in our own country.[15]

---

[15] *Desh ki Bat* (About the Nation), February 1927.

The racial arrogance of the British, exhibited in personal encounters and official protocol, has largely receded from public memory, enabling the nostalgic glow that has come to pervade memories of the Raj. In its own day, the racism and contempt displayed in such encounters fanned the fires of the national movement. The Indian-language press carried news of such acts of humiliation and summary justice beyond the borders of the local and the regional. A profusion of publicist pieces in Hindi, sparkling with wit and shot through with biting satire, was directed not only against the British but also against the helpless, often sycophantic, response of 'native' elites.

Harishchandra and his cohort, repeatedly punished for disloyalty by abrupt terminations of official subscriptions to their often tottering journals, also repeatedly indulged in mockery and farce which targeted both the oppressor and those allowing themselves to be oppressed. In *Bharat Durdasha* (The Sad State of India, 1876), one of Harishchandra's best-known plays, modelled on the Bengali but with its own variations, one of the most hilarious scenes is set in a library. A meeting has been called to discuss measures to ward off impending enemy invasion. A Bengali gentleman suggests:

> In my country a play called 'India's Uplift' has been written. Why don't we use the same remedy that is given there to throw out the British? It says that five Bengalis together will throw the British out. One of them will take some flour and fill up the Suez Canal. Another will cut bamboos and will make syringes. The third will use those syringes to throw dust in the eyes of the British . . .
>
> Or consider the response of yet another gentleman who suggests that their soldiers should simply dress up as women so that the British soldiers are thereby inhibited by the respect they are bound to feel for women. The obvious remedies occur to no one; as one of the native gentlemen says to himself: 'Too bad! Nobody here says that we should all get together, improve education, learn crafts so that we can really progress. Little by little we'll achieve all we want.'

Balmukund Gupta (1865–1907), one of the leading publicists of the post-Harishchandra era, is remembered today primarily for the satiric bite of his articles. Gupta was quick to challenge tyranny, whether of the magisterial Mahavir Prasad Dwivedi in the matter of correct Hindi usage, or even the viceroy, the aristocratic and imperious Lord Curzon. Gupta addressed a series of letters to Curzon—published between 1903 and 1905 in the Calcutta Hindi daily *Bharat Mitra* of which he was editor—on the occasion of Curzon's pompous Delhi Durbar (1903). Published later in book form, *Shivshambhu ke Chitthe* (The Letters of Shivshambhu) took the reading public by storm. Shivshambhu, the fictional letter-writer, takes on his mighty adversary, Lord Curzon, official representative of the Raj, sent out for the second time as the viceroy of India, even though

> Shivshambhu possesses not a single such certificate to validate him as a representative of the people. Nonetheless he maintains his claim to represent the subjects of this country who are dressed in tatters and rags. Why? Because he has been born in this land. His body is made of the very soil of India, and he wishes to one day return his body to this same soil. As a child he grew up rolling around in the dust of this country and it is the bounty of this land that keeps him alive.

The child Shivshambhu loved *bulbuls* (nightingales). He still dreams of them, vivid, expansive dreams, which send him soaring into the sky. There is no shortage of dreams. But when the dreams end,

> He sees his own house, his own bed, nothing more. The empire of the mind has come to a close. Have you my Lord, only been dreaming of bulbuls since you arrived in India, or have you done anything worthwhile? Have you merely been following through with your own ideas, or have you nurtured any of the duties you have towards the subjects of this country? . . .
> This country cannot be ruled by empty pageantry alone.

Myriad personal tales recounted acts of violence—the kind still perpetrated in rural India by caste-Hindus—as individuals and groups became the butts of an arrogance that quickly degenerated into physical abuse in trains, on pavements, and in public spaces. They triggered stubborn resistance and at times provoked counterviolence. These often momentous encounters were documented in the Hindi press, in short stories, reminiscences, and novels. Resistance to colonial rule, violent and non-violent, and accounts of life in prison would come to form a substantial part of Hindi literature from the 1930s.

The Hindi heartland, particularly the United Provinces and Bihar, had become a stronghold of Congress from the 1920s. UP would, in fact, soon acquire the leading position in nationalist politics that it would hold for several decades after Independence.[16] This was in no small measure due to Gandhi. His mode of address and model of personal austerity brought about enormous change in people's lives, especially among young people. At the height of the 1921–2 Non-Cooperation Movement, scores of young men left their colleges and schools in response to Gandhi's call to abandon British-run institutions. We have only to consider the well-known case of Premchand, Hindi–Urdu's best-known author, who resigned from his position as Second Master in the government-run Normal School in Gorakhpur, after he heard Gandhi speak in his city in 1921, to devote himself entirely to writing. Gandhi's impact on Hindi literature was far-reaching. A wide spectrum of literary genres—poems, short stories, novels, memoirs, sketches—would come to be pervaded with his ethos of personal sacrifice, social change, and pride in swadeshi.

However, the Gandhian impact is only the more obvious side of the nationalist movement. The second decade of the twentieth century was witness to several powerful trends which often pulled in opposite directions. The short-lived accord of the early 1920s fissured early, when, after the violence in Chauri Chaura (which saw angry peasants burn a police station causing the death of twenty-two policemen), Gandhi unilaterally called off the Non-Cooperation Movement in 1922. Many of those who had abandoned their educational institutions and professions in response to his call were left

---

[16] The UP Congress had a membership of 328,966 in July 1921, a figure which was exceeded only by Bihar, which claimed 350,000. See Sarkar 2001: 222. As Sarkar points out: 'Organized Non-Cooperation in UP was mainly an affair of the cities and small towns, as elsewhere, however, more elemental elements in the countryside were perhaps equally significant.' Ibid.: 223.

in the lurch. Several turned to communal organizations for direction, but others, particularly in the Punjab, took up armed resistance.[17] Branded as terrorists, and with the secret police hot on their trail, they operated entirely from the underground. A series of audacious acts of violence by Bhagat Singh and his friends and the Hindustan Socialist Republican Army, the organization they founded in Delhi in 1928, culminated in April 1929, when Bhagat Singh and Batukeshwar Dutta threw hand-made bombs into the Legislative Assembly in Delhi. This incident stirred the country's imagination as little else in political life. As Christopher Pinney has shown, a popular history of the national movement would be more likely to centre on the figure of Bhagat Singh and his companions rather than Gandhi, Nehru, and Bose.[18] The nationwide surge of patriotic fervour was reflected in the Hindi press and in the literature of the day. The special issue on *phansi*, or the hangman's noose, of the women's literary journal *Chand*, immediately proscribed, had a print run of 10,000 and became a treasured item in households lucky enough to possess a copy. The present anthology carries one item from this special issue, a satirical play questioning not only the hanging of so-called terrorists but capital punishment itself. It consists of a dialogue between Kanunimal, a lawyer, who has been dragged off to hell, and Yamdut, a messenger of Yama, sovereign of the kingdom of death. As Kanunimal tells the messenger: 'Everyone has the inalienable right to live peacefully in the tranquillity of life, property and honour. That right which may apply to everyone is considered a societal right, because society can be called the community of men . . .' The Indian Criminal Code serves only to instil the fear of empire. To

---

[17] For a particularly vivid account of this process in Punjab, see the memoirs of Yashpal, *Simhavalokan* (1951; rpnt Allahabad: Lok Bharati Prakashan, 2005). The book is also a mine of information on the activities of Bhagat Singh and other members of the militant Hindustan Socialist Republican Army, of which Yashpal (1903–76) was a key member.

[18] See Pinney 2004. Sumit Sarkar cites from the confidential Intelligence Bureau account of 'Terrorism in India (1917–36)' which noted that 'for a time, he [Bhagat Singh] bade fair to oust Mr. Gandhi as the foremost political figure of the day': Sarkar 2001: 269.

question and resist its autocracy cannot mean something as brutal as being deprived of life: 'this punishment is completely inappropriate because the people raise their voices against the empire when it has offended them in one way or another. Therefore, when the people are in this condition, the state should immediately find and correct the shortcomings which have created the grievance. This is how the crime can be reduced. There is no benefit from ridding the world of those who scream in pain, because the cause of pain is maintained in this way.'

The vast literary output in Hindi focusing on issues of violent resistance and prison experience is just beginning to be studied. One of the best-known novels of the period, a modernist *tour de force*, *Shekhar, Ek Jivani* (Shekar, A Life, 1944) by Agyeya (1911–1987), the major poet and novelist of this new generation, climaxes as the narrator, a student-writer-cum-political-activist in Lahore of the 1920s, finds himself sucked into the vortex of violence almost against the grain.[19] Prison confinement brings reflections on violence as a means of political resistance. Shekhar's friend Vidyabhushan proclaims: 'If you talk of violence, isn't it a form of violence to fail to protect one's honour out of fear? Violence inflicted on the self is the worst kind of violence, because it breaks the spine of the nation's self-respect, it breaks the nation itself . . . we owe the anger to the nation . . .' But, as Shekhar broods in his prison cell: 'Even to accept the immediacy of violence was to accept it in its entirety. Even if the human race protected itself through violence, it eventually lived under the shadow of this evil. The question was a simple one: was violence appropriate or not? Violence could either be completely accepted or completely rejected. In either case, however, the way ahead was unclear.'

The circles of resistance to colonial rule, non-violent shading over into violent, continued to spiral. The 1930s' Civil Disobedience Movement saw the entry of women and teenagers into active politics; they took to the streets and filled the prison cells alongside husbands

---

[19] Agyeya was also a member of the Hindustan Socialist Republican Army and was jailed for many years for acts of terrorism.

and fathers. A handful of women also turned to armed revolution—educated, thinking women, who broke out of the social moulds foreseen for them and who sought to lead a freer life, even if it was largely in the underground. Many more followed Gandhi's call. As a United Provinces police official reported in September 1930: 'The Indian woman is struggling for domestic and political liberty, at the same time . . . she has enormous influence over the stronger sex . . . many loyal officials including police officers have . . . suffered more from taunts and abuse from their female relatives than from any other source.'[20] This anthology carries the account by Shivrani Devi (d. 1976), Premchand's wife, of being transported to prison. She noted the response of prison guards in the lorry that was carrying the picketing women off to prison:

> I saw the guards sitting inside had tears in their eyes. I think their hearts were also tormented. They said to me, 'Mother, we receive twenty-two rupees here. If someone had offered us even ten rupees elsewhere, we would have given up this work long ago.' Another guard said, 'Mother, why should you go to jail for being so generous? But we shall take you straight there. The sad thing is that today we take the mothers and sisters we should be worshipping to jail for the sake of filling our stomachs.'

Shivrani Devi's response was: 'Son, you must pray to God that we have the strength to fulfil our duties. You remain my son and I, your mother. But our paths are different.' Shivrani Devi may have courted arrest without her husband's knowledge, but she worked within an ordered domestic world. By the 1930s domesticity was also beginning to change, even if in tiny steps.

Internal realignments and domestic reorganization were intimately related to questions of nation-formation. If the first decades of the nineteenth century had responded initially to missionary invective by pleading for social reform and legislative intervention—as in the calls asking for the banning of sati—later-nineteenth-century

---

[20] Cited in Sarkar 2001: 290.

concerns revolved around the fate of widows and the evils of child marriage, with heated debates for and against widow remarriage as well as raising the girl's 'age of consent'. The appellants directed their appeals and counter-appeals to the colonial government. There would be major changes in this mode of address from the early twentieth century.

The Hindi heartland had lagged behind the presidencies in the matter of social reform but was fast catching up. In the first decades of the twentieth century, for the first time, women began to make their voices heard. They addressed not so much the imperial legislature as men and women of their own community. And once again the press and journals, often with women as editors, played a major role. Thus *Stree Darpan* (Mirror for Women, 1909–28) published the address of Balaji, a Bengali woman speaker at the annual gathering of the Hindi Sahitya Sammelan in 1918, which raised the question of a 'Suitable Literature for Women':

> Since the introduction of new civilized manners and modern literature in India, various questions related to women have arisen and as a matter of fact, in the future, even more questions will be asked. At this time, many new thoughts and feelings are emerging in this country: all over the nation waves of emotion for the 'new life' are surging because the impact of national awakening is felt everywhere. Women are equally important members of the nation. They are mothers and supreme goddesses of the 'new life'. Thus it is both appropriate and extremely pressing to discuss suitable literature for women at a national language and literary convention.

In most popular writing, however, the emphasis continued to be on recalling the once-glorious state of women in Aryan India, the evils of Muslim rule, and the need for a reformed Hinduism which would do away with the superstition to which women were considered most prone. We see this clearly in the tract by Shiv Sharma, published by Arya Navyuvak Sabha in 1927: 'Because of the lack of Vedic education in present times, women are no longer as sensible as before. They fall very quickly into the trap of deceitfulness and debase their lives. They should remain firmly within their Hinduism so that no craftiness sways them. They must understand that the worship of graves and *tazias*, charms and amulets, the delusions of demons and prophets, fairytales and the getting of children through the spells of Muslim priests—all these are against the Hindu religion.' But the same tract could also display the kind of progressive activism, with a new empathy for the widow, which would be heard again and again through the century, even as the situation of the widows remained largely unchanged: 'Parents and in-laws of widows! You are aware of the calamities that befall a woman whose husband dies. Her whole world is filled with a grave void. On festive occasions and marriages, she feels great pain. It is very important to keep her heart and mind stable at such times. Could there be a greater sin than to curse a widow at such occasions?'

By the 1920s several aspects in the lives of urban women of the higher castes /classes were beginning to change, even if slowly. The most fundamental change was brought about by education. Even primary education, whether at home or in schools, opened up new worlds. Thanks to the efforts of the Arya Samaj, some women could go further and acquire high school or even college degrees. Even if marriage remained the one legitimate frame for an educated woman, education made for a new self-awareness within that frame.

Even if it was not possible to step outside the physical confines of the women's quarters, the print medium made it possible to question the legitimacy of secluding women socially. Once again, journals played a major role in opening up the public sphere to this new discourse. *Chand*, a journal which began to appear from Allahabad from 1922, proved to be one of the most daring with regard to the women's question. Its editor, Ramrakh Singh Sahgal (1896–1952), came from Lahore and it was as if he brought the progressive views of that city with him. He had a close relationship to Congress but also to revolutionaries such as Bhagat Singh and his comrades. His journal had a larger format (100 pages) than most women's journals; its pages were filled with a broad range of contributions—poems, short stories, serialized novels, news, editorial columns, readers' letters, reviews, cartoons—and it gained quickly in popularity and circulation. Not only did its special issues focus on women's concerns, it offered space to women themselves to articulate their concerns. The intention was less to reform women, more to educate society.

Most progressive male writers also took up the cause of women and the many evils which befell their lives. Amongst Premchand's most powerful novels were two that focused entirely on the horrifying consequences of obeying the dictates of caste in arranging marriages and the unholy consequences of dowry. For want of adequate resources, Suman, the young woman at the centre of *Sevasadan* (House of Service, 1918), is shackled to a much older man, living in straitened circumstance and suspicious of her youth and beauty. The young girl is driven to prostitution, berated for disgracing 'Hindu' womanhood, and eventually forced into a fate which could well be regarded as worse than enjoying the relative freedom of the bazaar: a reform house, where she is condemned to a life of austerity and relative solitude. The eponymous heroine of *Nirmala* (1927) is led to self-destruction for similar reasons. Unable and eventually unwilling to cope with her suspicious husband, many years her senior and jealous of her relationship to his eldest son, she ends by destroying the lives of the entire family.[21]

Alongside these novels focusing on social reform, where the initial defiance of lively and beautiful young woman is quelled and ends in calamity, 'the figure of the educated working woman—the unmarried teacher, social worker, or political activist—found a place in the collective imagination and began gaining social acceptance.'[22] From the mid-1920s this is apparent not only in the popular novels and short stories of Dhaniram Premi and Pandey Bechan Sharma 'Ugra', but also in the works of writers as sophisticated as Suryakant Tripathi 'Nirala' (1899–1961) and Jainendra Kumar (1905–88). That the fate of many of Jainendra's women would leave much to be desired does not detract from the fact that they were beginning to surface and claim not only new rights but also readers' sympathy.

---

[21] *Nirmala* was serialized in *Chand* from 1925 to 1926.
[22] Orsini 2001: 259.

For some who chose to, or were forced to, exist outside the marital union, in real life as much as in fiction, there was the *seva* (service) option. Gandhi's call to participate in the national movement had opened public spaces to women able to resort to this path.

> Sushila was sitting dejectedly, thinking that in such a foul state of affairs for the weaker sex, a spinning wheel would be so helpful. But where to get a spinning wheel? In the meanwhile, some volunteers knocked at her door. When she came outside, Sushila saw them holding a spinning wheel. They appealed to her to use the spinning wheel in the name of country and religion. It seemed to Sushila that the gods themselves had descended from heaven and were making the dream she'd had come true. She fell silent for a while, then blessed them with all her heart. She asked for two spinning wheels, and she and her mother-in-law both resolved to spin thread every day. From that day on they both began spinning, and from that very day on, joy and peace filled the house . . . The majority of women began to regard Sushila with great respect.

To take to the streets by participating in a mass demonstration undertaken in a worthy and noble cause or devote one's life to caring for the destitute was social service, not defiance.

Of destitution there was no dearth in the country. Though peasant unrests provoked by excessive taxation enforced by collusive zamindars had simmered for several decades, it took the hardships provoked by the end of the First World War to bring it to boiling point across North India. News of the successful Russian Revolution reached peasants and workers almost immediately, fuelling the fires of discontent. In Bihar and UP particularly, peasant activism, fanned by Gandhi's Non-Cooperation Movement of 1921–2, not only provided the first mass base for Congress, it went on to acquire its own dynamic, spilling into the very violence Gandhi decried, and carrying on even after he had called off the movement in 1922.[23]

Though Gandhi's charisma had a lasting impact and his Champaran Satyagraha remained long engraved in public memory, the strong

---

[23] Sarkar 2001: 239.

links of the Congress with landholding interests would eventually lead to disillusionment with the party and several peasant leaders would begin to call for radical action and the abolition of zamindari. Once again, it was the Hindi press which played an active part in building the bridge between urban and rural concerns. As early as 1919 it reported the peasant agitation in Bijolia in Mewar and gave wide coverage to the movement in Awadh between 1920 and 1922. The focus was not only on the oppression practised by landlords and village officials alike but on peasant perspectives and their relatively modest demands: the abolition of cesses and bonded labour; recognition of the refusal to cultivate land from which tenants had been ousted; the social boycott of oppressive landlords by denying them the services traditionally due to them.[24]

The Hindi press responded to the need of the hour. As Orsini has shown, through the 1920s and 1930s it was Hindi editors such as G.S. Vidyarthi in Kanpur, Srikrishnadatt Palival in Agra, Makhanlal Chaturvedi in Jabalpur, Dashrath Prasad Dvivedi in Gorakhpur, and Baburao Vishnu Paradkar in Banaras who made of the press more than a voice organ of the elite, addressing not only peasant issues but the peasants themselves.[25] The Hindi press had the power and widespread appeal which, for reasons too obvious to delineate, could only remain denied to the nationalist English press.

It was in this period that Premchand wrote the stories and novels for which he was to acquire lasting fame. Addressing peasant grievances with a poignancy and immediacy which was both precisely informed and unsentimental, he embedded his narratives in complex plots that spanned both city and village. He showed the obvious links between the urban conglomerate of power holders, absentee landowners, government officials, lawyers and judges, industrialists and zealous nationalists and, at the rural end, a brutalized and increasingly rebellious peasantry. Premchand's second successful novel, *Premashram* (1922), which was the first to highlight the peasant's plight in graphic detail, was written when Awadh was in the

[24] Ibid.: 203–4.
[25] Orsini 2002: 319.

throes of widespread peasant unrest. His *Kayakalp* (1926) featured an armed uprising by peasants, led by an idealist city dweller whose bold speech does not prevent the brutal repression of the rebels.

The relentlessly bleak plight of peasants was made bearable by the Tolstoy- and Gandhi-inspired utopian communities, with the founding of which all except Premchand's last novel, *Godaan* (The Gift of a Cow, 1936), concluded. *Godaan* became an all-time classic perhaps because it left the rebelliousness largely to its readers. It featured the internal politics of the village, the caste divisions that tore at its very fabric in a time of rapid social and political change. At the heart of the novel is Hori, a gentle peasant who, for all his clear-eyed understanding of the extortionist excesses of village leadership and colonial taxation, cannot help submitting to them, driven as he is by his notion of dharma, or righteous conduct.

Little support for the peasant was forthcoming from nationalist bodies, as *Godaan* also registered: swarajya or independence was only for the privileged. By the mid-1930s, the disillusionment with Congress politics had become relatively widespread, as Congress members, several of whom had been activists in the Hindi public sphere, won elections to municipal boards and legislative councils. Peasant organizations were not represented in the Congress leadership and peasants and peasant leaders found themselves increasingly abandoned to their own devices. 'The Congress . . . while fighting the Raj was also becoming the Raj, foreshadowing the great but incomplete transformation of 1947.'[26]

Swami Sahajanand (1889–1950), certainly the most vocal and powerful peasant leader to emerge from Bihar, turned away from the Congress after mid-1937 to demand economic justice and human dignity in the treatment of peasants. He saw these as fundamental requirements for swarajya and openly criticized the zamindari system as well as Congress collusion with the zamindars. As early as 1933, the British Raj made efforts to gag Sahajanand at the first mass rally of peasants in Gaya. He was issued notice under Section 144 to prevent him from appearing at the rally, an action for which, as he

[26] Sarkar 2001: 254.

reports, his peasant followers severely reprimanded him. In the years following he abandoned this restraint, assuming a more militant if non-violent posture in leading the peasants, including at mass rallies throughout Bihar and, by the late 1930s, in many parts of India. He was to write a vivid account of these years in his life story in Hindi, from which this anthology carries an extract. Reminiscing on the Gaya episode of 1933, Sahajanand says:

> The news spread like wild fire to the most remote corners of the district and we were astonished when we saw that lakhs of kisans had come to Gaya on the appointed day. Every street of the town was crowded with kisans. The people of Gaya were amazed to see such large numbers of kisans even when it was not the time of *Pitri Paksh*! This was a strange *Pitri Paksh* indeed! Little did they know that this was a demonstration of the growing power of the Kisan Sabha being offered for the benefit of Government on this day! The kisans had literally come to Gaya on the call of their Sabha to give expression to their anger at the vast climate of zamindar oppression in which they lived their lives.

The work of Kisan Sabha activists as much as that of novelists of the stature of Premchand has had a lasting impact on Hindi literature, which has produced powerful narratives of the peasant struggle for survival. From the 1940s a group of radical writers from Bihar, many of whom were involved in Kisan Sabha activities, were inspired by Premchand's work. Of this group Nagarjun and Rahul Sankrityayan are the best known. Given the vast stretch of the largely agricultural Hindi belt, with its relative paucity of dynamic urban centres, village-centred novels came in fact to form a defining feature of the Hindi literary landscape in the first decades after Independence. We have only to think of novels as different as Renu's lyric-ironic *Maila Anchal* (Soiled Border, 1954), set in the Purnea district of Bihar, which would also become a centre of radical Naxalite activity in the 1970s; Rahi Masoom Raza's poignant *Adha Gamv* (The Feuding Families of Gangauli, 1965), written originally in Urdu but finding its widest circulation in Hindi; and Shrilal Shukla's satirical novel of politics and politicians in the village, *Raag Darbari* (1968).

Just as peasant movements provided a counter to the middle- and upper-class orientation of the Indian National Congress, the rising communalism of the 1920s had its counterpart in the rise of radical movements in 'untouchable' or Dalit communities, which soon took over their own leadership. Gandhi's paternalistic stance, his use of the term 'Harijan' (Children of God), and his 1931 refusal to allow the British to create a separate electorate for Dalits came to be widely resented not only by a wide section of caste Hindus but, more importantly, by Dalits themselves. However, as always, it was his campaigns in the Harijan cause which made for the kind of publicity which few others could have achieved. There was no figure of Ambedkar's stature in the Hindi belt who could articulate the cause of Dalits with such eloquence and organize Dalit agitation to such effect, as he did in Maharashtra from the late 1920s. It was much less spectacular in the North, but voices are to be heard from as early as 1917:

> 'Oh Lord! What perverse justice is this
> That even if they choose to touch us
> We ourselves would declare impurity.'
>
> —from 'The Untouchable's Lament' (1916) in *Sarasvati*

The sentimentality of pieces such as these, particularly when written by caste-Hindus, would never entirely disappear, but from the 1920s there would be a political movement within Dalit communities which would throw up leaders such as Swami Achhutanand (1879–1933). Born into a Chamar (leatherworker), family, Achhutanand belonged to the second generation educated in his family. Disillusionment with the Arya Samaj and its *shuddhi* (purification) campaigns, which sought to 'uplift' Dalits by awarding them partial rights in caste-Hindu society, Achhutanand founded his own organization of *Adi* or original Hindus, as he called the Dalits, and edited his own monthly newspaper, the *Adi Hindu*, from the early 1920s. His play *Ramrajya Nyaya* was written in these years and has been continuously in print since then. Dramatizing a famous incident from the *Ramayana*, it stages the encounter between Rama and the Dalit Shambuk, who as a non-Brahmin was not allowed to continue his austerities and submitted meekly to the treatment dealt out to him. Shambuk's anger and defiance echo that of his generation:

> *Shambuk*: I don't believe that such Dharmasastras apply to me since at the time of their creation, the beliefs and advice of the *adi-vanshis* were not taken into account. The *Manusmriti* is a law made by a Brahmin by the name of Bhrigu, which has been spread under the name of Manu. It was this Bhrigu whose descendant Parashuram destroyed the *adi-nivasi* kingdom and, filling five tanks with their blood proudly bathed in them . . . I don't consider such scriptures to be religious scriptures, but rather irreligious scriptures, scriptures of sin. If Ram comes in support of *Manusmriti*, then let him come.

What kind of *Ramrajya*, or rule of righteous Rama—the term so often used by Gandhi—did the nationalist campaign seek? Would the new Indian nation reflect real social justice or continue the oppressions practised by the British, this time under the cover of a different kind of rhetoric?

From the late 1920s the Hindi literary world, and particularly its journals, reflected these concerns. Once again *Chand* was in the forefront with its special issue on Dalits, *Achut Ank*. Premchand's short stories and novels were replete with these issues. Temple entry for Dalits in Banaras, the holiest of holy cities, is a central episode of his novel *Karmabhumi* (1932). And in his last novel, *Godaan* (1936), the relationship of a Brahmin youth and a Chamar girl is treated not as commonplace, which it was in village life, but as a dramatic turning point in the life of the Brahmin boy. But it was left to Suryakant Tripathi 'Nirala'—the renegade Hindu, the brilliant poet and prose stylist—to sketch a portrait of Chaturi Chamar, in an eponymous short story, to which its Brahmin narrator could pay the sort of homage unthinkable since the days of the weaver-poet Kabir and the great devotional movements of the sixteenth and seventeenth centuries. Published in the journal *Sudha* in 1934, this is an exquisitely written tale of a friendship upheld between Chaturi and the Brahmin in defiance of caste taboos: 'Chaturi, in tones of a spiritual preceptor, reminded the others of any verses they forgot, and this is how I learned of Chaturi's great expertise in the songs of Kabir. He told me, "Uncle, even great scholars don't understand these nirgun verses", and then perhaps ranking me in a class with these same scholars, he continued, "the meaning of this verse . . ."' Devotees of the *nirgun* (attributeless) god and the school of verse attributed to them had several leading figures from Dalit communities, foremost amongst them Kabir. The reappraisal of these poets in the wake of a general ideologization of the medieval and early modern devotional movements tended to make of them an upper-caste affair, and Kabir had come to be revered as a great mystic. The verse of Kabir, translated by Rabindranath Tagore amongst others, was regarded as replete with esoteric references, which only scholars of great learning could be expected to unravel. It is in this context that we have to locate Nirala's gesture of restoring dignity not only to Chaturi but to Kabir himself as a poet of the people.

In the early twenty-first century, the situation has changed radically. Dalit problems may not have ceased socially, education and job opportunities may still remain a dream for most, but political power, precisely in caste-ridden UP and Bihar, has come their way and Dalit literature has become a major new force in the Hindi world.

After Gandhi's demise there was no leader of sufficient status to speak up for a people's language. Granville Austin (1966) has documented the debacle in the Constituent Assembly when the issue of Hindi as the national language was thrashed out amidst growing bitterness. Alok Rai has shown the course that 'Hindi' nationalism would take in the years before and after Independence, as a small but dominant coterie of conservative caste-Hindus came to speak for and then guide the destiny of official Hindi. Jyotirindra Das Gupta has analysed the role that institutions such as the Nagari Pracharini Sabha and the Hindi Sahitya Sammelan would play in the process.[27] In the meantime, however, Hindi as the people's language has continued

---

[27] Rai 2000; Das Gupta 1970.

to prosper, finding its course without the help of such institutions. The figures of the last census show that 400 million people, or 41 per cent of the present population of India, regard Hindi as their mother tongue. Meanwhile, official Hindi, stiff with the weight of Sanskrit-ridden words, virtually without meaning and without popular currency, staggers on, claiming a status which few accord it. And the gulf widens between on the one hand the all-India English-speaking elites, and on the other the vast mass of people who speak and think in Hindi, write creatively, and voice political concerns in it. Increasingly, the latter are from small towns, and women and Dalits figure largely among them.

This anthology opens a window into pre-Independence Hindi and Urdu. The immense galvanizing force of the literature of these intertwined cultures has become difficult to imagine today, when so much has come to be taken for granted and when the popular movements of the past have been overshadowed by the rhetoric of elite stakeholders. This volume provides a glimpse of what can be regarded as just the tip of an iceberg, giving some sense of a vast mass of powerful work which is still waiting to be discovered by readers, by literary histories, and by social historians.

References

Austin, Granville, 1966. *The Indian Constitution: Cornerstone of a Nation*. Bombay: Oxford University Press.

Dalmia, Vasudha, 1997. *The Nationalization of Hindu Traditions: Bharatendu Harischandra and Nineteenth-Century Banaras*. Delhi: Oxford University Press.

Das Gupta, Jyotirindra, 1970. *Language Conflict and National Development: Group Politics and National Language Policy in India*. Bombay: Oxford University Press.

Dodson, Michael S., 2002. 'Re-Presented for the Pandits: James Ballantyne, "Useful Knowledge", and Sanskrit Scholarship in Benares College during the Mid-Nineteenth Century', *Modern Asian Studies* 36/2.

Harishchandra, Bharatendu, 1883. *Hindi Bhasha*. Patna: Khadagvilas Press.

Jones, Kenneth W. (1976), 2006. *Arya Dharm: Hindu Consciousness in Nineteenth Century Punjab*. Delhi: Manohar Publishers.

Fischer-Tine, Harald, 2003. *Der Gurukul Kangri oder die Erziehung der Arya Nation: Kolonialismus, Hindureform und 'nationale Bildung' in Britisch-Indien (1897–1922)*. Wurzburg: Ergon-Verlag.

King, Christopher R., 1994. *One Language, Two Scripts: The Hindi Movement in Nineteenth Century North India*. Bombay: Oxford University Press.

Kumar, Jainendra, 1980. *The Resignation*. Delhi: Hind Pocket Books. Translated from the Hindi by Sachidananda Vatsyayan Agyeya.

Nijhawan, Shobna, ed., 2010. *Nationalism in the Vernacular: Hindi, Urdu, and the Literature of Indian Freedom*. Ranikhet: Permanent Black.

Orsini, Francesca, 2002. *The Hindi Public Sphere 1920–1940: Language and Literature in the Age of Nationalism*. Delhi: Oxford University Press.

Premchand (Hindi 1926), 1999. *Nirmala*. New Delhi: Oxford University Press. Translated from the Hindi by Alok Rai.

——— (Hindi 1936), 2002. *Godaan: The Gift of a Cow. A Translation of the Classic Hindi Novel*. Bloomington and New Delhi: Indiana University Press and Permanent Black. Translated from the Hindi by Gordon Roadarmel.

——— (Hindi 1918), 2005. *Sevasadan*. New Delhi: Oxford University Press. Translated from the Hindi by Snehal Shingavi.

——— (Hindi 1932), 2006. *Karmabhumi*. New Delhi: Oxford University Press. Translated from the Hindi by Lalit Srivastava.

Pinney, Christopher. 2004. *Photos of the Gods: The Printed Image and Political Struggle in India*. Delhi: Oxford University Press.

Rai, Alok, 2000. *Hindi Nationalism*. Tracts for the Times 13. Delhi: Orient Longman.

Raza, Rahi Masoom (Hindi 1966), 1994. *The Feuding Families of Village Gangauli*. New Delhi: Penguin Books. Translated from the Hindi by Gillian Wright.

Renu, Phanishvarnath (Hindi 1954), 1991. *The Soiled Border*. Delhi: Chanakya Publications. Translated from the Hindi by Indira Jhungare.

Sarkar, Sumit (1983), 2001. *Modern India: 1885–1947*. Delhi: Macmillan India.

Shukla, Shrilal (Hindi 1968), 1992. *Raag Darbari. A Novel*. New Delhi: Penguin Books. Translated from the Hindi by Gillian Wright.

Vak, 2007. 2/April–June.

Yashpal (1951) 2005. *Simhavalokan*. Allahabad: Lok Bharati Prakashan.

Index

acharya, 2, 152n2, 156n18, 167–68
Acharyaji, 145–67, 176, 179–81, 205
Agravals, 123, 130, 312, 340
Agyeya (Sachchidananda Hiranand Vatsyayan), 12, 305, 321–22, 329, 353
Ahmad, Aijaz, 310n2
Alam, Muzaffar, 92–93n4, 98, 314
Allahabad (Prayag), 10, 132, 159, 300, 303; as Hindu pilgrimage centre, 190, 294–95, 297, 301–302
Amherst, Lord William Pitt, 71–72, 78
Anand Krishna, 11, 191
Anchalik, 323–24
anthropology, 40, 85–86, 111, 113n4, 115, 124, 137, 288
antiquity, 29, 31, 110, 211, 219
Arya, 132
Aryans, 3, 32–39, 41–42, 54n15, 114, 132, 135, 346, 348, 355

Arya Samaj, 217–19, 220n11, 222, 226–27, 296, 299, 343–44, 356, 362
asceticism, 149, 151, 156–57, 160, 183; widowhood and, 186n11
ascetics, 35, 62n18, 295–96; women, 271–72
ashtachhap, 145, 155n16, 193
Asiatic Society, 27, 46, 62, 219, 253, 341
astrology, 53, 244
astronomy, 34, 47–48, 53, 61, 117
atheism, 53, 223
Avadhi, 313, 317n12, 318–19, 341–42
Avadhi literature, 319
Awadh, 92, 100; nawab of, 92, 93n4, 94–96, 191

Balabodhini, 252–57, 260, 264, 275, 280–81
Ballantyne, James R., 53–54, 55n15, 311–12, 339–40

Banaras (Benares), 2, 8, 14–15, 52, 76, 92, 94–97, 99–100, 102, 104, 108, 111–12, 114, 124, 136, 190–95, 201, 207, 211, 250, 253n3, 261; British presence in, 10; Hindi literature and, 6–7, 9–10, 13, 312–13; rajas of, 51, 62, 96, 99n17, 121, 218, 220; royal house of, 91
Banaras Hindu University, 11, 191n4
Bang Mahila (Rajendrabala Ghosh), 293–94, 300
Barz, Richard, 155n16, 176n4
Bayly, Christopher A., 97–98, 101n19, 113–14n4
Benares Sanskrit College, 10, 45, 48, 55, 62, 113, 311, 339
Bengal, 42n42, 54, 67–68, 300; Bombay film of the 1950s and, 323n20; devotional movements in, 173, 174n1; historiography and, 111; nationalism in, 112; partition of, 12; polygamy in, 276–77n48; sati in, 83; shastras in, 75; *subas* of, 95; women's journals in, 256–57n7
Bengali, 214n4, 254n4, 255–56, 275–76, 294n17, 317, 343, 349
Benjamin, Walter, 6
Bentinck, William, 3, 68, 82–83, 85
Bhagavadgita, 27

Bhagavatapurana, 144, 147, 154, 164–65, 167–68
Bhagyavati (Phillauri), 293, 295–301
bhakti, 9, 144n4, 148, 156–58, 163, 167, 178n8, 180, 182, 185, 204, 218, 223–26, 270; culture, 9; Hinduism and, 12; Krishna, 186; monotheism, 318; *saguna*, 142–44; traditions 12; Vaishnava, 9, 218. See also devotional movements
bhaktimarga, 176, 180
Bhav Prakash (Harirayji), 146–47, 153–54, 157, 159–61, 164–65
Bhumihars, 99n17, 100
Bihar, 95, 150n15, 224, 345, 351, 358, 360–61, 364
Brahmanas, 34–36
Brahmans/Brahmins, 11, 46–47, 49, 53, 55, 62n18, 72, 78–80, 83, 102, 104, 105, 106, 113, 132, 125n26, 142, 149, 150n13, 157, 161–62, 164, 166, 168, 181, 198, 215, 221, 225, 296–97, 301, 317n12, 362–63; of Bengal, 277n48; Goutam, 100; Kulin, 276, 279; lower-caste, 277; orthodox, 143n4; of Ujjain, 164; women, 68, 75
Brahmo Samaj, 219, 224, 226, 299
Braj, 173, 193, 201, 206, 266–67, 269, 318

Brajbhasha, 191, 194, 236n13, 255, 268–69, 309, 313n7, 318, 342, 345; literature, 145, 319; poetry, 261, 269, 276, 313, 316, 317n12, 319, 341
Brecht, Bertolt, 6–7, 8
British Raj, 242, 349–50, 360
Buchanan, Francis, 150n13
buddhi, 216, 218, 221–24, 226
Bulwuntnamah, 91–104, 106–108

caste, 13, 24n8, 49, 68, 74–76, 112–13, 115, 117, 120, 131–32, 142n1, 150–51, 174, 183, 206, 224, 277–78, 282, 291, 321, 326–28, 338–39, 350, 356–57, 360, 362–64. See also jati
caste system, 30
Chaitanya, 143, 173–74, 214
Chand journal, 352, 356, 357n21, 363
Chandra, Satish, 143n4, 173n1
Chatterjee, Bankimchandra, 135, 275, 277n49
Chatterjee, Partha, 330
chatuhsampradaya, 143, 169. See also sampradaya: Vaishnava
Christianity, 40, 53, 219; Evangelical, 87
Christian missionaries, 10, 22, 48, 121, 210–11, 213, 217, 219, 262, 295, 314; attacks on Hinduism, 86; conduct books and, 280; discourse of, 72; on sati, 72–73nn12–13

chronicles, 95, 117–18, 122–23, 127–29, 295n19. See also *Bulwuntnamah*
Chunar, 96; British in, 104–105, 106–108
Colebrook, H.T., 30n19, 56–57
colonialism, 7, 21, 141
colonial politics, 31
communalism, 10, 12, 14, 17, 97, 101, 108–109, 326n24, 351, 361; Vaishnava, 181
communitas, 291–92
community, 146, 148, 150–51, 154–56, 159, 177, 297–99, 302; devotional, 144, 160n20, 181; formation of, 143–44, 167, 180; Hindi, 341; imagined, 303; of men, 352; religious, 174, 176, 179–80; Vallabhite Vaishnava, 150n13, 155n16, 163, 175. See also *sampradaya*
Crook, William, 114n4
Curzon, George Nathaniel, 349–50

Dalit writing, 321, 326–28, 364
Dalits, 15, 175n2, 338, 361–65; Hindi, 323; separate electorate for, 14, 361
Das Gupta, Jyotirindra, 344n13, 364
Devrani jethani ki kahani (Gauridatta), 235, 241
*darshana*s, 33, 53
desha (territory), 123

Devanagari script, 310, 325, 326n24
devotional movements, 141, 173n1, 185–86, 315, 363. *See also* bhakti; *nirguna*; *saguna*
Dharma Sabha, 62, 120, 218, 220
Dharmasastras, 48, 115, 142, 167–69, 178, 179n8, 185n11, 186, 362
*dharmasutra*s, 142
digests, 142, 264, 286–88, 295n19
Dow, Alexander, 30n19, 104–107, 108
dowry, 13, 277, 282, 357
Dravidians, 3, 114, 310n2
Duff, James Grant, 118, 124–25, 130
Duncan, Jonathan, 48–49, 59
Durgacharan, 102, 104, 108
Dusanmalika (Harishchandra), 221–22
Dvarika, 152–53, 158–59
Dwivedi, Mahavirprasad, 316, 321, 342, 349. See also *Sarasvati* journal

East India Company, 22, 27, 52, 92, 94, 97, 105n26, 191, 310
East India Railway Company, 244
education, 1–4, 211, 238–39, 249, 332, 343, 349; Anglicist, 62; colonial, 3, 274; Dalits and, 364; English, 1, 10, 55, 115; European, 55; free, 49; hierarchies of, 331; native, 71; the novel and, 275; Sanskrit, 52, 55; in Urdu, 325; Vedic, 355; Western, 10, 121; of women, 77–78, 87, 259–60, 262, 264, 356–57
educational institutions, 321, 351
egalitarianism, 169, 174–75, 179, 258, 270, 281
Elphinstone, Monstuart, 119, 125–26
English, 1, 4, 9, 52, 56, 61, 118, 211, 214, 225, 239, 244, 302, 312, 340, 343; education, 1, 10, 55, 115; elites and, 329, 331, 338, 364; Hindi and, 309, 336, 344; nationalism and, 359; novel in, 231; as official language, 320–21; translation, 27, 92, 95, 214n4, 217n7, 232, 294n18; writing in, 22, 236–37, 329–30, 332
English literature, 1, 3, 9, 46, 52, 56, 60–61
Enlightenment, 3, 23, 25, 28n16, 86
eroticism, 261, 263, 270, 272–74, 281–83, 316

erotic literature, 243, 254–55, 261, 266, 319
ethnography, 28, 42n42, 113–14n4, 117n7, 122, 150, 297
ethnology, 4, 42n42, 114n4, 117, 122, 131, 134–35, 235
Europe, 1, 25–26, 47, 54n15, 70, 105, 116, 189, 196, 244; comparative linguistics in, 27n16; folklorists in, 254; Greek influence on, 26n11; historiography in, 111–12, 117; Indian history and, 42; Indian knowledge and, 63; the novel and, 234; progress and, 39; travel literature on the Orient in, 22; women and, 78, 86
European education in India, 56–63
European languages, 27, 116; Sanskrit as proto-language of, 28. *See also* English
European politics, 38
European society, 31, 39, 70
Ewer, Walter, 71, 77–79, 86n29

femininity, 86–87
folklore, 111, 115, 116–17n7, 124, 137, 254, 347
Fort William College, 236–37nn13–14, 310, 314

Gandhi, Mohandas Karamchand, 14–15, 286, 343–44, 351–53, 357–59, 361, 363–64. *See also* Non-Cooperation Movement
Gauridatta, 235; *Devrani jethani ki kahani*, 235, 241
Gaya, 190, 360–61
gender, 13, 86–87, 273–74, 277; differentiation, 252; interchangeability of, 271; representation of, 251, 261, 272
gender roles, 87n55, 235–36, 238, 254, 260, 280
genre, 95, 110, 118, 145, 175, 231, 234–35, 252, 274, 280, 296, 306; novel as, 245n24, 283; women and, 241, 255, 257–58n10, 265, 280, 296
German literature, 4
German Romanticism, 4, 26, 31; India's ancient past and, 21
Ghosh, Rajendrabala. *See* Bang Mahila
Girdharji Maharaj, 192–204, 206–208
Gokulnathji, 146–47, 154
Goldsmith, Oliver, 236–38, 245
Gopal Mandir, 121, 191–93, 195
Gosaimji (Vitthala/Vitthalanath), 145, 147n11, 148–49, 160–61, 166, 176, 198, 205. *See also* Acharyaji
Gosvamis, 186, 206
Greek, 27–28, 31; art, 23–24, 212; culture, 24–26; poetry, 29

Gupta, Balmukund, 349–50
Gupta, Maithili Sharan, 319, 346–47
guru, 143–44, 146, 152n18, 153, 167; authority of, 170; community and, 155; as mediator, 148–49, 151–52

hagiography, 144–46, 152n14, 175–76, 191, 207; Sikh, 155n17. *See also* Vallabha; *Vartas*
Halhed, Nathaniel, 69–70
Harakhchand, 193, 204, 207
Harirayji, 146–47; *Bhav Prakash*, 146–47, 154, 157, 159–61, 164–65
Harishchandra, Bharatendu, 6–13, 15, 112, 119n15, 120–31, 133–37, 193, 211, 218–22, 224–25, 227, 233, 252–57, 259, 263, 265–67, 269, 271–75, 280–83, 312–13, 316, 340–41, 349; *Bharat Durdasha*, 349; *Chandravali*, 255, 266–73, 280–81; *Dusanmalika*, 221–22; *Karmabhumi*, 13–14, 363; *Kulin Kanya, athava Purnaprakash aur Chandrapabha*, 255–56, 274–83; *Harischandra's Magazine/Harischandrachandrika*, 120, 253, 255; *Hindi bhasha*, 312, 340; texts on religion, 10. See also *Balabodhini*

Hariaudh. *See* Upadhyaya, Ayodhya Singh
Herder, Johann Gottfried, 21–26, 27–28, 30–31, 38
Hindi literature, 6–7, 11–12, 110, 216, 328, 330–31, 336, 344–45, 350; early, 242n22; Gandhi's impact on, 351; history of, 342; modern, 232n3, 252, 273, 317, 324, 347; periodization of, 319; post-Independence, 323; Premachand's impact on, 361. See also *Nayi Kahani*
Hindi Sahitla Sammelan (Allahabad), 7, 320, 344–45, 355, 364
Hindu gods/goddesses, 2–3, 5, 77, 198, 212, 214, 217, 290, 302, 327, 358
Hinduism, 1–2, 9–10, 12, 46, 106, 136, 189–91, 208, 210–11; modern, 9, 142, 169, 173, 226; reformed, 355; right-wing, 170; Vaishnava, 296
Hindu-Muslim antagonism, 12, 92, 94, 98–100, 104, 129, 346–47. *See also* mosque-temple dispute
Hindustan, 95, 126–27, 258. *See also* Bharatkhand
Hindustani, 314, 320, 339n5, 344. *See also* Ballantyne, James R.; Hindi; Urdu

Hindustan Socialist Republican Army, 352n17, 353n19
Hindutva, 142, 170, 227, 321. *See also* nationalism
Hindu women, 66, 75–76, 78, 84–85
historical essay, 111, 118, 122, 126
historicism, 22, 25, 63
historicity, 7, 57, 127, 137
historicization, 6, 58, 63
historiography, 111, 119–20, 123, 135–36; of Banaras royal house, 91n1; colonial, 117; of comparative linguistics, 28n16; European, 111–12, 117–18; of India, 7, 112–13; literary, 275; nationalist, 112, 136; vernacular, 119
Hitopadesha, 236–37, 242, 249

India, 5–10, 16–17, 24n8, 31–33, 35, 41, 47, 59, 67, 72, 95n7, 125n25, 141–43, 213, 217, 225, 258, 261, 322, 332, 340, 345, 350, 355, 360, 364; ancient, 58; androgyny in, 273–74n43; British, 135, 190; colonial, 136; Hindi and, 344; Hinduism and, 118, 129; historiography of, 112; Independence of, 3, 17, 66, 323, 329, 332, 336, 338, 351, 361, 364; literatures of, 231; medieval, 155n17, 187; Mughal, 314; nationhood and, 286; North (Northern), 189, 191, 293, 299, 310–11, 316, 328, 335, 358; novel in, 110; railways in, 301; Urdu and, 326n24; women's journals in, 254
Indian Antiquary, 115–16, 118, 122, 128, 134
Indian literature, 36, 56, 113, 127
Indianness, 3–4
Indology, 4, 6, 9, 15, 17, 39–40, 72

Jains, 123, 128, 133
jati, 100, 130–32, 135, 142n1, 150–51, 170, 303; hierarchies of, 164. *See also* caste
jnana, 218, 223–25
Jogis, 75, 115
Jones, William, 27, 46, 57, 69–70, 80, 128
justice, 2, 73n13, 109, 362; British administration of, 96, 106, 108, 349; economic, 360; law and, 70; social, 363

Kabir, 363–64
Kalidasa, 27, 127, 130
Kane, P.V., 262n22, 286n1, 288, 294n19
Kannada, 235n9, 329–30
Karve, Irawati, 288–92, 306

Kashi, 7, 13, 45–46, 156n18, 162, 190, 193, 194n9, 197, 201, 203–205, 211, 219, 222; merchants of, 62; teachers of, 48
Kashmirkusum, 128
Kayasths, 130–31, 164, 166, 168, 315
Kavivacansudha, 120–21, 126, 218, 222, 224–25, 233, 253, 256n6, 257
Khan, Fakir Khair-ud-din, 91–96, 100–104, 106–109
Khari Boli, 312, 316–17, 319, 323–24, 340
Khatri, Ayodhya Prasad, 316
Khatris, 123, 131–35, 152, 155, 159, 167–68, 312, 340
Kolatkar, Arun, 306
Krishna, 54, 173, 176, 186, 255, 266, 268, 270–72, 318; devotees of, 185–86n11, 327; Radha and, 174, 267; Yashoda and, 196. *See also* Vaishnavas
Kshatriyas, 30, 125, 130–35, 170, 224–25
Kumar, Krishna, 321, 329
Kumbh Mela (*Kumbh parva*), 293–99, 295n19, 301
Kumbh mem choti bahu (Bang Mahila), 294, 300–305

Latin, 4, 27–28
literature, 11, 35, 46, 52, 120, 211, 282–83, 330, 338, 342, 365; children's, 348; devotional, 219; "high," 322; "Hindu," 48–49; Indo-Anglian, 332; in Kannada, 329; Marathi, 237n14; national, 42; pilgrimage, 287–88; reform, 326; religious, 144, 178; Sikh, 133; Tamil, 237n14; travel, 22, 30n19; vernacular, 175, 216; Western, 332; women and, 281, 355. *See also* Avadhi literature; Dalit writing; English literature; erotic literature; German literature; Hindi literature; Indian literature; Sanskrit literature; Urdu literature; *Vartas*; Vedic literature
Lorenzen, David, 142nn1–2, 145n7

MacDonnell, Anthony, 314–15, 317
Mahabharata, 30, 33, 236, 346, 348
Maharashtra, 125n26, 126, 289, 362
Maine, Henry, 41, 114n4
Mahajun, Sewan, 97–98, 100
Mallika (Chandrika), 255–56, 263, 266, 268, 275–76, 277n49, 280–82
Mansa Ram, 91, 94
Manu, 30, 70–71, 179n8; *Law Books of Manu/Institutes of*

Manu/Manusmriti, 27, 33, 79, 177, 220, 362–63
Marathi, 237n14, 257n7, 317, 343
marriage, 38, 133, 186n11, 356; arranged, 277; child, 384; companionate, 281–82; upper-caste, 13
mayavad, 156–57
Mitra, Pramadadas, 55, 57–61; Thibaut's response to, 60–62
Mitra, Rajendralal, 219, 253
modernism, 6, 294n18, 322, 353
modernity, 6, 10, 12, 117, 136, 226, 299, 305
modernization, 112, 114, 293, 316, 343; bhakti culture and, 9; Harishchandra and, 135, 254, 259, 269, 272–73; Hindi and, 338; of Hinduism, 2; nationalism and, 14; Phillauri and, 296; religion and, 286–87; tradition and, 210, 227, 299; of Urdu, 327n24
monotheism, 38, 214; devotional movements and, 141, 318; Harishchandra and, 227; Hinduism and, 169; popular, 143n4; Vaishnava, 218–19
mosque-temple dispute, 96–102, 104, 108–109
Mughal period of rule, 12, 92n4, 97, 101n19, 127–28, 144n5, 295, 314; decline of, 190; emperors, 3, 92, 95, 173
Muir, John, 52–54, 56, 132
mukti (redemption), 156, 164, 180
Mukundrayji, 192–94, 196, 202–205, 208
Mukundrayji ki varta, 196–205
Müller, Friedrich Max (Max Müller), 21, 31–41, 42n42, 56–57, 59, 62
murtipuja (image worship), 210–17, 220, 222–23, 226–27
Muslims, 46, 69, 102–104, 114, 142n2, 295, 321, 337; conquest of India, 124, 128; electorates for, 12; as Other, 227; Urdu and, 310, 319, 335

Nagari script, 235, 314, 325, 344. *See also* Devanagari script
Nagari Pracharini Sabha, 341, 344, 364
Nathdvara, 191–93, 195–200, 202–205, 207, 267
nation, 7, 125n25, 238, 339; formation, 336–38, 354; India as, 286, 341, 344, 363
nationalism, 7, 10, 14, 61, 63, 112, 114
Naupatti Mahajans, 191, 193, 207, 252

nayi chal (new ways), 239
Nayi Kahani (New Story) movement, 323–24
Nirala, Suryakant Tripathi, 319, 357, 363–64
nirguna, 141, 142n2, 144, 145n7, 147, 151, 155, 168–69
niti-katha, 236, 237n14. *See also* Hitopadesha
Nizamat Adalat, 75–76, 80
Non-Cooperation Movement, 351, 358
North West Provinces, 10, 112, 131–32, 224, 253, 312, 314–15, 340
novel, 13–15, 110, 231–38, 241, 245n24, 246, 266, 274, 280–83, 287, 323, 336, 347, 350–51, 356–57, 359–61, 363; Bengali, 256; as genre, 245n24; Hindi, 274–78, 295, 305, 325; Irish, 324; social reform and, 246, 255
Nyaya, 48, 53

oral tradition, 6, 36, 132, 135, 144, 330
Orient, 22–26, 31
Orientalism, 45, 62, 112, 114n4, 118–20, 123, 128, 130, 135, 211, 219, 253, 332; Anglicist, 52; British, 27, 253; Western, 63, 113–14
Orsini, Francesca, 251n1, 252, 359

orthodoxy, 1, 71, 141, 143, 151, 157, 169, 220n11, 327n24

padas (devotional verse), 144–45, 164, 193
pamphlets, 72n12, 110, 112, 217, 280, 287
Pancatantra, 236, 237n14
Pandharpur, 288, 290, 292
Pandey, Gayanendra, 99n16, 101n19
pandits, 2, 47, 49–52, 54, 56, 59, 61–63, 69, 75, 113, 156n18, 189, 208, 210, 218–21; authority of, 17, 55, 63; Banaras, 45n1; Kashi, 121, 221; Ujjain, 164–65
Panini, 2, 4, 17, 34, 48
Pant, Sumitranandan, 320
parampara, 221–23, 225–26
Parasha, 262
Parikh, Dvarikadas, 146n9, 176n5
pariksha (trial), 237, 241
Pariksha guru (Shrinivasdas), 232–33, 235–246
Parliamentary Papers on Widow Immolation, 17, 66–67, 69, 73–74, 79–82, 84–85. *See also* sati
Parsi theatre, 268–70, 347
Pathak, Shridhar, 345–46
pativatra (virtuous wife), 178, 185, 241
patriarchy, 25, 36, 251, 254, 280, 282

patriotism, 61, 249, 345, 348, 352
patronage, 131n36, 207, 257; British, 48, 51–52, 57, 274; cross-cultural, 50; Muslim, 97; Rajput, 144; traditional, 62–63
peasant organizations, 360
peasants, 15, 41, 142n2, 323, 338, 358–61; protests/uprisings, 14, 351, 358–59
Phillauri, Shraddharam, 293, 295–96; *Bhagyavati*, 293, 295–301
philology, 5, 31, 41–42, 42n42. *See also* Vedic philology
pilgrimage, 152, 155–56, 167, 286–89, 292–93, 294n18, 296–97, 299, 301–303, 305–306
Poddar, Hanumanprasad, 1, 9
political economy, 60–61
polygamy, 265, 276n48, 279
Prasad, Jaishankar, 13, 347
Prayag. *See* Allahabad
Premchand, 13–15, 282, 305, 323, 325, 351, 356, 359, 361, 363; *Godaan*, 359–60, 363; *Karmabhumi*, 13–14, 363; *Kayakalp*, 359; *Nirmala*, 282, 357; *Premashram*, 305, 359; *Sevasadan*, 13–14, 282, 357
press, 121, 355, 359
Prinsep, James, 10, 46
priti, 154, 162
private, 251–52, 280

private sphere, 15, 149, 241, 251–52, 338
public, 15, 87, 251–52, 254, 280. *See also* private
public sphere, 337–38, 360
Punjab, 121, 131–32, 134–35, 295–97, 323, 343, 351
Puranas, 22, 33, 111–12, 117, 119, 121–24, 130, 133–35, 137, 164, 178n8, 185n11, 214–15, 220–21, 224–26, 295n19
purani chal (old ways), 239, 244. *See also nayi chal*
Puri, 152–53, 167, 306
pushti, 147, 156

radicalism, 144n4, 177
Rai, Alok, 309–11, 313, 315–16, 318, 320–22, 328–29, 332, 364
Rajputs, 47, 94, 100–101, 125, 130, 150n13, 183–84, 347; miniature painting, 11; Vaishya dispute, 17
Rajput states, 190, 207
Ramanandis, 150n13, 170n22
Ramanuja, 190, 199
Ramayana, 33, 122–23, 144, 318, 346, 348, 362. *See also* Valmiki
raslila, 266–69, 272, 281
Raza, Rahi Masoom, 325, 361
realism, 231–32, 234–36, 238, 243, 245–46, 267–68, 270–71, 323
reason, 78–79, 81–82, 86–87,

reason (*continued*)
224; *murtipuja* and, 213–14, 216–17; women and, 77
religion, 10, 16, 25–26, 30–34, 37, 39–41, 47, 49, 55, 81, 96, 102, 104–106, 111n2, 212, 216, 223, 263, 286–87, 305–306, 327, 358; bhakti, 142n1; communalization of, 109; comparative study of, 9; ecstatic, 214; enlightened, 71; European, 189; Harishchandra on, 211; Hindu, 47, 63, 72, 77, 95, 108, 219, 355; Indian, 29–30, 79; national, 9; politicization of, 92; superstition and, 81, 85–86; traditional, 136; Vedic, 32; women and, 66, 84. *See also* theology
Renu, Phanishwarnath, 323, 361
Rgveda, 32, 36, 38
rishis, 33, 37, 222
Roy, Rammohun, 82, 213, 214n4, 226; abolition of sati and, 82n21
Rushdie, Salman, 331–32
saguna, 141–44, 145n7, 147n11, 155, 159, 168–69; sampradayas, 154, 167, 169; Vallabha and, 152n14
Sahajanand, 360–61
Sakuntala, 24n8, 27
samkalpa (resolution), 288–89, 293, 299
sampradaya, 143–44, 145n7, 146, 151, 157, 168–69, 186, 208, 210–11; Chaitanya, 174; festivals of, 199; Girdharji and, 192–93, 195, 197–98; *nirguna*, 151; poets of, 155n16; *saguna*, 154, 167, 169; Vaishnava, 150n13, 185n11, 190, 218; of Vallabha, 121, 143, 145, 152, 169–70, 175, 176n4, 191, 205, 267–68. *See also chatuhsampradaya*; Ramanandis
Sangari, Kumkum, 175n2, 179n9, 251–52, 257n10, 262n19
Sanatana Dharma, 211, 218–19, 221–22
Sankara/Shankara, 35, 58, 156, 190, 213
Sanskritization, 74, 84, 112–13, 115, 135, 169, 259, 268; of Hindi, 311, 315, 317, 321, 323, 331, 336, 338, 344, 347
Sanskrit literature, 51, 55–60, 62, 113
Sarasvati journal, 294n17, 300, 316, 342, 346, 362
sati (widow immolation), 17, 66–68, 67n2, 71, 74, 79–80, 82, 175, 178, 182–85, 187, 261, 265; British regulation of, 67–68, 70, 72, 76–78, 82, 85; debate, 86n29, 186; coercion and, 67–68; history of, 67n4; "Hindu fundamentalism"

and, 66, 88; missionaries' attempts to ban, 72, 354; political implications of, 88; Sanskritization and, 74; symbolic value of, 84. *See also* Ewer, Walter; *Parliamentary Papers on Widow Immolation*
Schlegel, Friedrich, 21, 26–31, 32n21, 33n24, 36n27, 38
seva (service), 149–51, 154, 157, 160–62, 169, 174, 192, 196–98, 201–202, 217; *pushtimarg*, 199n17; women and, 357
Sharma, Ramvilas, 244, 273n42
shastras, 33, 55, 68, 75, 77, 156, 218, 286n1; as "Shasters," 70–71, 105, 214–16
Sherring, M.A., 122, 131, 189–91, 194, 208
Shivaji, 125, 130
Shivrani Devi, 354
Shrinivasdas, 232–33, 234n8, 235, 245n24; *Pariksha guru*, 232–33, 235–246
Shukla, Ramachandra, 232n4, 300, 319, 321, 342
siddhanta, 147, 150, 165
Sikh literature, 133, 155n17
Sikhs, 142n2, 295
Singh, Balwant, 91, 94, 95n7
Singh, Bhagat, 351n17, 352, 356
Singh, Chait, 45n1, 91, 94–97, 99–100, 108, 192
Sivaprasadsingh, 119, 121

social reform, 14–15, 211, 253, 257, 265, 279–80, 318–19, 354–55; novels and, 246, 254–55, 357
sovereignty, 111, 124n24, 127
Srinivas, M.N., 74n15, 113
state, 7, 70, 109, 170, 250, 289, 352; apparatus, 299; colonial, 92, 109, 112, 295; formation, 117; intervention of, 101, 108
stribodh, 236, 241
Subodhini, 147, 158, 167
Sudras, 130, 131n57, 132–33, 150n13, 151, 163
superstition, 23, 29, 36–37, 84, 117n7, 124n24, 296; religion and, 81, 85–86; sati and, 67, 70–71, 78–79, 82; women and, 87, 355
svarupa, 149, 158–62, 164, 192, 195, 197–98, 200–202, 204
Syed Ahmad Khan, 121, 222

Tagore, Rabindranath, 320, 364
Tandan, Hariharanatha, 176n4, 205n18, 206
Tantras, 214–16
Thapar, Romila, 117
theology, 25, 58, 70, 92–93, 96, 106, 108, 141, 147, 196, 198, 219; Hindu, 213; Shankara and, 156; Vallabha and, 157n19; women and, 174
Thibaut, George, 55–58, 60–62
Tilak, Bal Gandahar, 344

Tod, James, 118, 127–28, 195
Tulsidas, 9, 263, 276, 313
Turner, Victor, 289, 303–304
Tyler, Edward Burnet, 116n7

United Provinces (UP), 150n15, 323, 342, 343n11, 345, 351, 353, 358, 364
universalism, 58–59, 69, 85; Sanskritization and, 113
Upadhyaya, Ayodhya Singh, 317–18
Upanishads, 34, 35n26, 213, 224
upaya (ruse), 237, 243
Urdu, 12, 92, 119, 232, 275, 294n18, 317–18, 326–27n24, 344; Hindi and, 309–14, 320, 326, 335–37, 339n4, 341, 347, 365; Muslims and, 325, 335, 337; women's journals in, 254n4, 257n7
Urdu literature, 235n9, 319, 323, 325, 326n24, 351, 361

Vaid, Sudesh, 251–52
vairagya, 157–59
Vaishyas, 131–32, 134
Vallabha, 143, 145, 148, 151, 152n14, 168, 173–76, 192–93, 199n17, 218; on asceticism, 160; family, 200, 205; followers of, 176, 211, 217; theology and, 157n19
Vallabha sampradaya, 121, 143, 145, 152, 169–70, 175, 176n4, 191, 205, 267–68

Valmiki, 58, 123, 127
Varma, Mahadevi, 281, 328
varna, 130–32, 134, 142n1, 150n13, 190; affiliation, 125, 130; hierarchies, 168; society, 115
Vartas (Vallabha sampradaya), 175–77, 179–84, 195–97, 202, 205, 208
Vedanta, 35n26, 48, 53, 190, 213, 215, 221, 320
Vedas, 17, 30, 48–49, 164, 192, 198, 208, 213–17, 220–23, 225–26, 294n19; authority of, 199n17
Vedic canon, 220, 226
Vedic education, 355
Vedic gods, 3, 37
Vedic hymns, 5, 34, 36, 132
Vedic literature, 33, 36, 41, 132, 295
Vedic norms, 176, 179
Vedic period, 32–34, 36, 38, 41, 59, 129, 170
Vedic philology, 38–39
Vedic ritual, 190, 192, 197, 199
Vedic sacrifice, 37, 197–98, 199n17, 208
Vishnu, 29, 132, 150n13, 176, 214, 225, 318
Vishvanath, 126, 194
Vitthala. *See* Gosaimji
Voltaire, 22–23
Vyasa, 58, 127, 214, 216

Wilson, Horace Hyman, 52,

56–57, 128, 272n40
Winckelmann, J.J., 23–24. 26
woman question, 252–53, 273

Yadunath, 192, 207
yajna, 198–99

yatra, 288–90, 293, 297, 299, 306. *See also* pilgrimage

zamindars, 92n4, 99, 99–100n17, 358, 360
zamindari, 92n4, 358, 360–61

www.ingramcontent.com/pod-product-compliance
Lightning Source LLC
Chambersburg PA
CBHW071826230426
43672CB00013B/2766